AF251924

Ominous Portents

of the

PAROUSIA of CHRIST

By

R. Henry Hall

"Revelations of Brimstone"

"Also I say unto you, whosoever shall confess Me before men, him shall the Son of man confess before the angels of GOD.

But he that denieth Me before men shall be denied before the angels of GOD.

And whosoever shall speak against the Son of man, it shall be forgiven him: but unto him that blasphemeth against the Holy Ghost it shall not be forgiven!"

JESUS CHRIST (Luke 12:8-10)

Ominous Portents

of the
PAROUSIA of CHRIST!

By
R. Henry Hall

Inspiration & Motivation

The HOLY SPIRIT of GOD

Contributing Writers

Evangelist Oral Roberts
Evangelist Billy James Hargis
Evangelist Jimmy Swaggart
Pastor Gary Greenwald
Author Constance Cumbey
Columnist Lois Reed

Art Design

Denita Lambou

Chairman of the Board

The Lord GOD Yahweh

Author & Publisher

R. Henry Hall

Published & Distributed By

HALL PUBLISHING COMPANY
Post Office Box 19020 Suite 277
LAS VEGAS, NEVADA 89132
(702) 737-0040

COPYRIGHTED © 1984 ALL RIGHTS RESERVED
This book may not be reproduced in whole or in part, by mimeograph or any other means without prior written consent of the author! Submitted articles from contributing writers do not necessarily represent the opinion of Rick Hall or Hall Publishing Company!

ACKNOWLEDGEMENTS

I wish to express my sincere appreciation to the following persons and organizations for their physical and spiritual assistance in the making of this book. Without their contributions and the graces of GOD, this book could not have materialized!

EVANGELIST ORAL ROBERTS
(GOD Still Heals Today)
P.O. Box 2187
Tulsa, Oklahoma 74171
Prayer Line: (918) 495-6161

EVANGELIST BILLY JAMES HARGIS
(The Cross and the Sickle!)
Box 977
Tulsa, Oklahoma 74102
Prayer Line: (918) 663-5660

EVANGELIST JIMMY SWAGGART
(There's A New Name Written Down in Glory!)
Baton Rouge, Louisiana 70821
Prayer Line: (504) 769-8300

PASTOR GARY GREENWALD
Eagle's Nest
(Marijuana: The Heavenly Deception!)
1701 East Edinger
Santa Ana, California 92705
Prayer Line: (714) 953-1701

AUTHOR CONSTANCE CUMBEY
(Hidden Dangers of the Rainbow!)
2011 Park Avenue – Suite 500
Detroit, Michigan 48226
(313) 963-5387

DEDICATION

This book is devoted to my **GOD**...the Lord Jesus Christ, who awakens me each morning with His presence, assurance and the knowledge that He is indeed coming soon. To His Holy Spirit who has nudged, prodded and inspired the writing of this book; who has poured out His blessings on a most unworthy but faithful servant; who shed His Blood on Mount Calvary so that I might have eternal life by believing; and who has bestowed upon me the graces of a most loving and patient wife, Gail, and five wonderful gifts in the names of Philip, Heidi, Andrew, Nicholas and Natalie. May we always walk in His Light and worship Him eternally!

Special Testimony

"I will go anywhere, regardless of personal hardship, in the praise and witness of His name and the promotion of this inspiration, so that His message in this book may reach out to the multi-millions on this Earth that seek no supportive structure and walk in the darkest of darkness.

Those who will not perceive that the message in this book comes directly to you from the Holy Spirit of **GOD**... have not read it! Before you settle down to read it, become familiar with what **GOD** says in Proverbs 2:1-6, Matthew 16:24 and Matthew 11:27. May **GOD** richly bless you!"

TABLE of CONTENTS

Additional Inspirations

The following brothers and sisters in Christ are blessed individuals in the Ministry of GOD of whom I have the utmost regard. They are the present day inspirations who are acting on the graces of the Holy Ghost and are the nation's outstanding evangelists, pastors, preachers, priests and laypersons who have devoted their lives to the fulfillment of GOD's holy plan for humanity.

They are integral members of the Body of Christ (the church), and are fulfilling prophesy by preaching the gospel throughout the world as a testimony to all nations. I love them all and ask our Father in heaven to continue to richly bless them, their ministries and their families. They have been an additional inspiration to my family and me and are truly sons and daughters of GOD!

Oral Roberts	Billy James Hargis	Richard Roberts
Paul & Jan Crouch	Hal Lindsey	Jimmy Swaggart
Billy Graham	Pat Robinson	Dwight Thompson
Kenneth Copeland	Constance Cumbey	James Robinson
Gary Greenwald	Robert Shuller	Kenneth Hagin
Steven Bell	Fr Michael Manning	Fr Lawrence Farrelly
John Osteen	Demond Wilson	Roosevelt Grier
Dr. Benvenuti	The McDuff Bros.	Jerry Falwell
Daniel Schaeffer	Arthur Blessit	Zola Levitt
Efrem Zimbalist, Jr.	John Wesley Fletcher	Ben Kinchlow
Charles Taylor	Michael Braderick	Lavern & Edith Tripp
Pat & Shirley Boone	Richard Hogue	John Ankerberg
Doug Clark	Lester Sumrall	The "Buntain Bros."
Charles Stanley	Anita Bryant	DaNuta
Mother Teresa	Mother Angelica	Howard Estep
Joel Baez	Jerry Barnard	Demos Shakarian
C.W. Ward	R.W. Shambach	Buck & Dottie Rambo
Sonny Arguinzoni	Melvin W. Steward	Don Wellman
M.J. Gebhart	Jay Jones	Lloyd Ogilvie
Norman Vincent Peale	Pamela Cole	John Avenzini
Paul Crouch, Jr.	O.S. Hawkins	Jack French (KILA)
Rex Humbard	Heritage Singers	Robert Fierro
Meadowlark Lemon	Jim McClellan	Pope John Paul II

. . . . . And all the many thousands upon thousands in this world who hold the name of the Lord Jesus Christ above all else. To use this publication as a "love gift", please call Rick Hall at (702) 737-0040. . . May GOD richly bless them and their families. This book is independently published and distributed!

Coming in 1985

"1991: A GENESIS of HOLOCAUST!"

A Prophetic journey into end-time reality. An inspirational book on a world devoid of Christian influence after the RAPTURE.

What happens to mankind when God removes the restrainer and places the entire world on a "survival of the fittest basis" in which love and compassion are forgotten traits; homosexuality, murder and rape escalate in correlation with a depraved mind of man, and humanity enters the great TRIBULATION...the final seven years of mortal existence.

"Now learn a parable of the fig tree; when his branch is yet tender, and putteth forth leaves, ye know that summer is nigh:

So likewise ye, when ye shall see all these things, know that it is near, even at the doors.

Verily I say unto you, this generation shall not pass, till all these things be fulfilled.

But of that day and hour knoweth no man, no, not the angels of heaven, but My Father only.

But as the days of No-e were, so shall also the coming of the Son of man be."

JESUS CHRIST (Matthew 24:31-37)

INTRODUCTION

"Ominous Portents of the Parousia of Christ" is a book of faith and truths intended to awaken a sleeping giant – the United States of America. For more than three decades now our Country has been digressing economically, spiritually and morally...not to overlook the faith we are losing from our allies abroad.

This book will bring to light the factors that are underscoring our progress and subjugating our nation with the misinformations that are ripping at the very foundations of freedom.

Basically, what we have in the United States is a blatant failure of communications and the faults are none others than our own. For far too long we have allowed ourselves to become complacent in our views on the manner we should be governed. At the same time we have become naive to the presence of and the internal damages we have sustained to the communist cause in America. These subversive organizations and individuals threaten to overtake and destroy the liberty "real" Americans have fought for and died to preserve.

Because of this mass oversight on the part of all God-fearing Americans, we have subjugated this once powerful Country to the aggression, conspiracy and overt espionage of the Soviet Union. We have placed our precious sovereignty at the crossroads of despair.

Our Nation is on the precipice of losing the greatest battle in our 208 year history...the loss of freedom from external control! Throughout our two centuries we have decorated many great American patriots for heroism above and far beyond the expected limits of moral duty, warriors who have given up their liberty that we may enjoy the fruits of God's intentions for America. Since the late 50s and early 60s, we have watched these exemplary men of valor dwindle in number to but a few. This book may enlighten the many entities in this Country that have been drifting on selfish clouds of security. It will show the dire need to reevaluate our ideals and motivations while clarifying our present predicament in relation to the moral standards and codes of conduct that are indigenous to our current lifestyle.

For the past twenty years we have been sloughing and sherking our responsibility to this Nation. We've misused and twisted the definition of freedom and failed to recognize that any great nation is only equal to the strength of its weakest links.

Those who are not aware of the ultimate consequences we face as a result of this neglect in proper allegiance, should reacquaint themselves with the history books. You will find that every civilization since the world began has been devastated by GOD when the ominous elements of corruption have infiltrated their doctrines.

"Ominous Portents of the Parousia of Christ" will define these evil and historical designs. It uncovers their festering origins and will propose the real answers to our final alternative. America must awaken to these truths and reconnoiter that our failure to regroup and revive this loss in sanctity is more than essential for future prosperity and liberty; it is the only possible way to survival. The time is ripe NOW...we must get out of our easy chairs and reestablish our lost vigor to fight back under the banner of Christ Jesus.

As we are condoning the associations we have with Soviet inspired international organizations, we are in essence collaborating with demonic influence. By these memberships, we are compromising any future prospect for positive expectation and we are jeopardizing our ties to Almighty God as a result.

We have to realize that "no deals" with satan, or any of his allies of terrorism, "is" the proper approach for America. Regardless of the internal outcry for "peace at all costs," we must not make pacts with the un-Godly nations of this world and expect adherence to any treaty...it will not happen...it must not occur!

All we have come to acknowledge as a result from America's attempt at fair play with the Russians has been discord and misinformation in exchange for our good-willed intentions toward peaceful co-existence.

The Soviet Union represents the entity that is inclined and dedicated towards world demise as sure as its territory houses the residence of Lucifer. There will no peaceful detente as long as they maintain a deceitful nature towards such negotiations. There will be no harmony in this world as long as this atheistic nation outwardly propagates the free world with the evils of communism. The United States should not be expected to lower our self esteem and wallow in their filth that oppresses a free will to grow in this world created by God. It is not acceptable to propose that we open our gates to any country that fails to recognize the presence of our God, or any nation who supresses the worship of God from their countrymen.

America is not as strong as it once was, but that fact can be positively altered with the unified effort of every citizen. This book will pinpoint our decline in ethics and propose the only solution we have remaining to acknowledge.

This Country was not founded on the same principles as most nations. We were annexed upon the superlatives of the Lord God Yahweh and "no power" on the face of this planet has a stronger relationship than America. God's principles have made this Country what it is...elite among all nations on earth. With this allegiance to the Holy Spirit of God we have endured as a compassionate ally to those distant lands less fortunate.

In recent generations our people have outgrown humanity's only Hope. This inconsiderate blasphemy against the Spirit of God represents the prime elements of the unrest and discord in America today.

Since travel and knowledge have increased to epic proportion in the last century, we have become an arrogant, selfish and ruthless people. It is obvious we have forgotten our basic roots and in so doing, misplaced the true analogy of love. Without understanding the dire necessity for God's divine influence in our public school system, in our government and in our hearts, there can be no hope for any reversal of the deadly inclination on which we are traveling. Mankind must acknowledge that we are deficient of the necessary intellect to provide this world with even its basic needs, let alone the many extra essentials desired by most Americans. That fact is evident when you scrutinize the entire world picture.

"Ominous Portents of the Parousia of Christ" is also a book on Biblical prophesy. It will inspire and insure an awakening of those Americans who remain subjugated in spiritual darkness. It will afford you a documented reassurance that our God is alive and well on planet Earth and that He cares greatly for His ungrateful brethren.

This book's sub-title, "Revelation of Brimstones ," was carefully selected in accordance with the pre-destined prophesies of the Bible. It will renew the spirits of many and assist you to establish or reestablish a vigor and yearning to cope with today's ever changing ideologies. If it helps you to reacquaint yourself with the "Word of God and His Plan for the destiny of mankind," a design that is as old as time itself, it has tendered its commission.

One thing the book will do for you if nothing else; it shall open your eyes and shock you to the reality of the impending horrors that most inhabitants of this planet are ultimately facing in these final days.

If you know and accept God's Plan for humanity, this volume will bring you a much needed comfort and peace of mind. If you do not know "the Plan," or deny the presence of our Deity, you "will" take one of two possible pathways; the book will either put you on a "lighted course," or, if you harden your heart to its divinely inspired message, it "shall," in the very least, explain to you your eternal destiny!

"Revelation of Brimstones projects the "truths" that are the Bible's theme. By the time you have finished this book, you shall understand "just how true" it really is.

The prophesies in the "Good Book" are more than 80% fulfilled and it is my divine inspiration from the Holy Spirit of God that "prior to the turn of the century, not one shall be left unfulfilled."

It is prophesized in the "Word of God" that in the end times of the world, He will pour out His Holy Spirit on all flesh!

"And it shall come to pass in the "last days," saith God, I will pour out My Spirit on all flesh; and your sons and your daughters shall prophesy, and your young men shall see visions, and your old men will dream dreams."
ACTS 2:17

It is also said literally in Matthew 24:36.......

"But of that 'day' and 'hour' knoweth no man, no, not the angels of heaven, but My Father only."
JESUS CHRIST

Understanding these two scriptures, I tell you this: God's Holy Spirit is writing this book...I am nothing but an intermediary and have been commissioned to tell you in all honesty, we "ARE" in the final chapter of mankind.

Jesus said that "no man knoweth the "day or the hour," but GOD has given His graces to those that love Him...He has given us the "YEAR" that all these things will take place!

I tell you this in full acknowledgment of what would be my eternal damnation if I am bearing any false witness or proposing any erroneous or misleading testimony. The Holy Spirit of God is merciful and loving. He is giving us the year so that we may get our houses in order and with the hopes that those who read this book will understand the truth that "His Ultimate Plan for this World" is coming into fulfillment.

I am honored that He has given this hidden treasure to this unworthy servant, and I include this year in the book only after many hours of prayer. I have asked for this knowledge and He has given me what I have sought.

We must all realize that God has removed the mysteries in these days that have been sealed since the world was created. He has already informed me that many who read it...won't believe. Most will say that I have added the year for sensationalism. Those who will say that give me too much credit for wit. When you see the divine inspirational explanation of the year, you may change your mind and give all the glory to GOD! I love God...I could never be a deceiver of those He loves, nor would I do so for human profit!

Why our God has asked me to write such a book has been the object of much conjecture and prayers with my family and me. Prior to His calling, I had never even read the Bible, and although I had been a devout Catholic and have exaulted His' Name in my home, I was a professional gambler and a publisher of books on sports gambling.

When He touched me with His Holy Spirit last May, 1983, He also changed my ideas on life itself. As a Catholic, my opinion of worship was in the mornings as a brief thanksgiving and on Sundays in public worship. Now, He has given me a thirst for His word that cannot be appeased without around the clock worship throungh prayer.

GOD has promised Gail and me a ministry. Since we began this worthy project, the Holy Spirit of GOD has not left my side for a moment. He has given me His gift of tongues and the language in which to pray to Him through my spirit. He has given me wisdom and knowledge for interpretation of prophesy. He told me that the ministry will be taken care of in His time, but to be ready for public speaking.

My family and I have never been so close to the kingdom as we are today. I actually know for the first time what it means to be a Christian. He told me that all my past lectures at various gambling seminars were always meant for my public training and experience in public speaking. He told me to make this book available to other men of GOD...that they may use it in their ministries as love gifts and fund raisers...He even made sure that the artist, the printers and the proof readers were all believers in GOD. He did so much on this book...I felt unworthy of placing my name on its cover.

The prophesies in the Bible are not the product of either human inspiration, figmentation or of fantasy; they are of divine, fiducial knowledge, placed into the minds and hearts of bygone Prophets and wise men of that era. They were, and are, loyal servants from all nations who acknowledge His Gospel and witness throughout the world as a testimony to all the nations that Jesus Christ is much more than "a son" of GOD; He is the "Son of the Living GOD and GOD Himself!" (JOHN 14:7-9)

From the witness in this book, you will come to know that the Bible also represents a "way of life," as well as a "Way to LIFE!" It is a plan that shall lead believers to renew their broken covenant with GOD by accepting that the "only way to the Father is through the Son!"

The religion you profess is meaningless unless you accept that Key element to salvation of the soul within. The Bible is a true to life witness of God's understanding and mercy and a further testimony of His eternal love for humanity!

The decision you make today has far greater significance of judgment than any you have ever made. This book will make you understand that, as a nation, we have been misguided by devious influence and are being fashioned and programed by misconception.

The "liberal movements" in this Land, who threaten to choke our life's blood are outlined in gory detail. The advice that is offered comes not from the faulty mind of man, but from the mercy of Him that lives from everlasting to everlasting!

If this volume serves to awaken the lackadaisal, or is the cause for the saving of only one soul from the eternal agony of the lake of fire and brimstone – it is only to the glory of GOD that it shall be!

Our God is a divinely patient and caring Father, but it becomes more and more evident by current world events that His "Day of Judgment" is swiftly approaching.

HE APPEARED AS A DOVE!

Let me share with you brothers and sisters in Christ the elements which prompted the writing of "Ominous Portents of the Parousia of Christ." Whether you believe it or not....it's TRUE!

There was a time that I thought "I" was in complete control of my life. Because of my successes in forecasting the future sporting events, I thought there could be no vocation that I would enjoy more. I tell you this explanation so there will be no misunderstanding that this book was conceived for human profit or self-satisfaction. Without the graces from the Father in heaven, this book would never have materialized.

One day in May, 1983, while in the final stages of writing "Emotional Concepts of the Sports Investor," a book on sports gambling, a "dove" flew in and landed in the courtyard directly in front of my previous office space. I was wailing away on my typewriter and failed to notice the bird, nor did I look up from my toils.

It was at that time I had the most strange feeling envelope my entire body. It was almost as if the blood had been completely drained from my being and was filtering itself back into my veins.

The chills were dancing along my spine, then the most peaceful fibrillation took control. I felt a welling of emotion from deep within my very soul and I could not control the flow of tears which jerked from my eyes in an unexplainable stream of compassion for my fellow man. It was then that I heard the voice!

Speaking to my conscious mind, the voice asked me "what I was doing writing on things with no eternal value?" My first thoughts were that I was losing my faculties.......I later received the message that what had happened was an encounter with the Holy Spirit of GOD!

It was at that exact instant that I noticed this strange dove outside the door. I know I wasn't dreaming because the tenants in the neighboring suites were already commenting on the doves' peculiar behavior. I went to the door and opened it. Looking at the dove gave me the immediate impression that it knew that it wouldn't be harmed by anyone. It didn't even flinch at my close proximity. It just stood there with its head tucked neatly under its wing and remained motionless.

About that time my mind was transformed into a living computer and I was vibrantly inspired to write on a subject and venture into a realm that I knew little about. I returned to my office and withdrew the work I'd been consummating and inserted another paper. I then began typing a message, the words of which kept coming to me in an endless barrage. The more I typed, the more the tears rolled down my cheeks and continued for more than three consecutive hours. When I finally stopped and read what had been typed...I knew exactly what the Lord wanted me to do.

God not only took complete control of this project, He schooled me in the hidden secrets of Biblical prophesy. He gave me the knowledge that what He was giving me was something I had asked for more than thirty-three years previous...when I was but a child of 6.

He not only communicated through my mind, my heart and my soul on the book; He began playing with my leisure pastimes of viewing football and basketball games and made them seem so irrevalent to what I was about to do. He moved the channels on our television sets to a religious program called the PRAISE THE LORD Show on Channel 40 (6 in Las Vegas) and also the 700 Club on channel 28. It must be duly noted that previously I had watched this type of program sparingly. Now I couldn't get enough of the Evangelists, pastors and preachers who inspired the Christians on to great heights of praise in the Lord Jesus Christ.

The same day of the encounter, and because my family was in Oregon at my in-laws' ranch, I shared my experience with good friends, Lee and Lila Pete (Lee is the host of the radio sports talk show, "the Stardust Line" over KDWN Radio.) When they had listened to what I had read to them and told them of the strange dove, I got the expression they thought I had overworked myself and was experiencing extreme fatigue. That should give you an idea of how they viewed my previous dedication ..."What was an experienced sports handicapper doing writing on the workings of GOD?" That had to be what they were thinking, because I also thought that way

8

Everything in this book has fallen into place...all in its proper sequence...all at the right time. Any slight reasonable human doubt I may have had before my encounter with the Holy Spirit, was completely wiped away and replaced with the love and confidence that can only come from the Father of Creation...GOD!

It is my desire that everyone who reads this book of truths will have the sense of logic to comprehend the magnitude of its purpose. Regardless of your professed faith or practice of religious belief...this book has an important message for you - one intended to either introduce you to everlasting hope or bring you closer to our heavenly Father in this final act in the dominion of satan!

Although I have written other books, many of the words that came to me in the production of this volume had to be referenced for meaning in the dictionary...believe me, I'm not that sophisticated, - but He accepts us as we are.

I sincerely believe that if you are honest with yourself; you will not take the book's purposes lightly!

If you are an atheist, a socialist or one of liberal practice, if you allow it, it will straighten out your preferences on the existence of one greater than thee.

If you are a humanist and believe that the destiny of mankind rests with each other's personal merits, your ideas may take on an abrupt new understanding!

Whoever you are or whatever your belief in a hereafter, "Ominous Portents of the Parousia of Christ" should change your spirit and set loose your bonds to the outer world of emptiness. I know it shall restore your awareness in the myth that GOD doesn't exist, or, if He does exist...doesn't care for humanity. If you knew me, then you would realize that I could not have written a book of this nature in only eight months without assistance from the Holy Spirit.

You may accept this book's value as factual, or, be foolish and fail to recognize its eternal significance. Either way, you shall come away with the acknowledgment that it contains no false hopes for the future, no misconceptions or misinformation and was certainly not conceived with any sensationalism for selfish benefit.

Whether you believe the truth or not...Christ Jesus is at the Door and is knocking...you'll either let Him in or bar the entrance and lose your only chance for eternal happiness.

We know from experience that the wizards of human intellectuality don't possess the necessary solutions to the world problems...Why not give GOD the chance?

WAKE UP AMERICA, IT'S LATER THAN YOU THINK!

R. HENRY HALL

CHAPTER ONE
Seeking The Source of Blessings!

I remember a time in my life when I walked in extreme darkness. I hated living and detested myself even more. I've had many tests in my life and I suppose I've failed most because of trying to work my way through the maze of life on my own. I didn't need anyone's help, specially not someone that I could not see or hear. I had all the answers and everything I thought I needed in life,- but I wasn't happy!

Somehow I had outgrown a need for God. I don't quite know when it happened, but it materialized just the same. I remember when I was young how impressed I was with anyone that represented God and how I had had a special relationship with Him as a child. Now, I had gotten into the swing of things with the motto "live life to the fullest for when you die you're dead for a long time." Even without going to church as a teen, everything went well for me and I had the idea that "if you need a doctor, you go to the hospital; if you need God, you go to church", personally I didn't need either. Or so I thought.

When I went to church it was always a drudgery. I'd go to weddings, funerals, occasionally on Easter and sometimes on Christmas when I didn't have something better to do; but I would go only for two reasons. The first was to be seen and the second was to check out the girls. The scriptures were always boring to me and I'd much rather be watching a ballgame than trying to stay awake in church.

I remember the unhappiness of my first marriage. Although we were married in a church, we never attended Mass except on rare occasions. The only bright spot of my five year marriage was the birth of my two oldest children. Although the five years was full of animosity, quarrels and other discord, I derived much satisfaction in my children and had planned to stick it out for their sake only. To me then, it was always the other's fault, surely "I" couldn't be the cause of an arguement. I knew she was wrong and she was positive that it was I. What we had was a five year failure to communicate and the reason was the absence of God in the marriage.

When we divorced in 1973, I became extremely depressed. Not because I missed any union, but now I couldn't come home each night to the children. I got an apartment and chased everything in skirts to occupy my free time. The more girls I dated, the unhappier I became. Depression was an every day occurrence and the only time I could forget how much I hated my life was on alternating weekends when I had both of my children with me, but even the love I had for them wasn't enough to fill my deepening void.

Surely there had to be more to life than existing. Although some months I would date 10 different girls, most were either looking for a father for their children or didn't appeal to me for other reasons. None possessed the morals I was looking for. I was convinced that I would not make another mistake and waste another five years. All this time I was walking in darkness and growing deeper in despair.

One evening I was alone in my apartment and turned on the television. An evangelist was preaching the word of God. Under normal circumstances I would have changed the channel for something more exciting, but for some strange reason I sat and listened to his message. I know now that it wasn't fate that the preacher was describing exactly how I was living my life. If he would have had a script of my autobiography, he couldn't have pegged me more accurately.

The preacher told how it was possible to fill my void in life and everything he was saying was true. I could not find one flaw in the words that flowed from his mouth. What I had to do to change my life was to accept Jesus Christ into my heart. I had to ask for His help before I would receive it and be totally sincere about my request. He described the emptiness I was feeling, named all the characteristics I was experiencing and proposed the ultimate solution to my problem. What did I have to lose!

Although I had always believed in God, I was not practicing His Laws. It was always, do as I say and not as I do. Looking back on my life from that point, I could see that what I had done by outgrowing my God was to remove my protective shield on life. I realized at that time that I was thankful for the patience God had with me and prayed to Him that very night. I sincerely wanted help and was surely willing to give up the life I had been leading in search of more peaceful surroundings. My prayer went something like this:

Dear GOD, I have sinned against You and my fellow man. I ask that You come into my heart and change the voids I now feel. I thank You for the patience You've had with me and for the blessings You've given me in spite of the life I've lead. I humbly ask You to send me someone who will truly return the abundance of love You know I have to offer. I accept the fact that Jesus died on the cross for the atonement of my sins. I humbly ask You to send me someone that will make my earthly life more bearable and I ask these things in the name of Jesus. Amen & Amen

The prayer was my way of asking God to forgive me for leaving Him out of my life all those years. I don't know how I strayed from Him, but I did and it resulted in decreasing moral and spiritual values in my life. Now I had asked to be forgiven. The prayer was not taken out of any Bible because at the time I didn't own one. They were my own words, but they were sincere.

From the moment I accepted God into my heart, things began to change in my life. Almost immediately I had a surge of energy; my eating habits improved and I immediately stopped dating old girlfriends. God told me in a dream that if I wanted a girl with pure substance, then I should go to church and obey His Commandments. That made a lot of sense to me but it didn't work out the way I had planned it. I felt God was telling me that I would find the girl for me at church, and each week I kept looking for Miss Right. If you notice the words I was still using you would pick out "made sense to ME"; the way "I had planned it" and "I felt". What I was doing was practically the same as I was doing before. "I" was looking for the girl I needed, but I was failing to understand that "I" wasn't qualified to select her. God had told me that 'HE' would take care of everything if 'I' played the game in His way. I decided to give it a try, and asked Jesus to have His way in my life totally. "That's when the real changes began happening!"

To the unbeliever it must seem strange when I mention that I have been carrying on direct communications with God since 1973. Sometimes I don't listen as I should, but He has told me His plan for my life. You see, "we" are not qualified intellectually to give our lives the fulfillment we seek. Only God can do that! When you give Him the reigns, He does as He pleases with your life and, although you may not always agree with His ideas, they always work out for the best. I'm convinced of that fact. You say God is not real? I got news for you! He is as alive and well today as He was in the days of the Prophets. Some people say, "if He is alive today why doesn't he talk to us?" He does talk to us, but people are so caught up with "themselves" and trying to manage their own affairs, they fail to listen!

I decided to give my life to Him and would obey His Laws. I found that the closest church was only a block away, - the Del Amo Baptist Church! I went to the rectory and introduced myself to Pastor Cain. He understood and sympathized with my problems. We knelt and prayed together. I was surprised that the roof of the church didn't fall in when I attended service that Sunday. Everyone was nice to me and I got the impression their fellowship wasn't the least bit plastic.

12

My confidence grew by the day and I found that there was indeed something else in the world to live for, - and that was God! The more I prayed with sincerity, the more wisdom God would give me. I had every bit of confidence that it wouldn't be long before God would show me. I had every bit of confidence that it wouldn't be long before God would send me someone that would be capable of truth and love, only this time I wasn't looking for her.

On March 19th, 1974, two days after my 30th birthday and two months from the time I made my sincere commitment to Jesus, it happened. God placed me in the right spot at exactly the right time. He sent me His gift in the package of a blonde-haired, green-eyed, seventeen year old by the name of Gail. Three days earlier she had only been sixteen and this presented a large problem. Here I was a divorced, thirty year old man with two children and she was a naive girl which was still in parochial school. God's test to insure that I would be His forever was at hand and He made my intentions for the girl pure.

I met her at a place called "Hamburger Henry's" in Belmont Shores, California, and she was with her girl friend, Janet. I'd asked them what was good on the menu and, later, if I could join them. It seemed that all three of us hit it off well from the start, but when I found out how old they were I backed off a little. When I parted company with them, I gave them my phone number and didn't request theirs because of their age. I mentioned that if they would like to visit me at my apartment, they were welcome, but come together. Although I had faith in my new ideals, I didn't want to push it and especially so, I didn't want any temptation to break my covenant with God. What did I know? The girls were nice but maybe this wasn't God's answer to my prayers. By not having their phone numbers, God had complete control. I couldn't call them if I wanted to. If it was to be, God would make the move through them.

About a week later they called and asked if they could come over. To make a long, happy story short, the three of us became inseparable and went everywhere together. We had one fantastic time and it was all platonic in nature. I had been noticing that Gail was the more domestic of the two, showed more interest in my children and appeared more conservative. Janet was very nice too, but Gail turned out to be my Gift from God. She was everything I wanted in a girl. She had a good heart, believed strongly in God, was attractive, pure, domestic and truthful. What more could anyone ask for, but the rest wasn't that easy.

As you would guess, right from the time she introduced me to her parents, the problems began. They despised me and thought I was some pervert, but I couldn't blame them. In my eyes they were wrong, but the circumstantial evidence heavily favored their side of thought. If the same thing happened to one of my daughters I would react the same way they did, and possibly not as understanding.

At first they restricted her from seeing me, but we had already known each other for more than a month, and were good friends. Gail rebelled against their wishes. Her father had me investigated thoroughly, going so far as to personally visit my ex-wife. Surely he would find something there to convince his daughter that I was wrong for her. He didn't find it! He researched my personal history, back to my home town in Massachusetts, but turned up nothing. After quite some time and trials, we were permitted to date within their guidelines. As long as she was under eighteen, I had to have her in by midnight on weekends and for a year we stuck to their rules. All this time my heart went out to them both. The right thing would have been for me to back off, but the friendship was so fulfilling and my respect for her too strong to allow it. I really understood how Gail's parents felt about the situation and prayed for them every night that God would inform them that everything was in His hands.

Two months after we had met, God told me that Gail indeed was the one He had sent me and I asked her to marry me. I wanted things to be right in her parents eyes and made an appointment with her father to ask him for Gail's hand in marriage. Her father made it clear that they didn't like me and would not give their blessings for such a union, but would not stand in our way of getting engaged as long as I respected her tender age. I told him that I loved her very much and would respect his wishes. He told me that if it was God's will then it would happen in God's way and in God's time. I felt like a wolf stealing his prize sheep and nothing I could say would have been appropriate at that time to convince him that my intentions were good!

For the next ten months my relationship with God grew stronger. Many times during that span I mentioned to Gail that maybe she should have someone closer to her own age, but she wouldn't hear it. If it had been left up to me only, instead of God's Will, we would have never been married. I loved her so much that I would have given her up, rather than to continue defying her parents wishes. As it worked out, I'm glad it was God's Will to bless the union.

Gail's parents were (and are) devout Catholics and projected this fellowship with their lifestyle. Both Grace and Andrew (Chub) were married in the same year I was born and at the time, had been married for thirty years. Although Gail loved and respected them very much she was determined to become my wife. During the next year we had many trials in our relationship but with the help of Almighty God we endured.

One of our severe tests was also a most rigid obstacle. If Gail was to marry a divorced man she could not receive the blessings of the Catholic Church. This seemed to represent an impossibility. What we needed was an annulment of my previous marriage and because I had been married for five years, with two children, it looked as though that would not take place. I visited two different priests who both indicated that it just wouldn't be allowed, but as mentioned before, "with God anything is possible" and the impossible was in the divine process of happening.

Gail remembered a young priest she had in one of her classes at St. Josephs, in Lakewood, and made contact with him. He indicated that nothing was impossible, but this would surely be difficult. He said that we would have to prove to the tribunal at the Diocese of Los Angeles that my previous marriage, in all sense of the union, did not exist during the five years. I knew in my heart that it didn't, but how was I going to convince them and most of all, prove it?

I marveled at the energy of my naive, but determined fiance. Finally in March of 1975, after completing the required psychological testing prescribed by the Church and successfully convincing a Tribunal of Priests at the Diocese that a marriage never existed (the existence of the bond of real love), we received the blessing from God in the form of the Diocese's affirmative approval to marry in the Catholic Church. God had worked another miracle in our brief relationship. I mailed a copy to her parents, (not facetiously), so they would know their daughter was not living in sin when we were married. In April, 1975, Gail and I were married at St. Cyprian's Catholic Church in Lakewood, California.

Although Gail's parents were extremely slow to accept me, they recognized the findings of the Church. All my prayers of previous years were coming to fruition and when we were invited to Thanksgiving in 1975, I was indeed nervous. I continued to pray that they would not think badly of what I had done to their family unit. I wanted them to bless our marriage and to look upon our relationship "as not losing their daughter, but gaining a son", to coin an old phrase. It took place, but not in the time span I had wanted. It took place in God's time, which is sometimes slower than mere mortals enjoy.

Although the first couple of years in our marriage were shaky, our faith and prayers to God saw us through our period of adjustment. Gail matured into a most precious gift from God and I thank Him everyday for His kindness to His undeserving servant. In 1977, He blessed our holy union with

Andrew (now 7), in 1978, He blessed us with Nicholas (now 6) and in 1983, He blessed us with Natalie (now 1). The children blend amicably with my other two children, Philip (age 14) and Heidi (age 13) and the entire credit goes to God. He also blessed my ex-wife and her new husband with His presence – they,too,are strong advocates of Jesus Christ!

God changed my entire life by altering my belief in His powers. He brought me out of a world of darkness and into a beautiful realm of earthen-happiness, working many, humanly impossible miracles in the process. I love Him more and more for what He has done with my life each day. He will change your life,too,if you let Him have His way. To have a full life, with all the wonderous joys it can hold for you, you must first ask Him for this goodness.

If you are tired of living in the outer world, a life filled with horrendous voids, I urge you to accept Jesus Christ into your heart right now. Say a prayer like I said in early 1974, or make up your own. But be sincere and know you will receive your deliverance from evil when you do so.

Since accepting Jesus into my heart I have been extremely happy. We have had many trials since that time, but nothing we couldn't handle with God's assistance. When you sincerely acknowledge God, He also acknowledges you. Like any child, you will still have temptations to do evil and even experience your many imperfections from time to time living as a Christian. But with Jesus in your heart it is impossible to stray to the outer limits of His Kingdom. You may refer to me as you would like. You may slander this testimony of truth, but you may not even infer that my testament bears any false witness. You see, – as long as we have the presence of God in our lives and give Him His Way – satan no longer controls our destiny!

GOD Never Lies!

When GOD makes a promise...He always keeps His Word! Although we are children of GOD, created in His Image and recipients of all the blessings anyone could ever ask for...our human nature does not follow our royal heritage...that is, until we receive the Holy Spirit in our souls.

One classic example of GOD always keeping His promises was telecast over Trinity Broadcasting Network on the "Praise The Lord" cable television program. I didn't need any verification of GOD's word, but it was surely a most powerful documentation of the only ethics GOD observes with His ungrateful children!

Understanding the thinking of GOD will never take place! It is an impossibility! Satan tried once and look where he is. Yes, GOD will talk to us, nurture our outreach, give us what we ask for and continually show us His love...but, it would be dangerous to ever say that YOU KNOW WHAT GOD IS THINKING! With all the miracles GOD has done in the sight of man, it really surprises me that only 25% of the earth's population lays claim to Christianity. It also would seem strange that, of that percentage, less than 20% of these professing Christians really believe. What does that tell you? It tells me that only 5 of every hundred (and it may be less than that) people really believe in the miracles of GOD!

In May, 1984, a visiting pastor told of an incident which lowered me to my knees with my face down in reverence to GOD. I could not control my emotions when I heard the factual story.

When you trust in GOD, giving Him your entire life to do with as He wills, wonderous things begin transforming both you and your family's future. If you are to believe on the Lord Jesus Christ...not only you receive eternal life, but GOD has promised that your family (those family members in your house) will also live eternally.

> "And they said, Believe on the Lord Jesus Christ, and thou shalt be saved, AND THY HOUSE."
>
> ACTS 16:31

Simply stated, that passage means that GOD promises to give your family graces, based on your belief in Jesus Christ.

This pastor told the heart rending story of a aging married couple; the woman believed and raised her family to believe on Jesus...the man did everything in his power to make sure that his family was uncomfortable whenever his wife would take them to church for worship. I mean...he would rant and rave and throw all kinds of fits because he didn't want his family believing on anything he couldn't understand.

One day while the wife was at work she received a phone call from the hospital. The administrators told her that her husband had just died of a heart attack. Grief-stricken, she left immediately for the hospital. For many years she had been familiar with the fact that GOD never lies and recalled the scripture in the Book of Acts when GOD promises that her whole house would be saved. If her husband had died without knowing the Lord Jesus...one...her husband would be going to hell and..two...that would have made GOD go back on His word. She prayed to GOD all the way to the hospital.

When she arrived at the hospital she was met by the

attending physician who made a valiant, but fruitless, attempt at reviving her life's mate. With tears welling in her eyes and and a mighty strong faith in GOD, she asked...

"Where's my husband?"

"I'm very sorry Ma'am, we did everything we could for your husband..." explained the doctor sympathically.

"Where is my husband?" she asked the doctor again.

"He's in this room, Ma'am."

Going into the emergency room she saw her husband on the slab. Already his pigmentation had changed.

"He is not dead!" exclaimed the woman. "He's not dead!"

"I'm sorry," explained the doctor again moving to further console the woman. "He has been dead for more than fifteen minutes!"

"GOD promised that my husband would not die...he's not dead!"

The doctor knew differently...but he showed her the body. Sure enough all vital signs were gone.

"Where are those things you doctors use to revive the heart?" asked the woman. "Get them and place them on him...he's not dead!"

"To satisfy the woman, the doctor took the difibrilators and placed them on the man, giving the man a good shock...nothing happened.

"Do it again!" the woman commanded!

The doctor reciprocated, but still nothing...

"Do it again!" said the persistent woman...

Again nothing happened....

"Step aside," commanded the woman, "I know he's not dead cause GOD doesn't lie!"

Placing her hand on her dead husband's head, she tearfully petitioned GOD to keep His word.

"Father GOD, you told me that if I believed in the Lord Jesus Christ that my husband would also be saved. I do believe and he's part of my house!" said the woman, as the tears rolled down her cheeks and onto her dead husband. "In the name of Jesus Christ I command you to rise!" said the woman confidently.

At that moment...the man's hand twitched. Being shocked out of his mind, the doctor backed up against the wall.

"I command you to come back in the name of the Lord Jesus Christ!" she said again.

With that command, her husband's eyelids began slowly opening.

"Jesus loves you, honey," the woman exclaimed. "He loves you very much!"

In a feeble whisper the man said, "I-I-I know it!"

"Repeat after me!" said the woman. "Father GOD!"

"F-F-Father G-GOD!" came the almost incoherent words.
"Forgive my sins against You."
"F-F-Forgive my s-sins a-a-against You.
"I accept Jesus Christ as my Savior!"
"I-I a-ccept Jesus C-Christ as my Savior!"
"AMEN!" said the woman tearfully.
"Amennn" came the low voice.
"Jesus wants to come into your heart," explained the woman.
" I knooow...there Heee is...gooood bye!"

With those final words her husband passed on to eternal life with Jesus in His Father's House.

That testimony is a classic example of how much you are loved by our GOD. Even death will not interfere with His keeping His promises to us. That is something we are not worthy of...but it just shows that Jesus will take us JUST AS WE ARE. He will accept us with all our blemishes and unrighteousness...because...HE LOVES US MORE THAN YOU WILL EVER KNOW!!!!!!!

Now, read on and understand that with our GOD...anything is possible.

CHAPTER TWO

Truth Through Grace;
Discernment of the Spirit World!

Passing through the outskirts of Ventura on the northbound 101 Freeway, the sheer elegance of God's plush landscape can make one acknowledge that our historical struggle for liberty has been well worth it. The breath-taking views from roads that knife their way through natural rock cliffs along the Pacific Ocean lull the senses to a tantillizing state of euphoria. Tomorrow was to be a monument of spiritual awareness and the short 90 minute jaunt up the coast to Santa Barbara seemed unusually endless.

Mankind's reluctance to believe in that which he cannot see or hear was on my mind that day and it was a cause for bewilderment. There were many times in my life that I had faltered in my spiritual beliefs and sometimes questioned reality, but I found it difficult to understand why so many people in this world fail to place God number one in their lives. I recalled how as a little child I had been raised to respect the principles of God and cried when I was shown how badly He was treated by man. When I'd see a movie about Christ, I would yearn to be like Him. I secretly wanted to heal the blind, raise the dead and cure the sick with my touch. What a wonderful influence He is.

Although there were many times that my actions didn't show it, I couldn't recall a time that I didn't love God. I suppose many would consider me unsophisticated and possibly naive among the flow of the intellectual, but I have always had His gift of common sense. God has been good to me! He has given me so many wonderful blessings and like an unruly child, I knew that I had given back nothing in return. It's peculiar what will run through your mind when it's at ease.

This weekend was to be the first time we were away from our children since the birth of our son Nicholas, and our anticipation was overwhelming. My wife, Gail, and I had carefully planned our trip to Santa Barbara for months and it was to consist of two days of relaxation, fine dining, a tour of the famous Dutch Village in Solvang and an appointment with a spiritualist - Reverend George Daisley of Hallowed Grounds Fellowship. It was while skirting the town of Carpenteria that my reticent mood was awakened.

"Isn't it beautiful," Gail said with awe, "These cliffs must have been around since the beginning of time."

Nodding assuringly, I mentioned how nice it would be if we could have been around to see all the changes that took place over that time. I pondered to myself if humanity realized just how beautiful the world really is or could appreciate God's natural wonders.

"I wonder if Grampa Jake will speak to us?" Gail inquired, "You mentioned that your mother had difficulty making communications to you and your brother, Jim, last year!"

"If it's possible, I'm sure he will." I said with confidence, "God gives powers to those He loves, honey, I'm quite sure you will agree when you meet Reverend Daisley."

The trip to Santa Barbara was my second in less than 18 months, and I began recalling how exciting my first spiritual reading was with Reverend Daisley.

Two years earlier, I had been reading a novel by the famous Taylor Caldwell and noticed a reference in the book to her own experience with George Daisley, as well as a meeting between the Reverend and the late Bishop Pike. Although it was already late in the evening, I had decided to confirm Daisley's existence with a phone call. Requesting that the operator give me information for Santa Barbara, I quickly learned that there indeed was a party with the same name located on San Ysidro Road. I dialed the number and listened to what seemed to be around ten tones before making the connection.

"George Daisley heah!" came the refined English reply. I caught my breath. Half apologizing for the late night intrusion, I said, "Are you the same George Daisley that was mentioned in Taylor Caldwell's book?" Knowing quite well that the last name wasn't common.

"I'm that exact one," came the reply, "I do remember Mrs. Caldwell's meeting quite well. Lovely lady, simply lovely!"

I informed Daisley that I had read about him in Caldwell's book and inquired whether a commoner would have the opportunity for a sitting. "I must apologize to you, but it would be impossible to fit you in until the first part of March," he said sympathetically, "If you would like me to put you in my book for a date, I most certainly will.

I confirmed that I would indeed enjoy a meeting, set the date on my calendar and bid him adieu.

When our meeting neared, I called to assure him that I would be there and requested if it would be permissable to bring my brother with me. Receiving an affirmative reply, I informed Jim and spent over a half-hour on the phone discussing how difficult Reverend Daisley's job would be the following day.

"Have you told him anything about you? Jim said with a leery tone. "You know there are many quacks around and they have a tendency to use trickery when they have something to work with!

I assured him that Daisley was going to start from scratch. He didn't even know my name, where I was from or who I had wanted to contact. The appointment was made simply with the name Richard.

Bright and early the next morning I picked up Jim in Anaheim and proceeded north to Santa Barbara.

When we arrived, we discovered that Reverend Daisley's directions were most precise. Proceeding inland from Pacific Coast Highway, we followed the winding road through lush greenery. Set back from the road in dense foliage, we could make out a home nearly 50 yards from the street. As we pulled up the drive, we saw a middle-aged gentleman striding towards us. Daisley appeared to be a man in his early sixties, very neat and gave you the immediate belief that he indeed was no fortune-teller or palm-reader. The closest I could describe him would be to say he could possibly stand in quite effectively as a Gary Grant understudy.

After exchanging introductions, he led us down a wooded pathway to an unusual-looking cabin. (We later found out that it was a 163-year old converted well-house) Although it was late morning, a chill lingered in the central-California air and I couldn't swear to it, but it might have only been my eager anticipation. After we informed Daisley that he need not warm the building with a fire, he motioned us over to an antique divan.

"Have a seat and let me explain what you may expect." he explained. "First, I must make mention that my only purpose here is that of a receiver for the spirits that wish to make a connection with you. Is that understood?" We said that it was. The room seemed somewhat eerie and I was thinking about how frightening it would have been near the bewitching hour. My earlier thoughts of some seamy-seance by the full moon were quickly dispelled by the mid-day sun that was shining through the old window.

All the way up to Santa Barbara, Jim and I were exchanging frivolous jest that Daisley would have to be some fraudulent medium and any likelihood of his being anything else was the furthest from our minds. With a strong faith in God, I wasn't even sure that I should've been there and over the previous months I was tempted to cancel the appointment, thinking it might be construed un-Christian. Anyway I was there.

Reverend Daisley seated himself on a metal chair approximately ten feet away. Facing us he said, "When I make the contact between the spirits, please remain silent," he went on, "If you would like to ask questions, you may ask them through me as if I am the actual spirit. Is that understood?" We nodded affirmatively.

Although I came there sceptical, knowing fully well that Daisley would indeed have to be gifted to convince me otherwise, I left with another attitude altogether. George Daisley was everything I thought he wasn't.

"When the spirits appear, I will be able to see them, describe them to you, and in some cases, when permitted, I will give you their names and give you their messages. Do you know what I mean?" We indicated that we did. Daisley cleared his throat, relaxed his body, loosened his tie and slumped forward as if in a form of meditation. After a moment he leaned forward and gave us the impression that we were in a room with someone quite different.

Looking directly through me, he said, "Richard, you have a beautiful aura with all the colors of the rainbow in it. Standing near your left shoulder is a large woman, not too long ago departed from this world." Daisley went on, "She says that she is glad you came here today. She knows you had many reservations about coming, but she is glad you have. Do you know what I mean?" Not impressed as yet, I said I did.

"She says that she was your maternal grandmother," said Daisley in a crisp English monotone, "she says that she is in a wonderful place where there is no sorrow...only extreme happiness. She says that she is with you both many times during the day and that everything in your lives will work out if you seek your answers in the proper order. There is nothing you boys can not accomplish if you set your minds to it. You have healing powers within you that you do not know of. You must work hard to find these answers." With that Daisley seemed to change his glance and thoughts.

Glancing back and forth between Jim and myself, he said that there was a small woman with close-cropped hair and diminutive features that is trying frantically to reach both of you equally. "She says she is your mother and although it is not clearly communicatable, I believe she is saying that you both ought to have more self-confidence with yourselves, in answer to the question you were talking about on the way up this morning. Do you understand? queried the Reverend. Again we said we did.

"I was very happy with you boys on earth, but there is nothing there that can compare with anything here. Don't go visit the grave, - I'm not there!" With that the communication broke off. Jerking, ever so slightly, Daisley seemed to come back from a distant place, losing receivership with our mother.

It is needless to say that I was shocked and in awe of his powers. Chills were doing funny things to my spine and tears began welling in my eyes. I had just witnessed something that twenty minutes ago I thought was an impossibility. From that moment on there wasn't the slightest notion of disbelief in my mind about the existence of a Hereafter. It had been proven to this doubting-Thomas that Heaven existed after life, and everything was beginning to come into focus. I remembered what Jesus had said in the Bible in reference to His Father in Heaven and now I had proven, to my own satisfaction, that God was telling the truth. How could I have ever had doubt? I felt so small, weak and helpless, but at the same time renewed in faith. I vowed that I would never doubt God again and silently asked Him for forgiveness.

On the return trip to Anaheim the joking was missing from our conversation. I got the impression that Jim wasn't as sure as I was about what we had heard. Maybe his faith was already stronger than mine on the existence of life after death or maybe he thought it was the result of trickery.

"What did you think about Reverend Daisley?" I said expecting exhilarance.

"Okay I guess," he said, "I guess if he was a crook he would have charged you for the sitting."

"That's another thing I didn't understand," I said, "I was totally satisfied with what he did accomplish. He said that he would not accept a donation because he couldn't clearly reach Mom. Daisley said that he did nothing on his own and without his gift from God he would not experience any reception with the spirits."

We left it at that, but I badgered him all the way home and must have talked his ear off with my excitement. I couldn't wait to get home and tell Gail all about my new experience. I still was in shock at communicating with my mother. It was March 1979, and our mother had died of cancer on August 16th, 1975. Now, when I pray for the soul of Merle Grey Hall, I do so with extreme assurance that they have indeed been answered. There was no questioning the fact that God exists. I felt so wicked as to have ever only half-believed in what I heard in church or read in the Bible, but I guess I was one that had to be shown.

I could see from my wife's eyes that she was experiencing that same doubt as we manuvered the final stretch to Santa Barbara. She knew full well that I would not lie to her, but she still had a degree of scepticism about the venture.

Arriving at our destination, we checked into the Best

Western and unpacked. That evening we had a candlelite meal at the Chart House and the queries were rampant. I knew what she was thinking even before she said it.

"Honey, do you think we ought to go tomorrow?" she said with reservations, "I'm not so sure the church would approve. What does the Bible say about this sort of thing?

I couldn't recall whether it said anything about communicating with spirits but I quoted what Jesus said in the Bible. "Jesus said that we should test every spirit as there will be many wolves that will come in sheep's clothing." I reminded her, "He said that good trees do not bear bad fruit. I feel that Reverend Daisley is surely gifted and to my estimation, he passes the test of the spirit."

Evidently that was good enough for her and we finished our meal. Arriving back at the motel, we showered and retired early.

The next morning we rose at about 7 a.m., dressed, ate a light breakfast in the motel cafeteria and prepared for our 10 o'clock appointment with Daisley. I wondered if he would recognize me when we arrived.

At precisely 9:45 we pulled into Daisley's driveway. Almost mechanically he was there to greet us warmly. I introduced my wife to him and we were off to the well-house.

Gail is one lovely person and if she has any shortcomings, it's her penchant to interrogate new acquaintances. She was no different that day. I once told her that she had missed her calling and that she should have been a detective. The questions were flowing, but to my surprise they were met with much patience by Daisley. Maybe her questions were her way of disguising her nervousness, but never the less they came out in an endless stream. By the time we were seated on the couch for the meeting, she knew more about Daisley than I had known previously. As I looked at her I thought how good God had been to His undeserving and sometimes unfaithful servant, namely me. My statuesque, California-girl had a rare beauty found in so few. Her glamorous features only hinted at the goodness in her heart, and I indeed felt blessed.

Once again Daisley placed himself directly across from us, explained what we could expect for my wife's benefit and began. He explained something I had missed in our first meeting. The metal chair he used made reception more clear. Maybe my earlier thoughts were on being deceived and could have resulted in a different frame of mind. Anyway, Daisley cleared his throat, wiped his face of expression, lowered his head and relaxed for a moment, fidgeting with his palms on the chair. When he had achieved the state of reception, he again appeared to be somewhere distant and at the same time possessing a power to look through some invisible veil between the living and the world that lay beyond.

"Gail! There is a gentleman here that wishes to speak to you. He says that he is your paternal grandfather. Do you know who I mean?" said Daisley. Gail said she did. "He says that he heard you on the way up yesterday morning when you were talking about how beautiful the landscape was. He also mentions that he is in a place that is much more beautiful than you could every try to imagine. Do you understand?" said Daisley. She again indicated that she understood, but this time with her voice almost muffled in tone. "He says to tell you that he is happy that you came today and that your father will never believe you when you tell him you spoke with me, but tell him this." the spirit went on, "Tell him not to worry about the land deal. It should all work out favorably in time. Tell him he worries too much." At this I could see that Gail was taken aback. She said that she didn't know of any land deal but nevertheless she said she would tell her father upon her return. Daisley continued with Gail.

"There is someone else here," Daisley went on, "Her name is Mary Elizabeth, but she says that you would not know her, however your mother would. Do you know what I mean?" inquired the Reverend. Gail indicated that she did not know of anyone in her family by that name. "Tell your mother about me. Tell her I said hello! Do you know what I mean? was Daisley's repetitious query. Gail again said that she would pass along the message, but again said that she did not know the spirit.

Turning to me quickly, Daisley said, "There is an Indian, possibly an Aztec Indian near your left shoulder. He says his name is Ahmed and you would not possibly know who he is." Daisley went on, "He says that on your last visit you were told that you had an aura about you that would allow you to be a healer of many. He says that since that time you have not made any attempt to learn this gift. He will help you in that quest. Do you know what I mean?" asked Daisley. I said I did, but really wasn't aware of the meaning. When all this was said, Reverend Daisley came back to where we were, refreshed himself and smiled faintly. He later explained that it was exhausting in many ways to contact the spirit world. He said that so many try to get through all at the same time, and when that happens it's difficult to sort them out, and is physically draining.

To me there was no question about the authenticity of Reverend George Daisley. As Jesus said "to test each spirit", I believe I did just that. I did not supply any advanced information to him and the odds against the chance of selecting the information at random seemed impossible. I am not that naive as to fail to recognize that this world is full of con-artists and charlatans who, with a little to go on, can systematically build on an average base on which to project lifestyles. Such was not the case. Jesus said that in the 'end times' He would send great prophets, wise men and scribes among the people of the world. Judging from what I witnessed in Santa Barbara, Reverend George Daisley at least appeared gifted, if nothing else.

All the way back home, Gail and I were praising God for His sign to us. Our outlook on the future was somewhat more sure and it is difficult at best to describe the inner glow we possessed. Even though our faith in God had been strong before, this experience seemed to reinforce what we already believed. The next question we posed to each other was, who would believe what we had seen? Most of our acquaintances would possibly think we had lost some marbles. We decided to tell only those who had strong faiths, believed in the power of God and that circle of close friends and family.

When we arrived back in Downey to pick up the children, Gail was anxious to let her parents know of the good news. She told her father about the land deal that her grandfather had mentioned and he was surprised. Both of Gail's parents have a strong commitment to serving God and know of his wonderous miracles, so it wasn't surprising that they didn't exhibit our same enthusiasm about Daisley.

Gail appeared to be saving the best for last. She had never heard her mother, Grace, ever mention a person by the name of Mary Elizabeth and we had already thrown out the possibility of Reverend Daisley selecting a name at random, let alone two names for the same person. If there was indeed a person by that exact name that Grace knew, it would solidify our beliefs that much more.

Seated at the kitchen table Gail asked, "Mom, do you know anyone by the name of Mary Elizabeth?"

Without a moment of hesitation her mother said, "Mary Elizabeth was my grandmother. She was my mother's mother and died long before you were born. She would have been your great-grandmother had she lived. Was she speaking, too?"

"Yes!" Gail exclaimed, "She said that I wouldn't know her, but you would. She said to say hello."

I had a lot of trouble believing at one time in my life. I was caught up in material wealth and thought I had all the answers necessary for happiness. I was wrong! The average person lives to about 75, but what is that compared to an eternity. I know that God's Word is Truth, and I thought I had seen part of it.

"Discerning The Spirit"

That is the way I felt with both of my experiences with George Daisley. Gail and I were overjoyed and felt that the Lord GOD was giving us a message to further our spiritual beliefs. I cannot explain the power that came from Daisley nor did I understand his accuracy, but my GOD-given common sense told me that something still wasn't right.

Even though at the time I felt that I had tested the spirit as Jesus told us to do, maybe I hadn't done it to His satisfaction. My answer came years later...the answer was from GOD upon my request. Although I thought I was well verse with the Bible, GOD's Commandments and prophecy, He instructed me to the effect that I had made an error in judgement, an error in "testing the spirit" and in the course of writing this book I should make the proper adjustment.

All Christians know that GOD works within us in peculiar ways. He will allow us to experience good and evil so that we will know the difference. Many times what appears to the mortal as good can often turn out otherwise. My testing of the spirit of George Daisley was not thorough. My error in judgement came as a result of my ignorance of scripture.

One of my brothers in Christ, Pat Robinson, of the 700 Club, sent me some material that started me thinking. When I started this book in 1983, I began each day by praying that every sentence of the volume would be divinely inspired. I did not want to misinform anyone and I have not done so. According to the overlooked scripture, GOD does not want His people to contact the dead through any medium. In Leviticus 19:31 GOD makes it very clear:

"Do not defile yourselves by consulting mediums and wizards (fortune tellers), for I am Jehovah your GOD."

In 20:6 GOD says, "I will set my face against anyone who consults mediums and wizards instead of Me and I will cut that person off from his people." In 20:27 He says that mediums and wizards are causing their own doom.

In Isaiah 8:19 GOD says, "So why are you trying to find out the future by consulting witches and mediums? Don't listen to their whisperings and mutterings. Can the living find out the future from the dead? Why not ask your GOD?" Although I did consult a medium (Daisley) and felt an emotional surge from what was said, I must believe that it would be extremely possible that I did so naively. Satan also has influential powers that can appear innocent at first glance. I don't know what the case would be with Daisley but recently I tested his organization further. This time according to Isaiah 8:20 which reads, "Check these witches,words against the Word of GOD! If their messages are different than Mine, it is because I have not sent them, for they have no light or truth in them."

Daisley couldn't come to the phone but I talked with his administrator. He informed me that Hallowed Grounds Fellowship was formed in "1963" and confirmed my belief that Daisley was indeed a "medium." (The emphasis on 1963 will come clearer as you read on in this book) According to the aide, Daisley inherited the title "reverend" and was never ordained as a minister. The organization was non-denominational and, although they believed in GOD, they failed to recognize Jesus as anything other than a good prophet...that caught my ear more than anything else that was said in the half-hour conversation. My belief that Jesus is GOD is firm, (John 14:7-8) and when the aide explained that they believe in "reincarnation," that man could control his own destiny and that the New Age Movement is "Okay if that's what man wants," it brought me back into reality. I remembered a scripture that says, "the way to the Father is through the Son" and also "those that deny the SON, "DO NOT" have the Father." Their opinion on JESUS told me that no good could ever come from any further association; now or in the future.

In 1 Corinthians 12:3 it is said, "But now you are meeting people who claim to speak messages from the Spirit of GOD. How can you know whether they are really inspired by GOD or whether they are fakes? Here is the test: No one speaking by the power of the Spirit of GOD can curse Jesus and no one can say, "Jesus is Lord," and really mean it, unless the Holy Spirit is helping him. Because their belief only recognizes Jesus as a prophet, and because they also feel that Budda or Krishna were all possibly equal, I feel that the test has been completed and my inspiration tells me to obey GOD, and no one else. I will never return to consult any medium as GOD wishes.

Corinthians 12 explains the gifts GOD gives all. Everyone does not receive the identical gifts. In 1 Corinthians 12:27 GOD explains them and calls them all necessary components of the church body: they are Apostles, Prophets who preach GOD's Word, teachers, those who do miracles, those that heal, those who help others, those we can get others to work together and those who speak in languages they have never learned. Mediums are not mentioned. If it was GOD's Will that man should speak with the dead, I am conviced that He would have said so.

My experience with Daisley was good and I saw no evil in what he did; however GOD explains that we should not seek out the dead through any mediums...that's good enough for me!

George Daisley believes in life after death, in GOD and in the power that is healing, so my feeling is that he means well with his intentions. Daisley does not "curse Jesus", but failing to recognize Him as GOD tells me that all is not right. I realize that there are good people in this world who have not as yet accepted Jesus as the Christ for whatever reason. It is my inspiration that GOD allowed my wife and me to have that experience to solidify our beliefs in Him. I also believe that GOD allowed the experience to tell us how easy it would be (if that was the case) to become mislead by emotional feelings. I do not feel that my association with Daisley was anything but right, but it is not my decision to make. It is written that man should not seek the dead through mediums. As I love GOD, so let it be written, so let it be done!

We must recognize the fact that GOD gives wonderous miracles to those who love Him. Many times these gifts defy our mortal senses of logic and reason, but we should not be naive as to believe that we know all the answers or that these miracles only were existent in the days of the Prophets. If we want happiness to enjoy a full life on Earth, we must be willing to give ourselves to GOD and only obey His every wish!

CHAPTER THREE

"When The Salt Loses Its Savor!"

*"Ye are the salt of the earth: but if the salt have lost his savor,
wherewith shall it be salted? It is thenceforth good for nothing,
but to be cast out, and to be trodden under foot of men."*

JESUS CHRIST (Matthew 5:13)

Ask any brick mason or carpenter of the need for
stability in construction and they will tell you that the
longevity of any dwelling is dependent on a firm foundation.
Just so is the like foundation of man necessary for prosperity.
Without acknowledging this eminent truth, the mind and body
will erode.

Many times throughout the Bible, Jesus calls His believers,
the "Salt of the earth" and the analogy is most appropriate.
Salt is more than a seasoning for food, it is a preservative
and the reasoning behind the analogy is that Jesus came to
Earth for the preservation of the human soul. Today we see
'wolves in sheep's clothing' almost everywhere we look. They
would have you believe that either there is no God or if there
was one, He is dead or hasn't yet arrived! It is difficult for
any real Christian to understand such idiocy. God is as alive
today as He was in the days of the earliest human. He is not
the prefabrication of human thought, but the representative of
all that is good in this world and the Creator of everything
that exists.

In keeping with the projections of Karl Marx, our
sciences are trying to feed our youth the theory of evolution,
a process in which the whole universe is a progression of
interrelated phenomena. It would be hard to top such an
untruthful contention. The very meaning of the word "science"
dispels and betrays its validity. Science is the "limited
knowledge" covering "general truths!" The word 'general' tells
us that these truths are not confined to "any specialization or
careful limitation!" In essence, science is the end product of
"man's intellect" and we already know the imperfections of our
species, don't we? Because science is "limited to the knowledge
of mans fabrications" it should be evident to common intellect
that the possibility of the human being evolving from the
creatures of the ocean or progressing from the ape, is utterly

absurd.

In the only recognized history of origin, the Bible, it says that God created man from the clay of the earth, the dust of this planet. When the body's vital signs cease to function, a decomposition takes place which eventually turns the body back to the state of origin...Dust - not fossils. The next time your Science or Biology teacher tries to push the unfounded theory of evolution down your throat, tell him your Bible says different. Give only to science what is accomplished in the name of God, and nothing for proposed accomplishments of man's creations without this grace.

It has been determined by scripture that God gave man the mental capacity to comprehend, reason and engage in activity that requires the creative use of his intellect. This capacity, although intended to be unlimited, is indeed narrow and un-imaginative in relation to its God-given potential. When God bestowed the power to man to govern over all the creatures on earth, this power was unlimited in capacity. The only limitations placed on man's use of this power was that it was to be used for the betterment of fellowship with God and for good only. Mans faith in the power of God is his downfall. Because of this deficiency of understanding these facts, the knowledge of man shall remain limited until that time when he is reintroduced to the "Tree of Life!"

Jesus said that in the end times of the world there would come many false prophets, who, through deceit, would lead many astray from the truths. They shall come in the name of liberty and will deceive all who have not been written down in the Book of Life. It becomes more and more obvious by the day that the times Jesus spoke of are indicative of this generation.

The seed of anti-Christ had its festation in the early fifties. Today he stands with his satanic creator at an age near 33. The deceiver is here as sure as you breathe! If you have eyes to see, ears to listen and the intellect to decipher good from evil, you can relate to this surety. We have regressed in true knowledge at the same time of proposed advanced technology. The gifts from God are being misused, abused, defiled and degraded, while the credits of man are being praised for truth and logic. All a good man needs to know can be found in the Bible.

As the mustard seed will grow into a mighty tree, the seed of man (sperm) when introduced to the egg from a woman's ovary results in the life form known as man. This sacred gift from God was never intended to be defiled or degraded as it has been in recent generations. God gives man the right to life, and also determines when it physically ends.

All the worthwhile discoveries can be directly attributed to God only, so why all the credit to science?

Can man create living organisms without first using God's existing elements? No! Why waste all the time and money on unworthy projects when God has said that He will provide all the knowledge man needs in life? All man can create is a robot, incapable of love or compassion for another. What good is that? Why are God's gifts being so blantantly abused?

Abortion by any other name is still murder! Man does not have the God-given right of deciding the fate of another living human regardless of the advancement in the life cycle. Where do we draw that line between the two? Is a fetus not described as a "developing human?" The Laws of God say...THOU SHALT NOT KILL! Why does man have to be so disrespectful before the Lord? Everyone who kills another faces judgement as sure as you are created by GOD. Without repentance our Father shall have His vengence on the perpetrator. God have mercy on their souls.

This sex abuse must stop now or the ones that are doing the tempting will be facing certain and swift judgement. Humans have been promiscuous by experimentation for ages but sex wasn't intended as an act of pleasure outside of wedlock. The streets of America and the world are littered with pornography. Since the early 1960's, the devices of pleasure have multiplied to sickening proportion and now many legislators want to legalize the debasing of a womans' body through prostitution. They want to open "red light districts" in the United States and tax a union so conducive to God's infinite love for mankind. Because man wants it, it will materialize!

Homosexuality is a prime sign that America's salt has reached dangerously low levels. In the early sixties this degenerating influence on society began making itself known to the world. They came out into the open with sympathetic pleas for recognition, formed organizations, lobbied their infectious disease in front of America and asked that their ways be overtly tolerated. America condones this perversion because of liberal views. "If they don't bother me, I don't care what their preferences are," is one such careless observation. Now we have them as policemen, school teachers, preachers of the word, newspaper publishers and writers with the power of the pen, guidance counselors of our youth and in every facet of our environment. They stage annual parades and the American people transude this degeneration of human will and encourage defilement of the mind in so doing.

It is not my intention to mislead anyone into believing that I am holier than thou, or that this author is anything more or less than a common sinner, however this world is not turning out as God had intended. We must acknowledge that to be fact and appreciate all that we have while we still have His blessings here on earth. I remember an age when the weaker sex known as woman was respected by most men and admired for her ideals of chastity. I remember a time when the aspiration of the female agenda was to include homemaking and caring for our Countrys youth with guidance. And I remember my childhood when it was not an uncomon occurence for a girl to be a virgin when married. It seems that all ideals have been twisted in nature. Anything that was good is now deemed to be bad!

I can faintly remember a period of my youth when the main idea of dating the opposite sex was for companionship and friendship with truthful overtones. Most can recall a time when men would make haste to open the door for a female and four-letter words were only occasionally uttered in the confines of locker rooms, unheard of in the presence of females.

Has man really been progressing in fruitful knowledge? Or, can we assume that we have progressed to the lowest form of primitive culture? Are we that naive as to look to this generation for future positive expectation? I don't think so. Everyday we witness negative vibrations with many end products of violence. It has been carefully programed into our culture. Those that believe in the meliorism of this age are not realistic. Standing alone, man cannot make anything better, specially not the world we live in or the communities we call home. A Christian's spirit is not of this planet and if he is oblivious to this reality, he is falsely calling on the name of Christ.

In the early sixties the American people witnessed a new generation that evolved through deceit. It marked the beginning of a sexual revolution in America and the pangs have only grown in dimension since that time. Although the onslaught of the sexual liberation was through devious means, we didn't have to usher it in, but we did. The mini-skirts and bikinis of the late fifties signaled a robust beginning but the influence of the cinema and porn magazines escalated and venesectioned the world with its smut. Because of this outpour of liberal thought, the treasures of once admired ideals were subverted into submission. The Communist design was taking hold in America and their evil plans were aimed at the family unit. By removing the woman from the home it would become that much easier to reprogram the children and disillusion the parents. Divide the family and you conquer the country from within and because Americans were oblivious to what was taking place, it worked in the favor of our adversaries. Now that liberal thought was foremost in the minds of their capitalist enemy and flourishing, the onslaught continued.

The ultimate Soviet conspiracy of getting women involved in our economy, came to the forefront with the conception of the women's rights movement. If the women were equal in industry it would cause greater competition between the male and female. Capitalists love material possessions and more money could lead to more greed within the family. The more money the family would have, the more they could buy and by having the woman in the business district, instead of caring and guiding the child, many male breadwinners would be unemployed. They were right in their assessment and accurate as well of the turmoil it would cause.

We didn't realize that what we had previously was best. We didn't understand the consequences we would be facing with this liberal movement. What transpired was that women were filling the positions that were held by lower income male heads of household. Many people with lesser education were losing their opportunity to provide for their families, because higher educated women were moving into the job markets. The myth that 'more money for the family budget would make all members more happy' spread throughout our country like an epidemic but more capital did not lead to happiness.

The more possessions the family would acquire, the more it wanted. Children were being left behind with less caring entities and without proper guidance, they searched for ways to cope with lost love and found illusion with drugs. Conservatism within the family was shelved and the world moved into a era of radical behavior. Credit became widely abused. With more income projected, the family began living three to five years ahead of their budget and when recessions caused layoffs in industry the family could no longer meet their obligations. Family discord rose along with the divorce rates. More and more broken homes; more and more unhappy endings; more and more independent heads of households in the market places of our country. Gone forever were the conservative ideals of family life. Gone was the love in the family with money as the root of all evil. Money replaced GOD.

By no means do I intend to project a feminist or anti-female image. In its proper place, the female has every right to equality in compensation for equal output. What I contend is that God didn't plan it that way. God had been placed on the back burner of the family unit with greed to the forefront. Cherished ideals of the female raising the child had been subverted and extravagance replaced conservative budgeting without the female in the home. The male image became inadequate and his effectiveness, motivations and goals stagnatingly dormant. Time for God and raising offspring dwindled rapidly and now more money was needed, but the desire was missing. Material objects became burdensome, wearing out before they were paid off and family bankruptcy became commonplace. At every crossroad the presence of Soviet design was winning and the precious standards of God were misplaced.

The once admirable role of the female as the homemaker dissipated with the birth of liberal reform in our society. Many new opportunities were being opened to females everywhere but unfortunately many of these new careers were sexually-biased and debasing in effect. By the mid-sixties the motion picture industry began giving the world what the new liberal attitude desired and old world ethics became outmoded. The new ideology of the film makers was that 'sex and nudity sells' and a once precious commodity was being carnally exploited. The chastity of the country girl became passe, unless of course she was sans apparel. Pornography was in and poisoning the minds of America with lustful imagery. Gone forever was the concept of 'living happily ever after,' - the country wanted more.

Before many could realize what was happening to our basic standards, communism struck again with subversive tactics as distraction. Since the preservation of liberty was the capitalists' dream, communism had to divert the goals from the homeland to the distant shores of Southeast Asia. Moral ethics in the United States were already submerging when Vietnam broke into full fervor. America to the rescue! The distraction from our heartland cause and the Soviet travesty came to fruition. It was once inconceivable that such a deviously conspired strategy would be successful on our country; however, the vile smokescreen worked and morals plummeted in despair. Mass misinterpetation of South Vietnam's strife came to the minds of the liberal element and the gap widened between what was right and what was not. We were engaged in another's battle for free thought, but one that was destined for failure.

America was engaged in two wars again and was losing both, fighting for Vietnamese rights and at the same time losing many of our own in the process. 1963 was indeed not one of America's better years.

The Soviet subjugations had succeeded in removing the woman from the home, alienating the child in so doing. They were degrading the female image and at the same time were placing the male bread-winner in no-win predicaments, further degrading the American way with deception. Lust and greed were festering on the home front and they saw to it that illusionary influences were readily available to further cloud the picture. Liberals everywhere wanted drugs legalized and penalities reduced for their consumption. Because Americans are so cherishing of liberty, the communists attacked these freedoms with intensity. Every atheist in our nation came out of the darkness to further disillusion and twist these freedoms in their favor.

The Atheist Deceivers!

"Take care that no one deceives you; because many false Christs (anti-Christs) will come using my Name and they will deceive many!"

JESUS CHRIST (Matthew 24:4)

The vile, liberal thought-process was only simmering in our Judiciary branch of government when a failure to communicate poisoned the minds of true justice in 1962. The United States Supreme Court incompetently allowed the anti-Christ a foothold in America when they ruled against freedom in the case of Engle vs. Vitale (370 U.S. 421). A hearing was given on school board action which, under New York law, directed the district's principal to cause a prescribed prayer of 22 words "to be said aloud by each class in the presence of the teacher at the beginning of each school day." Our illustrious, liberal court deemed this to be "part of a governmental program to further religious belief."

"Almighty GOD, we acknowledge our dependence upon thee, and we beg thy blessings upon us, our parents, our teachers and our Country!"

"Hence, the fact that the prayer (is) denominationally neutral...(and) that its observance is voluntary...(cannot) free it from the limitations of the Establishment Clause.," was the findings of the Supreme Court.

In 1963, the question of Bible reading was again presented to the "High" Court in the case of the School District of Abington Township (PA) vs. Schempp (374 U.S. 203). A companion case, Murray vs. Curlett was pressed by atheists and combined with it. The chief justices reviewed a Pennsylvania law requiring that "at least ten verses from the Holy Bible shall be read, without comment, at the opening of each public school day." Any child could be excused from such reading upon written request from a parent or guardian, but these liberal atheists, Jews and Unitarians felt that their children would be set upon by the majority if that took place and were determined to remove prayer completely and our liberal-thinking justices agreed.

"This," the Court said, "transgressed the prohibition against the enactment of any law respecting an establishment of religion as included in the First Amendment and embraced within the due process clause of the Fourteenth Amendment."

In its decision the Court noted that no one version of the Bible would be acceptable to all sects and concluded that, "to be valid under the Establishment Clause" governmental requirements must have "a secular legislative purpose and a primary effect that neither advances nor inhibits religion." The Court could not believe that insistence on such neutrality "collides with the majorities' right to free exercise of religion." Nothing in its decision would prevent "study of the Bible or religion...as part of a secular program of education."

The prayer was so-called a nonsectarian prayer, composed of 22 words by the New York State Board of Regents to meet objections to the recital of sectarian prayers in the State's public schools. Suit was brought by a group of 'parents' - including one atheist, members of the Jewish faith, the society for 'ethical culture' and the Unitarian Church. Although their children were allowed to be excused from any participation in the prayer, the Supreme Court overruled the ruling by the State court - all justices but one concurred.

"We 'think' that using its public school system to encourage recitation of the Renent's prayer, the State of New York has adopted a practice wholly inconsistent with the Establishment Clause. There is no doubt that the prayer is a religious activity. It is a solemn avowal of divine faith and supplication for the blessings of the Almighty," was the OPINION of Justice Black and the other justices.

Can you imagine any doctrine adopted by the highest court in God's Country, a free democratic society, ruling in favor of a total religious minority? Because of anti-Christs our children have been deprived of their rights. The atheists, who believe in the exact same non-religious preference as the Soviet Union, caused the removal of GOD from our public school system! Without being presumptuous to the hopes that I will be included in the 'Rapture', all I can say to that is, "Come on Rapture, Come Lord Jesus - come now for your people and let me be one of your witnesses when you destroy the atheists of this country and the world. Let all the innocent children that have died from drug overdoses or from atheistic persecutions be in the front row when you come. What a day that will be!"

The decision of the Engle case clearly established 'the

principle,' that requiring the recitation of a State-written prayer in a public school is unconstitutional, but the question remained unanswered was whether the recital of a non-sectarian prayer, not written by a State agency, would likewise be held unconstitutional.

The answer was given as a result of both the Schempp vs. Abington School District and the Murray vs. Curlett cases. The decision in this instance made it clear that religious functions of any kind cannot be carried out in a public school.

To further 'appreciate' that illogical opinion from the Supreme Court, you must first understand a few glaring facts that the court didn't consider to be important.

First, the dissidents were representative of a minority religious preference. The Schempps were members of a Unitarian Church with doctrines towards 'liberal thought.' The Unitarians express the use of human "reason" with their religion, believe that the Deity consists of one person, stress individual freedom with their church and exercise 'freedom for liberal social action.' The key word there is 'LIBERAL!'

Secondly, Madalyn Murray (O'Hair), acting on behalf of her son William, is a professed atheist, a practice indigenous to that of the Soviet Union, and is currently defiling the great State of Texas with her infestation of American atheists, where she serves as founder and president. In the composing of this book, I sent to that organization for some of their literature. When I received it, I could only read the first paragraph for reasons of nausea. Their material is so sick, so un-American, so un-Godly perverted that I cannot understand why they haven't been run out of Texas on a rail. I didn't believe that America would allow such vile propaganda within this precious territory. In their filth (literature), they mention of how they have been persecuted by believing Christians everywhere they have been. They are indeed fortunate that I am not in a public office of that State. They would find out what persecution is all about,---right pronto! Nevertheless, our high court ruled in their favor!

It was evident that our Country's founding fathers were religious people whose institutions presupposed a Supreme Being. When the Constitution's First Amendment was written, there were only a few undesirable entities in this new country. Taking the Constitution literally, decisions were made favoring anti-Christian beliefs by liberal justices who had absolutely no insight as to its future ramifications. There was no regard for the majority's established practice!

Man took it upon himself to 'go against GOD and His decision that all government was His. (Romans 13:1) On that hideous day in 1963, - GOD as His justice was not served! In retrospect, to the delight of so few, so many since have been damaged brutally. It has been twenty years since that debauchery of injustice and true Americans are still feeling its pain.

On that dark day in 1963, the atheists made a shambles of God's principles. Madalyn Murray O'Hair had the initial laugh against our God and country. I'm sure the Soviet Union applauds her efforts at debasing our country's moral and spiritual values, but if there is one thing certain-something she will not escape, without repentance is the judgement of the God - whom she's certain doesn't exist! The significance of having the "last laugh" is in His hands only! It is the opinion of this author that Murray and her satanic brood will not find jest in GOD's Wrath.

President Reagans' devotion to cleaning up America is righteous. A good starter would be to restore the meaning of liberty in our Country and renew patriotism among all Americans. The reestablishment of "VOCAL PRAYER" is necessary in the public schools. Many liberals are pushing for silent prayer, as an appeasement to Christians, have always had in America. We must put GOD back in our schools and His Law back into the minds of our people. President Reagan said that "as far as I'm concerned, God should have never been kicked out of the public schools in the first place!" When you vote for him this Fall, you also cast a vote for GOD!

In 1935, Joseph Stalin made reference to what it takes to overthrow capitalism. He indicated that communism must attack a country's weakest link, religion, and remove it from their society. Next, subversion will be easier on the nation through their music, removing patriotism. Stalin thought that America had so many religious beliefs they would be easily blinded. What he didn't take into consideration was that you can subjugate people with doctrines or ideology, but the Christian's heart cannot be changed by communism. A man's soul is real. You can destroy the body and mind, but the soul is everlasting with Christ.

The deterioration of the moral and spiritual fibers of our nation can be traced directly to the un-American organizations we have allowed to thrive. Our patriotism and our adherence to the principles of God should be one and the same. This is GOD's Country, no one else's. An atheist is a person who denys the existence of God and all religious faith or practice thereof; therefore, we should not tolerate any of these anti-Christian organizations in this Country. If we are to remain a free nation, everyone must take an active part against radical, un-Godly activities. Allowed to organize and fester in the midst of our people, good will always lose out to evil, while the liberty we seek will be lost forever.

These organizations are the seed of satan. They thrive on adversity while promoting negative cultures and beliefs. They twist everything that is good and prey on our freedoms. To eliminate these viperous entities, we would tend to threaten the same liberty we all hold sacred; and they know it! Communism, socialism, atheism, liberalism, negativism and satanism are closely linked in harmony. They are also an exact opposite of Christianity. In Revelations 12:4, there is mention of a Red Dragon with seven heads and ten horns and a tail that "dragged one-third of the stars from the sky and dropped them on the earth." It has been written that faithful Christians will shine like the stars in the evening sky for their belief in Christ. It has been fairly estimated that one-third of the world's population is currently under the (Reds) control of communism. I believe this prophecy is already fulfilled! The dragon (anti-Christian communism) already has one-third of the world!

What we witness each day is the continual loss of the (salt) preserving elements. This can be directly attributed to un-American activity. What does it take to make Christians and Jews everywhere stand up and be counted? Haven't we lost enough to the powers of darkness? When a government allows any subversive (anti-American) organization within their border, it is wrong and must be corrected! It is time to present the proper legislation to forever rid America of these vipers, - tomorrow will be too late.

We cannot afford to be a people of much talk and little action. The communists have given us ample warning of their intention and they are accomplishing what they have set up as goals. We must fight every liberal element that surfaces. Our Country is worth it, our children are worth it and our God deserves it!

Dissolving American Perception

The early 60's did much more harm than just the debasement of spiritual values. That period witnessed the birth of America's dissolving perception. It was a time in our history that many would relish an opportunity to replay. It was the birth of illusionary drugs and the initiation of our youth to the darkness of the outer world.

By now you should have come to a fairly accurate conclusion that this author is 100% down on liberal beliefs. It is not fiction, whether through design, neglect or deceit, who are the cause for the free thought that drugs were no worse than alcohol or cigarettes. It was the liberal who fought for the legalization of marijuana in the early sixties and it is that same element who stand firm today for legalized abortion (murder). I don't have to name them in this book. All one has to do is pick up a newspaper to see who they are.

Bad seeds are the same today as they were in the sixties; always for evil...never producing positive expectancy in their deeds. Many of these same liberals oppose vocal prayer in the public schools. Who are they protecting? Surely it can't be the 10% who don't want their children worshiping God! If we can eliminate the idea that they are not protecting the majority or the minority, who's left? You guessed it! I feel sure that many of these liberals are direct or indirect correspondents for the Soviet Union. We know they are in the State Department, the House of Representatives, the Congress, the Senate and on the Suprene Court, as well as firmly entrenched in State government. Their calling cards are adversity and their motivations are for the separation of church and state (or shall we safely say the elimination of religion), and (ist) reform. America wake up! We've been subverted by wolves in sheeps' clothing. We have been taken to the cleaners by liberals calling themselves Americans.

When I say we should be against reform, I talk about liberal reform. There is a dire need of reorganization of standards in this Country and if that is reform, that's what I contend. The power of the people can bring about the needed alterations in ideology. It must be done this Fall with your vote. (See chapter fourteen)

This period in our history is not the product of chance, but of design. The correlation between the removal of public school prayer, the civil rights and womens liberation movements, the sexual revolution, drug and alcohol abuse and other related difficulties were astutely programed into our culture by a sinister design with the ultimate aim at eliminating capitalism. When socialism gains, liberty is the only loser! When these standards of despair are prevalent, everyone loses and America is primed for its infestation. We are losing our preserving elements by the ton. The answer to reversing this trend is so simple...it will be overlooked by most.

What we need is God back in the public schools. We need GOD foremost in the minds of Americans everywhere and GOD in our hearts. The current luke warm attitude is not good enough to save America. With GOD at the forefront....we can't lose. To reverse any momentum, we must stop it first with sincerity. To get our Country going in the right direction, we must make the 1984 elections our stepping stone. President Reagan can't do it alone, he needs our support through prayer and the power of our vote. We must weed out the liberals and replace them with men who have GOD foremost in their hearts. Don't fret, they're around and ready to step in to do GOD's Will for America. They need your vote if anything positive can come out of our darkest hour.

"Not All Who Appear Religious, Are Godly Men!"
(Matthew 7:21)

Psalms 127 tells us that "Unless the Lord God builds the house, the builders' work is useless." If Mondale, Hart and Jackson were men of God they would not be condoning that man has the right to decipher who lives and who doesn't. The Psalm goes on..."Unless the Lord protects a city, sentries do no good. It is senseless for a man to work from early morning until late at night worrying about making a living!" Jesus tells us in Matthew 6:25 that we should not worry about where our subsistence will come from, it's in the hands of GOD. In Matthew 15:18, God speaks about the Democratic candidates and others without mentioning their names. "Things that come out of the mouth are from the heart; and it is these that make a man unclean!"

Abortion is wrong...those that are for it are wrong. GOD says in Psalm 127:3, "Children are a GIFT FROM GOD; they are His reward." GOD gives blessings to those who give Him reverence and trust in HIM! There is no other way to look at it. You are either with GOD all the way or you are against Him. There's no middle of the road. Those who feel it is right to have anyone but GOD decide if His Gifts are acceptable are WRONG!

It would be wise indeed to trace the primaries and candidates from the year 1960 through the present. You will find that that year was THE year most of these debasing influences took seed in America. There is no question that it was all contrived and connived by the Soviet Union in order to dilute spiritual beliefs, corrupt the moral structure in our Country and eliminate any form of American patriotism! Drug abuse has reached epidemic proportion and no end seems in sight unless we can eradicate liberal thought.

A recent government-sponsored study into the use of drugs indicates the heavy burden its use has had on our economy. In loss of production, 4.9 billion was lost through absenteeism, slowdowns, mistakes and sick leave. Drug-related deaths another 1.3 billion, imprisonment 2.1 billion and leaving employment for criminal careers to support the habit topped off at 8.3 billion. Medical expenses for treatment in rahab centers, hospitals and for doctors' care cost us 1.9 billion and the administration costs for the treatment programs, research and proper technological training cost taxpayers another 367 million.

The losses from drug related crime soared through 1983. Federal, State and local expenditures for the courts, police and prisons were 5.2 billion, alarm systems and other preventive steps for businesses and other individuals cost 1.6 billion and property destroyed during criminal acts was 113 million. The total reflection on the US economy tilted the scales at 25.8 billion dollars. To say that America was not in the middle of an epidemic, would be like burying one's head in the sand.

Recently Dr. Mitchell Rosenthal, the President of Phoenix House, America's largest residential program for the treatment of drug abuse, was interviewed by USA Today columnist, Barbara Reynolds.

Dr. Rosenthal, a noted psychiatrist and lecturer, indicated that they were seeing more and more cocaine users who were successful businessmen with high earning capacity. Salesmen, stockbrokers, lawyers and even some clergymen, who had gotten involved because they were disillusioned into believing the drug was relatively safe and fun, sexy and part of the scene.

"The potency of the drug compels people to continue using it," said Rosenthal, "It is so powerful to the system that it will command the person to continued addiction. Cocaine and alcohol, although both drugs, are not the same. Both have very different effects on the system. If you look at the effect on 100 people that use alcohol, of that amount only a few will go on and abuse it. Of a like number of cocaine users, a very high number will become serious, dysfunctional cocaine users, where there is spending a disproportionate amount of their personal money on the drug."

"Many of the drug users are very ambitious, very upwardly mobile, have thought that cocaine is going to do nothing but increase their mobility and make them more successful in both the bedroom and the boardroom," Rosenthal went on, "What has happened though is quite the reverse. They really become dysfunctional in their work and their bedrooms, so that it turns out to be neither a boost to their private or professional lives."

Rosenthal went on to admit that there is no particular profile as to the cocaine user. The poor, the rich, the well educated and the poorly educated are all subject to its use, and that no particular location in the United States is escaping its influence. Individuals are spending hundreds of thousands of dollars on the drugs, losing their jobs, their wives and their homes. Cocaine is deception and disillusionment because it makes one feel that he is well on his way to success when in reality the feeling is a myth.

"Cocaine is a dangerous drug from a physical point of view," says Dr. Rosenthal, "Often the people who do not use the drug by sniffing it, or tooting it, begin injecting the drug or freebasing it, which is smoking it. When they do that they are able to get much higher concentrations in the lungs and in the blood. Those people become more out of control, become extremely nervous, irritable and paranoid. Far from feeling good, these people feel out of sorts. They are jittery, jumpy and uncomfortable and what started out as a pleasure trip ends up in a nightmare.

If America is to recover the precious resources of mental health, personal hygiene, moral and the spiritual balance of ethical practice, there can by only one alternative, and that means man must seek the fulfillment he lacks through the acceptance and adherence to GOD. Remove the Spirit and faith becomes diluted. Remove faith from an individual and a decaying process materializes.

Humanity alone does not possess the intellectual power necessary to alter this deadly inclination. Nor will the majority ever seek out the truth. Jesus said that faith comes from hearing and hearing from the word of God. Unless a man is to allow Jesus into his heart, he will always walk in darkness. If you are dissatisfied with your direction in life, and have a thirst to partake in fruit from the 'Tree of Life' you must acknowledge that the way to God is through His Son, Jesus Christ. The decision is of an individual nature and no mortal has the power to sway the heart once Jesus resides within its confines.

Jesus said that in the end times there would come many false prophets who will deceive many, and with the increase of lawlessness, love in most men will grow cold; but the man who stands firm to the end will be saved. The Good News of the Kingdom will be proclaimed to the whole world as a witness to all nations. And then the end will come.

MATTHEW 24:11-14

The time to accept Jesus Christ as your Savior is now! Before I personally accepted Jesus, my life was in turmoil, I was certainly not happy and I had no real meaningful direction for my life. I used to think it odd that some people could outwardly proclaim Jesus as an entity that was actually alive. To communicate with Him was unrealistic at best. FROM THE MOMENT that I sought Him out, He was there to assist me; from the instant I asked Him to change my life and give it meaning, He was there for my fellowship.

This personal testimony is not a quirk of fiction, it is a reality. God is as alive as you and I are breathing. Don't be deceived by the atheist factions in this world. The good tree will bring forth only good fruit. Jesus is your answer. Accept Him and you, too, will understand the true meaning of peace and joy.

If you are on drugs – with Christ's assistance you will be healed. If you are crippled – your faith in Jesus will heal you and if you are hungry, Jesus will see to it that you are fed. If you really want to have a life of meaning, pray the following prayer in earnest, and you will receive that of which you request.

DEAR GOD
FORGIVE ME FOR I HAVE SINNED AGAINST YOU AND I AM SORRY. I am unhappy with my present lifestyle and I ASK THAT THE LORD JESUS CHRIST WILL COME INTO MY HEART and take over completely. I ask that you will assist me with my family, my business and help me to LOVE MY NEIGHBOR AS I DO MYSELF. I acknowledge that Jesus died on the cross for my sins and I am seeking His Total Guidance and Love. I ASK THIS IN THE NAME OF JESUS.
AMEN and AMEN.

CHAPTER FOUR

"Educational Demission of Our Youth!"
Twenty years after removal of prayer.

In a survey completed last year (1983) by the U.S. Department of Education, not one of the States in the Country escaped the effects of decreasing intellect. Over the ten year period 1972-1982, there was only one State in the U.S. displaying any rise in the test score, 49 plummeted! Twenty-two states and Washington D.C., use the Scholastic Aptitude Testing procedure (SAT), while the remaining twenty-eight use the American College Testing (ACT) for college entrance examinations.

SAT Tests are given in the following states:

California	Connecticut	Delaware
Florida	Georgia	Washington, D.C.
Hawaii	Indiana	Maine
Maryland	Massachusetts	New Hampshire
New Jersey	New York	North Carolina
Oregon	Pennsylvania	Rhode Island
South Carolina	Texas	Vermont
Virginia		

Of a possible perfect score of 1,600 points, the tate of New Hampshire scored the highest overall grade with 925 points, while Oregon was the runner-up with 908. Put these figures into percentile and the SAT National Leader comes up with a bland score of just 57.8%.

The ACT tests are given in the states of:

Alabama	Alaska	Arizona	Arkansas
Colorado	Idaho	Illinois	Iowa
Kansas	Kentucky	Louisiana	Michigan
Minnesota	Mississippi	Montana	Nebraska
Nevada	New Mexico	North Dakota	Ohio

Oklahoma   South Dakota   Tennessee   Utah
West Virginia   Wisconsin   Wyoming   Missouri

A perfect score with the ACT Test is 36 points. Wisconsin (20.4) and Iowa (20.3) were the front-runners, but placed again in percentile scores, their 56.6% showing again is indicative of failure.

In the previous decade, which has shown vast technological and scientific advances, these indicators of education development with our youth are devastating. Of the 50 States, only Washington, D.C. showed any improvement with the testing over the last ten years. The other States showed marked declination of intellect. Those liberal procrastinators who continue to remain optimistic of America's future leadership had better re-evaluate our present programs on educational development. Never in the history of this Country have American youth scored so low in development of basic skills.

The cause of such a delimma will become the object of great conjecture among our educational wizards. They will toss around the scores, re-evaluate programs and maybe even soften the examinations for the next groups that will be taking the tests. That will of course give many reason to be optimistic. What they won't do is evaluate the program in relation to those of pre-pray removal days, when discipline and standards were much higher than they are today, one thing that has to be understood before any positive, constructive reform can be accomplished in our Country. GOD MUST BE RECOGNIZED! GOD must be replaced as our foundation of future promise. Remove a sound foundation of the child and, like removing salt from the earth, erosion of the brain function materializes. America has been lowering standards ever since prayer was removed from the public schools in 1963, and instead of scores being higher with easier examinations, they are working in reverse. GOD is the answer, but our society is so crammed with liberal scientists and educators, they will never admit the fact. They would rather teach your child the arts of sexual perversion or basket-weaving, and grade them accordingly, than raise the standards of education. Eliminate those liberal teachers and get back to the basics of GOD!

What causes such a mass of degraded wit? Are the educators as concerned as they should be? Is the negative trending the result of bored youth in search of ultimate distraction? WIth the blessings of President Ronald Reagan, Education Chief Terrel H. Bell (U.S. Secretary of Education) launched the current school reform movement three years ago. He founded the National Commission on Excellence in

"ATTENTION STUDENTS! COURSES IN WITCHCRAFT, SEX EDUCATION AND EVOLUTION WILL BE HELD AT 3PM IN ROOM 666...CHRISTIANS AND BELIEVING JEWS REPORT TO THE DETENTION CENTER WITHOUT YOUR BIBLES!"

Education.

In its report last April (1983), they discovered a "rising tide of mediocrity" within our school system and it has caused such national furor among concerned citizens, that it has become a front-runner as a national issue. Bell prided the teachers, the board of education members, the legislators and the college deans that voiced their concern at the national forum of education last January in Indianapolis. In return they gave Bell an "A" for his effort. What really was accomplished, aside from hedging the validity of the scores that were compiled by the N.C.E.E.? This current society seems to sweep problematic areas under the bureaucratic rugs, rather than face up to alarming controversy.

When the Presidential Scholars met with Bell to discuss problems in education, it became evident that the commission found no correlation between the recession or poverty for the decline in aptitude. When the statistics were attacked by detractors, Mrs. Yvonne Larsen Vice-Chairwoman of the President's N.C.E.E. Program) defended the figures and voiced a plea for educational reform, mentioning that it need not cost additional revenue.

Florida's Education Commissioner, Ralph Turlington, hailed Bell's rankings of school quality as a major "breakthrough" that would inspire educators to try harder. Other educators tried to justify a need for a bigger part to be played by the Federal Government. Not surprisingly, GOD wasn't mentioned by one educator as a solution. With the intellect of this prize grouping of educators, showing a need to replace some salt into the system would hint that man couldn't make it on his own, and that would be reason for ridicule! You see our educators are so intellectual, they fail to understand the basic fundmentals. "The more they call themselves philosophers; the more stupid they grew!" (ROMANS 1:22)

One doesn't have to believe in God to acknowledge His positive influence on any society, but failing to recognize Him at all will contribute to further voids in knowledge. When you really believe in GOD and the influence He projects on the world picture, you come to the only logical conclusion that man cannot go it his way, even if he did have the intellectual capacity, which he doesn't! If we desire prosperity and hope for future generations, we must plant the "God Seed" today. Replace GOD back into the classrooms of America and watch the ACT and SAT test scores rise! When GOD is reestablished in education, raise the standards for college entry, don't lower them. With GOD on the minds of our youth any higher standards will be surpassed ten-fold, and you can count on it.

When you lower standards, you also lower potential. Place more emphasis on the spiritual values and the rest will follow in line!

There is also a pressing need to remove the undesirable educators from the classrooms. When you have overly liberal teachers in control of the child's mind, the child will assume an identical role in society. Our present liberal school boards have allowed teachers to influence our children with socialistic views and this must be curtailed immediately. We don't need homosexual teachers pressing their beliefs on our offspring; we don't need sex education classes in school and we don't need the A.C.L.U. dictating their policies in support of these minority liberals. If we don't take affirmative action now, we cannot complain about the future. It is time that America speaks out against these perversions and begins upholding the rights of our children. As far as I am concerned, homosexuals, socialists, communists and any other subversives have no legal rights to the education of my children, and there's no liberal organization on the face of this earth that can tell me otherwise!

Before children began receiving sex education classes in school, teenage pregnancies were minimal and before the standards were lowered to include the free-thinking elements, our graduating seniors knew how to read at a level higher than the fourth grade. When GOD was a prime influence in the schools, we didn't have 275,000 major crimes in our school yards each month. Our daughters used to be able to go to school without fear of being sexually attacked and raped. Times were surely better when higher standards were observed and kinky elements were not to be found at the head of the classroom.

Over 82% of our nation is in favor of returning vocal school prayer to the public schools, but that vast majority didn't even insure its passage through our liberal Senate. Because it didn't pass, you should remember the leaders opposing vocal school prayer in the next election. The opposition leader in the House is Rep. Pete W. Rodino, (D) New Jersey, who is also the Chairman of the House Committee on Judiciary. The opposition leader in the Senate is Sen. Lowell P. Weicker (R) from Connecticut. You must remember with your next vote who the liberal politicians are that oppose GOD! Remove the evil and you give the future of America a fighting chance! (See Chapter Fourteen)

What our children need in school in lieu of sex education, is a class on Biblical study with credits for excellence. By removing the homosexuals, atheists and socialists from our schools, we will have taken a most positive step toward the future. We should replace the perverted influence and install spiritual leaders with old fashion ethics and ideals.

This procedure is not as difficult as it would seem, but it requires parental attention in conjunction with cooperation from the school board and superintendents. Knowing that the quality of educators is poor, we must go that extra mile to eradicate this un-American practice of hiring liberal teachers, regardless of their supposed liberty. Where our child's future prospects are concerned, they have no liberty! If your present education system is just, they will assist a group in this quest.

With this liberal outlook on education of our youth, we have seen a national dropout rate of better than 1 in 4 students that reach the ninth grade. Those who deviously relish this beginning of socialism are the same ones that are incompetently in charge of this educational demission, and our children are the losers.

I would examine the credentials of any teacher who professes liberal views towards American ideals on your next PTA Meeting (Parent-Teachers Association). Query the educators about their long term goals for your children's future. In a friendly manner, discover their religious beliefs, their political preferences and their feelings on returning GOD to the classrooms. Many of their ideas will shock you with their bold and illogical gameplan. To know your children's teaching influence is to know your child much better.

The national test scores are declining while the dropout rates continue to rise in alarming proportions. In California alone, the dropout rate has escalated from 20% in 1972 to over 30% in 1982. In Michigan the current dropout rate is 26%, up from 19% ten years earlier and in Colorado where 84% graduated in 1972, only 73% received a sheep skin in 1982. The trend must be reversed but without GOD as a foundation for your child, it's impossible for improvement.

High school graduates have significantly higher lifetime earning capacity, are less likely to inhabit unemployment lines and are the most unlikely to wind up in prison due to a life of crime. There is a commercial that warns you "a mind is a terrible thing to lose!" As parents we must be more observing and protective of our childs' future and be willing to invest in the future of our Country with their education.

Mrs. Larsen was most accurate in her assessment that positive school reform need not cost added revenue. Parents can and should assume an active role in education. In New Hampshire, the State that is ranked number one nationally (SAT), expenditures per child are 28th nationwide. Idaho ranks 44th in pupil expenditures but is tied with Kansas for

10th in ACT scores and is 19th nationwide in graduating their seniors. South Dakota is 37th in spending per child, but 8th in aptitude. The higest spending States are not necessarily the ones that are achieving, but spending cannot be considered irrelevant to the cause for higher education.

In the small State of New Hampshire there are over 6,000 parental volunteers assisting limited school teachers. The community spirit is one of the prime reasons for that State's higher level of excellence. The States of Idaho and South Dakota were recently cited by the government for getting the most out of each school dollar. Officials in these three States have cited strong community involvement, their rural atmosphere, strong discipline and a focus on basics for their success rate. Their students seem to have a thirst for education and respect for good ethics of discipline. New Hampshire's 158 school districts are funded eighty-five percent by local taxpayers and because of this, the taxpayer is interested in where his tax dollars are going.

The teachers in many States are complaining about low salaries and laying the excuse that because of it they do not have the proper incentives to educate. Maybe there are some educators who are underpaid, but it has been my witness that most are not equal in caliber to the compensation they now receive. Bring back the non-liberal educators of the 40's and 50's and with the graces of GOD America will overcome this dilemma. I would rather have my children educated entirely from the Word of GOD than have them become intellectual in the liberal teachings of present day man. It would insure a better tomorrow for all if we can reinstall His graces in the minds of our children through parental participation, more spiritually inclined teachers and less undesirable entities in control.

More federal intervention is not the answer, nor is it more revenue or higher salaries for teachers. We should be willing to pay for premium educators, but not in the sciences, government or economics. GOD must get back into our children's curriculum, their activities and their goals in life, to insure their promising future successes.

If you have the desire to see your children aspire to greater heights, you must be willing to take an active part in that future and let your actions speak louder than words. The forces or evil surround your child each moment of the day. Why not subject them to the most powerful education they could ever receive and let the chips fall where GOD places them. I can guarantee that you'll like the outcome! If your religious preference is Jewish and you are not a believer in Christ, what harm will it do your child to learn His Ways?

I know the New Testament is not part of the Kabbala but the wealth of experience your child will receive from this exposure cannot be measured.

The decision of believing in Christ is one of an individual nature. Because you do not believe is not sufficient cause to deprive your children the learning experience. Regardless of your religion, there's only one GOD. If you are truly His servant, pray to Him and ask for guidance in your decision - don't act on your own! When the scriptures were read in the public schools, the children that took part prospered! If your child hears the Word of GOD each morning, his ideals will become more positive and regardless of the Biblical version, isn't it better to have some spiritual guidance than none at all?

Think of your own youth. How many teenagers did you know that were dependent on drugs or alcohol to get through the day when the teachings of GOD were foremost in their minds? Our children are in the hands of irresponsible liberals. As long as this is their influence, parental respect will not be realized. Many children are indeed on illusionary drugs and addicted to its realm of darkness. How many children are receiving psychiatric care for being unable to cope with peer pressure and life in general? How many teenage suicides does it take to tell parents that we are not on the proper course? How many crimes must be committed before parents everywhere will unite and fight back for precious lost liberty?

A recent report on Americas' youth indicates that one in sixteen drink alcohol daily and their reasons vary as do their brands of liquor. Many of these children have cited low self-esteem, isolation or the inability to keep up with the pressures found in today's high schools. That didn't happen when GOD was in the classroom, and you know it! The whole world is depressed and the effects of liberalism are being pushed down our childrens' throats until they can no longer endure the pressures of society. Yes, our children can no longer cope with present social conditions, NOR SHOULD THEY HAVE TO! Before anything can be realigned, our priority must be set straight. If we love our children as we would like others to believe, that time is now! If a person chooses to be a socialist, let them become "social outcasts in our Country," and we should not stand by and see them teaching their filth to impressionable future American leaders. If they desire to become homosexuals or any other degenerated low form of life, let them burn in hell, but do not allow them to drag our offspring into the abyss with them!

When you have twelve-year-olds thinking about their next sexual encounter, instead of dolls and sports, we have a major problem in ethics. When our children have to "shoot up" or

54

"smoke a joint" to cope with reality, our society is perverted. Positive and immediate reform is necessary.

Our youth are being admitted to psychiatric wards by the thousands, drug rehab centers and hospitals by the hundred-thousands, and not one can say they are really enjoying their lives unless they have a special relationship with the Almighty! If you think the liberal pressures will just go away in time, you are not logical! According to Dr. Joel Mishalow, Ph.D., a school psychologist from Las Vegas, many of his patients suffer from extreme depression, inner anger towards society and guilt complexes, many times brought on by either a drastic sudden change in their environment or a void in proper supportive structures.

All troubled teens seem to have one common trait. They are all searching for ways to hide their feelings in dope and alcohol. Most are lonely, are extremely impressionable in lieu of leadership qualities, and are astute in devising ways to trick their unsuspecting parents. Many will tell you that they come home as late as possible so their parents would not find out "how wasted they were!" When questioned as to why their eyes are so red, many will exclaim that they have been drinking and in this society of drug abuse, that "relieves parents!" Can you believe that parents would be relieved to know that their children are on the bottle instead of drugs? That's like saying, "Am I glad I only lost half my brain in the accident!"

All around America children hear their parents arguing about "lack of money," how different society is today and how great things used to be. What they don't hear too often is good sound principles to remedy the problems. People are great authorities until it comes time for action! Many parents forget that the peer problems being faced today by their children are much more severe than when they were young. They think their child is going through a stage and that they'll grow out of it with maturity. It won't happen and you must realize it before your child winds up on a slab in the morgue.

Violence has become a "way of life" and its influence is programed into the child from early life. On television and in the movies people get stabbed, shot, burned up, and vaporized with laser guns. This form of entertainment predestine the child to be immune of compassion, less lovable and terrorist by nature. Even the cartoons on Saturday morning have themes on violence and the occult. Good versus the powers of evil. Where are the programs with positive substance? Why are good "happily ever after" movies being shelved in favor of murder mysteries and acts of terror? There are a few positive influences like CBN's "Superbook" and "Flying Horse". Most of the entertainment lacks substance.

What many of us fail to recognize is that "the child of today is the leader of tomorrow!" What they witness in formative years will become their design for what comes later. Children are small, human computers. How they are programmed will more often spell their successes or failures in life. There's no better time to start guiding your child than the present. If you desire a positive outlook in your offspring, you had better supply the positive training aids and proper attention when they are young.

Children learn what they live:

If a child lives with criticism,
He learns to condemn.
If a child lives with hostility,
He learns to fight.
If a child lives with ridicule,
He learns to be shy.
If a child lives with shame,
He learns to feel guilty.
If a child lives with tolerance,
He learns to be patient.
If a child lives with encouragement,
He learns confidence.
If a child lives with praise,
He learns to appreciate.
If a child lives with fairness,
He learns justice.
If a child lives with security,
He learns to have faith.
If a child lives with approval,
He learns to like himself.
If a child lives with acceptance and friendship,
He learns to find love in the world.
If a child lives with the principles of GOD,
He can do no better!

Although the previous metaphor is not original, it is most appropriate for the youth of today. As most humans will act and react to stimulants, both positive or negative, the need for sound principles of living is ever urgent in our present day. In Matthew 5:13, Jesus said that His believers are "the world's seasoning to make it tolerable. If we are to lose our flavor, what will happen to the world?" We are slowly losing this precious commodity He spoke of and without His tender influence, hope is lost!

We parents must spare no means to educate our children. We must raise them with love, kindness and compassion and instill in them a thirst for the Word of GOD. The greatest gifts you can give your child are your time, your love, your understanding and most of all the respect for the blessings of the Almighty. GOD is like a Divine Buffer on our Lives. Accepting Jesus Christ into your heart doesn't guarantee that nothing will ever go wrong with your life. It does place a permanent shield around you and filters all aspects of your life, never allowing more burden than one can hold up to. Your child deserves that same knowledge and protection!

If you yell and scream at your spouse, show disrespect for your fellow man or are incapable of accpeting GOD in your life, your children will generally adopt a similar attitude. Don't worry about your tomorrows, GOD said that He would take care of them and He never lies! Recognize Christ by your every action, display His influence in your home and teach His principles to your children. If you say that you love your family, but do not accept GOD's Will, you are walking in darkness and Oh how dark it can be!

With GOD nothing in your life will be an impossibility and no task insurmountable. He is the only answer to problems we all face in this world. When you acknowledge this fact He bestows on you great wisdom and strength. And His positive influence will be passed along to the future of the world....our children!

CHAPTER FIVE

''What's Happening To Planet Earth?''

"There will always be temptation to sin —
but woe to the man who does the tempting!"
JESUS CHRIST (Luke 17:1-3)

When was the last time you picked up a newspaper and read something really positive? If you are one of the concerned citizens you would have to say that it has been a mighty long time! What's happening to our world? Has everyone gone insane? What's causing everyone to be so heartless and cold? Where is the trust that used to be so prevalent? Are we really in the 'end times' of the world mentioned in Biblical prophecy? Are there any solutions that can reverse these tendencies and revive the world we used to love and took for granted? Is a thermonuclear war unavoidable? These previous queries are the most frequently asked among this generation. There is only one answer to all the questions but it is so simplex in nature, so fitting to the problems and so obvious to the mind that it will not be considered by the vast majority of world members. "The answer is Jesus Christ!"

Those that say I do not know what I am indicating are blind. If you will allow your heart to soften, your mind and body to be at ease and read this chapter carefully, you will no doubt come to that same conclusion.

What's happening to our world?   The love and wisdom that comes only from Jesus Christ has been removed from our society. We have been cleverly deceived by false prophets. Without these divine acknowledgements by the people, man has indeed become insane. He has become heartless and uncaring, self-centered and grasping; boastful, arrogant and rude; disobedient to parents, ungrateful, irreligious, unappeasible. They slander, they are profligates, savages and against everything that is good; they are treacherous, reckless and demented by pride and have preferred their own pleasures to those of God's. They keep up the outward appearance of religion but are rejecting the power within. Does that sound like the world problem? Are those the people you see in the

THE UNITED STATES OF AMERICA
IN GOD WE TRUST
Then said Jesus, "FATHER,..
FORGIVE THEM; FOR THEY KNOW
NOT WHAT THEY DO."
— Luke 23:34

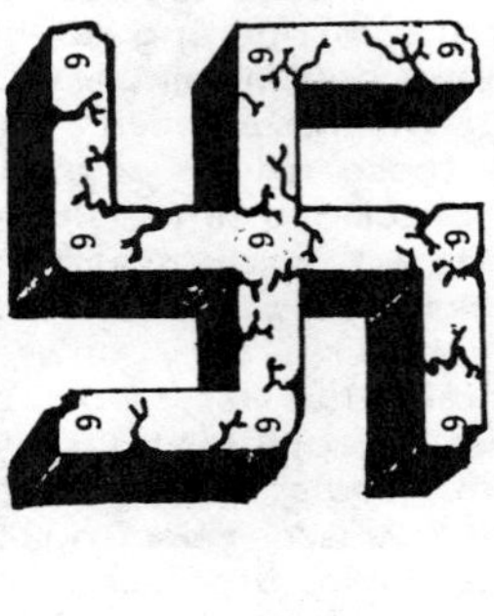

stores? Is that example conducive to our current generation? Does it describe your personal attitude? If you are like 75% of the world's population, then it describes you to the note! That figure represents the multitudes that do not know Jesus Christ and it could be much higher. Many who call themselves Christians do not know the meaning of the word.

The previous paragraph accurately describes our current generation but the words do not originate merely from my observations. They have their origin and it is from the Mouth of God. (See II Timothy 3:1-5)

If by a miracle of God, you could have been alive for the last six thousand years, you would indeed be bored by the world's repetitious and vile nature. You would be watching our current events and feel like it was the part of the movie that you had seen before. Your common expression as you yawn would be, "this is where I came in." It is just possible that our God's patience is running out with man's six thousand years of rejecting His covenant. We should be rejoicing that the Lord God Yahweh is a most caring and loving Creator, and be searching for ways to please Him. We should be fulfilling His covenant with mankind by obeying His Laws...but we do not! We should feel blessed that our God does not have the patience and wisdom of mortal man.

Overlooking the world picture we see wars and rumors of war. In over forty countries around the world there is war and the rumor of a world shattering thermonuclear confrontation is foremost in the minds of men. (See Matthew 24:6) After you read that verse and acknowledge that the prophecy was made nearly 2000 years ago, you should be gathering the message of where we are in world history.

In our generation of advanced knowledge and travel (See Daniel 12:4), we have learned nothing of eternal value. Our great scientists are searching for answers to questions God never intended to reveal. Astrology has become an in-thing and the "super powers", as they refer to themselves, are attempting to find other planets to pollute after they destroy this one with world-wide corruption. "Oh you foolish men of little faith", to take a phrase from the Lord Jesus Christ. Man is searching for answers in a dark room without a candle; flying a plane in a dense fog without benefit of radar; and squandering billions of dollars of hard-earned money on un-Godly projects with no physical need. Because we are looking for answers to world problems in wrong quarters, we will find none.

We humans are a procrastinating lot. If we discover the whole universe and even ways to land our crafts on distant planets, what have we gained in so doing? God gave us an earth to live on, to mutiply and fill it with our love, to govern over all animals of the land and to love and respect Him for this blessing. We are a unique being, made by the hands of God with the clay of this planet only and in His likeness. If He wanted man to use their wisdom in outer space, He would have said so in the Bible. If God wanted man to experiment with His creatures of the earth, to clone another human with mortal hands or to create devastating weaponry, He would have said so. But He did not! Science is venturing on Holy Grounds and desecrating it with the filth they call intellect while proposing anti-Christian ideology with their insinuation of the evolution process. Man has indeed reached a point of insanity.

Things have never been great on planet Earth, but there was a time when our priority was realistic and our foundation was centered on the presence of God. We must face up to the surety that America and the world are not progressing towards any peaceful co-existence. Prior to World War II, only a handful of countries were under communist control. Now, less than forty years later, more than a third of the world's population is subjugated. What that should tell you is that evil is festering over truth. When you have two-thirds of the world passive to communist agression, it's only a matter of time before the stage will be set for a one world government. When that is set up, there will be no recourse, no mortal hope for any revival of old and treasured culture and absolutely no individual freedom. What you will have is slavery of the mind, the body and the human will to live.

Regardless of many inspired efforts from past generations, communism is spreading over the world by leaps and bounds. It is firmly imbedded in America today and thrives in the governmental offices throughout the land. They are in the Supreme Court, the Legislature and also have their messages heard in the Executive Branch of our Nation. These parasites call themselves "liberals" and spread misconception and discord wherever they can under the misused term of democracy. What they represent is social reform, many times referring to themselves as 'peacemakers". By any other name these liberals are socialists, and the difference between socialism and communism is little, if any.

Can you really say we are progressing as a nation when we have 'potential mass murderers' running for election to the highest office in the Country? We have a country that was founded by our forefathers on the principles of God and our children cannot even pray in our public schools! These same Democratic hopefuls, save one, are pro-choice in abortion and AGAINST PUBLIC SCHOOL PRAYER. They use misconception as their trademarks and actually have the gall to voice their opinions of 'human rights' and 'social reform' directly into our living rooms via television. As Jesus said to 'test every spirit', you wouldn't think these 'Democrats' would receive a single vote, but they will deceive many along the way. Evil people vote for their own kind. You won't find Satan casting his ballot in favor of President Reagan because he is a good man, wants vocal prayer restored to the classrooms of America and is a strong anti-abortion advocate.

Because the world has removed the "Prince of Peace" (Jesus Christ) from His rightful rule, the doors have been opened to the Abyss and evil will continue to reign in the hearts of men. The only chance mankind had to reverse his eminent demise, has been cast out in favor of worldly pleasures. Man doesn't need help, he chooses to formulate his own destiny, researching unchartered regions with less than adequate intellect. All the good from past generations is being undone is this generation. How great things used to be.

The vast majority of our citizens know little of what is taking place in this 'modern' civilization. Many of those that do understand the situation are hiding themselves in closets and fear the horrors that are soon to overtake humanity. Only a few brave men are doing something about it.

America wake up! Face up to the fact that the 'end times' are here. Knowledge is increasing while morality and spirituality are in retrograde. Goodness is being dominated by evil around the world and the motivating forces of darkness originate from the Soviet Union. Their propaganda will tell you of the many churches they have behind the iron curtain but it will not show the persecutions they inflict on their countrymen for practicing their faith in God.

Religion to the Soviet Union is representative of an unwanted crutch, a weakness in their coat of armor and a blinding cog in their quest for world domination. The liturgy in their churches is carefully screened and those that attend the services are harrassed, ridiculed and are susceptible to imprisonment for their beliefs in Christ. No Russian citizen may attend the services and also be able to hold any position of authority in the Kremlin. They teach their children from early on that there is no God, and that those who believe in Him are enemies of the people. Their children are indoctrinated to believe that science and production are all that matters and nothing else is important. The spirit of anti-Christ thrives in the filth known as Russia.

The official ideology of the Soviet Union is a doctrine based on revolutionary Marxian-socialism and Marxism-Leninism. Their totalitarian form of government has one party in control and governs a state-owned means of productivity with the professed aim of establishing a stateless society. In reality, the goal of communism is the elimination of all private property and the establishment of a system in which all goods are owned in common and are available to all in need. Considering the words only, the system doesn't appear all that bad until you evaluate the entire scope of the practice and discover that the results all lead to a negative expectancy for all citizens involved.

One who advocates this form of government is referred to as either a socialist or a communist and as stated earlier the difference is minimal. Many of our present day Democrats with their "liberal views" would have been tarred, feathered and run out of town on a rail, had they voiced their opinions back in the 1950's. The left-wing revolutionaries in this country must be singled out and removed from public office and it is the voters that are responsible. Liberal democrats like Walter "of pro-choice in abortion & silent prayer" Mondale must never be placed in the position of the Presidency. Just the idea that he was a vice-president tells the American people that the average voter knows little about the candidates that get into office.

What Americans have to comprehend is that our government is already infested with these left-wing liberalists. If you want a country you can be proud of and realize the security we all seek, then you must use the power of the vote this Fall. You must know the value of the candidates running for office. A good seed will produce good fruit, but a bad seed cannot conceal the adverse tendencies he projects. Weed out these liberals on your ballot and vote for a sound America.

Communism, socialism and liberalism are all degenerating influences on society. Be attentive at the next anti-nuclear demonstration and you will find all of these entities present, with many in leadership roles. The ones that are yelling the loudest for 'reform' are the exact same that would lead you to despair. It would surely be a laugher to see these same liberals leading a demonstration in the Soviet Union. Two years ago the Russians had a demonstration against nuclear weapons. One person showed up and he hasn't been heard of since.

If it was not for the United States and capitalism the Soviets would have starved a long time ago, along with much of China. Tell me communism is a progressive influence on the people and I'll show you someone that is misinformed. In a nutshell, communism fails in any world society because it removes personal motivation from the laborer. All individuals do not perform equally therefore th aggregate productivity stagnates due to uneven output. Need some first hand proof?

Take a close look at the labor unions in the United States if you want a view of what communism is like. Every member of each separate unit within the union receive equal pay and few produce a justified workload in compensation. The unions are a strain on the economy when they can dictate to management inflationary wage demands and withhold their labor if they are not met. Look at all the corruption in the unions from the top down to the lowest business agent. The rank and file (laborers) being mislead and misrepresented into biting the hand that feeds their families and with one party in control their recourse is non-existent. Those who oppose union doctrine may file with the American Civil Liberties Union (ACLU) and that's the biggest laugh yet. That organization has had their noses in every "liberal" reform since it was organized and could care less for the motivation known as free enterprise. Any organization against free enterprise is unAmerican. I say three cheers to Ronald Reagan for his stand with the air-traffic controllers and may it be received as a message to other liberal organizations with intentions of destroying American standards. When unions were first formed their cause was righteous in respect to eliminating 'sweat-shops' in our country but their present version is overstepping their bounds with political overtones. Free America cannot withstand such debasement.

One question the liberal element may propose is; if socialism (communism) is so unAmerican, why has it spread like wild-fire throughout the world in the past 40 years? The answer to that is not easily arrived at, however you may scrutinize the fact that its origin is being force-fed through internal subversions on weaker nations. No country desires communism because the most treasured liberty among men is to be free. There is no freedom where communism is concerned. If it were not so, the communist bloc countries would not need walls to keep their countrymen confined. There are no liberties behind the 'iron curtain' or any country that is an advocate to a one party system of government.

Although a third of the world is under communist control, the entire planet feels the effects. No country in the world has escaped communist subversion and that includes our own. Communism infiltrates under the banner of social reform, liberally altering the ideals of the countrymen and coerces the people with misinformation. Remember that misery loves company and the best analogy of communism is misery. In America, a country formulated with the recognition of God, we are losing the preserving elements so necessary for liberty. As the attitudes become more and more liberally inclined, the salt is being extracted from the earth, and decomposition is swift without this vital ingredient.

Communism is not acceptable where freedom reigns, so the Soviet Union has changed the label to read "liberalism" and the people are buying it. The difference here is that the Soviets are at a major disadvantage because of their inability to understand the word of God. By following the principles of communism and professing their allegiance to atheism they are the anti-Christ. The word of God is clear and simple to His own people. God Protects those that love Him, and will punish those that hate Him! (Deuteronomy 5:9)

The Soviet Union's objective is the elimination of capitalism and world subjugation to communism. For over 60 years they have assumed the role of an unrelenting aggressor and the United States has been an advocate of passive resistence, in lieu of a conquer and takeover theory. We believe that we can achieve our objectives through kindness and compassion to our foreign neighbors. When that cannot be accomplished our passive resistance takes on the form of censorship and embargos and this hand-slapping is cause for ridicule from the Soviet Union. By utilizing acts of noncooperation in lieu of violence and active measures of opposition we have lost effectiveness as a world power.

When the Soviet Union enacts a takeover, they remain and establish their perverted totalitarian government, enforcing their evil tyranny on the victims. Our country made a grave error at the end of World War II when we allowed the Soviets the occupation rights to East Germany. They remain there today as a lasting memory of their oppressive nature. Whenever the United States has associated with un-Godly nations or negotiated with them in good faith, we have come up the loser.

More recently they have set their carnal throne in Afghanistan which is representative of a strategic Soviet foothold to the Middle East. From that region they are now in position to springboard their oppression to the jugular vein of the world,-the Persian Gulf, the Suez Canal and the oil-laden countries of Iran, Iraq and Saudi Arabia. They realize that they must control this area to bring their objectives of world conquest to fruition. You can't say that it will never happen, it has already begun and was prophesied centuries ago!

Only the extremely naive would lay trust in the testimony of Russian leaders. They have violated every arms accord ever established by treaty. Why our country's leaders are expected to establish detente for constructive agreement with the Soviet Union is beyond comprehension.

The Soviet Union provided toxins and other chemical weapons to their allies in Laos and Cambodia and used chemical weapons in Afghanistan that were banned by the 1925 and 1972 international agreement. They have conducted military manuvers without properly notifying the western nations in violation of the 1975 Helsinki Final Act. They have built an anti-ballistic missile radar system in central Siberia in direct violation of the 1972 anti-ballistic missile treaty. They have disguised data on the testing of missiles needed to verify compliance with the 1979 Salt II Treaty,and tested a new intercontinental ballistic missile outlawed by SALT II, and have deployed the SS-16 ICBM, also banned by SALT II. And they have exploded underground nuclear tests above the 150-Kiloton level permitted by treaty.

By these gross infractions of international treaties, it is unrealistic to assume that the U.S.S.R. is capable of reliance for peaceful co-existence. They have been documented as saying, "agree to anything the capitalists propose that will afford us the time and resources in our goal to eliminate capitalism. When it's in black and white, are we to assume that the United States will achieve any positive expectations from future negotiations with that nation of anti-Christs?

We must come to realize that what we have in the Reagan Administration is a firm foundation of hope for future Americans. Ronald Reagan is not a yes man, he is the epitome of what America has stood for since our beginning. With the changing of ideals so prevalently favoring the liberal sector, it is a wonder that the United States is blessed with such a natural leader. Ronald Reagan is a God-fearing Christian who cares greatly for the stability of all Americans and his commitments towards the revival of precious American standards and allegiances should be warmly recognized by all. We should be praying that God will preserve and enhance the Reagan Administration in our fight to restore our lost liberties. We must pray for our enemy that they might see the light and reverse their negative tendency.

The next time you complain of the President's foreign aid programs consider this: The Soviet Union's military support to subjugate nations amounts to three times what the United States invests towards their freedom from outside control. Our humanitarian contributions far surpass that of all other countries combined in the areas of food, clothing and medical care to the underprivileged, but it is not enough to maintain control or reverse the onslaught of communism. It should be every Americans concern to assist the cause of freedom for our world neighbors sovereignty and this support is our common bond that will insure our future liberties and those of our children.

"The Middle East: Problems of Real Estate!"

Since the re-establishment of the State of Israel in 1948, there has been a marked escalation of subversive elements filtering into that area. Although these actions have taken on a diversified battle zone, their main intentions are ultimately the devastation of the Holy Land. Israel's main ally is the United States and the preservation of this alliance should assume more stability in the next few years. Our support of the State of Israel should remain foremost in the minds of all Americans for many strategic reasons. Israel can easily be construed by the U.S. as the gateway to world peace as its geographical location is near the Suez Canal. Control of this region is essential for world peace or world subjugation. The United States and the Soviet Union are well aware of this and according to Biblical prophecy it is in this location that World War III will take place.

It is also a well known stratagem that the abundance of oil and natural resources in this location would be essential to maintaining armored vehicles and control of these precious elements would almost (humanly-speaking) insure world victory. However, the most important decision the United States will be faced with, in future years, will be exercising the defense for Israel we have agreed to. As long as the United States remains united in our efforts to head off the flow of communism, we will remain a powerful deterrent against foreign agression into Israel. But are we that Strong?

In the United States we are foremost a Nation of God's People and Israel is the home of God's Chosen People. It is more than coincidence that God's people recognize their own kind and the allegiance is justified. Our strength in nuclear capacity is not in question; however our moral and spiritual values are. Due to internal subversions over the past twenty-five years, the United States has been weakened considerably and the extent of any futuristic aid, involving our commitment of combat troops, is indeterminable. We have always been a peace loving people but the difference with this generation is that too many are incognizant of the need to fight for these liberties. When a nation is not willing to fight to perserve their precious sanctuary, it's imminent demise will be forthcoming. We must re-evaluate our priorities and realign our hopes for the future with a unified effort today. We must be allegiant to our Nation or else we shall lose Her and the defense of Israel will be of tantamount significance to our efforts of unity. America should defend Israel with every fiber we possess with the assurance that our God will justify every action. We must not allow our past failures in defense of liberty to deter our objectives. We must rally our people to the unity that can only be from God and defend His Sacred Holy Land at all costs. As you become more versed with Biblical scripture, this necessity will become more clearly acknowledged by all Americans.

We do not need to be hit by a train to recognize certain trends within our world. The Soviets invaded Afghanistan for strategic purpose. They are aiding the Syrian cause in the Lebanon crises to gain allegiance from the Arabic Nations and they are lurking in the shadows of the Iraqi-Iranian war to pounce on the eventual winner. They don't care who wins the war because the spoils of which will be theirs in the end (or so they think). The withdrawal of American troops from Lebanon has assured Russia that the United States is no longer the committed nation she once was. We can thank the liberal elements in the U.S. for that decision among others. If you can't acknowledge the significance of Soviet momentum and motivation in the Middle East sector, then the recording of historical events in our past has no meaning.

Consider this scenerio. All through Biblical history there have been holy wars. In a nutshell the distress in this region is a matter of real estate and religious hatred against the State of Israel. We are dealing with the transplantation of an entire race of people from the place they called home for centuries to being without a homeland. Consider that and you have a festering and irreversible malignancy. The Palestinians say the land is theirs and the Israelis know the land was given to them by God.

By the end of the second millennium A.D., the population of this planet has been astutely estimated to double and because it represents a period of only sixteen years, it becomes extremely alarming. How can anyone be that naive as to suggest that a war of epic proportion is not on the horizon. Based on current technology, the surety of confrontation is apposite for future world endurance. We cannot be that optimistic as to project any economic recovery without a major world war preceding it. Scripture says it will be the final confrontation between good and evil; - the end of the dominion of Satan.

It is evident that the world powers are building forces and stockpiling most destructive super weapons. With all the world's great intellect, they will never find the answer to a peaceful co-existence, because they don't seek the truth. President Reagan knows the answer is God, but few other world leaders will acknowledge this only logical choice.

If you were to place all the world's intelligence and

common sense in juxtaposition, it wouldn't amount to an ounce of human logic. Man has lost the ability to reason because he has lost his desire for God. With the acknowledgement of God you receive the true wisdom that surpasses all intellect; without God, mankind gives up their only possible hope for peace. The only answer to the world's problems is a mass revival to this Holy Allegiance, however most do not see it that way.

Since the beginning of time, man has shown the reluctance to accept God's Way, opting instead to go it alone. He has exercised his own illogical expertise to receive full credit for his own accomplishment, while bypassing the origin for success.

We see this common practice on a lesser scale in our own family units, therefore we won't challenge its validity. God created man in His Own Image and on a lesser scale we see ourselves in the offspring He gives us as blessings. God gives us many blessings and expects very little in return. We should be able to relate here as well with our own children and what we expect from them. When we anger God He punishes us according to the severity of the infraction; we do the same with our own children - if we love them. God rewards us when we obey His covenant; we do the same for our children. If you can logically agree to these previous facts, is it that hard for you to understand what is happening to Planet Earth?

As we were given the capability to love our own children, can't you feel the love God has for us and experience it with your life's blessings? There is no good deed from the hearts of men that God Almighty has not planted! But the evils that come from a cold heart are the infestations of satan.

The foolish man says that "there is no God" but can't explain why "wise men still seek Him!" As long as man refuses to allow God His Way in their lives, there will be no positive expectancy; no fruition of effort; no hope for the future!

There should be no question that God is the answer to all the problems man is facing. When mankind realizes this fact it will be past the point of reversing his destiny with satan, - but he will know! It is written in the Bible (Luke 17:1-3) that Jesus said, "There will always be temptation to sin, but woe to the man who does the tempting!" It is also written that man will not turn away from sin. He will continue in his evil ways and drag many to the abyss with him. Never truer words can be spoken than those that come from the "Book of Truths!"

The Bible was written by the Prophets, who were inspired by the living God. All the answers to life in general and to eternal life specifically can be found within the Good Book. We know that which we have been taught and to

Christians, it means God never lies. He is more than fair with us and has always given us an ample warning before punishment. The Bible not only gives us truths, knowledge for loving fellowship and a way of life, it also forewarns us of what the future has in store for the human race and allows us to make our own decision on which road we choose to take.

We can either go north to Heaven or south to hell and there's no inbetween. There's no purgatory, no suspended animation and no reincarnation. You make your own destiny by believing in Christ or not!

According to Roman Catholic doctrine, upon death the souls of those who die in God's grace are put in a place or state of temporary punishment, where they are allowed to 'atone themselves' for their sins in life and justify God in so doing. In relation to God's Kingdom, I consider myself a Christian first and cannot justify the existence of this proposed "state of atonement." Jesus Christ died at Calvary for our atonement and I believe that our faith in that fact forgives our sins and purges our soul for everlasting life.

I believe in the communion of saints, the forgiveness of sins and life everlasting. I don't believe in a purgatory, or any other form of suspended animation. If we have lived a Christian life, have obeyed the Commandments of God, and most of all believe that salvation is through Jesus Christ, we have already been forgiven for our sins. The Blood of Jesus....wipes away 'all' sins!

As far as reincarnation goes, there are two ways to believe; only one is right. Many Hindus believe that when you die you keep coming back to this world with different bodies until you have perfected the soul to such a state that you are worthy of God's Kingdom. I believe that man can be reborn "in faith" with Christ Jesus during this life and believing in Christ, inherit rebirth with a new body only in God's Kingdom. As far as coming back into this world as another "form of life" (cat, dog, monkey, etc.) that may seem fitting to a nonbeliever, but the Good Book says that man is made in the image of God. When God allows man to reproduce, the offpsring are human beings. Just so, even the most unsophisticated logic will tell the theory of reincarnation if a lie.

The trouble with Planet Earth is caused by too many diversified beliefs in conjunction with too many who don't believe at all. In the end times, when a one world religion is institutionalized, it will pit the Christians against the rest of humanity. We know from census that there are approximately 4.7 billion inhabitants on this planet. Of those only a little more than one in four profess the Lord Jesus Christ as his

Saviour (25% or 1.2 billion Christians). Of these Christians, many who profess to the saving graces of Christ are indeed deceivers and are a non-practicing entity, thinking they have found an easy way to cope to life's problems.

Today, more than ever before in our history, the United States is an object of disgust within the world picture. The cause for this despicable viewing is due to our luke-warm support to allies around the world. It is true that the United States has done more for the rest of the world than any other nation, but when you build a powerful name for yourself you must always live up to it.

Due to the many unAmerican activities within our boundaries, our people have become mislead and assume this luke-warm attitude as a result. This attitude will become colder and the results more degenerating in effect, by the late 1980's.

The fig tree that did not bear fruit was banished by Christ; (Matthew 21:18,19) just so is our need to rid America of these vampires. The freedoms mentioned in the Bill of Rights were intended to include all of "GOD'S PEOPLE"; there is no mention that we must stagnate ourselves and dilute the minds of our children with anything less. Our freedoms have been taken advantage of for far too long. If America is to regain the prestige we had and lost, there can be no other alternative.

You can well understand how wonderful the world would be if every man loved God and abided by His Laws. There would be no mass murders of unborn infants, there would be no crime; no child molestation, no homosexuals, no incest, no hate, no rape, no lies, no deceit, no pornography, no bigotry, no collusion and no war. There would be peace among men. Communism is closing the free world and the sentry is the fallen angel himself. We must give to satan what is his and give to God our love; with all our hearts, with all our strength and with all our souls. Then, and only then, will it be possible to love our neighbors and enjoy eternal fellowship with our Maker!

It doesn't require the intellect of Einstein to see what is happening in our world. Jesus tells us that in the end times of the world there will be a great revival and there will be evangelizing throughout the globe (Matthew 24:14). The evangelizing is happening as you read this book. "This Good News of the Kingdom will be proclaimed to the whole world as a witness to all nations. And then the end will come!" How much more clear can the Word of God be?

We are at a most critical crossroads in time and we must understand that God's hourglass has but a few grains left. We

We must comprehend the reality of the saying, "united we stand and divided we fall" and know the significance of allegiance to our God and Country. We are a most divided nation and are certainly not "under God" with our present national discord.

Since the late 1950's, the Soviets have been planting their vile seeds in the heartland of America - the Family! They knew that overt expression of their doctrine would not be acceptable to the capitalist, so they set to undermine what we viewed most preciously - Our God, our Family and our freedoms of expression. Twenty-five years later they are winning that battle on our very own shores. They aimed their aggression through internal subversion and scored a direct hit. They succeeded in removing our expression of religion in public schools and that has contributed greatly to both moral and spiritual decay. Because of our love for freedom, we are enslaved by its misused projection. Our courts allow too much, to so few and in truth it was never meant that way.

In our current society we stand by and let the atheists dictate what the majority should hold true. With united vigor we must once again rally around the flag, learn the meaning of forgiveness and give our fellow man the deserving respect we seek for ourselves.

The liberal element would have you believe that Ronald Reagan is a monger of war and that his firm hand with the Soviet Union may cause a thermonuclear confrontation. It isn't so. We have had our share of unrighteous statesmen over the past twenty years, but Reagan isn't one of them. Reagan realizes the previous concessions we have made to prolong peace were wrong, and there comes a time when we must stand up and fight. For the first time in more than 38 years America has the Presidency working for the people and not around them. We must realize this with our prayers and with our action. If the young people of this Country could see the atrocities that go on in communist bloc countries they would get down and kiss the ground we walk on in America. They would shelve their ideas of liberal reform and take up their share of the war for sovereignty with pleasure. We are losing the cold war and many are covering their eyes. Anyone who thinks that freedom is free to anyone who seeks it hasn't been across our borders.

We finally have a President that sees the trend and has the gumption to change it. He can't do it alone or as long as he faces direct opposition from the House of Representatives and the Senate. He knows to have proper growth and prosperity in the future, we must tighten the purse string today. The defense budget is necessary, our foreign aid is not enough to halt the flow of communism and one of the biggest deceivers of our people in this country is the leader of the "House", "Tip" O'neil. He has opposed everything Reagan stands for so you could construe O'Neil as opposing what is good for America.

Liberals like O'Neil, Mondale, Hart and the other marauders of righteousness must not receive second terms in "serving" the publics needs, and by no means should anyone but Reagan be in leadership. We need another four years of Ronald Reagan and then we must search high and low for one of the identical pattern.

Reaganomics initially hurt every American, specially the poor, but it was inevitable that the action took place. Had the Presidency taken a back seat, as so many other previous Administrations have done, we would currently be in one of the world's biggest depressions. The inflation rate under Reagan has decreased and prosperity is on the rise. Judge the Democrat candidates by their ideals and they wouldn't receive a vote. The incumbent has proven his leadership qualities and deserves our support.

The Reagan plan for uniform taxation is justified. For too long now the rich have escaped taxation because of loopholes and tax breaks. The national debt can be decreased if everyone, regardless of deductions, payed just 10% of their annual income to the Federal government. Higher taxes is not the remedy to our dilemma; even taxation is! Every human that earns a dollar should pay ten-cents in federal taxes, - no more-no less. The Democrats are right on course with the predictions of the Communist Manifesto (see Chapter Nine for that farce) when they propose that the American people need a tax hike. What America needs is less government, not more. We need less paychecks to liberal politicians and less liberal politicians.

President Reagan is the first president in this country that has tackled the economy head-on, in lieu of public opinion and has come out a winner. We are on the road back economically, but he is not satisfied. He is pushing the anti-abortion and the right for vocal school prayer issues in the Senate and Good Lord Willing we'll win that right back too. Judge Reagan for his good deeds and not by what you hear the liberals say about him. They are deceivers and all a deceiver can do is spread misinformation and discord. That's not what America needs when she is on the road to recovery. We need the support of everyone.

The Bible says that in the 'end times' God will send prophets, wise men and scribes throughout the world. President Reagan is one of those wise men and with this

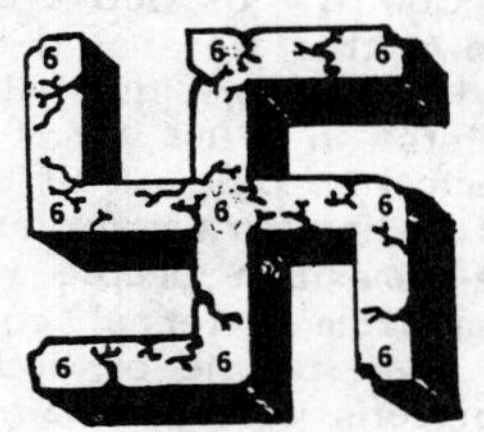

"YOU MUST UNDERSTAND, COMRADES, IF REAGAN GETS ANOTHER TERM...HE WILL STOP "FREE ABORTIONS," HE WILL PUT GOD BACK IN THE CLASSROOM...WE DON'T WHAT THAT...THE COMMUNIST PARTY CAN NOT HAVE THAT!"

prophet, you must recognize him while he is still here. He is a man of God leading a Country of God's people back to God! Reagan has made it known that we should be out of the United Nations by late year. Hooray for insight! That organization, inspired by the Soviets in 1945, has been the biggest draw-back for the American people of all time. The conspiracy that goes on within its walls is rampant and controlled by the U.S.S.R. It's time the American people wake up and realize our dreams of freedom from external control are dwindling rapidly. We must have good people of God in our government if we are to see new horizons without chains. Knowing that the Soviets don't want Reagan for another term should be cause enough to put him there indefinitely, but surely for another four years. The Soviets and the liberal democrats of this world have much in common. They both want the United States to reduce its nuclear capabilities, while Russia uses theirs for blackmail of the human race. It won't happen with Ronald Reagan.

What's happening to America? Too many liberal-thinking, non-doing Democrats, that's good for a starter. Without this free-thinking element in the country we would be removing the road block to prosperity. Judge for yourself, but be astute and let no one deceive you with neatly wrapped packages called freedom. Freedom costs dearly and if you can't understand that, you don't deserve to be free. Those that take offense to what I am saying are the same that the shoe will fit perfectly. We need God back in our schools, back in our families and everywhere else in the land of Liberty. There can be no other alternative!

WHAT IS AN ATHEIST?
"SICK-SICK-SICK"
6-6-6

How many people really know what it takes to make a person an atheist? To understand that, you must first realize just who (or what) these creatures really are. In the making of this book, I felt that it would only be fair to the reader to investigate one of these dens of iniquity and I went directly to the "horses hind end" to find out what makes these people tick. I sent for some of their "literature."

I found out about the "American Atheists" during research into library files concerning the Supreme Court decision that removed as unconstitutional vocal public school prayer in 1963. I discovered that a woman by the name of Madalyn Murray O'Hair organized an outfit in Austin, Texas, to promote the filth known as atheism. She's so successful at denying the Lord Jesus Christ that her son, William, became a Baptist Minister. Nevertheless, I requested some material from the organization and when it arrived...I have to admit – I was shocked!

When I was a child I used to think that the word atheist was just a person who didn't believe in anything. I was wrong! Atheists do believe in something. They believe in "freethinking," "the supremacy of reason and the aims at establishing a lifestyle and "ethical" outlook verified by experience," "materialism," "secularism," "that man can create his own destiny," "social philosophy," "humanism," "no existence after death," "the separation of church and state," "the belief that there is no god" and interdependence on man!" I believe that these people are in the darkest of the dark. They are very blind and are trying to organize other people with narrowed vision to lead into the depths of hell.

The first material I received was direct from their national chapter in Austin, Texas. The content was so obscene and sickening, I placed it in the circular file after reading only a paragraph. Recently I was mailed an application for membership to their northern Nevada chapter in Reno (sure glad they're not in Vegas), along with some of their highlights from one of their meetings. Here's what they ask for on their membership card.

AMERICAN ATHEIST MEMBERSHIP APPLICATION

Name (last) _________________________ (first**) _______________

Address (street, apt. no. or p.o. box no.) _______________

City _________________________ State (or country) & Zip _______________

This is to certify that I am in agreement with the "Aims and Purposes" and the "Definitions" of the American Atheists (see left). I consider myself to be a Materialist or Non-theist (*i.e., A-theist*) and I have, therefore, a particular interest in the separation of state and church and the American Atheists' efforts on behalf of that principle.

I usually identify myself for public purposes as (*check one*):

☐ *Atheist* ☐ *Objectivist* ☐ *Agnostic* ☐ *Realist*

☐ *Freethinker* ☐ *Ethical Culturalist* ☐ *Rationalist* ☐ *Secularist*

☐ *Humanist* ☐ *Unitarian* ☐ *I evade any reply to a query*

☐ *My own appellation as given* _______________

However, I am an Atheist and I hereby make application for membership in American Atheists. Both dues and contributions are to a tax-exempt organization and I may claim these amounts as tax deduction on my income tax return.

_______________   _______________
Date   (This application must be dated and signed by the applicant to be accepted)   Signature

All memberships include a monthly "Insider's Newsletter" and the *American Atheist* magazine. Memberships are available in the following NEW categories:

☐ Individual, $40.00/year ☐ Family/Couple, $50.00/year**

☐ Student, $12.00/year* ☐ Sustaining, $100.00/year

☐ Age 65 or over/Unemployed, $20.00/year* ☐ Life Membership, $500.00/lifetime

(For those of you who wish only to make a partial commitment by subscribing to *American Atheist* magazine, orders for subscriptions alone are available upon request for one-year terms only.)

☐ 1-year subscription, $25.00 ☐ Sample magazine, $1.00

I enclose my check or money order made payable to American Atheists or

charge my ☐ VISA or ☐ MASTERCARD   Bank No/Code letters

Number _______________ Expiration Date _______________ _______________

Date _______________   _______________
                                                  Signature

Mail to: **American Atheists, PO Box** _______________

This application must be dated and signed by applicant to be accepted. Upon your acceptance into membership you will receive a handsome gold embossed membership card, a membership certificate personally signed by Dr. Madalyn Murray O'Hair, our special monthly "Insider's Newsletter" to keep you informed of the activities of the American Atheists, and a subscription to American Atheist. Your name will be sent to the chapter in your local area if there currently is one, and you will be contacted so you may become a part of the many local activities.

*Photocopy of ID required.
**Spouse Name _______________

I eliminated their address just for the sake of disallowing them any special...free advertising space in this book. They don't deserve it.

Can you imagine that you "really" get an autographed "gold embossed membership card" from the nation's highest ranking antiChrist, when you become an associate of satan? If you don't know who Madalyn Murray O'Hair is, she's one of the prime reasons our children cannot have spoken prayer in our public schools. It was that 'being' that joined with other liberals (at that time about 2% of the population) to make sure their children would not be "hurt" by hearing of the saving graces of GOD!

"There will always be temptation to do evil, but woe unto them through which these evils come!"
It were better for them to have a millstone hanged about their neck, and then cast into the sea, than they should offend one of the children of GOD!"
LUKE 17:1,2

According to the atheists, "religion is a denial of reason, and as such, hinders "progress" towards real solutions to our problems."

I am asking every reader of this book to pray for these misguided souls. Pray that their ranks will be infiltrated by the Holy Spirit of GOD and they will awaken and find the real truth. They say that Christianity "hinders the progress towards real solutions to their problems." Can you imagine that! They have bypassed their only chance.

I'll tell you how my feelings go. I will try to reach out to anyone in search of the real meaning of life (GOD), but Jesus also said not to give holy things to evil people...they will trample them, turn and attack you! I believe these lost souls need our help. Many of their members have been grossly misinformed and are on a collision course with the eternal Lake of Fire and Brimstone. These people must repent or they're doomed, and that's real sad. They are foregoing their eternal life...something that is free for the asking. For that misunderstanding they need our prayers. We must forgive them for their lack of proper knowledge...do not call them the enemy – they're just in the dark and misery loves company.

Madalyn Murray O'Hair did a humanly unforgiveable sin against both GOD and Country in 1963 and she has persisted to build her army of anti-Christs ever since. We are not of this Earth, therefore we are not considered human beings.

We are sons and daughters of the Living GOD and we

must sincerely forgive them with all our hearts. Pray with me this following prayer. If you are one of these atheists and desire to have a real meaning for living, not to mention the importance of saving your eternal soul, pray it with sincerity and for the first time in your life...be free!

Dear GOD,

I am agreeing with Rick that the atheist is a lost soul and in need of extreme prayer. They are some of Your lost sheep and need a way back into your flock. They have been deceived by the king of this earth (satan). Without Your special graces they will be doomed to eternal torment. In the name and power of Jesus, I bind the evils of satan and command them to leave immediately, never to return to their bodies. By the power of the Blood of Jesus, who has no equal. . . be free and sin no more. Amen and Amen.

This Prayer is For Madalyn Murray O'Hair!

Dear GOD,

I have sinned against You and my fellow man and I am sorry. I realize that I am unworthy and deserve nothing. As You said that anything I ask in the name of Jesus will be granted and I am asking to be forgiven and made whole.

I accept the fact that Jesus died on the cross for all the sins I have ever committed and I ask that Jesus will come into my heart and give me a reason to live. For most of my life I have been against You; now, with the power of the Holy Spirit, I will use my remaining days to witness for Jesus Christ. Give me this chance and I will campaign twice as hard FOR YOU as I was previously against You. I ask this is the name of Jesus. Amen and Amen.

When you have prayed that prayer you'll be free. Call someone and tell them about your new life. If you prayed that prayer Madalyn...welcome home and GOD bless you!

CHAPTER SIX

GOD'S TEN COMMANDMENTS

"Think not that I am come to destroy the law, or the prophets: I am not come to destroy, but to fulfill.

For verily I say unto you, Till heaven and earth pass, one jot or one tittle shall in no wise pass from the law, till all be fulfilled."

JESUS CHRIST (Matthew 5:17,18)

Nearly thirty-five hundred years ago the Lord GOD Yahweh summoned His Prophet Moses to the holy ground on Mount Sinai. There, speaking through a burning bush, GOD gave His commandments and made His covenant with His Chosen people. He issued Moses a set of majestic principles we know today by the name of the Ten Commandments of GOD.

GOD told Moses to tell the people that they would surely be blessed if they obeyed them. GOD said that He would dwell with them and they with Him for ever if they would adhere to His principles for close fellowship. He would be the enemy of their enemies and give them His blessings in the Promised Land of milk and honey and would be their GOD.

He told Moses that to have this fellowship, the people would have to renounce the pagan gods they worshipped while in captivity in Egypt and worship Him only. Unfortunately for the seed of Jacob (Israel) and the world, His commandments fell on deaf ears and hardened, lustful hearts.

Regardless of the supernatural miracles the Jews witnessed on their exodus from Egypt, their minds were clouded by evil practices and the Chosen people of GOD had no intentions of fulfilling their initial promise to Yahweh. Even while Moses was on the Mountain of GOD, they coerced Aaron to build them a god so that they could see who they were worshipping. They collected all their gold earings, bracelets and necklaces and had Aaron construct a golden calf and worshipped the man-made image who could neither see, nor talk nor breathe.

After fourty days on the mountain, Moses returned with the tablets of GOD's covenant and in his fury, smashed the stones of GOD's commandments. Moses drew a line and asked who would be on GOD's side...thus was the division of the

Chosen people. Those who chose to follow Moses and agree to GOD's principles prospered...Those that chose to worship their pagan god were punished and didn't prosper. They chose darkness and GOD gave them what they asked for.

Today, as knowledge has vastly increased throughout the world, the carnal hearts of men remain despicable before the Lord and this despiteous desecration of GOD's commandments remain as a curse on all humanity. Today we have some who choose to worship evil and tasteless gods and we have those few who choose to seek the face of GOD in their lives. I can tell you this with assurance...I have never met a happy and content man who didn't know GOD!

Even GOD's beloved Moses altered many of GOD's commandments, demeaning their principles and diluting their holiness in compensation for the evil hearts and uncompromising opinions of the people at that time. Many of our churches today are altering GOD's principles and even preaching false truths to their congregation. Unless your church is preaching the gospel and taking the Bible in its literal sense...you are the ones that are being lead away from your GOD. If any preacher or priest tells you that Jesus was not GOD, that His birth was not an Immaculate Conception (virgin birth) or if your church leaders are begining to tell you that the Bible is not to be taken literally....STAND UP, GET YOUR HAT, GET OUT AS FAST AS YOU CAN and find yourselves another church...one that preaches from the Word of GOD only! If they choose to go to hell - that's their choice. But don't be guilty by association!

Nineteen-hundred and eighty-six years ago (2 B.C.), GOD decided to come to earth and witness first hand of the temptations of man. He wanted to see why man couldn't adhere to His guidelines for fellowship. What He found was hardened hearts, lust, fornication and every other evil conceiveable. Surely this confirmed to GOD that mankind was destined to hell unless they were given another form of saving grace.

Animal sacrifice was man's only form of atonement prior to Jesus. GOD saw that man was not adhering to this covenant either. Simply put, man had to atone for himself prior to GOD dying on a tree at Calvary and it wasn't enough to reverse their evils.

> "For GOD so loved the world, that He gave His only begotten Son, that whosoever believeth in Him, should not perish, but have everlasting life."
> JOHN 3:16

During GOD's thirty-three years in the body of a mortal (Jesus), He gave mankind a new reason for living...a fresh

"For GOD so loved the world, that He gave His only begotten Son, that whosoever believeth in Him, should not perish, but have everlasting life!"

JOHN 3:16

start and a renewed spirit. Jesus rejuvenated man's lost faith but many of His own (Jewish) people could not find it in their hearts to realize that the fulfillment of their Prophet Isaiah was at hand (Isaiah 53)...the First Coming of the Messiah.

Today there are more and more Jews coming into the Light. Jews from across the face of the earth are beginning to understand that their Messiah was the Lord Jesus Christ. This understanding by the Jewish people was also prophesied for the final times of the world and it's happening as you read this book. Messanic Jews are forming organizations all over the United States and in Israel there are approximately 15,000 who have come to know the truth. If that's not a miracle...I don't know what is.

Think about it. The Jews are the Chosen people of GOD. For centuries they chose to believe the deceitful priests of that era who lied about the ascension of Jesus after the crucifixion. They made up stories and bribed the Roman sentries who were guarding the tomb to say they fell asleep when the stone was supernaturally rolled away. There were at least 10 and maybe twenty Roman guards on the tomb...No one saw the stone moved, but Jesus wasn't there in the morning of the third day! PRAISE GOD! He has risen! Praise God for the Jewish brothers in Christ who are beginning to see the truth after almost twenty centuries. That's a miracle in itself! For you other Jews that believe in GOD, but not in His Son, read Isaiah 53, then read the Books of Matthew, Mark, Luke and John in the New Testament...These Books of the Bible were written by Jews, not Gentiles!

When Jesus was questioned on which of the commandments were the most important, Jesus told him:

> "Thou shalt love the Lord thy GOD with all thy heart, and with all thy soul, and with all thy mind.
>
> This is the first and the great commandment.
>
> And the second is like unto it, thou shalt love thy neighbor as thyself.
>
> On these two commandments hang all the law and the prophets."
>
> Matthew 22:37-40

How much more powerful can words be? If man would follow these two commandments, all the rest would fall into place. Obeying only two allows you to adhere to them all!

It would be an impossibility to love GOD and not obey His commandments. To understand just how far off the beaten track we are, let's analyse these ten special laws and measure our own individual allegiance and faithfulness...But understand this first. GOD knows it is more than difficult for

"AND THOU SHALT WRITE THEM UPON THE POSTS OF THY HOUSE, AND ON THY GATES."
DEUTERONOMY 6:9

man to remain sinless in this dominion of satan...it's impossible to aspire to perfection in GOD's eyes. But it is not impossible for us to make the attempt to follow His commandments and pray to Him all the time for the needed strength in doing so. Anything you ask of GOD in the name of Jesus...He will grant you, and it's all to His glory!

The TEN COMMANDMENTS!

"And thou shalt teach them diligently unto thy children, and shalt talk of them when thou sittest in thine house, and when thou walkest by the way, and when thou liest down, and when thou risest up.

AND THOU SHALT BIND THEM for a sign upon thine hand, and they shall be as frontlets between thine eyes.

And thou shalt WRITE THEM UPON THE POSTS OF THY HOUSE, and on thy gates."

DEUTERONOMY 6:7-9

"THOU SHALT LOVE THE LORD THY GOD WITH ALL THINE HEART, AND WITH ALL THY SOUL, AND WITH ALL THY MIGHT, THOU SHALT HAVE NO OTHER GODS BEFORE ME."

We live in a world of hate and contempt, of prejudice and deceit. And on an earth where man can not even say that they love their fellow man...without loving your brother whom you can see, how can you ever hope to love your GOD?

Many today give the outward appearance of religion and all the piety that goes along with it, but much of what they do is for earthly credit in the eyes of man. There is only a shadow of love in their hearts – they will smile to your face and spread vicious gossip behind your back.

The existence of compassion for the less fortunate is almost non-existent, an admirable trait long lost in our society! Their evils know no limitations and few, a very small percentage of the people, really TRY to reach out for the knowledge from GOD with all their hearts. Without repentance of sin, no mortal can say they love Him.

Without adhering to His principles we all fall short of His wishes...but He already knows the kind of a world we all live in. When you pray, ask GOD to help you in your everyday life...truly seek Him and you will find HIM! If you look at your fellow man with compassion, even when they say they hate you, you will find the better parts of him. You will pray for those that hate you and by so doing...GOD will shine on your every undertaking in life...GOD will then know that you are truly seeking Him.

> "THOU SHALT NOT MAKE UNTO THEE ANY GRAVEN IMAGE, OR ANY LIKENESS OF ANY THING THAT IS IN HEAVEN ABOVE, OR THAT IS IN THE EARTH BENEATH, OR THAT IS IN THE WATER UNDER THE EARTH:
>
> THOU SHALT NOT BOW DOWN THYSELF TO THEM, NOR SERVE THEM: FOR I THE LORD THY GOD AM A JEALOUS GOD, VISITING THE INEQUITY OF THE FATHERS UPON THE CHILDREN UNTO THE THIRD AND FOURTH GENERATION OF THEM THAT HATE ME;
>
> AND SHEWING MERCY UNTO THOUSANDS OF THEM THAT LOVE ME, AND KEEP MY COMMANDMENTS."

When any man places his family, material wealth or any other worldly possession in front of his love for GOD, he is worshipping a false idol and desecrating commandment number two. GOD should be the "head of each household, involved in all family decisions and every ounce of trust should be given Him." GOD knows what's best for us!

In most of the nation's homes, GOD is not so much as a secondary preference. Most are storing their treasures where they will rot. A good rule of thumb in making our priorities is, "IF YOU CAN'T TAKE THEM WITH YOU..........IT ISN'T A FIRST PRIORITY! Material wealth should not be placed above spiritual richness.

Most people of this world are not their brother's keeper...or so they give the impression. As long as we can feed our families...nothing else seems important to us. That's not the way GOD had planned for us. The darkness that many are presently serving will not be met with any real hope for future prosperity. The idols they worship are going to "burn" right along with those who worship them. If you want GOD's favor...put Him first above all else and pray that He will count you worthy. There's only one way to get to heaven and that's by recognizing that Jesus Christ died on the cross for the redemption of your sins. Those who deny the Son...do not know the Father...because the SON is the Father! (John 14:7-9)

> "THOU SHALT NOT TAKE THE NAME OF THE
> LORD THY GOD IN VAIN; FOR THE LORD WILL NOT
> HOLD HIM GUILTLESS THAT TAKETH HIS NAME IN
> VAIN."

Why is it that we always have to attack innocence when things do not go as planned? Jesus said in Matthew 5:34, that man should not make any oath using the heavens, the earth or upon His Father's name. Simply say "yes I will" or "no I won't!" If you have to "swear to GOD" on the vow...something has to be wrong with what you are saying. Your word is enough to suffice.

In the courts of law we swear to our word on a Bible. Few today will not perjure themselves when put on a spot...so why all the reverence to the sacred Bible when even the justices do not even stand for equality and fair play.

All you seem to hear nowadays is "Goddamn" or "Jesus Christ" when someone is mad...shouldn't that be "satan-be-damned?" Most don't even have to be mad to take the Lord's name in vain...they use it in their regular speech when in conversation with most anyone. GOD says that He will not find the offenders guiltless who use His name in vain...and He never lies! We're all guilty of using His name in vain in our lives, but if it slips out in a fit of anger...train yourself and control the words you use vainly. Ask for forgiveness!

> "REMEMBER THE SABBATH DAY, TO KEEP IT
> HOLY.
> SIX DAYS SHALT THOU LABOUR, AND DO·ALL
> THY WORK:
> BUT THE SEVENTH DAY IS THE SABBATH OF
> THE LORD THY GOD: IN IT THOU SHALT NOT DO
> ANY WORK."

Through the advancement of technology we have destroyed our economy. What we have created is a seven day, round the clock world and if that's advancement...you can have it!

In worship of material wealth, man has left no time for the most important things in life...their GOD, their Family or their Country.

Sunday for most is no longer the day to rest and praise the Lord for His blessings to us. This monster we call the economy has perverted America's ideals and has caused, in most homes across our nation, a family "in need of two incomes to break even!"

GOD never intended for the woman to work outside the home. Their purpose was to care for the children and be a homemaker...not business executives, policepersons and Judges in the courts.

May GOD have mercy on those liberalists and communists who were the cause of placing the woman in business and taking her from where she was sorely needed. You Christians should come down to earth. Throw away your credit cards and if possible get your wife back in the home watching over and caring for your children. Don't do as the world does...you're not part of it...you are a son of GOD and a most unique being. Place your burdens on GOD and give Him full control. When you do that you won't worry anymore. GOD said that He would provide and He will do just that...if you let Him. Give credit where it's deserved and it will go nowhere else but to the glory of GOD! Make the seventh day holy with you and your family and GOD will bless you for your wise decision.

> "HONOR THY FATHER AND THY MOTHER: THAT
> THE DAYS MAY BE LONG UPON THE LAND WHICH
> THE LORD THY GOD GIVETH THEE."

How many in this present generation really show honor and appreciation to their parents for their sacrifices they have made in our favor? I would say a very small percentage!

Today, more than any other time in world history, children are more disobedient and disrespectful to their parents and show little, if any, regard for their affection. Much of this disrespect comes directly back on the lap of the parent who is so selfish they would rather be playing golf with buddies or working an extra day, rather than spending a few hours to love and guide their child.

The three greatest gifts a parent can give their child are 1.) "the knowledge of GOD," 2.) "their precious time and attention to their children," and 3.) their understanding and patience! Anything less and you DON'T DESERVE RESPECT AND HONOR!

Mankind has evolved into self-centered egomaniacs, caring less and less for the things in life that have true value...opting instead for their own pleasure. They have no time to get down on the floor and play with their children when they are young...then they expect a close relationship with their children when they become teens...Forget it! The

The time to nurture a relationship with your child is when they are young...and I don't mean when they are two or three. I mean from the moment you bring them home from the hospital. If you want honor, do something to deserve it, but nevertheless, our GOD says for us to give our parents honor and respect. If we truly love our GOD, we must forgive our parents if they were not the best in our childhood. Love them while you still have them...they need it more than you could possibly know!

"THOU SHALT NOT KILL."

Anyone that says they have never killed anyone is not cognizant of the meaning of the sixth commandment. The literal analogy of the word is only one meaning...and possibly the more honest of the two expressions.

Abortion by any other name is still murder. You can not condone the killing of "developing human beings," regardless of the advancement in the life cycle and still say you have not broken the sixth.

If you have ever "killed anyone's spirit or will to live," you are also guilty and subject to judgment.

The physical act of murder in our country has escalated in the last twenty-five years. The further man regresses from GOD, and His principles, the more the vicious crimes of humanity will increase. In bygone days when someone got mad they were ready to fight...now when people get mad...they want to kill!

The value of human life to man has decreased to lower and lower levels in the past two decades and the reason always comes back to the same area...GOD has been taken out of the society! The salt has been removed...thus decaying will take His place.

If you are a girl with an unwanted pregnancy...don't kill that little one. The courts of our land condone abortion, but GOD doesn't, regardless of their 12-1 vote. Can man save your soul? If not, you'd better get back to Him and start practicing His ways!

"THOU SHALT NOT COMMIT ADULTERY."

Regardless of one's chastity, not one above the age of reason can truthfully say they have adhered to this commandment as well. The "Law of Moses" said that a man could divorce his wife by merely giving her a letter of dismissal. That was an altered commandment to suffice for the hardened hearts of that era. It was certainly not the intentions of GOD for man to divorce his wife, except for fornication.

Jesus expanded on the Laws of Moses when He said, "Any man who even looks at a woman with lustful eyes, has already committed adultery with her in his heart." Can you now say that you are guiltless of desecrating this commandment?

> "Whosoever shall put away his wife, saving for the cause of fornication, causeth her to commit adultery: and whosoever shall marry her that is divorced committeth adultery."
> Matthew 5:32

It is relatively doubtful that anyone can say that they have truthfully not looked at another with lust in their eyes. GOD bless us. We're not doing very well on the first seven commandments...are we? Let's see how we stack up to the final three.

"THOU SHALT NOT STEAL."

As you progress in this book you will see how GOD has multiple meanings for most all of His commandments, covenants and "Plans" for humanity. Commandment number eight is no different.

You do not have to physically remove another's property to be guilty of judgment here. If you have ever stolen another's idea...you've broken number eight. If you have ever lied on your income tax...your wrong again.

Crime figures are not decreasing in these modern times. Many citizens feel the "world owes them a living!" Welfare fraud has reached a peak in America and when President Reagan tries to do something about it...his righteousness is attacked by these very same freeloaders. Some of the people in this nation really have a need for assistance...most are able-bodied and still don't want to work!

If man cannot be trusted with small things...he surely cannot be trusted with larger.

"THOU SHALT NOT BEAR FALSE WITNESS AGAINST THY NEIGHBOUR."

The admirable asset of honesty has swiftly become a forgotten trait among men. Mankind will spare no means whatsoever in the justification of falsehoods.

They will refer to lies as fibs, procrastination,

exaggerations and prefabrications. In actuality what they are really saying are lies...always untruthful in content unless it is the exact truth!

Some will lie to make themselves more desireable to others, while many lie for acceptance as a veil for their inferiority complex.

They will call lies by many names...each time failing to understand that these untruths can never grow smaller in context. Lies will always get bigger and soon they are lying to cover up misinformations.

You can say that you were only telling a "fish story" but unless what you say is exactly as it happened...you're a liar! If we look for honesty in this world...we must begin with ourselves and project this desire in our individual actions. Your word should be your creditability and it's only as good as your exports. Be dependable...don't lie!

"THOU SHALT NOT COVET THY NEIGHBOR'S HOUSE, THOU SHALT NOT COVET THY NEIGHBOUR'S WIFE, NOR ANYTHING THAT IS THY NEIGHBOUR'S."

If you have ever looked upon another's material wealth and desired it for yourself...you've missed again. Most of us have done it and it's wrong. Be happy for the prosperity of others but never try to put yourself in their shoes..."they may not be what you really want...the grass is not as green in the other fellow's yard, especially if you have the riches of knowing the Lord Jesus Christ when your neighbor doesn't! He would be the poor one."

It's not wrong to dream or to work hard to attain that which others already have...it's wrong when this desire becomes an obsession with you and you begin worshipping false principles.

No mortal ever owns anything except a relationship that can be free for the asking. GOD is the only thing you can take with you when you go to your final destiny, so, why all the clatter about treasures you can only store on the earth. Money can be stolen...cars can be ruined...family can die...houses can be burnt to the ground...but...the love of GOD cannot be lost if you work for this relationship. The love you have for others will live on long after your body has turned back to dust...Store your treasures in heaven where they cannot be taken by a thief.

The Ten Commandments

"And thou shalt teach them diligently unto thy children, and shalt talk of them when thou sittest in thine house, and when thou walkest by thy way, and when thou liest down, and when thou risest up.

And thou shalt bind them for a sign upon thine hand, and they shall be as frontlets between thine eyes.

AND THOU SHALT WRITE THEM UPON THE POSTS OF THY HOUSE, and on thy gates."

DEUTERONOMY 6:7-9

★

"Thou shalt love the Lord thy GOD with all thine heart, with all thy soul, and with all thy might, THOU SHALT HAVE NO OTHER GODS BEFORE ME!"

★ ★

"Thou shalt not make unto thee any graven image, or any likeness of anything that is in heaven above, or that is in the earth beneath, or that is in the water under the earth.

Thou shalt not bow down thyself to them, nor serve them: For I the Lord thy GOD am a jealous GOD, visiting the inequity of the fathers upon the children unto the third and fourth generation of them that hate Me;

And shewing mercy unto thousands of them that love Me, and keep My Commandments!"

★ ★ ★

"Thou shalt not take the name of the Lord thy GOD in vain; for the Lord will not hold him guiltless that taketh His Name in vain!"

★ ★ ★ ★

"Remember the Sabbath Day, to keep it holy.

Six days shalt thou labour, and do all thy work;

But the seventh day is the Sabbath of the Lord thy GOD: In it thou shalt not do any work!"

★ ★ ★ ★ ★

"Honor thy father and thy mother: That the days may be long upon the land which the Lord thy GOD giveth thee!"

★ ★ ★ ★ ★ ★

"Thou shalt not kill!"

★ ★ ★ ★ ★ ★ ★

"Thou shalt not commit adultery!"

★ ★ ★ ★ ★ ★ ★ ★

"Thou shalt not steal!"

★ ★ ★ ★ ★ ★ ★ ★ ★

"Thou shalt not bear false witness against thy neighbor!"

★ ★ ★ ★ ★ ★ ★ ★ ★ ★

"Thou shalt not covet thy neighbor's house, thou shalt not covet thy neighbor's wife, nor anything that is thy neighbor's!"

No man on earth can truthfully say they stack up to GOD's covenants, however this fact is no reason to quit trying to adhere to them and continue to ask GOD for His divine help in our lives.

Those who "give up to the pressures of society will never know the joys of success." My idea of success is anything that comes out of my relationship to GOD...anything less and it's not material to the growth of my family or myself...In other words, I don't want or need anything that doesn't come from the Father.

You'll be totally surprised when you find out "how much" GOD really wants for you to have. People are so caught up with making a living on their own that they have forgotten how to live. Money has become so important to them that they fail to acknowledge where all blessings come from. What you "sow in life you will also reap." If you use GOD's money wisely and find the meaning of charity to others, you will be taken care of by the Father. Don't be afraid to help others for lack of resources...have faith and they will be given to you by GOD as a reward for your compassion.

The next beggar you see on the street...don't pass him by because he may just be our Lord. Lend your assistance and show love where there is none, but don't do this to be seen by man. Jesus passed the blind man when the crowds were near and returned later to give the man sight.

Planet Earth is indeed in bad times but this fact shouldn't alter the manner in which you treat your fellow man. Do what Jesus asks of you. When someone does you a wrong...tell them you love and forgive them. Love is forgiveness and forgiveness is GOD's Wish.

Start out your day with thanksgiving to GOD for His mercy and kindness....and never fail to recognize that He already knows what you need before you ask for it. Some of the most heard prayers you will ever make are not for yourself, but for others. If someone asks you what you want from them...Tell them that you want them to pray for you.

All the earthly sins we will ever make have already been paid for in full when Jesus died on the cross. They were atoned and death was defeated by the mercy of GOD for mankind. All He requires from man is to accept it and live. We cannot make it to heaven on our earthly merit!!! We can only dwell in our Father's House through believing in the Lord Jesus Christ.

We don't stack up to GOD's wishes...but keep trying...practice cannot be made perfect on earth...but it will lead to perfection in heaven!

CHAPTER SEVEN

"Do You Believe In Miracles?"
You can perform them — if you believe!

". . .And those who believe shall use My authority to cast out demons, and they shall speak new languages. They will be able even to handle snakes with safety, and if they drink anything poisonous, it won't hurt them; and they will be able to place their hands on the sick and heal them!"

JESUS CHRIST (Mark 16:17)

Have you ever had a secret desire to be like Jesus? I think many who are compassionate, overly emotional and inclined to the spiritual have had dreams of walking in the shoes of Jesus. Being able to possess the divine gift of healing the sick, the blind, the lepers and using these blessings in the advancement of spiritual faith in GOD, has always been in the back of my mind. I believe in every word from the mouth of GOD! If He says it can be done by mortal believers, there should be no question of its validity. Mere mortal human beings can perform wonderous miracles but you must have at least the faith of a mustard seed!

"If you only have faith in GOD, this is an absolute truth, you can say to the Mount of Olives, 'Rise up and fall into the Mediterranean,' and your command will be obeyed. All that's required is that you really believe and have no doubt. You can pray for anything, and if you believe, you have it, it's yours. But when you are praying, first forgive anyone you are holding a grudge against, so that your Father in heaven will forgive you your sins too!"

JESUS CHRIST (Mark 11:22-25)

Those words are directly from the Power that Is, GOD Almighty, and you can believe in His Name. Jesus performed many wonderful miracles while in human form and renewed a long lost faith in GOD among many. But even when many of the wicked of His day saw His great power, they still did not believe He was GOD; just so is the faith in our world today! The tomorrows of the non-believer are indeed limited.

Lazarus was already gravely ill in Bethany when the word reached Jesus. Yet He remained where He was for two more days before going to his aid. By the time Jesus arrived, His friend was dead and entombed four days. Upon death the body goes through a chemical change that eventually will result in the body turning to dust. After three days the body begins to rot. When Jesus arrived at the home of Lazarus (2 miles outside of Jerusalem) he was met by Mary's sister Martha.

"If you had been here my brother would not have died, but I know that even now, whatever you ask of GOD He will grant you," Martha said confidently.

"Your brother will rise again," Jesus told Her.

"I know he will," said Martha, "at the resurrection on the last day."

Then Jesus said,   "I am the resurrection. If anyone believes in Me, even though he dies, he will live, and whosoever believes in Me, will never die!" (John 11:26)

"Do you believe this Martha?" asked Jesus!

"Yes Lord, I believe that you are the Christ, the Son of God, the One who has come into this world." said Martha.

"Where have you put him?" asked Jesus. Jesus was moved with compassion and wept for His friend Lazarus. "Take the stone away," He commanded as He approached the tomb.

"But Lord; this is the fourth day," said Martha, "he will smell!"

Jesus said solemnly, "Have I not told you that if you believe you will see the glory of GOD?"

When they rolled the stone away from the entrance to the cave, Jesus lifted His eyes to the heavens and prayed.

"Father, I thank you for hearing My prayer. I knew indeed that you always hear me, but I speak for the sake of those around Me, so that they might believe that it was You who sent me!"

When He had prayed this, He cried out in a loud voice, "Lazarus, here! Come out!" The dead man came out in his burial cloth. Jesus said, "Unbind him, let him go free!"

I am the Resurrection
and the Life
JOHN 11:26

To me this scripture holds a special meaning. It tells me that believers in GOD are never dead, only resting. Every time I read it, tears well in my eyes, I find it difficult to catch my breath and chills run up and down my spine from joy. Anyone that cannot appreciate the Powers of GOD, is a fool!

That miracle is only one of many that Jesus performed in the presence of witnesses. This gift of healing is available to all that hear the Good News and believe in the message He gives to the world. You must not have doubt. Many of us do because we have been programed by the work of mortals into believing otherwise. In the shallow mind of man, 'everything must have a beginning and an end.' This is false - it just isn't so!

Ordinary death to the non-believer is a darkness, a permanent cessation of all vital signs. Basically it is passing out of existence. To the Christian, death is none of the above. Jesus says that those who believe in Him "will never die," and He never bears false witness. If Lazarus had not believed in Jesus as being the Christ mentioned in prophecy, he would not have risen. Because he did believe in Jesus as the Messiah, he was only asleep and resting, waiting for GOD's command to awaken him.

I realize that when I said "being like Jesus" in the opening paragraph of this chapter, I was walking a thin line. I certainly do not suggest that a mere mortal can be GOD, nor do I entertain that anyone should have that aspiration. I meant that man can be "like" Jesus if his worldly deeds are righteous, his heart compassionate and his actions promote the Will of GOD! The powers that GOD has given those who love Him are unlimited and awesome. They are given to those who truly love GOD, obey His Covenant for fellowship and will use them in promotions of the Spirit.

Jesus said, "If you have the faith you will be able to do great miracles, even greater than the ones I do!" He also promised that "anything you ask for using My Name and believe that you will receive, you will be given!" Christians can receive these powers only through acccepting Jesus into a reborn heart and practicing your belief with the end product of goodness. If you want to experience "real power," and be able to work wondrous miracles in His Name, you must be willing to give up all evil ways and follow Him with no reservations and no doubts.

Even the evil can be swayed to goodness when touched by the Holy Spirit. Saul was a man whose heart was hardened. He was against everything that Christ promoted and even tried to slaughter Christ's disciples, ridding the world of the earliest Christians. In the Spirit, Jesus spoke to Saul and drove the demons from his heart. Saul became Paul in name and was blessed by GOD. Paul became the first Disciple to preach the "Good News" to the Gentiles and was possibly the world's strongest support of early Christianity. Don't even hint that the atheist element cannot be changed in spirit. With GOD anything is possible. Don't give up on someone because they seem alienated from GOD's ways...When you finish with this book, give it to them as a gift!

Jesus said that in the end times He would send "great prophets, wise men and scribes" (Matthew 23:34). He has already completed this prophecy. Oral Roberts, Billy James Hargis, Pat Robinson, Billy Graham, James Robinson, Dwight Thompson, Jimmy Swaggart, Robert Schuller, Paul Crouch, Hal Lindsey and Jerry Falwell are but a few of GOD's prophets and wisemen. Many qualify as scribes as they have written their testimonies in great books in promotion of GOD.

In Daniel 12:4, GOD told Daniel to seal up the prophecies until the end times! If you feel we are not in those "times," explain to your own satisfaction why the "seals" have recently been broken and most all of GOD's prophets are proclaiming that His Kingdom is at hand. Only a fool will overlook the importance of getting back to the Ways of GOD. In sports you back the team that is the strongest; just so should you get your action together and place your family and friends on the winning team with GOD!

If you have kept one eye on scripture and the other on present miracles in the world, you should have a rather keen insight on the actual power that is GOD's.

Recently a woman gave birth to a healthy baby boy under seemingly impossible (medically speaking) circumstances. She had expended all hope of ever having a child of her own and had been told by numerous doctors that it would be an impossibility for her to become impregnated due to her surgery years earlier that removed her fallopian tubes. (passages that carry the egg from the ovary to the uterus for fertilization) Without fallopian tubes, it is humanly impossible for a woman to become pregnant as the eggs would become sealed in the ovary without such a passage. She had no hope, except to place her attention to the scripture where it is said, "with GOD anything is possible!"

She believed in GOD and prayed for such a miracle in the Name of Jesus. Her faith was her reward, much to the surprise of the medical world. GOD didn't only give her one gift, she is presently pregnant for the second time in three years!

Our family babysitter had an advanced case of

emphysema. For twelve years she had to sleep in a sitting position in order to breathe. She was slowly dying a most miserable death. A friend of hers told her of a Charismatic Mass at a local church and with her faith in GOD, experienced a total healing. Her doctors told her that it would only be a matter of time; the Lord GOD had other ideas for her life. After the healing, she went back to the doctor for an x-ray. The doctors could find no logical reason for the fact that her lungs were perfectly healthy and showed no signs of the disease!

One circumstance that holds back some from seeking the gifts of the Spirit is an almost morbid fear of Satan. They will see demonic power and delusion everywhere.

There are many deceiving spirits on this earth, it is true, but the scriptures give us the means to test these deceiving spirits and discern which are not from GOD. Moreover, one of the gifts of the Spirit is designed to detect the presence of evil powers. Those who fear that if they sought the gifts of the Spirit, they might receive something from the devil, should remember Christ's Words in Luke 11:11:

> "If a son shall ask for bread from any of you that is a father, will you give him a stone? Or if he asks for a fish, will he give him a serpent? Or if he asks for an egg, will he offer him a scorpion? If you know how to give good things to your children, how much more shall your Heavenly Father give the Holy Spirit to those who ask Him!"

Jesus healed lepers, the blind, the deaf, the crippled and the ill. He told the believers that if they have faith, they will be able to do all these great miracles and even greater ones.

Even though people become devoted Christians, there is always the possibility that they may be mislead by some plausible, but self-deceiving leaders who happen to win their confidence. God's people need teaching by GOD-anointed men-men who can discern between the true and the false as Paul shows in the following verse:

> "That we henceforth be no more children, tossed to and fro and carried about with every wind of doctrine, by the sleigh of men and cunning craftiness, whereby they lie in wait to deceive."
> Ephesians 4:14

The main purpose of these gifts is for the edification (instruct and improve the moral and religious values) of the church and the beautification of Christ Jesus as one with GOD. We are told that the church is the body of Christ and each of us are members in particular. The point is this, that as long as Christ was on earth, He could only be in one location at a time. He could only minister to a few at a time. However, after the gift of the Spirit had been poured out, it became possible for Jesus to manifest Himself through an unlimited number of believers. These members of His body could go forth into all parts of the world and minister to people, even as He ministered when He was on earth. "As He is, so are ye in the world!"

Can The Gifts of God Be Counterfeited?

In Matthew 24:24, Jesus said, "For there shall arise false Christs, and false prophets and they shall show great signs and wonders, insomuch that, if it were possible, they would deceive the very elect." The answer to that question is–yes, miracles can be from the evil one that waits in darkness to deceive anyone that is without Christ in his heart. Christians, the true believers will be able to see through the haze and devious candor of these false-Christs through the Will of God.

These false-Christs are plentiful in our world today, but more are on the way for tomorrow. If you gain one positive reflection from reading this book other than coming to Christ, it should be learning to discern the spirits. Some are good, – many are bad! If you remember that parable from Jesus that says, "test each spirit. A good tree never bears bad fruit and a bad tree cannot bear good fruit," you will have gained much. Remember that love is infectious and breeds a like quantity. Hate and jealousy can only make you miserable, keep you in darkness and breed discord. To have the gift of healing, or any gift from our Lord Jesus, you must only have love in your heart. So if you have an enemy, forgive him and make him your friend. If you have a friend, treat him justly and treasure the friendship. Friendship knows no barriers. If you say that you are a Christian, but hate anyone you are lying, and GOD will not bestow His gifts upon you.

Those who are opposed to the ministry of healing, and there are many, have on occasion challenged those who teach healing to make a demonstration of their healing power. They are like Herod who "hoped to have seen some miracles done by him. "(Luke 23:8) But Jesus would perform no miracle to gratify the curiosity of Herod. Nor would He comply with the mocking request of the chief priests who said, "If He be the King of Israel, let Him come down from the cross, and we will believe Him." (Matthew 27:42) GOD has no miracles for the mockers or curiosity seekers! Unless a man accepts the Lord Jesus Christ as the Son of GOD, who died on Calvary for the redemption of the human soul, he will not receive the gifts from the Father.

> "Anyone I lay My hands on will receive the Holy Spirit!"
>
> (Acts 8:19)

> "They will lay their hands on the sick, who will recover!"
>
> (Mark 16:18)

It never ceases to amaze me how little faith there is in this world. In a time when GOD's miracles are needed most, the ones that give the appearance of being educated and sophisticated are the first to deny the fact that GOD's miracles are happening all around us.

"TONY AGPAOA, The Living Legend!"

In our most recent past, there lived a man in Baguio City, Philippines, who used GOD's full power to heal the sick, cure the crippled and performed surgery with absolutely no anaesthetic no pain to the patient and no side effects. The man many called the "Living Legend" was Reverend Tony Agpaoa. Reverend Tony died recently but in his wake he left many healed in the Name of Jesus Christ. His ministry of healing continues to heal the heavy laden in the Philippine Islands. Reverend Agpaoa was by far not perfect and by his own admission, but because of his extreme faithfulness, he was granted gifts! Tony Agpaoa loved his GOD with all his mind, strength and soul and lived in the manner prescribed by the Almighty, as close as humanly possible. Because of Tony's love for GOD, he was given the gift of healing. What harm can come to the rest of us if a group of people choose to believe in GOD so fully that their faith will carry them thousands of miles to seek a man who uses GOD's direct power?

Have you ever had such an emotional flow within your being that you could not control the tears of compassion for GOD's blessings to others? If this has happened to you – then you are a prime candidate to receive the Holy blessings of healing! In the last year, especially since the time that GOD commanded me to write this book, I have had such emotions. It is unfortunate that the normal reader will not understand what I am saying, nor will he attempt to comprehend its significance. GOD touches each believer in different ways and

"Rise, your faith has healed you!"

bestows on those that truly love Him special gifts. To receive these gifts from GOD one must open his heart to the Lord, pray for understanding GOD's Will and be willing to follow His leadership.

Tony Agpaoa received the Holy Spirit while still a youth. His Protector-Comforter, as He referred to GOD, spoke to him and told him that He had selected Tony for a gift of healing. GOD's exact words to Reverend Agpaoa were as follows:

> "It is time for you to know, Antonio, that you are to heal others of their afflictions. You will open wounds and bind wounds. But you are to search your soul to find the ways of healing. You are to depart from your people during the search. You will harken only to what you hear inside you."
> (Taken in text from the book "The Living Legend," the true life story of Reverend Antonio Agpaoa!)

The very words of the One made tears start. In Tony's words, "Tears were close to my eye lids much of the time, but never tears for anything else. I knew I had to follow His Will. Where it would lead me, I did not know, but I was determind to obey!"

"I will go," said Tony. "I will tell my people."

"They have already been told," came the Word, "You have already left. When you return you will be as old as the ages, wise in the ways of nature, mindful of every living thing as every living thing should be mindful of but isn't. The need for healers is great!"

"How do I begin, Sir?" was Tony's reply, "I am eager but I do not know where to start."

The Protector-Comforter pointed and Tony saw the fluttering bird, wondering how he had missed it or not heard its fluttering.

"Take it in your hands, Antonio," said the One who was speaking. "It does not fear you-or me."

Tony stepped from the path, taking the bird from the tangled twigs of the thorny bush. The delicate thing rested in his hand. Then Tony placed his other hand over it for a moment. He had had many birds in his hands before, but never had it occured to him to breath upon any living thing that he held in his hands. But he breathed on the bird through his fingers and opened his hands. The bird looked up as if to ask permission, or to murmur a thank you. Then it flexed its wings, stood for a moment and flew, circled around Tony's head, as if to leave an assurance that his broken wing was completely healed.

Tony looked about him, pleased and happy, filled with questions to ask GOD, but there was no one to be seen. Tony studied the dust along the trail. No fresh footprints save his own were there. Had he actually heard and seen his Protector-Comforter? Had he only hoped that he had, and therefore believed that he had actually talked with and saw Him.

Tony turned back home, but a Force he could not see, pressed against his chest, holding him motionless. He could not go any furhter - not towards home. He felt a touch of fear and pushed against the unseen hand. A bird, perhaps the same bird he had held in his hands moments before, circled his head singing, then flew away towards the deep woods. Tony felt the urge to follow and did. Tony did not understand what was happening but was not about to question it. He had a thirst for the knowledge GOD said He would give him.

To discover the workings of the human mind is beyond mortals. To understand the mind takes eternity. Despite Tony's strong Christian beliefs, there was always hesitation. Once near a berry bush, GOD told him to eat of the berries so that he might learn faith. Tony knew well that the peasants in his small village held those particular berries as poisonous, but he tasted the berries and did not die. He ate of the berries and knew from the pains in his stomach that faith would be a comfort. But he insisted on living, and when he knew that he was alive, he ate of the same berries in order to learn more. Though he wept often in loneliness, he remained true in his search. How could man disobey the laws of nature and even live at all?

Tony roamed throughout the territory. Through dense forests, mountains and valleys, all the time learning the laws of nature while listening and reading the words from GOD. He sought the answers to questions that most men wouldn't have even thought of and by trusting his GOD, he learned, by seeking he found and by asking he received.

Anyone watching him roam, seemingly aimlessly about, would have reason to believe that Tony was devoid of his facilities, but such was not the case. Because he was different than others, he was also blessed. Because Tony did not seek his answers from man, he learned GOD's true knowledge of nature. Because he listened to GOD, he could also hear His messages.

God told young Agpaoa that the gift He gave Tony had conditions. GOD told him that his heart must be in his work wherever it takes him and that Tony would work with and for GOD! GOD told him that Tony would be ready for his ministry when his heart, body, mind and spirit were cleared of hatred, fear, impatience, resentment, greed, envy, covetousness and inequity...Tony told GOD that he was filled with all of those. GOD told him, "Who is not? But, at least in your case, you know."

Tony appeared and disappeared among the barrios, the small clusters of neighboring huts of hill people in his widening domain. He was welcomed everywhere he went helping menfolks in their small patches of grain fields and ate but little of what he helped produce. He managed to procure food as most people had forgotten how - taking it from the trees, melons and berries. He joined in their work and play and religious rites. Somehow he managed to keep secret that he was as young as their youngest and yet as old as the oldest of them when in study. Someone once said that Tony slept deeply, while his eyes remained unblinkingly open.

Young men followed Tony wherever he led them, sometimes to their dismay for not knowing. A youth by the name of Pedro Gonzales fell from a tree and bounced on his limbs as he hit the ground. His meager clothing was torn to shreads showing his brown body streaked with blood. He screamed and cried from his wounds. Tony remembered what his Protector-Comforter had told him..."You will open wounds and close wounds!"

Tony reached out to the boy and covered the wound with his hands. When he removed his hands, the deep and bloody gash was closed and seemed to be healed. There was no scar. There was only blood where the wound had been. For a moment there was silence among the onlookers. Even the winds seemed to have stilled their murmurings. Then all of those who had witnessed this miracle of GOD began scurrying away to tell the story - to report this miracle...

Tony told them that it was not a miracle. "Others had closed wounds and have not done miracles." He insisted. "But not at the age of nine and with naked hands,"the legendmakers insisted. Tony fled back into the wilderness, but it only added fire to the legend and increased the circle of his first domain. Tony was not the most fleet of foot and they caught him and returned him to the village where Pedro called home. Others were waiting at the Gonzales hut.

The villagers insisted that Tony would also heal them. "If you do not think you are a miracle-worker, heal us then," said many of the neighbors, "and earn the name."

"Not for miracles' sake, but for your sake," said Tony. "I do not say that I can heal you, for only GOD heals. But I can touch you as I touched Pedro...perhaps GOD healed him through me."

Tony touched each one, after each had told him what

they believed they're sicknesses were. After touching them all, each one believed they were healed and felt better. And Tony began to believe.

"I have the most dreaded disease of all," said an old and emaciate man. "I am afflicted with leprosy."

Tony saw no signs of it in the man, though he knew the signs.

"You are afraid," said the "leper" who insisted he was one. "Afraid they you will also have it? Do you really have faith that GOD heals through you?"

"I have faith," replied Tony, "but you do not have leprosy. You are well. You are not sick.

"You are afraid," the man insisted, "afraid to touch me and prove you tell a false tale."

"I've claimed nothing," said Tony.

"I challenge you to touch me, Antonio Agpaoa!" said the man.

"Do not accept, Antonio," he seemed to hear his Protector-Comforter say. "To accept is to agree that you are proud..and fearful."

But even as Tony heard his Protector-Comforter, he touched the naked chest of the challenger. The man screamed in pain and terror as much as his brown-skinned chest turned fiery red - seared by Tony's touch.

"Why had his touch burned the chest of the man who had challenged him?" was his thought.

"Deep within you," said the Voice from within him, "you were angry. Your pride could not endure questioning. You wished somehow to punish the tormentor. And you did!"

Children in the Philippines would often go barefoot, many times because they could not afford shoes, and Tony would heal their stubbed toes, their bleeding bodies from thorns and whatever afflictions they had...most all were healed. The bleeding would stop when Tony placed his hands on them. Thorns and splinters came easily free to Tony's fingers. The splinters would simply come to Tony's fingers, never leaving a festering sore, nor any scars. The wounds were instantly closed and healed.

"It hurts right here," a half-grown girl said, indicating a spot in her abdomen, the location of which, that first time, caused the brown-skinned face of Tony to blush red - to the amusement of even the half-grown girl. "Touch it. Take it out of me."

Tony touched it and there was waiting. Tony waited to see what, if anything, would happen. The girl waited. Her parents waited, watching the touching fingers, the blushing face of Tony. Tony could not keep his fingers motionless.

"Take it out through the navel," came the Voice within, and Tony moved his fingers towards the child's navel.

Tony moved his forefinger until it hovered over the small deep mystery of the navel - and the small infection came forth. It came forth much as a marble might if held somehow in hiding. The "thing" was soft, uncomfortable to look at, and spread across the girl's abdomen. Tony turned away. The girl's mother took over and examined the "thing".

"The pain is gone," said the girl.

"You have enticed the devil out of her," said the girl's father.

"I never saw the devil in any man save he placed him there himself," said Tony with confidence and knowledge far beyond his years.

Tony never turned anyone away, he knew he couldn't. He loved animals and even healed them when they were brought to him by the villagers. He was a mere ten-year-old from a peasant family and as the days and years passed, the legend grew.

Obviously there were miracles he could not perform. Notwithstanding that he made no claims and promised nothing. GOD had told him he was not compelled to heal all, but Tony said, "Rightfully, I work only in Your Name."

One woman, old enough to be his grandmother, followed him wherever he went. She had been one that young Tony could do nothing with. She continued to accuse and badger him wherever he went. Finally Tony got the message to try again with her. He told her to lay down in one of the huts and examined her body by circling his hands over her. Almost like an x-ray machine, he located the infected area beneath her skin, but whatever it was it would not come forth. He told the people that had gathered, "If I were a surgeon, I would make an incision right here," he said pointing to a section of her stomach. Then a man that was present said, "why don't you place your fingers close to her skin? Maybe the growth will come out if the skin opens up? Tony did what the man said and the skin opened up as if a pore were stretched wide. He removed the growth and as soon as that happened, the skin closed, leaving only a small trace of blood where the opening had been. There was no wound and no scar left.

Tony turned to the man who had lent him the advice but he was not there. He went outside to thank the man, but he wasn't outside either. Tony wondered who the man was or how he could have run away faster than any man could run. Who was that man?

Many people tried to pay him for his healings with livestock and produce, but he refused any compensation. He gave the food to the ones who were needy from the ones who were well off, taking only what he needed to eat at the time.

In his healings there was one thing that he soon discovered - one thing that he must be careful when faced with. His Protector-Comforter warned him of this early enough, "Do not touch a woman or a girl newly pregnant. You will cause miscarriage if the pregnancy is under two months!"

As happens in many societies, young girls will become pregnant by their boyfriends and such a shame against the girl's family was immense. Nevertheless, the Lord GOD told Tony, "Do not do it. It is their honor against your soul!"

Once when he refused a girl to stop her shameful pregnancy she said, "If you won't I will say that it is your child."

"Let's go to your parents then" said Tony. The girl did not follow through with her threat.

With no knowledge of medical science, Reverend Tony Agpaoa performed many great miracles in the Name of the Lord. Brain tumors, open heart surgery, cancer and incurable diseases responded to his touch and came to his fingers for removal from the afflicted bodies he would work on.

Tony Agpaoa was to become a living legend among the peasants in his own land. The fact of his healing spread far and wide, even as far as Manila, the Visayan Inlands and Mindanao, then even farther, in lands he'd never heard of. To those lands he carried what he knew of love in that love is the power behind the greatest of healing. But as healers before him were rejected, so was he rejected by the unbelievers. This grievous rejection, though it took him a long hurting time to learn the wisdom behind it, became his greatest victory over what his Protector-Comforter referred to as the adversary.

Have you ever seen the movie "Oh GOD!" or maybe "Oh GOD, Book II" starring George Burns as the Almighty in human form? If so - what was your initial reaction to the many actors who doubted the contentions of John Denver? Did you relate to those who did not believe that GOD had visited him, or did you side with those of us that wept in reaction? If you were emotionally moved by the climax that saw Burns (acting as GOD) appear to the non-believers and do wonderous miracles, - you are closer than you think to the Power that IS!

Why is it so hard for many to understand that there is much that we mortals do not know. The human mind of man and his sciences say that everything "must" have a beginning and also an end. To man, thinking otherwise is nonsense. Or is it? The Bible gives us all direct eye-witness accountings of great faith healings by Jesus and later by many of His

Disciples. Why must we always have to see for ourselves before we will believe? There is so much in this world that man will never experience because he will never seek the answers from GOD.

The mirror we look at ourselves in, works two ways. Can we look at ourselves each day and like what we see if we are unable to forgive those around us for wrong doing? Man has always found it difficult to forgive others and this represents another reason why we do not learn from our own mistakes. GOD says that we must forgive so that we, too, may be forgiven! That accomplished, there is nothing GOD will not give you as a reward.

The great priests, rabbis and pastors, store managers, reporters and even his own wife did not believe that GOD had spoken, let alone appeared, to John Denver. They ridiculed and criticized him for his "lies," even so much as costing him his occupation. A wise man once said, "how can anyone listen and learn when they are always preoccupied with gab and gossip." If you will take time from each of your days and listen for GOD's message to you - you will learn much of His Ways!

We humans are big on retaliation when our feelings have been hurt. When it happens, we never consider that we could possibly have some part for the action or reaction of our neighbor. Why is it so difficult for earthlings to say, "I'm sorry?" Jesus said that you will receive what you ask for in His Name! It is true! But if you ask for forgiveness, you must truly mean it with no reservations. If someone doesn't wish to forgive you, that's their millstones to carry around their neck, but you must at least try earnestly to reach them. If more would think before they act, the world would be much better for it! Words can sometimes hurt more than actions, so we must be careful with the feelings of others. You must believe and have no doubt that GOD is around you all the time. He waits for you to call on Him. To ask Him for blessings. You must believe that. "Happy are the peacemakers; they shall be called sons of GOD! (Matthew 5:9)

Nearly all of the 33 years Jesus spent on earth was used in spreading the "GOOD NEWS" of the kingdom. He cured all kinds of diseases, sicknesses and afflictions. Those who were possessed by demons, ones with leprosy and boils, epileptics, the crippled, the blind and the deaf were all healed in the sight of men. Why was the trust and faith non-existent in man of that era? Why is it missing from this very generation, when it is needed sorely?

I must admit that I become irate and impatient when I hear of non-believers that denounce everything they do not understand. They would have you believe that nothing is possible unless it is man who does it. We have made many great strides in the sciences, but what has been accomplished without the graces and knowledge that can only come from the Almighty? What can doctors do for you except prescribe medicine, operate and remove an afflicted portion of our bodies and give us their estimate of damage (diagnosis).

Miracles are all around us but we fail to see their significance. They are always something that happens to others, but others won't even believe that which they see. I see GOD's miracles every day of my life, especially when I look upon my lovely wife and five healthy children. If birth isn't one of the most precious gifts from GOD, I certainly don't know what is.

The previous non-fiction accounting of Tony Agpaoa was a closely related test to my own beliefs. Trust is not something we can inherit from our parents; it is a wonderful trait that has a close relationship to faith when in juxtapositioning to each other. As it is impossible for truly good to export itself from an evil heart, it is also illogical to assume that GOD is not working His miracles in our present age. Tony's story is absolutely true and he has many responsible witnesses to that effect.

I know a fine woman from Joseph, Oregon, who, before October 15th, 1973, was destined for an early grave. Pearl Ingle, a real estate broker from Wallowa County in Northeast Oregon, was engulfed with cancer and her heart was cause for five separate attacks. She had a bad valve in her heart for most of her life and to further complicate the matter, she had malignancies in the lungs, the liver, the urinary tract, the lymph glands and in both breasts. Thousands of dollars were spent with research and treatments throughout the United States, but because her heart could not withstand an operation, her diagnosis was determined to be terminal. Her doctors at the Mayo Clinic in Rochester, Minnesota, and also at the Good Samaritan Hospital in Portland, informed her to go home and get her house in order.

One day while servicing a client on some property, she was told of Reverend Agpaoa. Her client was a wealthy industrialist who had had a malignancy removed by a healer in the Philippine Islands. After he explained his story, Pearl, with no avenues of recourse remaining, decided to make the contact with Reverend Tony. With a strong belief in GOD and a sound knowledge of His ways, she listened to the businessman intently, believing earnestly that the man had no reason to be telling her anything other than the truth.

Armed only with her faith in the Almighty, she embarked

on her trip, arriving in Manila, Philippines in late 1973 where she met the "Living Legend." You have already heard of the Holy Spirit that works with Tony and Pearl Ingle was about to be added to his many healings.

With absolutely no anaestheic, no scapel and no loss of blood, Reverend Agpaoa performed an open heart surgery, repairing the valve while curing a lasting heart murmer. On the same visit, and three subsequent visits to the Philippines, Mrs. Ingle was totally cured of all cancer and to this day is living testimony to the Power that is GOD. She speaks the truth. I know the woman personally.

"Tony explains that in himself he can do nothing," says Pearl, "the faith he has in Jesus Christ does it all. I experienced no pain and have no scars whatsoever from the operation. My skin just opened to his fingers and the diseased organs came to his hands as if magnitized."

I was amazed when I first heard of the miracle from my wife's parents at their home in Downey, California. I more than realized that Chub (Andrew) and Grace Hohn were not given to the bearing of false witness. Their devout faith in GOD would never allow such travesty and deceit.

For most of their lives they endured minor ailments like most, and they had made provisions to visit Reverend Agpaoa themselves. Chub, a rancher and a hard working sort all his life had been continually bothered by hemorrhoids for 40 years. Fearing the imminent painful surgery, he had never had the operation. Grace suffered from a broken coccyx (tip of the tail bone) from as early as her teens, and it proved extremely painful when seated for extended periods of time. They were sure that GOD would also work His miracles on them through Agpaoa.

With a brief stop over in Hawaii, Grace and Chub arrived in Manila, Philippines in January, 1977. Taking a short ride to the hamlet of Baguio, they came to know the Faith Healer known as Tony.

The next morning Reverend Agpaoa removed the hemorrhoids and at the same time removed a potentially dangerous growth Chub didn't even know he had. Agpaoa cured a colon disorder, also unbeknown to the senior Hohn.

In the afternoon Agpaoa got around to Grace and healed her coccyx without pain or after effects, blood nor scars. For the first time in forty years, Chub and Grace could rejoice in the Lord with no physical pain.

"While in the operating room (as it was referred to), we both had the inner assurance of a deep spiritual awareness," said Grace in awe, "in the presence of Tony, there was an emotional feeling of true peace!"

Their testimony was not the figment of prefabrication or exaggeration. I can witness to their ideals and highly respect their values in relationship to GOD Almighty. I know them well, but their close proximity to GOD as the head of their household is the only witness they need. Praise the Lord for His mercy and kindness.

The works we humans perform in the Name of Jesus will dictate how much we are to learn of His Ways. The Almighty works in supernatural fashion and it is not to the mortal to dispute His precious gifts to anyone of us. God has a plan for us all. We can either accept or reject His graces, but they are there for the asking.

In my forty years, He has worked many wonderful miracles to me. It wasn't by chance that as a five-year-old He spared me from certain death when I plunged 25 feet off an old bridge, landing squarely on my head in jagged rock and 6 inches of water. Even the doctors exclaimed that it was a miracle that I was alive, let alone still walking and capable of logical reasoning.

He also warns His people of impending perils. If we are listening, WE WILL HEAR HIM!

For as long as I could remember I held animosity towards my father for divorcing my mother when I was but two. Inwardly I despised him and only tolerated his visits for the benefit of my children knowing their grandfather. While in the process or this book's writing. I became truly touched by the outreach of GOD. He told me to forgive my father. Cut him loose from the bondage that was imbedded in my heart towards him and pray for him to have peace. I stopped typing the book as I fought the tears that streamed and jerked from my eyes. I wiped my eyes and gritted my teeth in defiance of GOD's wish and tried to return to the matter at hand. But it became fruitless. My train of thought had been broken, I could no longer find the references I needed in the scriptures and I sat looking aimlessly at the typewriter.

I prayed to GOD and asked why He would request this from me. The harder I prayed, the more I cried. I remembered how selfish I had been in my childhood, never realizing that life is always a two-way street. I had inwardly cursed him for leaving my brother and me fatherless when we needed him the most. I thought of the loneliness my departed mother had gone through with her voids and how hard she labored in support of the two children she loved. I remembered how hard it was as a young child to embrace him and call him "Daddy" when he visited us once a year and how much I missed his presence at the baseball games I had played in as a youngster. Others had fathers in the crowd, why not me?

GOD indeed works in strange ways. When you love Him, you cannot refuse Him! I tore the paper out of the typewriter and proceeded, as if guided by Someone quite dear to me, to write my father. I hadn't even communicated with him for more than two years and wasn't even sure that he was in the same locale.

Choked by emotion with tears clouding my eyes to the point of haze, I wrote him a letter of forgiveness and asked him to forgive me for my selfish and unwarranted attitude towards him. When I said that I loved him very much, I meant it from my heart for the first time in my life. I truly loved him and could not explain the inner warmth that I had for him at the moment. I suddenly knew what GOD was doing with me and thanked Him for the blessing of forgiveness.

It was New Years Eve and I was alone with my thoughts when the phone rang. It had been two weeks since I had written my father and he called to say that my letter had been the best Christmas gift he had ever received. I cried when I told him that I meant every word and his voice seemed distant and in sorts, almost noncoherent. He did not say that he was in the hospital when he received my testimony, nor did he say that he was fighting for his life at the time he spoke.

When I wrote him I sincerely believed that GOD also released my own bonds and made me a whole person for the first time in my life.

Three weeks after his phone call, I received the message that Dad was in Abington Memorial Hospital and was not expected to live. Both of my brothers, Jim and Carl, had called to notify me and said that if it were financially possible, I should come back immediately. I called McCarran Airport and was on the midnight flight to Philadelphia.

On the plane I recalled the many years I had lived with a hardened heart and thought how senseless it had been. I prayed most of the way back east and asked my Father in Heaven to forgive me for my shortcomings and also that my father and I would experience peaceful unity when we would meet. Life is sure strange. A month earlier I had no intentions of ever going to visit my father again and I had had total resentment for him.

Through the powers of GOD's mercy, I was now on a plane to visit him 2500 miles away on his deathbed. All the while I was recalling the scriptures and wanted greatly to be able to work a healing upon my father. At one time I had made the expression to my wife that I didn't need my father anymore as a grown-up, the time I had needed him was when I was a child. How wrong I had been. I wanted and needed him to live! Talking to the doctors at the hospital gave us no encouragement. He would not eat and because of his weakened heart, complicated by various afflictions within his body, they could not operate on him. His heart was weak and the vital signs were diminishing rapidly. The doctors indicated that if he continued in this manner, death would come shortly.

I moved towards the remnant of the man that was partially responsible for my birth. I bent over and kissed him and asked him to forgive me for not honoring him over the years. Tears welled in both of our eyes as he looked up and noticed who had come all the way from Las Vegas to see him. We hugged each other for a long time and I began to fully realize why GOD had brought us together for the last time on earth. He too had had guilt through the years and thought that it was forever hopeless of ever having his son forgive him in his lifetime. I never thought that it was possible to forgive him, let alone ever love him...but I truly did. By the grace of our ever-loving Lord it happened and I thanked Him for letting it happen while my father was still alive to acknowledge it.

Holding his weary hand, I searched my memory for the words of petition to the Lord that would allow my father to recover. I prayed with my father that Almighty GOD would show His divine mercy and not allow him to suffer any needless pain. I asked Jesus to forgive my father for his worldly transgressions and if it was His Divine Will, spare him with a complete healing. I thanked GOD for bringing us together after so many years in discord. I thanked GOD for the father I never had the opportunity to know or understand.

On February 13th, 1984, GOD's mercy was shown my 79 year-old father. After a brief period of recovery, he passed into the Divine Hands of his Maker. Although my father and I had made peace with each other, - all too many in this world are not as fortunate. As on August 16th, 1975, when my mother accepted GOD's new beginning, my father is now beginning his peaceful life in eternity. The power of prayer is an unlimited quantity. They are always answered, but many times not as we mortals expect. As we are His, and He is ours, GOD's way is both merciful and just! Who are we to deny or question the Will of GOD?

Yes, GOD grants gifts to those who love Him. Mortal man can perform miracles in the Name of Jesus, but only in His Name. It is impossible for an infected seed to sprout a healthy plant. Witchcraft, sorcery, astrology and socialism are being taught in our universities, homosexuals are pushing their filth upon our society and in some factions they are being accepted as "normal." Christians are being persecuted by the hundreds of thousands and computers know more about your actions than

114

you do. Lawlessness is rampant and injustices prevalent and the cause is a GOD-less society.

Just recently the Senate voted down our right to vocal prayer in the public schools by a 56-44 vote (56 for prayer - 44 against...needing 67 to pass), and without His divine guidance the depravity will continue to escalate in proportion with the growth of these left-wing radicals known as liberals. We lost the battle when 80% wanted the prayer restored.

The liberal students who were pushing the legalization of marijuana in the sixties are now our Senators, Congressmen and governors. Illusionary drugs are as plentiful as candy in a dime store. Rape, incest, and other perversions are as common to our culture as it was in the days before Sodom was destroyed. False-Christs and other demons receive more respect than lawbiding citizens and are allowed to fester their untruths through their partner the Press. The injustice will not decrease as GOD's judgement day moves closer.

Life, one of GOD's greatest miracles, is being defiled and degraded. Many of the "leaders" of our own country are either pro-choice or for the extermination of millions of our babies each year. Every Democratic candidate, except Askew, is condoning these murders of developing human beings. The five eldest members of the United States Supreme Court are the same who voted in favor of this criminal act in the 1973 Roe Case.

The American College of Obstetricians and Gynecologists (ACOG) disputed the fact that an aborted fetus feels pain. When a syringe is inserted into the growing human (fetus) it squirms eratically...tell me there's no pain! One who takes the life of another or condones abortion (legalized murder) is an anti-Christ. Only GOD has the right to determine expendability!

The word "democrat" no longer stands for democracy. It stands for "demon-rats" and our Country is infested with their liberal jargon. The A.C.O.G. does not represent intellect, their messages are clear...They are A COG in the worlds' quest for human survival. A broken cog messing up the wheel.

Recently the (Jesse) Helms Human Life Statute was dismissed after only a two week filibuster. The Hatch Amendment to overturn the Supreme Court decision came up 18 votes short of passage and Senator Jepsen's attempt to attach a human-life amendment to the civil-rights commission's authorization never left the ground. Ronald Reagan personally lobbied the Senators who were undecided on school prayer and we came up 11 short of passage.

Our Country is filled with "takers," when what we need are more "givers!" Miracles can indeed be performed on our society but these graces from GOD cannot be obtained when the hearts of men are being subverted by the politicians we have placed in control. We must first consider this election year a pivotal period in American history. We must "weed out" these "demonrats" with our voting power and set higher standards to prevent them from ever reattaining these vital positions of leadership.

The miracle we should be asking GOD for with all our heart is that He will change the ideology of the Soviet Union and reverse their anti-Christian stance against the world. We must recognize that purity and miracles are synonomous with the graces from GOD. We must set worthy examples for others with our actions and reactions in the heartland first, then strive to overturn injustices on the world theater. We must thirst for the Word of GOD and replace Him at all costs to His rightful throne over humanity.

If we are to be sons of GOD (peacemakers) we cannot compromise on His demands of us. We should move forth to new frontiers with positive and firm foundations of knowledge and stand behind our President in his war against the socialists in government. If we want a free America for all GOD fearing individuals we have to uncover the liberal cloak of deceit that is our newspaper, our lawmakers and our teachers. If the ideals of capitalism were good enough for our forefathers when times were more secure, we should understand that they are good enough for our present generation. Liberty is for those who will fight for it; it is not for those who wish to remove it!

The onerous situation is not one of hopeless despair in America. Man can change his destiny, but not without Divine assistance from the Almighty. If that avenue is not approached with reverence, GOD will not respond favorably to our plea. If we can understand the "cause" of a predicament, we should also understand that the "solution" is GOD! Don't give as the world gives and don't compromise your soul in search of earthly pleasure. Those times the Prophets spoke of are here. Anti-Christians and humanists are the cause; Jesus Christ is the answer!

CHAPTER EIGHT

Morality, Pornography & Punk Rock!
By Columnist Lois Reed

"And I heard another voice from heaven, saying, Come out of her, my people, that ye be not partakers of her sins, and that ye receive not of her plagues."

REVELATION 18:4

Recently my family and I were viewing a Jimmy Swaggart Crusade on television and his topic that evening was based on an article that appeared in a southwestern newspaper. When the author's name was flashed on the screen as a reference to Swaggart's theme that evening, I had my chapter nine. I contacted Mrs. Lois Reed through the newspaper and asked her if she would submit some material for this book. Lois is much more than just a journalist. She is a past president of the Arizona Committee to Combat Huntington's Disease and has also devoted much of her life in a crusade against pornography and for individual integrity and the preservation of morality. She's one fine lady and sold five articles to me of which I assembled for this chapter.

****

I believe that there is an even greater threat to humanity than nuclear war. During the 1950s there were some who saw the danger in pornography and urged parents and those who care about the future of America to do something about it before it was too late. But we buried our heads in the sand and let those who profit from the filth, while preaching about their freedoms, create the problems we have today.

The youngsters whose lives and values were warped by the proliferation of filth during the 1960s are the educators, the lawmakers, the publishers and the parents of today, and GOD help us during the 1980s if we don't wise up.

Ten years ago the production and sale of pornography was a half-million dollar industry. Today there is an estimated $5 billion U.S. pornography market!

The number of lewd and salacious books and magazines has increased extensively in recent years and most are easily acquired by any child through direct purchase, snitching from big brother or piled on top of trash in the alleys. For those who can't read, there are photos depicting bondage, sado-masochism, beastality and every conceivable form of depravity known to man. Competition among the pornographers in this low-investment, high return business, was bound to lead to child pornography and incest. In the United States, one child is molested every two minutes.

In one of the magazines there was an accounting purportedly written by a 38-year-old father of three teenage children, describing graphically, using every vulgar word possible, weekly sex orgies participated in by this man, his wife and their three children. With all five members present they engaged in every form of kinky sex imaginable. He describes his family as a typical American family and states that, "They're good kids and never get into trouble. Why should they when they are having so much fun in the home?"

Another magazine includes a letter from a 15 year-old girl describing, in vulgar detail, sex activity between herself and her sixteen-year-old brother. The girl is advised to visit a birth control clinic but not to mention that her sex partner is her brother as it - "might upset the counselor!"

There are stories of fathers who initiate their daughters into the "beauty" of father-daughter sex. Sex psychologists write about the "benefits" of incest, calling it the "last taboo!"

What has happened was forseeable. Child abuse and murder of children has risen directly in ratio to the magazines describing incest and child sex. How could a nation built on family, decency and morality have come to this? The answer is greed, apathy and ignorance. I doubt that we can eliminate greed, but we can make the smut business less lucrative by getting rid of our own apathy and ignorance.

A remark frequently made by sincere and moral people is, "I don't read the stuff, but it's okay for those who like it." They fail to realize that if the community condones pornography and it is readily available at the corner store, the child feels that society approves even if his own parents do not.

Today's children are being taught that self-gratification and sexual performance are the goals of adult society. They are being taught about bondage, sado-masochism and homosexuality before they have a chance to discover for themselves that gentle heterosexual relationships are normal.

A very real and sincere fear of censorship among publishers and the ordinary citizen has been responsible in large part for the inability to control pornography. But we must not be mislead by talk about "infringement of rights." What the pornographers are saying is, "Don't infringe on my right to make a lot of money." Our children have rights too!

The "Citizens for Decency Through Law" have come a long way in their fight against smut, but they can not win the battle without a unified effort. Recently three Chris-Town book stores were the targets of complaints for display of sexually explicit magazines. Reaction among many were that tax-dollars should be spent in other ways than trying to ban "girlie magazines," and reiteration of the asinine theory that, "we have no right to deprive those who like it from reading and viewing the material."

Some people like to drink and drive. Do we have a right to deprive them of their wishes?

There is no longer any doubt among thinking people that there is a correlation between both TV violence, pornography and anti-social behavior. People don't like to look at such material – or talk about it – because if they look at it and think about it, they suspect they will have to do something about it. It's easier to bury their heads in the sand while pursuing their own selfish pleasure.

This so-called "gray area" is far more damaging to children and adults than the "adult sex shops and arcades," simply because many people who would never visit one of the "peep shows" (and children who are banned from the X-rated movies and such places) are becoming addicted to pornography through the magazines so readily available to both adults and children. You don't have to view an X-rated movie or visit an adult bookstore to learn about voyeurism, pedophilia or necrophilism.

Penthouse, Oui and the like are no longer "girlie magazines." They describe in graphic detail and encourage every form of sexual perversion found at the hardcore porn shops. Their advertisements make it easy for children to order "phone sex," X-X-X rated books, sex devices and "Swedish Erotica" materials. If you don't know what "Swedish Erotica" is, you'd better learn; it is one of the many forms of pornography used by John W. Gacy in the sado-masochistic sex-torture and murder of more than a score of youngsters.

Experts in the field are convinced that sexual deviations and perversion are learned through modeling, classical conditioning and desensitization (see chapter fifteen), all of which occur through exposure to pornography. Because cable-TV and video cassettes have become a status symbol, parents are bringing material into their homes which may someday turn their child into a John Gacy, a Thomas Schiro or an Elmer Henley.

I find it ludicrous that the National Committee for the

Prevention of Child Abuse, supported by tax-payers, has for several years, run a full page advertisement in "Hustler," a magazine which also carries a cartoon titled "Chester the Molester." I also feel that companies who advertise in Penthouse or any other degrading influence on society are supporting the pornographers.

There can be no neutrality where pornography is concerned. You are either for it or against it. By refusing to take sides, you are on the side of the smut peddlers and against America's future and our children.

Child abuse is not decreasing in our Country. Approximately one in four abused children admitted to hospitals are victims of incest or sex abuse by a family member. The victims include infants with venereal disease and impregnated children who have not yet reached the age of reason.

The "Rene Guyon Society" now boasts nearly 9,000 members. Its slogan is, "Sex before eight or else it's too late." Articles are being published describing the beauty of incestuous relationships and in many cases, children are being forced to view films or magazines depicting child sex or incest to persuade the child.

Estimates of the number of sexually abused children in the United States vary from 500,000 to a million a year. The Criminal Justice Institute reports that probably 20 to 25 percent of the nation's prostitutes are juveniles.

How many horrors such as five-year-old girls being sexually mutilated and murdered must occur before we admit that there is a connection between pornography and such acts? And now the stuff is in our homes, or at least in our neighbor's homes, via cable and subscription TV.

What about the video cassettes? Adult titles like "Daddy's Little Girl," "Family Fun," Oriental Babysitter" and more than 15 volumes of "Swedish Erotica" are sandwiched together with family favorites like "Old Yeller," "On Golden Pond" and "Superman." I wonder who is buying the pornographic cassettes. If you buy such filth, or patronize any company which deals in pornography, you must accept your share for the increase in sex crimes.

Those who say we have no right to "deprive" others their right to view such material are wrong. We do have a right, and a duty, to deprive others of reading and viewing pornography.

There is perhaps an even greater problem than the correlation between obscene material and crime; it concerns the tone of society, now and in the future. Public exhibition of obscene material, or commerce in such material jeopardizes our right to maintain a decent society.

120

Penthouse publisher, Bob Guccione, says: "Everyone has a right to his own personal morality." WRONG! A society must adopt moral codes and members of that society must conform to these standards.

Ernest Hemingway wrote: "What is moral is what you feel good after and what is immoral is what you feel bad after." WRONG AGAIN! Using that code of ethics, Hitler could have proved that, for him, slaughtering 6,000,000 Jews was a moral act.

J.D.Urwin of Cambridge University made a study of 80 civilizations ranging over 4,000 years and concluded: "Any human society is free to choose either to display great energy, or to enjoy sexual freedom; the evidence is that they cannot do both for more than one generation."

Nevertheless, I doubt that censorship and prosecution of the smut peddlers will be very effective as long as there are those who buy it. If you subscribe to any company which offers such programing, you are promoting pornography even though you may not subscribe to the "adult" portion.. If those who profess to care about our young people or America's future would cease patronizing, or advertising via any establishment which handles such material, it would be eliminated within a few months.

""Punk Rock Is Not A Rock 'N' Roll Movement!""

A recent TV channel ran a series on adolescent and teen-age suicide, which has risen dramatically in recent years. I can't help wondering where the "punk rock" movement that is spreading over our Country fits in.

In 1966, author James Michener wrote an article for the New York Times defending rock 'n' roll music, but there is little resemblance between punk rock and that which Michener was defending.

In the begining there were the Beatles and Elvis and the Dave Clark Five, followed by hard rock and acid rock. Then came punk rock and my neighbor's 15-year-old daughter began combing her shortly-cropped hair forward when she went to the shopping mall or other places where she might encounter other"punk-rockers."

When I tried to discuss with her parents the punk rock which has filled Sandra's life almost to the exclusion of all else for the past year, their response was: "Our parents didn't like our music either when we were young; it'll go away like other fads if we just ignore it." When I tried to tell them about the lyrics, they said: "But no one listens to the words –

it's the beat they like."

The kids I have talked with say it is indeed the beat they like, but they also admit that they do hear the words. If so, it is probable that they are subconsciously being influenced by the lyrics (see chapter fifteen).

Recently, Sandra's mother conceded that it is dangerous and that it may already be too late to save her daughter (see chapter fifteen...With GOD, it's never too late). "I suppose it will go away in time," she said sadly, "but I wonder how many children it will take with it!"

Sandra has become rebellious, furtive and terribly depressed. She seems totally alienated from her family, and even her friends, except for a small group of youngsters who are also "into" punk rock. She has secretly pierced a second hole in her ear lobes to accommodate safety pins and has assured her parents that if they refuse to allow her to buy punk rock albums, she will leave home.

The very names of the groups lend some insight into the scatalogical and rotten obscenity of punk rock: "GERMS," "GOBSHITTES," "SAVAGE REPUBLIC," "CIVIL DEATH," "CORPORATE WHORES," "SLUTS," "URINALS," "LIFE SENTENCE," AND "NECROS," to name but a few.

While acid and hard rock had to do with sex, drugs and satanism; punk rock is concerned with rebellion against parental and civil authority, anarchy and a sickness worse than eroticism or drugs.

In both punk rock lyrics and punk literature, frequent references to corpses, blood, scabs, phlegm, etc., take precedence over erotic and four-letter obscenities. Many punk rock bands hang out in graveyards. The Los Angeles VooDoo Church band gets its ideas for new songs by sitting in a cemetery.

The articles, photos and illustrations in a publication called "No-Mag" are more disgusting and obscene than any found in Hustler or Penthouse, yet it is sold at record stores such as "Roads to Moscow" which are frequented by children.

In one published interview, a band leader talks of a future system of masters and slaves, a pending bloodbath, and the Earth being regurgitated.(Editor's Note: that punk rocker is right about the earth regurgitating the people...what he fails to recognize is that it is his kind that gets regurgitated...see Leviticus 18:25 in the Holy Bible) According to another, their purpose is to tell the kids the truth: "That America sucks," and to encourage kids to go against the police, the establishment, and the "so-called preachers and the Christians." The same issue contains an article about a 40-year-old female pornographer who is intrigued and obsessed with "castration and fondling teenagers,"accompanied by graphic photos.

Two pages are filled with illustrations, photographs and discussion of keeping food costs down by COOKING HIGH-PROTEIN "FETUSES" with "amniotic fluids and membranes" cooked in a special sauce.

"Life Sentence" ridicules education, comparing life with being a "chained up dog fenced up in a yard." One titled "The Equalizer" maligns the work ethic, and splashed all over a sheet distributed by Thunderbolt Record Distributors are the words, "Life is ugly so why not kill yourself?"

I find it awfully hard to accept the fact that thousands of young girls and boys are listening to such putridity, often through head phones for many hours each day. I find it even more appalling to accept the fact that the parents of these youngsters are actually buying the filth for their children through generous allowances and failure to supervise and investigate what is being purchased.

I am reminded of a communist leader (Joseph Stalin in 1935) who described how easy it would be to take over America by simply corrupting our youth with music and drugs. I don't know whether the punk rock movement is communist inspired (Editor's NOTE: it most surely is!) or not, but I think parents would do well to investigate the material their money is furnishing for the kids.

EDITOR'S NOTE: Joseph Stalin's words in 1935 were: "If we can enslave just "one generation" in any country, that country will fall to Soviet Communism. The way to enslave that generation is by means of IMMORALITY, MUSIC and DRUGS!" He said it...He meant it...and it has been accomplished!

Mrs. Reed is indeed accurate in her assessment of the punk rock movement in America. This movement is also inspired by the Soviet Union and promoted by liberals, socialists and communists from right here in our own Country. Don't miss chapter fifteen "Desensitizing the Children of GOD!." Pastor Gary Greenwald's study has been added on to that chapter.

I ask you who have any doubt that the Soviet Union isn't directly behind the punk rock movement, "Who stands to gain the most if capitalism is destroyed?

For those readers who don't know what the punk rock band "NECROS" is short for, listen to this:

NECRO means one that is dead!
PHILIA means an abnormal appetite!

"IF WE CAN ENSLAVE JUST ONE
GENERATION IN ANY COUNTRY,
THAT COUNTRY WILL FALL TO
SOVIET COMMUNISM. THE WAY
TO ENSLAVE THAT GENERATION
IS BY MEANS OF IMMORALITY,
MUSIC AND DRUGS!

JOSEPH STALIN (1935)

124

NECROPHILIA means <u>sex</u> <u>with</u> <u>the</u> <u>corpse</u>
NECROMANCY is sorcery and witchcraft
NECROPHAGIA is the practice of <u>eating</u> <u>corpses</u>

So, either way their band name stands for satan.Where else but the Soviet Union, the residence of lucifer and his antiChristian Chernenkos and company, could such travesty originate? They said they would do it as early as 1935, and they are presently succeeding in their effort to enslave our young boys and girls, and even some misinformed adults. Our society is being taken over by these ignorant rock bands who contribute absolutely nothing but filth to our society.

America must rise up in unity. We must replace the liberal lawmakers in the judiciary branch of the government and spead local legislation to rid society of these ignorant misfits who paint their faces and yell out their obscenities and call it "music!"

We must wake up to the coercion, the subversion and the conspiracy that is infesting our Country before it's too late to save our young children...If we save our children - we can prolong the sovereignty of the United States. What we need to seek is GOD! Without His graces, America stands no hope at all!

Witchcraft, voodoo, necrophagia, satanism and all the rest of America's degenerating influences can be run out of our country with a one-way ticket to the Soviet Union with a united concern of both parents (voters) and Christian statesmen. Many drug-crazed misled children need our help; they will be lost without it!

Recently in Bedford, New York, there has been a rash of teen-suicides, but it doesn't represent only isolated instances. Since 1970, the suicide rate among young people in America has risen 41% through 1983 and unless we listen to the American children's pleas for help, that rate will increase ten-fold by the year 1990.

Witchcraft is even being taught in many universities across the nation...what in the world does it take to get the public's attention? Many psychiatrists and psychologists feel that the criminal element exists in many children and some indicate that regardless of early treatment, this element will surface sooner or later and transform the strong willed child into tomorrows horror stories. I don't buy their "learned logic."

If your child's attitude has been swayed by evil influence, there is an answer with knowledge far surpassing anything from mortal minds. The answer is GOD! Why won't the supposed "wise men of this age" seek Him for the solutions. The only really wise people I know believe in Jesus

Christ and are doing quite well with this intelligent allegiance. If your child has become possessed by evil spirits (and don't remain naive to their existence)...your only answer is turning to the One and only answer...Jesus Christ! If they are into drugs, alcohol or the evils of punk rock...GOD, not psychiatrists or any other science of the human mind, IS YOUR ONLY ALTERNATIVE!

You don't have to have to be a man of the cloth to devise a prayer to talk with Him either. He'll listen to you regardless of your language, your current religion or your race or color...What GOD is is an equal opportunity Deity and loves everyone. If you are really interested in saving your son, your daughter, your spouse or yourself...PRAY TO HIM...HE'LL ANSWER YOU IN THE ONLY WAY HE KNOWS HOW...THE TRUTHFUL WAY!

Lois Reed's accounting of human tragedy is tame compared to where it will be if left unattended. Satan is very real...he's not just something someone thought up. Pornography, morality and punk rock must not be ignored in America. It's satan's tool that's aimed at this current generation to overthrow every freedom we still have left. Don't allow it to happen by doing nothing!

Most people who don't know the Lord Jesus Christ have no idea of the "POWER of PRAYER! If everyone that's reading this book right now would pray all at once...satan would grab his filthy hat and go back to Russia for a break in action. We could give the devil a heart attack and send him running to regroup!

I don't know how much proof Americans need to tell them that when GOD is missing from any level of society...satan moves in with all his tools of despair. If your child has gone astray, get on your knees and pray this prayer with your hands raised in worship of your only hope...your Lord GOD!

Dear GOD, I'm a little new at this but I seek Your divine assistance. I don't have the answers. . . but I know you have them all. I'm a sinner unworthy of any graces but You said that anything that is asked of You in the name of Jesus the Christ would be granted and I know You never lie! My (son-daughter-husband-parent-friend) have gone astray and I ask You to come into my heart and into the hearts of the ones I have mentioned and make them whole. I accept Jesus into my heart RIGHT NOW and know that when he died on Calvary, He did so for all my sins. I ask that you come into our lives and make them real in the name of Jesus. Amen & Amen! NOW WELCOME HOME YOUR FAMILY!

CHAPTER NINE

Satan & His Punk Rockers!
By Pastor Gary Greenwald

This punk rock craze which is sweeping our nation has affected our young people in many startling ways. Take, for instance, the following incident reported in "The Journal" by David Noeble of Summit Ministries which occurred in Milpitas, California. It appears to be typical of the callousness of punk rock behavior.

A FOURTEEN YEAR OLD GIRL NAMED MARY CONRAD WAS STRANGLED TO DEATH BY HER BOYFRIEND. AT LEAST THIRTEEN STUDENTS WENT TO LOOK AT HER BODY.
ONE GIRL PICKED UP THE MURDERED GIRL'S JEANS, CUT OFF A PATCH PROMOTING A LOCAL ROCK STATION, AND THREW THE JEANS DOWN ALONG THE SIDE OF THE ROAD. ONE STUDENT TRIED TO COVER THE BODY WITH LEAVES. ANOTHER TOOK HIS EIGHT-YEAR-OLD BROTHER ALONG TO SEE THE BODY. ONE BOY WENT TWICE. THOSE WHO SAW THE BODY WENT BACK TO CLASS OR TO THE PIN BALL ARCADE. ONE WENT HOME TO BED. TWO DAYS LATER ONE STUDENT FINALLY CALLED THE POLICE.
ANOTHER STUDENT SAID HE ONLY CARED ABOUT COLLECTING THE MARIJUANA CIGARETTE HE HAD WON ON A BET THAT THE BODY WAS REAL.

Cruel? Small? Indifferent? This negative behavior is indicative of the satanic spirit influencing punk rock music. These actions are all symptoms of the punk rock syndrome.

What Is This Craze?

The punk philosophy in the simplest form is a type of "nihilism." This is the belief that there is no meaning or purpose in existence. It's the general rejection of customary beliefs in morality, in religion, and in all of society's standards. Take, for instance, the punk rock group BLACK FLAG. In their song "No Values," they sum up the philosophy of punk rock. The lyrics go, "I don't care what you say. I've got nothing to give you. Why don't you just go away? I don't care what you say."

Another group called BLONDIE has a little blond bombshell named Deborah Harry who sings her song "Rapture," and the lyrics show the simple insanity of punk rock. The lyrics say:

> "Rapture is pure.
> Take a trip through the sewer;
> Don't strain your brain;
> Paint a train.
> You'll be singing in the rain...I said,
> Don't stop, do punk rock."

Anyone who has ever come in contact with "punkers" will never forget the experience. Their activities are bizarre, crazy and totally rebellious. In Hollywood, there's a Christian group called the HOLY GHOST REPAIR SERVICE, led by brother Charles McPheeters, that goes out on Hollywood Boulevard to witness. In one of their latest reports, this is what Charles said:

> On Friday, April 10, 1981, three of us (Scott, Jason and I) were out in front of the Whisky-A-Go-Go after midnight, proclaiming the love of Jesus Christ to the gathering of punk rockers.
>
> There they were in all their regalia: bleached and multicolored hair, modified mohawks, burr haircuts; hard, vicious eyes staring, 'David Bowie-ish' through the deep dark eye-shadow, caked around their eyes; leather jackets with all sorts of jangling beads, buttons, chains and punk paraphernilia; large chains wrapped around their legs and arms; pierced ears and gawdy red lipstick; and make-up that enhanced the well-rehearsed aura of defiant nihilism that was the binding force. While we told some punk rockers on the strip that Jesus loved them, one of the girls ripped my glasses off," Charles said, "and spit in my face. She kept spitting on all of us and cursing Jesus and us. Then her very large boyfriend towered over me and told me how much they disliked being told that Jesus loved them. He really began to grow more violent when I mentioned the precious Blood of Jesus. He pushed me back and threatened to "bust my head open" on the sidewalk. We suddenly felt 'led' to move across the street. We pray that GOD will open their hearts to realize that He really does love them."

Of course this demonic repulsion to Christians and Jesus is nothing new. Matthew 27:30 says:

And they spit upon Him (speaking of Jesus), and took the reed and smote Him on the head.

verse 3l says:

They mocked Him.

And even in the Bible, speaking of the last days before the return of Jesus, Second Peter 3:2 and 3 reminds us that the Prophets, Jesus Himself, and the Apostles predicted this end time of rebellion.

II Peter 3:3

Knowing this, first, that there shall come in the last days, scoffers, walking after their own lusts.

Romans l:30

They will be disobedient to parents.

II Timothy 3:2 and 3

For men shall be lovers of their own selves...proud, blasphemers, disobedient to parents, unthankful, unholy...without natural affection...fierce...and despisers of those that are good...

Why Do We Have All This Rebellion?

First, we have to understand that punk, and new wave music, as they are sometimes called, are basically a mutation of the rock 'n' roll that started in the fifties. Way back in the early 1950s, there was a Cleveland disc jockey by the name of Alan Freed who was one of the first whites to play a rhythm and blues type of music over the air waves of his radio station. The reports that came back to Freed were bizarre. People said that this new, wild music was turning the kids on and getting them frantic and aroused. Freed wanted a term to describe this music so he adopted a term used in the ghetto for premarital sex in the back seat of a car...rock and roll. As the car rolled, they were rocking in the back seat. As this new 'rock and roll' music became more popular through the fifties, in 1956, a young southerner, named Elvis Presley, was ushered into world fame when he stepped before the cameras of a national telecast. With his hair flapping in his face, he got up and began to punch out the wailing, emotion-packed lyrics that made him famous.

Elvis Presley had such an impact on the American scene that great crowds of young people followed him everywhere he went. Riots broke out, and theaters were demolished as young people were driven to a frenzy by this new type of music.

Last Days Violence

As Christians, we should see satan's hand in all the violence of today's rock music. In Genesis, it speaks of the days of Noah.

Genesis 6:11

And the earth was also corrupt before GOD and the earth was filled with violence.

This type of violent activity is being repeated dramatically through rock and roll, and punk rock music today.

Matthew 24:37

But as the days of Noah were, so shall also the coming of the Son of man be...

Jesus will return to an earth filled with violence, the Bible predicts. I believe that satan is stirring up this kind of violence as a form of worship for himself.

Iggy Pop of the STOOGES would spew out raunchy, gut-rending lyrics, while performing violent acts of mutilation and debauchery on the stage. For instance, he would regurgitate on stage. Finally, he would dive head first into the frantic audience. As I said before, punk rock has become a nihilistic protest of rebellion against all social standards.

The group, The RAMONES, would sing, "Beat the brat, beat the brat, beat the brat with a baseball bat...Oh, yeah!"

Another group, TOMATOE DuPLENTY, had a lead singer who sang, "I wanna hurt, I wanna hurt." This was sung at regular intervals while a girl in zombie makeup would emit piercing wails. Despite this type of performance this group has continued to be one of the most famous L.A. punk groups.

Proverbs 4 describes the young people that follow these punk rock groups:

For they sleep not, except they have done mischief, and their sleep is taken away unless they cause some to fall.

For they eat the bread of wickedness and drink the wine of violence.

Violence seems to be the key word to the attitude and activities of the punkers. Some characteristics typical of many punk rockers include staying out all night at the punk clubs, sleeping very little, and causing all kinds of trouble. In New York, there's a club called the Mudd Club. At the Mudd Club, they had what they called a "Mommie Dearest" Party. Everyone came dressed like Joan Crawford personalities, or like innocent school children. During the party, infant baby dolls were tied into little cribs; then, these Joan Crawford clones pretended to beat the school children.

Satan Behind The Music

All you have to do to see satan's involvement with this music is listen to the lyrics of their songs. Many of the lyrics play up the glories of going to hell, telling the young people there will be sex and drugs and parties, and all their friends will be there. The young people are blinded to the fact that satan hates them and he wants to destroy them with the same tools which destroyed him.

II Corinthians 4:4

In whom the god of this world hath blinded the minds of them which believe not, lest the light of the glorious gospel of Christ, Who is the image of GOD, should shine upon them.

Satan has blinded the eyes of these young people so that they may not come to the Lord Jesus Christ and have their sins forgiven and have their lives changed. It's interesting that satan is called the god of this world. (II Corinthians 4:4). He always wanted to be like GOD.

Isaiah 14:12,13,14

How art thou fallen from heaven, O Lucifer, son of the morning...for thou hast said in thine heart, I will ascend into heaven...I will be like the most high...

Satan wanted to be like GOD. He wanted worship. GOD's judgment upon his rebellion and pride and iniquity was in Ezekiel 28:17:

> Thine heart was lifted up because of thy BEAUTY. Thou has corrupted thy WISDOM by reason of thy BRIGHTNESS: I will cast thee to the ground, I will lay thee before kings that they may behold thee.

Now, it was because of satan's pride and violence that GOD cast him out of heaven. Since rebellion, pride and violence were the cause of his fall, what tools do you think satan will use to destroy the young people today, and cause their fall? You guessed it, rebellion, pride and violence!

Take , for instance, a song sung by the DEAD KENNEDY'S, a group which sings a song called, "I kill children." It starts out:

> "GOD told me to skin you alive." (I wonder which GOD?) The lyrics continue...
> "I kill children, I love to see them die.
> I kill children, I love to see their mommas cry.
> Crush'em under my car.
> I wanna hear them scream.
> Feed'em poison candy,
> to spoil their Halloween."

You may ask, "Is satan really killing our children through this punk rock music?" Sonny Arguinzoni's wife, Julie (the Director of Public Affairs at Channel 40, in Southern California) went to the L.A. county morgue to investigate the traffic deaths of teenagers and drug abusers. She was sent to interview the chief medical examiner, Doctor Naguchi. Julie wanted to question Naguchi about runaway teenagers and violence-related deaths. She was led into the autopsy room, past open refrigerators filled with dead corpses with tags on their toes. She said the sickening stench of death was everywhere. It was so overpowering she felt like she might pass out.

As Julie was escorted down the hallways to the doctor's office, to her shock and amazement, the halls were stacked and piled with dead bodies, hundreds of corpses, because there was no room in the refrigerators Julie read the tags on many of the dead bodies. Some said Jane Doe, Others said John Doe. There were hundreds of unclaimed, unnamed bodies. Julie, in absolute amazement, asked where all these bodies came from. She was told that these were primarily runaway teenage young people. Young people who had died in violent deaths, where nobody knew who they were. In total, there were over 650 bodies stacked in halls. These bodies, she was told, are held for six months, and then they are cremated if not claimed. As Julie was walking out among all the pathetic young murdered bodies, satan whispered in her ear, "There, take a good look. These are my trophies! This is my trophy room!" Satan was sneering over his victory. I have to agree with what Paul Crouch, Sr., said on national television. He cried, "Christians, we've stayed inside the four walls of our churches too long. The militant body of Jesus Christ has got to rise up and get out into the streets, singing 'Onward, Christian Soldiers' and wrecking satan's kingdom. Satan doesn't own these young people. They belong to GOD and Jesus, if we the Church will go out and do battle for them."

Satan Possessing The Children!

Satan not only kills the children, he possesses them. This week a mother brought me her little girl's last letter before she ran away. She ran away to join some punkers. The letter went"

> Mom,
> Sorry, but I have to leave the world. If I live here, he will punish me. I love you. Don't ever forget Deana, because I am no longer her; he is in control.

Then she scribbled her name, but it was not hers.

The handwriting was totally different from her own. Very possibly one of satan's demons had invaded this sweet little girl. Christians, we must and we can stop satan's violence against these kids. If we don't, GOD's fury will be unleashed against them in judgment.

> Ezekiel 8:17, 18

> Is it a light thing...that they commit the abominations which they commit here, for they have filled the land with violence, and have returned to provoke Me to anger;and lo, they put the branch in their nose. Therefore, will I also deal in fury. Mine eyes shall not spare, neither will I have pity, and though they cry in mine ears with a loud voice, yet will I not hear them.

Satan is driving our children to violence!

Psalms ll:5

> But the wicked and him that loveth violence, the Lord hateth.

Many of the young people have come to believe that death is a glorious way out of this life. Their violence usually ends up in death. Many of the rock and punk groups advocate death. The group BLONDIE with Deborah Harry sings:

> "Die young, stay pretty.
> Die young, stay pretty." over and over again...

In other words, why grow old and wrinkled while you can die young and stay pretty? This self-destruction is the underlying theme of punk rock.

Satan's followers often cut themselves as an act of violence and rebellion...... Remember when Elijah had challenged the prophets of Baal in l Kings, chapter 18? And when they could not call fire down from heaven, and he did, the Bible records:

> And they cried aloud, and cut themselves with knives, till the blood gushed out upon them.

Another satanic symbol is the number 999. That is satan's upside down mockery of the anti-Christ symbol 666 (see chapter 21). The spirit of murder and homicide lurk behind many of the punk groups. The punk group, 999 has a hit record called, "Homicide." Over and over they repeat "Homicide, homicide, homicide." Paul Crouch Jr. said he saw one girl at the punk club, with a 999 shaved into her hair. While Paul was filming the group singing, the fifteen year old leader of the group pulled his pants down to his knees and danced around the stage totally exposing himself. Paul was absolutely shocked and stunned by this blatant promiscuity, but the kids around him seemed totally unimpressed by what was going on, and not outraged at all.

Backward Masking Of Satan's Music!

Almost all rock music is dangerous. The rock group K.l.S.S. (KINGS IN SATAN'S SERVICE) has an album called "God of Thunder" in which they have placed satanic messages in the music. This is satan's most popular way of communicationg with the young people of today.

Satan doesn't want the kids to know that they are indirectly worshipping him when they listen to rock music. According to Paul Crouch, Jr. - Doctor William Urell, a neurologist from U.C.L.A. in California, the brain is a most unique organ. Conditioned response mechanisms are stored in the reticular activating system at the base of the brain. In other words these mechanisms screen out unwanted or unacceptable information we don't want programed into our minds. If someone told you satan is GOD, you'd say "NO WAY," and this mechanism would screen out and discard that information, nor would it store the information for future recall.

Your memory banks would not receive that message and would reject it right away. But when these messages enter the brain backwards, they pass through the pulmonary screening area without being rejected subliminally (subconsiously) and they are stored in our subconscious mind for further and future access.

Your mind would not accept: Satan, he is GOD!
but, it may accept the reverse: DOG si eh ,nataS

The brain accepts these words because they are disguised. Satan knows he can get you to believe and receive them into your minds if he can get them into your minds backwards.

When you listen to this music and a lot of these lyrics that "you don't know are backward programed onto the music begin to be fed into your mind...you are begining to not only receive this information...but you'll slowly begin to believe it!"

Let's say you don't like brussel sprouts. Let's say mother put it in your records to say, at low decibel levels or by backward masking:

Maybe brussel sprouts are delicious?
Brussel sprouts make you grow up to look good.
Brussel sprouts make you healthy!
Brussel sprouts taste good everyday!

Before long, you will begin thinking, "brussel sprouts aren't so bad after all!" Now, neurological studies of the brain have proven that your taste can be changed through subliminal programing.

Paul Crouch, Jr., (son of Paul and Jan Crouch...founders of Trinity Broadcasting Network) tells of a department store who placed a similiar message in the music at their store saying:

> You will not steal!
> You are an honest person!
> You don't want to break the law!
> You are a good person who does not ever steal!

After they played it over their speaker system, their thefts dropped 80%

What satan is doing is programing the young people to not only worship him by listening to the rock music, but to desensitize the youth to readily accept the anti-Christ when he says to worship him and receive his mark (666).

When the anti-Christ places his messages over television or radio, that, "satan is GOD...satan is the anti-Christ...your mind will process these words and find the information in your brain lobes...it will tell you that..."satan isn't bad at all!

K.I.S.S.: "God of Thunder!"

The backward secret message on the album "Gods of Thunder" is:

> I don't want to go to that place!
> I gather darkness to please me!
> I command you to kneel before the god of thunder!
> The spell you're under will rob you of your virgin soul!

Aptly put, there's a spell on almost all rock 'n' roll music currently being made. K.I.S.S. leader, Jean Simmons, as seen on the album cover, is overly gross. He extends his tongue in another satanic symbol (the snake) and rushing around the stage, he will lick the blood off anyone that's bleeding. He will then puke out blood-like colored water as he does so. Millions of young people are listening to this servant of satan. In Ephesians 5:12, it says:

> "For it is a shame even to speak of those things which are done of them in secret."

In Revelation 12:12, it is said:

> "Therefore rejoice, ye heavens, and ye that dwell in them, Woe to the inhabiters on earth and of the sea! for the devil is come down unto you, having great wrath, because he knoweth that he hath but a short time."

Satan knows that his days will be short and he is trying to gather in as many young people as he can before his time is up!

136

In the Second Book of Thessalonians, these rock stars and rock fans are described by GOD as complete fools who refuse the truth in favor of falsehoods. Because of this, GOD will send them additional delusions.

> "And with all deceivables of unrighteousness in them that perish; because they received not the love of the truth, that they might be saved.
> And for this cause GOD shall send them strong delusion, that they should believe a lie:"
>
> 2 Thessalonians 2:10,11,12

These punk rock stars are pervertedly evil. When asked by interviewers whether many of them really worship satan, they say...naw, it's just for "fun" man. They flaunt every perversion known to man including homosexuality, transvestism, beastality (sex with an animal), necrophilia (sex with a corpse) and overtly propagate cannibalism as well as promoting every kind of violence and rebellion among their following. They outwardly tell their fans that if they can't cope...use dope or if the world's too much...there's always suicide!

On the cover of BLACK SABBATH'S album, "We sold our Souls for Rock 'n' Roll" there's a picture of a woman who has been impailed on a cross and recently after a concert in Ontario, Canada, this very same group gave an altar call for satan. Thousands of misled young people flocked to the stage and gave their souls to the devil.

PINK FLOYD blasphemes the Holy Spirit in their album "Animals," in a song called "Sheep." The lyrics are almost uninterpretable to the conscious mind...but the subconscious mind would have no problem picking up the message.

The actual words to the 23rd Psalm are:

> The Lord is my shepherd; I shall not want.
> He maketh me to lie down in green pastures:
> He leadeth me beside still waters.
> He restoreth my soul: He leadeth me in the
> path of righteousness for His name's sake.
> Yea, though I walk in the valley of the
> shadow of death, I will fear no evil: for
> thou art with me; thy rod and thy staff
> they comfort me.
> Thou preparest a table before me in the
> presence of mine enemies: thou anointest
> my head with oil; my cup runneth over.
> Surely goodness and mercy shall follow
> me all the days of my life: and I will

> dwell in the house of the Lord for ever.

On the album jacket cover, the lyrics are as plain as the nose on your face:

> The Lord is my shepherd, I shall not want.
> He makes me down to "lie."
> Through pastures green He leadeth me,
> The silent waters by.
> With bright knives He releases my soul,
> He makes me to hang on hooks in high places.
> He converteth me to lamb cutlets,
> For lo He hath great power and great hunger.
> When cometh the day we lowly ones
> through quiet reflections and great dedication,
> master the art of karate.
> Lo, we shall rise up and then we'll
> make the BUGGER'S eyes water.

I looked up the word "bugger" in Webster's Dictionary. It means a 'sodomite,' a pervert, a very contemptable person. They are saying GOD is the lowest form on earth. You can't call anyone worse than a bugger.

These punkers blasphemed the Holy Spirit of GOD when they turned the 23rd Psalms around to say that "GOD is a great, wrathful, powerful and hungry GOD who's going to eat us alive. They said that He's going to convert us to lamb cutlets and hang us in high places...He's going to destroy us and mutilate us. Then they are going to rise up against GOD and make His' eyes water.

Revelation 13 describes what these punkers are doing today in verse 6:

> "And he opened his mouth in blasphemy against GOD, to blaspheme His name, and His tabernacle, and them that dwell in heaven."

They are trying to make the young people believe that GOD is cruel and that He will rip them apart. They are also trying to make satan appear as an angel who cares for them with great love. They are twisting everything around and it has all been prophesied that they would do just that. That's the picture satan wants to paint of GOD.

In Luke 12:10, Jesus says that if any man speaks against the Son of man...it will be forgiven: but unto him that blasphemeth against the Holy Ghost IT SHALL NOT BE FORGIVEN!

138

The anti-Christ in the Bible is associated with the numbers 666...it is also a trademark of this punk rock movement.

In the album "Sabbath Bloody Sabbath," no one would have any trouble understanding their mission. The numbers 666 are in plain sight on the album cover. Backward masked on the song "Who Are You," are the following subliminal messages:

> Yes, I know the secret that's within You...speaking to Jesus...
> You think all the people who worship you are blind. You're just like big brother, giving us your cross. And when You have laid it up, you'll just cast our souls into the dust.

There's no question that these punk rockers are in the service of satan. In order for satan to get people to worship him, he has to put down Jesus Christ. The more they worship the "beast," the more blind they will become.

The young people of this Country must turn to Jesus right now...before they are too blinded to understand that their souls are slowly being taken over by satan. The more we worship Jesus, the more power He will give us...We must pray to Him all the time for these lost souls.

In Revelation 13:4 it is prophesized:

> "And they worshipped the dragon (satan) which gave power unto the beast: and they worshipped the beast, saying, Who is like unto the beast? who is able to make war with him?

Elton John has a song called "If there's a GOD, what's He waiting for?" The lyrics go like this:

> "If there's a GOD in heaven, what's He waiting for. If He can't hear the children - then He must see the war.
> But it seems to me that He leads His lambs to the slaughterhouse - not to the promised land!"

It's people like this that our young people are going into a frenzy over. Satan doesn't care if you understand the words of the songs frontward...he wants to program your minds through his devious subliminal backward masking...you'll get the message he intends to give you.

E.L.O. (Electric Light Orchestra) has an album by the name of "El Dorado" and the secret, backward message on their song is:

> He's the nasty one...he's the nasty one...
> Christ your infernal...

What these punkers are saying is that Jesus Christ is evil. They are saying that Jesus Christ is INFERNAL. That means abominable..contemptable...inhuman or inferior. They are trying to tell the young people to accept the mark..."everyone who accepts the mark will live for ever...

The punk rock band S.T.I.K.S. has a song called "Snow Blind," which promotes the snorting of cocaine.   It is often referred to as "snow" and they advocate staying blind by taking it in. I don't think this group actually realizes that in this song they are praying to satan when the secret message played backwards says..."satan..move in our voices" S.T.I.K.S., by the way, is the legendary river encompassing Hades...it is the river of hell.

These punkers think that it's good to be debaucherous. They think that it's fun! They are blind and don't realize exactly what they are doing.

Satan has to do everything deceitfully. He knows that this generation is not dumb. If he placed these messages up front...no normal thinking young person would even listen to the songs. He has to do it deceitfully, backwardly concealing his messages to the youth so only the subliminal consciousness will be picking up the messages. He's planting his evil seeds in the minds of our youth, where it will be stored and will eventually be used. Satan is altering young people's minds and winning more souls for his unrighteous cause.

In their song "The Day Electricity Came To Arkansas," the punk band BLACK OAK ARKANSAS has the hidden words in their "Raunch and Roll" album. Played backwards, the words are quite clear:

> After demonic laughing you hear...

> satan, he is god. satan, he is god.
> satan, satan, satan...he is god....

Listening to their song frontwards, you'll hear...natas - natas - natas...dog si eh...dog si eh...dog si eh, dog si eh...natas.

You young people must understand that all rock 'n' roll music in this age is bad...the intentions are all evil. When the anti-Christ comes in the next few years and asks you to worship satan,your mind will have already been programed to accept him. Your mind will find the lobe where "satan, he is god" is stored and you will freely accept the "beast." You will feel that "he's not so bad" and you'll be worshipping the devil and lose your eternal soul in so doing.

Alister Crowley was one of the most feared satanists of the sixteenth century. People called him "the beast" and "mr. 666" in his day. He wrote a book on black magic called the "Manual on Magic" and on pages 481 and 482, Crowley tells the reader to think backwards and that one of the ways of truly getting insight into the next world is to program yourself to think in reverse. You should teach yourself to write backwards and listen to phonograph records and learn to speak backwards. All the warnings for our young people are in the open today...what they have to do is listen with their ears and understand with their brains.

E.L.O. doesn't even try to conceal that their song "Fire on High" has reverse messages. They make it obvious when you play the record frontwards. Their message is:

> The music is reversable
> ...but time isn't! (then it says...)
> TURN BACK..TURN BACK..TURN BACK!

According to Paul Crouch Jr., the Beattles were possibly the first rock band to use backward masking. In their song "Revolution Number Nine," the subliminal message of "TURN ME ON DEAD MAN" is repeated excessively when the record is played in reverse.

The punk band Queen in their record "Another One Bites the Dust" tells people that "it's fun to smoke marijuana."

I have a question for you right now. If satan isn't behind this phoney, backward masking of lyrics..why aren't there any positive messages about Jesus Christ? We know that satan is the god of this world, but if these punk rock bands aren't his own infestation, why aren't there good and Godly messages in the songs???

There are a few good messages on Christian songs too. GOD is also mentioned subliminally and humanly unintentionally on Dottie Rambo's song..."Behold the Lamb!" On the PRAISE THE LORD program, there was a segment where Paul and Jan Crouch were talking to their son, Paul Jr., and when they played Dotty's song backwards, sung by the PRAISE SINGERS, the words "Lamb of Glory" were very clear.

Also, Randy Stonehill's song "Rainbow," in his album "Between the Glory and the Flame" the backward message is "Jesus shall reign forever!"

One of the biggest selling deceits of all time was Led Zepplin's "Stairway to Heaven." This album sold nearly 38-million copies. It's lyrics were almost spontaniously

SATAN'S EARTHLY DEMONS

142

received, according to an interview with its writer, Jimmy Page (who also owns the largest occult bookstore in London.) "It was almost as if the lyrics came to me from "somewhere else!"'

You'd better believe they came from somewhere else!!! The fires of hell and more than 38 million young people have the message of "my sweet satan, the one whose little path makes me sad...whose power is satan" imprinted on their sumliminal minds! Why do you think satan made this song a #1 best seller? Some more of the lyrics say: "I'll build a stairway to heaven..." Who else built a 'stairway to the heavens? You're exactly right...Nimrod...just before the "tower of Babel" was destroyed by GOD!

> "And be not conformed to this world: but be ye transformed by the renewing of your mind, that ye may prove what 'is' that good, and acceptable, and perfect, will of GOD."
> Romans 12:2

> "That at what time ye hear the sound of the cornet, flute, harp, sackbut (trombone), psaltery (stringed instrument - guitar), and all kinds of music, ye fall down and worship the golden image the king hath set up:
> And whoso falleth not down and worshippeth shall the same hour be cast into the midst of a burning fiery furnace.
> Therefore at that time, when all the people heard the sound of the cornet, flute, harp, sackbut, psaltery, and all kinds of music, all the people, the nations, and the languages. fell down and WORSHIPPED THE GOLDEN IMAGE that Nebuchadnezzar the king had set up.
> Daniel 3:5,6,7

> And all that dwell upon the earth shall worship him (anti-Christ), whose names are not written in the book of life of the Lamb (Jesus) slain from the foundation of the world.
> Revelation 13:8

GOD is making it very clear of what He intends to do with those that worship satan or his deceitful ways (music). The young people are being programed to bow down when they hear the music. Those who present their bodies to satan...will lose their life everlasting and be thrown into the fire along with their music.

On the album jacket of Led Zepplin's "House of the Holy," there are nude bodies which are worshipping satan and all of his signs (pentagram, onyx, etc) are present...May GOD have mercy.

Do you remember what satan wanted from Jesus?

> And the devil, taking Him up into an high mountain, shewed unto Him all the kingdoms of the world in a moment of time.
> And the devil said unto Him, All this power will I give Thee, and the glory of them: for that is delivered unto me: and to whosoever I will I give it.
> If Thou therefore wilt worship me, all shall be Thine.
>
> Luke 4:5,6,7

This really shows you the ignorance of satan. Why should GOD give up anything to the devil. Satan didn't even know that he was talking to GOD. Those young people who are following satan and his tool of music don't know what they're doing. Satan is the second most powerful force, but compared to our GOD...he's a wimp!

Satan wanted GOD to bow down to him...maybe satan would also like to try to "make His eyes water as well?" I can't wait to see that one first hand and front row center!

Although these rock stars make jest of worshipping satan, they are to whom they obey...

> Know ye not, that to whom ye yield yourselves servants to obey, his servants ye are to whom ye obey; whether of sin unto death, or of obedience unto righteousness?
>
> Romans 6:16

I don't care if they are doing it for fun – they're doing it for satan and they're his for eternity...they belong to him because the "one" you work for...is the "one" you belong to! He's programing you right now...to ACCEPT THE ANTI-CHRIST! Believe it!

One of the most startling backward masking is in the "A Child is Coming" album by JEFFERSON STARSHIP. In a song "Blows against the Empire," (Guess Whose Empire it blows against?) the lyrics go like this:

> I've got a surprise for you...
> a child is coming...
> a child is coming...

> a child is coming... (over and over, then)
> a child is coming for you...
>
> it's getting better, everything's getting better;
> people are getting brighter; they're getting
> smarter; getting finer;
> this childs gonna do everything...
> he's going to open it all up... (etc.)

To find out which child they are speaking of, the record has to be played backwards.

"SON OF SATAN...SON OF SATAN....(etc.)

Of course the innocent young person received this message when it was played in its' normal manner. The innocence of children is being deceived and many will not understand...they won't even listen. How duped are we going to be? At this very time you read this book, according to Time Magazine, it is known that there is a church of satan operating with 12,000 members in San Francisco. It was opened by satan's highest priest - Anton Levy, in 1969. It is nothing but a coven of witches and warlocks. Who knows how many other chapters they have in the United States, but have you noticed the increase in occult bookstores? How many Americans can't wait for their daily horoscope in the newspapers? These people believe in cooking body parts in a vat! Is that sane? Is the world sane to allow such debauchery?

We can either follow GOD; the Lord of all flesh, or, we're going to follow satan who has a complete different language in his songs.

The best way...the only way to be free of satan's influence is to destroy all your rock posters, your heavy metal albums and get them out of your house and out of your lifestyle. In Acts 19:19,20, it is said:

> Many of them also which used "curious arts" brought their books together, and burned them before all men: and they counted the price of them, and found it fifty thousand pieces of silver.
> So mightily grew the word of GOD and prevailed.

Acts 19:19,20

Get the cursed things out of your house. Be free at last with the Lord Jesus Christ!

Lucifer has used this punk rock music to speak to this

end time generation. I don't think that there's a better media than rock 'n' roll to speak to the masses.

In BLACK SABBATH'S album "N.I.B." (Nativity in Black, which is a blasphemy against Jesus Christ and His virgin birth), there's a "love song" in which satan sings to the youth of America. The lyrics are like this:

> Some people say my love cannot be true...
> Please believe me, my love, and I'll show you
> I'll give you those things, you thought were unreal; the sun, the moon, the stars all bear my seal
> Follow me now and you will not regret
> leaving the life you lead before we met
> You are the first to have this love of mine
> Forever with me, till the end of time...
> Your love for me has just got to be real,
> before you know the way I'm going to feel.
> Now I have you with me under my power,
> Our love grows stronger now with every hour;
> Look into my eyes, you'll see who I am,
> My name is Lucifer, please hold my hand!

Is that what you want for eternity? If it is, then you shall not be interferred with by GOD! Before you make up your mind, finish the complete chapter...especially the accounting of the place you will reside with Lucifer...HELL!

Read the eyewitness accountings of people who were unfortunate enough to have temporarily died and came back in a frenzy of total horror.

Another real "sickie" is Alice Cooper, a man who claims to be the reincarnation of a 7th century witch. He comes on the stage dressed in mascara and many times...women's clothing.

In the early months of his act, he would include the vile live killing of a chicken...biting its head off and with the smashing of watermelons on stage.

One of his favorite 'tricks' for desensitizing the children was from his "Killer" album, entitled "Dead Babies!"

Cooper would walk on stage with a life-like looking doll...with a hatchet he would chop it to pieces - gleefully throwing the apendages into the audience who were raging with frenzy. Blood capsules were attached to the doll's back and when hit by the cleaver would squirt blood in every direction. Afterwards, Cooper would stand holding the head of the doll, like a decapitated enemy. With one final demonic thrust...he would impale the head on the microphone stand.

If that were not enough, he allows a six-foot boa constricter to wrap around his body which he kisses and sings to the symbol of satan. He drives the crowd into such a frenzy by biting off these chicken heads and the tearing apart of innocent rabbits and other animals, the audience cannot be controlled. You'd think the audience would be sickened...right? Wrong! He drives them into such a frenzy that when he tosses these harmless little animals into the audience the crowd rips them to shreds...throwing their little body parts high in the air. The kids become like their idols because the spirit at these concerts is depravity and degeneration.

How sick can these concerts get? Try Alice Cooper's song "Cold Ethel,"...the lyrics go like this:

> One thing...no lie;
> Ethel's fridged as an eskimo pie.
> She's cool in bed....
> She ought to be...cause Ethels DEAD!

That's how disgusting Alice Cooper is. Ever wonder how he got his stage name? How he gets away with his disgusting behavior? Do you think that those ideas just come from him in a night vision?

Originally his name was Vincent Vernier. He was raised in a southern baptist church, as the pastor's son. In school he felt ugly and rejected..he craved fame and fortune...he wanted people to notice him...he wanted to be popular

> And they worshipped the dragon, WHICH GAVE POWER unto the beast; and they worshipped the BEAST (music rock stars)...
> Revelation 13:5

Satan will give power to these rock stars..he will give them all the fame and fortune they want as long as they continue to bring him fresh souls to corrupt.

In a copyrighted story published several years ago nationally, Cooper said, "I went to a seance where a spirit was conjured up. The spirit promised us worldwide fame if he was allowed to possess my body. The spirit (demon) gave me my name at the seance...Alice Cooper." That's why Alice Cooper is so popular...the spirit was satan!

> While they promise them liberty, they themselves are the servants of corruption: for of whom a man is overcome, of the same is he brought in bondage.
> 2 Peter 2:19

Many of these punkers write songs that propose death and suicide for their teenage following, but that's standard operational procedure for satan. His major aim is to kill the youth before their souls can be saved by the Lord Jesus Christ. Many of these misled children are dying without saving grace and satan is hysterical about it all!

In the BLUE OYSTER CULT'S record "Don't Fear the Reaper," the song praises what Romeo and Juliet did as a pact of their love. The lyrics go something like this:

> Don't fear the reaper (someone who gathers)
> Romeo and Juliet forever in eternity,
> 40,000 men and women everyday...
> 40,000 men and women everyday...
> ...over and over...

What do you think Romeo and Juliet did by making a love pact? What do you think 40,000 men and women do everyday? Right..They are committing suicide! The song goes on...

> Come on and take my hand,
> Baby I'm your man...
> (doesn't that sound like satan)
> I'll take you down to the promised land!
> (Yeah..to the bowels of the earth for eternity)

Young people are being subliminally influenced by much of the music and they are being attacked from both sides. Frontwards and in reverse. These young people could follow them to suicide and to hell – but we care and we're going to pull them out of the pit!

> He that walketh with wise men shall be wise: but a companion of fools shall be destroyed.
>
> Proverbs 13:20

If you follow these rock stars, you are a companion of fools and by the word of GOD, you will be destroyed.

Another one is Ozzie Osborne In his album "Diary of a Madman," Osborne describes himself as a raving lunatic...When you have heard more, you'll be convinced that he knows what he proposes about his nature. He tells the kids, "When you play with satan, you cannot escape the reaper...here's some of the lyrics:

Song: The Suicide Solution

> You might as well kill yourself,
> It's the only solution:
> when you're following the devil,
> you can't escape the master reaper!
> You're living a lie, such a shame..
> You're wondering why.
> Why don't you just kill yourself,
> because you can't escape the master keeper!

Osburn is a natural leader for the kids today. I think that he's a born leader for the kids who follow rock music...

In Rolling Stones magazine, in their 1984 yearbook edition, I quote..."When it comes to sick, Ossie knows his stuff – just ask the folks at CBS, where in the midst of a marketing meeting, Ossie plucked a harmless little dove from his pocket and in his words, chewed its 'blanking' head off and spat the remains on the table. His explaination? "I was tremendously jet-lagged!"

You say that's absolutely gross? Well Osburn majors in gross!

At one concert in Iowa, he wanted to outdo his dove routine and bit the head off a bat. Afterwards, in another concert in Illinois, he actually collapsed on stage. The doctors rushed in and assumed that he had rabies, because most bats are rabid; you bite their head off and you GET rabies. They took him to the hospital and gave him rabies shots. That's the kind of leader our kids are following! A rabid monster!!!

Now here's a guy that a lot of people thought was "Mr. Cool." Even though he's been dead for years, his music is still popular. Jim Morrison was the leader of the "DOORS." In many of his songs, Morrison advocated that people should seek suicide as the only "out!"

He was found dead in a bath tub and people say that he constantly took LSD trips...constantly filling his body with drugs of all kinds. Doctors simply said that his heart gave way under all the drugs and his satanic behavior on stage.

In his last album, "L.A. Woman," he advertised with posters showing a nude woman crucified on a telephone pole. Then, in one of his very last songs in performance, he screamed to the audience..."Cancel my subscription to the resurrection!"

He blasphemed Jesus Christ and I believe that satan had another trophy because when you live for satan, your life is his at any moment he desires to take it.

One thing I know with Jesus, as my life is under the Blood protection, and he says, "My life shall be long and happy!"

Here's what Newsweek says about his performance in their

issue, April 7, 1969: "He starts out shrieking, eating the microphone, pressing his leather legs against the stand and there are incredible sexual groans from the girls down the aisles at his very whisper. I think it's because you can tell by looking at him that HE IS GOD! When he offers to die on the cross for us, it's okay, because he is Christ!" That's what one of his fans said about Jim Morrison.

In March 1969, he broke all boundaries in a performance in Miami, Florida. At the time, the DOORS were giving a performance before an audience of 14,000, comprised largely of 12 to 14 year old kids, mostly girls who paid $6.00 to get in.

In front of these 14,000 children, during his act, according to the charges that were filed by the state attorney's office against him...Morrison did lewdly and salaciously, expose himself sexually and did simulate the sexual act and did 'blank-blank' upon another member of the band. Said the plaintiff of the defendant, "He was using unlawful and utter profanity and indecent language. This man was obscene!"

The article went on to say that he beat his girlfriends and that he was a total failure in bed...he was impotent. This big sexual thing he did on stage was to make up for his failure in bed. He was a monster off stage and the girls feared him. It's no wonder that satan took his prey at such a young age of 27.

At the age of 12 to 15, kids are in the time of their life when they are sexually becoming mature. They are going through the stage of puberty and are coming into an awareness of their sexuality. These punkers know it and play on it. They use these sexual movements to bring these young people to that excitement they know they can stir within them - and so sex is a big seller in rock music.

For The More Casual Stuff, There's Olivia!

We have a gal by the name of Olivia Newton John who has a song called "Physical." It has been for long periods on top of the charts in many areas of the country. On the cover she gives the impression that it's all for fitness of the body..."don't judge an album by its' cover!" The lyrics are like this:

> I took you to an intimate restaurant,
> than to a suggestive movie.
> there's nothing left to talk about...
> unless it's horizonally... (laying down)
> Let's get physical...physical
> I want to get physical, let's get physical

Let me hear your body talk..your body talk
Let me hear your body talk.....

Does that sound like a song about the physical fitness of weightlifting and jogging? I really don't think that she thinks she was fooling anybody, especially not the kids. Years ago she said that she wanted to break out of her sweet little girl image...Olivia...You have succeeded!

> This know also, that in the last days perilous times shall come.
> For men shall be lovers of their own self, covetous, boasters, proud blasphemers, disobedient to parents, unthankful, unholy,
> Without natural affection, trucebreakers, false accusers, in continent, fierce, despisers of those that are good.
> Traitors, heady, highminded, lovers of pleasure more than lovers of GOD;
> Having a form of godliness, but denying the power thereof: from such turn away.
> For of this sort are they which creep into houses, and lead captive silly women laden with sins, lead away with divers lusts,
> Ever learning, and never able to come to the knowledge of the truth.
> 2 Timothy 3:1-6

These people will hate the good and it has also been determined that punk rockers hate Christians as well as they do Jesus Christ.

The Rocky Mountain News on April 26th, 1977 carried a story explaining the lusts of the group K.I.S.S. (Kings in satan's service):

> "Their depravity seems to know no end! Their album "Love Gun" contained a song dedicated to "Plaster Casters." Rock music prostitutes and groupies who make plaster of paris replicas of the genitals of famous rock stars!"

Marvel comics produced a special edition comic book of the rock group K.I.S.S. The group drew their actual blood samples and smeared it on the plates so they could literally say the comic book was printed in their own blood.

Marvel editor, Steve Gerber, deliberately aimed the magazine at 8-9 year olds, stating that the decadence of K.I.S.S. would enhance sales because of the bands appeal to the basic qualities of human nature (the babies). Gerber adds, "At first the parent's reaction will be total revulsion, then, they'll shake their heads and go back to watching their TV sets."

The K.I.S.S. comic was the biggest selling comic in history. It contained every debauchery, sex, perversions, every kind of grossness in the magazine and the kids bought it. Some of them might have it in their bedrooms right now!

The devil is laughing at our faces as the parents are saying; "Oh! That's so bad! Oh, let me go to church and pray about it...then I'll pretend it's not there anymore.

Gerber was right! The parents will do nothing about it. Praying is good and we need prayer...but we also need positive action. We have to awaken our children. Winston Churchill once said, "The only thing necessary for evil to triumph, is for good men to do nothing!"

> Wherefore GOD also gave them up to uncleanness through the lusts of their own hearts, to dishonor their own bodies between themselves:
> Who changed the truth of GOD into a lie, and worshipped and served the creature more than the Creator, who is blessed for ever. Amen.
>
> Romans 1:24,25

These punk rockers glorify everything that GOD stands against. They exault the homosexuals, every perversion known to man, sado-masochism, beastiality, violence of every kind and lawlessness. If you don't know what beastiality is...it's sex with animals! Our children must wake up or they will go to hell with these rock stars...for eternity as a servant to satan! If you care about your child...get up and do something. Find out where they are at night and show them that you care with discipline...honest, fair and just! Eternity is a very long time to be spending apart from love and kindness!

What Can You Expect Next!

A friend of mine was seated next to a punk rock manager on a plane a few years back. He knew right away that something was quite different about the man he sat next to as soon as he saw the real expensive sports jacket worn over a 'T' shirt and jeans. Every satanic symbol hung from this man's neck. This manager told the pastor that the church was blowing their opportunity to get to the kids...and, that the new rock age had no intentions of blowing their chance to take over where we left off. This punk rock manager said that the Christians were losing our people...because we had standards and principles...they didn't. We said things and didn't fulfill them...They had nothing to fulfill because they didn't say anything.

He told that pastor that the rock movement was soon to involve themselves with spiritual healings through this "music." The church has had these healing powers and hasn't been using them. WE HAVE TO START before it's too late. GOD has poured out His spirit on all flesh...that means great healing power...Let's use this overpowering faith and get our children back into the fold.

> Even him, whose coming is after the working of satan with all power and signs and lying wonders,
> And with all deceivableness of unrighteousness in them that perish; because they received not the love of the truth, that they might be saved.

The punk rock group has an appropriate song for the poor souls who are physically alive today...but spiritually dead. The name of AC-DC's song is called "Highway to Hell." Unfortunately, satan is claiming many of our young people and much of the thanks go to these profligates known as rock stars. There is not one positive expectation that can come from this movement. Wake up young people..begin working along a pathway that will lead to heaven...not hell.

Father GOD,

We pray to You in the name of Jesus that Your word and Your will has been glorified by the writing in this book. We pray that this chapter has helped many out from the grip of demon power and that all glory will be Yours for the souls that are saved as a result. Father, we agree that there is no power on the earth, under the earth or under the seas as powerful as Yours and we ask that You channel Your glory through us today that we may fulfill Your wishes and save many souls from the grips of satan. Lord we bind the powers of satan and command him to loose his spell on the many young people who are into drugs, rock music and other degrading influences. We ask that they will see the Light that only comes through Your grace. And we ask all this in the name of Jesus. Amen and Amen.

THE EAGLE'S NEST

P.O. Box 19038, Irvine, CA 92714   (714) 540-2056

Pastor Gary Greenwald is the dynamic young minister at Eagle's Nest Christian Fellowship located at 1701 East Edinger, Suite B-7, in Santa Ana, California. For those in the Southern California area who need a spiritual home, I highly recommend Brother Gary's Ministry. He has been instrumental in the making of this book and we love him and pray that GOD will continue to pour out His blessing on his Ministry, his family and himself. Brother Gary began the Eagle's Nest Ministry in 1978 and he presently ministers to an average Sunday attendance of 4,000 brothers and sisters in GOD. I thank you, Gary, for your contribution, for your love and prayers that this book reaches its intended audience and that many new souls may come to know the Lord Jesus Christ as a result. GOD Bless you!

Pastor Greenwald has written three dynamic books and the readers of this book may obtain copies directly from Eagle's Nest Ministries. The prices are reasonable but the content is essential to a meaningful spiritual life. Brother Gary also has two cassette tapes on the punk rock movement. Pray for him and the great work he is doing in the name of our Lord Jesus Christ.

____
Name

____
Address   City   State   ZIP

Dear Pastor Greenwald,
Please send me the following books and tapes. I am enclosing my money order/cash/or check of $__________ to cover the full price of the books, tapes, slides and shipping and handling charges.

▷ "THE PUNK CALLED ROCK!" @ $4.00 each
▷ "THE ROCK THAT DOESN'T ROLL!" @ $3.00 each
▷ "MARIJUANA: THE HEAVENLY DECEPTION" @ $4.00 each
▷ "ROCK-A-BYE-BYE-BABY" (2 tapes) $8.00
▷ Please mail me your FREE tape catalog!
▷ I would like to be a faith partner with your ministry. I
   will pledge __ $10.00 __ $15.00 __ $25.00 __ other per month

CHAPTER TEN

"AMERICA: Infested With Liberal Thought!"

"Happy is the man who never follows the advice of the wicked, or loiters on the way that sinners take, or sits about with scoffers, but finds his pleasure in the Law of YAHWEH, and murmurs His Law day and night!"

(PSALM 1:1)

In 1945, Americans were rejoicing their triumphs over the Germans and the Japanese – two victories on two separate fronts – neither initiated by American aggression, but both won in the name of freedom. It was a great year for all Americans and the promise for the future indeed looked bright. It was a year of patriotism; a time for great spiritual thanksgiving and a period when our allies relished the association they had with a winner. Well, most of the allies anyway! Through all the glitter and jubilation, the stages were being set in motion for a deviously designed organization that would see to it that such future engagements would never be won again. The United Nations was conceived that same year as a dark cloud that would forever smother the cause of liberty.

In 1945, the United Nations was formed under the disguise of providing a means for maintaining peace and security on an international scale. Its purpose was to develop international "cooperation" in humanities, economic, "social," and cultural affairs. Of the 5l charter member countries, only six of the governments were socialistic in nature, but of these few it soon became known that one – the Soviet Union, had more sinister aspirations.

According to noted Evangelist, Billy James Hargis of Tulsa (Christian Crusade), the Charter of the U.N. was either written or proposed by Alger Hiss and Molotov. In essence the foundation and principles of the organization would have been adopted from the constitutional ideology of the Soviet Union. Hargis contends that its inception was the result of subterfuge

- careful and deceitful scheming by the U.S.S.R., and it poses a dire threat to the sovereignty of the United States. Reverend Hargis' early assessment and my research of the historical inception are identical.

"The United Nations is the beginning of the end for the United States," says Hargis, "the enemy marches on our shores from that organization!" His findings intertwine with my earlier contentions of Soviet espionage and subversive tactics against our Country. Hargis confirms my understandings of both my conjecture on the subject and its correlation to Biblical scripture.

Its formation was a direct result of a declaration from Moscow. That in itself makes its inception un-GODLY. "The present day concept of the brotherhood of 'all' men is not a Christian principle," says Hargis, "properly understood, the concept refers to Christians only. The de-emphasis of nationalism is dangerously un-Christian. If this Republic is to be saved, we must rebuild the shattered walls of loyalty and devotion to our nation."

"Our primary threat to the U.S. is internationalism," explains Reverend Hargis, "and conversely, it is the United States and not the United Nations that is the hope of free men everywhere."

"From any viewpoint," contends Hargis, "the U.N. is bad for America. The 'hideous house that Hiss built' exists to take away from America even its right to determine where its money will be spent, by whom it shall be spent and whom it should benefit." Both Hargis and I agree that its presence represents the final attempt at a one world government, prophesied in the Bible.

In Revelations 13:1, John saw through the Spirit of Prophecy a great dictator arising in the end time, - a one world government. "Since the empire of the anti-Christ is identified with communism, and the United Nations is part of the communist plot, - the U.N. should be viewed as a phenomenon of Satan; the anti-Christ," concludes Hargis, "For this reason more than any other, the fledging "Parliament of man" must be denounced as part of the total satanic plot against GOD!"

"By the exclusion of GOD in this organization, the U.N. is atheist," Hargis goes on, "by its inclusion of communist nations, it is anti-Christ, pure and simple. Quite apart from the matter of prophecy, the United Nations is incompatible with Christianity on the basis of its record. Scripture warns us to "test each spirit" to see if it is good, if it is from GOD, or of satan. You will find that the U.N. is not for America."

"The GOD of our fathers who granted us victory in World War II is being ignored in the U.N. chambers," says Billy, "as a Christian I protest this shabby treatment of the World's most important Source of peace...Almighty GOD. By being yoked together with un-GODLY member nations, the United States is sinning against GOD."

"In peaceful co-existence between opposing ideologies, the more sinister will triumph," explains Hargis, "You cannot do business with the devil. If Jesus Christ couldn't co-exist and work harmoniously with the forces of evil, why do many of our liberals think we can?"

"The U.N. Military Staff Committee was responsible for the strategic direction of the United Nations armed forces in Korea," states Hargis, "because our hands were tied we were not allowed to win that war. We actually surrendered our right to win because we were members of that organization. The U.N.'s activity in the Congo was nothing short of lunacy. They sent troops in to prevent self-determination of a civilized and Christian province which did not want to be part of a Communist-controlled Congo. They were also responsible for the Cuban 'Bay of Pigs' affair. Our defeat in the abortive Cuban invastion can be laid directly on that organization's doorstep, as the U.N. treaty prohibited us from engaging in any military operation without first acquiring approval from the security council. Because of our involvement with the U.N., Cuba today is an atheistic country."

"The enslavement of the human race has been progressing steadily since the U.N.'s inception," Reverend Hargis goes on, "and it is the major reason why the Kremlin and other communist cohorts have not worked to destroy the organization. In fact, that is why they want to retain and strengthen it."

Reverend Billy James Hargis' research of the United Nations has been astute. He says that UNICEF is a sinister scheme and its collections are deceptive. Unless it is stopped, our children will become tools of one world internationalists now, and ultimately the slaves of the communist dictators in the future.

UNESCO has furthered communism more than any other agency. This wing of the U.N. is polluted with communists, pro-communists, fellow travelers, sympathizers, dupes and one world government dreamers. Hargis says that it is a deceptive propaganda arm of the U.N. and if allowed to be maintained, will brainwash the American public.

Reverend Hargis indicates that the U.N. stands for centralization, one world government, internationalism, foreign entanglements, atheism, secularism, social gospel, compromise and above all...the anti-Christ! The only alternative for the United States is to withdraw membership. "We must get out of the U.N. and the U.N. out of U.S. (United States)," concludes Hargis.

Fortunately for true Americans, President Reagan is well aware of Reverend Hargis' study. He has publicly stated that the United States will be out of many of that organization's committees by the end of 1984. We can praise the Lord for His giving us a leader with insight, astute awareness and the gumption to follow through with his necessary policies regardless of liberal (socialist) pressure from the Senate, Congress and the House of Representatives. If we are not out of the U.N. committees by the end of this year, don't blame Reagan. The fault would lie with his opposition, a cog in American justice infested with liberal and socialistic thought.

Currently (1983) the United Nations has 161 member nations that contribute. The largest benefactor by far is the United States supplying 25 percent of its total revenue. The next largest contributor is our chief adversary, the U.S.S.R. with only 11 percent. If you consider the contributions of only five of its members, you discover that the U.S., the Soviet Union, the United Kingdom, West Germany and Japan supply almost 60 percent of the total revenue for the organization's maintenance.

The present (1984) Security Council of the U.N., which was formed in 1946, consists of only five permanent members (United States, Russia, United Kingdom, France and China) that comprise its ruling body, with the ten remaining members of the assembly elected for two-year periods only. This assembly was formed to provide the structure for promoting international peace and security in all parts of the world. Judging from our current status, the United Nations has failed in this attempt and has allowed ludicrous injustices in each corner of the globe.

The United Nations: A Prostitute For Terrorism!

Recently the Reagan Administration added Iran to its growing list of terrorist countries. Already included are Syria, Cuba, South Yemen and Libya. All terrorist nations (save Syria, and that's subject to debate because of being allied with the Soviet Union) are listed as socialist governments. They are all members of the United Nations with seats in the various committees, and it is not by chance that all have close ties to the Soviet Union.

If the U.N. was so concerned with maintaining peace and security on an international basis why have they not expelled these radicals? The U.N. professes their desire for the development of humanitarian cooperation among all member countries. If that is their goal, why have they tolerated the actions of these terrorists against other member nations? Syria, Cuba, South Yemen, Iran and Libya contribute only one percent of the organization's revenue so we can discount as a motive the loss of necessary operating capital. Condoning the terrorist activities by their neglect of issuing any condemnation against the nations, bolsters Reverend Hargis' research and confirms my contentions that the U.N. is indeed the right arm of the Soviet Union. I believe it's high time the United Nation's largest benefactor pulls out, support and all! Those countries are not being ejected from the organization because the Soviet Union, and not the U.N. assembly, simply would not stand for it. And Soviet Union does control the United Nations - hook, line and sinker!

Behind the initiatives of Ronald Reagan, the United States has finally come awake to the realization that nothing positive can ever materialize from this association. By the end of 1984, President Reagan will (without liberal intervention) pull the United States out of U.N.E.S.C.O. (U.N.'s Educational, Scientific and Cultural Organization). The move is one of the more positive actions we could be taking under the historical circumstances. Reagan also signaled a possibility of quitting the U.N. Committee on the Peaceful Uses of Outer Space because of the group's insistence on disarmament. They are preaching disarmament while another member (Soviet Union) continues to violate the Salt Treaties with massive stockpiling. Sounds fair doesn't it? We shelve our weapons and Russia uses their edge as nuclear blackmail!

U.N.E.S.C.O. has been responsible for overt and invert espionage on our very shores. They have infiltrated every meaningful organization we have, and American liberal sympathizers are their crutch. The United States has undertaken an inquiry into the organization's politicking and shady business transactions. Their financial practices are corrupt, and recently there was a major fire at UNESCO Headquarters in Paris, France, that was "believed to be an attempt to destroy documents crucial to the inquiry."

UNESCO was the only one of the many U.N. organizations that did not meet U.S. concerns that priorities be set and activities scaled to meet economic reality.

The most bitter controversy involving UNESCO in recent years has been the attempt by Third World and communist nations to use it to promote what they called a "New World Information and Communications Order." Don't tell me that this is just another organization that is for the betterment of world relations! There is no question that it involves the "New Age Movement" which ultimately will result in "one world government." Constance Cumbey, a Christian lawyer from Detroit, infiltrated the "movement" and outlines the "New Age Movement" in her best selling book <u>Hidden Dangers of the Rainbow</u>! That book is highly recommended to all caring

American Christians and Jews as it confirms much of what has been written in <u>Ominous Portents of the Parousia of Christ</u>.

The fire was possibly set because many UNESCO officials have been trying to conform to the request by the United States that major changes be observed before the end of 1984. Secretary of State George Shultz said the twelve month period (from December 1983) before the pullout takes place will give UNESCO "a potential opportunity to respond to the serious concerns that are cause for our withdrawal."

Another U.S. Official, Gregory Newell, Assistant Secretary of State for international organizations, said, "There's no conceivable way that UNESCO could change its policies, its direction, its practices, such that we would be enticed to remain." He went on to say that President Reagan would reconsider his decision to withdraw if "significant" and "permanent" changes are made in the fundamental policies of the educational, cultural and scientific agency of the U.N.

"Our conclusion is firm," adds Newell. "The decision to withdraw is not a negotiating tact or a ploy of any sort." U.S. officials conclude that for the time being those changes are just not in the offing. State Department spokesman Alan Romberg said, "With regret we have been forced to conclude that we are not now able to effect these major alterations in policies of UNESCO and that we cannot participate as a member without them." After a six-month review, Reagan and his advisers have determined "that continued U.S. participation in UNESCO does not serve the interests of the United States."

Romberg said the United States contends UNESCO has:
- "Politicized virtually every subject it deals with."
- "Exhibited hostility toward the basic institutions of a free society, especially a free market and a free press."
- "Demonstrated unrestrained budgetary expansion."

Whether other member nations feel it is a ploy or not, no concessions on the part of the United States should be made. President Reagan may not be in the position to say what he and his advisers really mean, but this author can. I say, "Git out while the gittin's good and don't look back or else you'll turn to salt!" That's how evil the organization really is!

In a recent meeting of the U.N. Security Council, the Soviet Union and their Soviet republic Ukraine (just another way the Russians get another vote) vetoed a French proposal to replace the Western multinational force in the Beirut area with U.N. "peacekeeping troops." The vote in the 15-nation security council was 13-2. Soviet Ambassador Oleg A. Troyanovsky said beforehand that the Soviets would be voting against the move because, "the reasons are pretty obvious." He said that the Americans have tried to impose an agreement that would put Lebanon in the American sphere of influence. He said that the United States government "using Marines and warships were dictating how Lebanon should run its affairs." Can you imagine that? The Soviets are assisting Syria and all the other radical terrorists in the region and "WE" are dictating how Lebanon should be governed? As you would have guessed, a compromise was in order. The Lebanese government wanted the peacekeeping forces of the U.N. in "all" of Lebanon, but as a further concession to the Soviets the United Nations proposed an alternative plan that called for a cease fire in all of Lebanon, however, the forces would remain only in Beirut. When you compromise or deal with the "devil," liberty will always lose out!

No compromise should ever be made with the Soviets as long as they represent terrorism in the free world. We wouldn't recognize Arafat and the PLO so why should we make any attempt to play square with their "big brother and trainer?" Regardless of liberal pressures, the U.S. must pull out of that (U.N.) alliance. We made a mistake in 1945. The assurance of that fact was the formation of N.A.T.O (North Atlantic Treaty Organization) in 1949. We remained as members of the U.N. for reasons of diplomacy and for the sake of insulting atheists and rebel nations; we remain today linked with the "right arm of satan!"

Our allies in N.A.T.O. are basically friendly nations to the cause of freedom. They are: Belgium, Canada, Denmark, France, the Federal Republic of (West) Germany, Greece, Iceland, Italy, Luxembourg, Netherlands, Norway, Portugal, Turkey, and the United Kingdom. Many of these same allies are presently receiving air defense missiles from the U.S., much to the dismay of their internal subversive and radical elements. N.A.T.O. officials have tried to appease the many protests by switching to conventional air defense in the Netherlands, but the attempt does not diffuse the constant harrassment from protesting commies.

The U.S. is investing in the Dutch arms industry as a result of their agreement to purchase long range Patriot Missiles. Our nuclear Cruise missiles are already installed in West Germany, Belgium, the Netherlands, Italy and Great Britain. My protest is for better security against these internal elements through the enactment of stiffer laws and penalties against these protestors. Get their leaders and you'll have mostly communists, pro-communists and radical liberals.

Our President has been continually accused of "destroying any future hopes for detente with the Soviets." So what! They are nothing better than LIARS, professed atheists and have broken every signed accord and treaty ever presented to them. The Soviet Union stands tall for deceitful practice and terrorism. To hell with diplomacy where they are concerned; it's time to call it as it is!

Liberals, Socialists and Other Anti-Americans

The Soviets have "always agreed to disagree," and our Administration's justified hard line with them should be construed as patriotic, nothing less. We should not allow any subversive organization or any un-American activity to organize within our borders. Ronald Reagan is 100 percent justified in his stance, and it's about time good Americans began understanding that as fact. Don't listen to the newspapers. They are mostly communist and atheist sympathizers and will print and exault only that which is detrimental to the cause of freedom. Talk about "freedom of the press," they've got it now! They don't understand that by printing their present rubbish, they are supporting un-American activities. They'll be the first to lose this liberty when the socialists take over.

In the previous decade since the devious ousting of Richard Nixon, we have been sliding and slipping in the arms race. While we were freezing our arms, the Soviets were racing for the advantage. Originally Reagan had support for his defense spending and build-up of nuclear weapons due to the Soviet's deployment of increasingly accurate, many-headed SS-20s. Now, thanks chiefly to radical opposition by many of the same "Americans" who opposed vocal public school prayer, liberals are accusing and abusing the only real president this nation has known in this century.

Americans must wake up and understand that, regardless of the rights of a few liberals and potential terrorists, they must be thoroughly investigated when our security is in jeopardy. We cannot withstand another Watergate. If one is proposed, or if anyone continually attacks sound Administrative policies, therein will be your subversion. You can bet on it! The communists want Americans to have a "panty-waste" and a "yes man" in our highest office. The future prosperity of our nation and the security of our people depend on the strength of our allegiance to our President. Reagan must have our support!

These liberals are compromising our security and encouraging the Soviet effort in America when they protest against our defense policies. Many of the liberals are being misled by the communist element in our society, and because we are the "Land of Freedom," nothing is being done about it! How long would these radicals last if they tried the same tactics in the Soviet Union? That's a question that answers itself.

The Soviets don't want a nuclear war any more than we do. Believing otherwise is ludicrous and utter nonsense. Even a partial demonstration of this form of warfare would affect the entire civilized world. They know it as well as we do. The United States and the Soviet Union are playing chess, and Reagan astutely awaits the Soviet's next move. I can guarantee you their move will be connivingly well thought out. When you look at the leaders of the next demonstration against nuclear power, you can be assured that their energy comes from the abyss. These liberals are the enemy of the American people. Don't forget it for one short moment.

As the 1984 elections draw near, expect further attacks on the integrity of our President and his justified policies aimed at peace. The "liberals" will twist these policies in front of your eyes and deceive many with their perversions and untruths. You will see no compromise from the Soviets prior to election day. The stalemate will continue and their aggressions will magnify in proportion. The liberals and the communists want anyone but Reagan in office. The "biggest liberal" in the House, Tip O'Neil, has made a stand against Ronald Reagan and 'all' his proposals. What a great American O'Neil makes himself out to be. As you guessed it, he endorses ole Walter "pro-choice in abortion" Mondale, the best "yes man" in the country. With citizens like Mondale and O'Neil, we admit defeat before we begin. Ironically O'Neil backs the same candidate that all social reformers applaud...the same choice the Kremlin would vote for given the opportunity. Had it not been for O'Neil and the rest of the "liberal Demon-rats," our children would now be praying to their GOD in the public schools and America would be headed towards greater spiritual understanding. It's sure nice to still have the right of opinion, isn't it? Leaders as such, we can well do without.

Since the death of Soviet leader Yuri Andropov and the "election" of new chairman Konstanin Chernenko, many Americans have assumed an optimistic attitude towards the resumption of favorable peace talks. Understand this! The Soviet political transition should not be cause for the presumption of any positive expectancy, now or in the future. Chernenko is more hell-bent on the enslavement of the world than was his evil predecessor. They are both from the same atheist mold, with identical motivations. It's either their way, or no way. To me that's just fine, and hopefully that's the way our policy will evolve towards association with these un-GODly entities.

Chernenko has already made political waves with his radical and unfounded statement that Reagan and his Administration are aggressive and imperialists. That "bone-head" remark should substantiate my contention that no positive detente is on the horizon. It also exposes his illiteracy for an accurate assessemnt of the very "word."

Imperialism is the policy and practice of extending the dominion and power of a nation by direct territorial acquisitions, through forceful or political means. Common sense tells me that Chernenko has accurately described the tactics of the Soviet Union - not the United States. Our country's intentions and cause are aimed towards allowing a nation to decide their own form of government through free elections. If that proposes a threat to the Russian conspiracy, too bad! Compromise in this area is totally insane.

Capitalists we are. But "Imperialism" has never been the policy of the United States. They claim that the U.S. is interfering with the internal affairs of Central American nations. Tell that to the people of El Salvador and Nicaragua, whose rights are being violated by the day from communist insurgents from Cuba and the Soviet Union. All El Salvador desires is to be left alone, but the Soviets need their land to encompass the last outpost of the free world - the United States. Our intentions are bent on freedom, while the Russians are intent on its removal.

The Soviets remain steadfast that no further arms talks can materialize until N.A.T.O. removes the missiles from Western Europe. In the same respect they feel we should overlook their deployment of missiles in the eastern sector. This will never come about as long as we have a leader that cares for his people and their liberty. Something Russia fails to comprehend, whether through ignorance or design, is that you can enslave a nation but you cannot change the heart. Future positive co-existence between the United States and the Soviet Union can only be obtained through non-aggressive means. In other words, that attainment is currently beyond the scope of realization and will not happen in this generation or any other.

If the Soviets really feel that their technology is of equal par with ours, why have they continually coerced and connived in their search for American technological expertise. The fact be known, America is far superior to anything satan and his brothers can manifest. Why are they so intent on undermining the United States in search of our knowledge, if theirs is so advanced? The Russians and their ideologies cannot even feed their own without our support and assistance, nor do they have a solution to their escalating illiteracy rate.

I do not refer to myself as an intellectual. On the contrary, I praise the Lord for the inspirational common sense He gave me. I would rather be unsophisticated with the human capability of reasonable logic than to fail to acknowledge the dire need of His intervention in world affairs.

The "negotiation of any peaceful co-existence" among alien religious beliefs should not take place. GOD does not have the desire to place His people in association with anti-Christians. He will not permit such an alliance. Where GOD is banned, the spirit of anti-Christ thrives and infests the logistics of the human mind. Obviously, it has done just that with the leaders of the Soviet Union.

Let that atheist country continue in its evils, professing the idiocy of their Marxian-Leninism doctrines to the unsuspecting. Let them continue with their foolish prospects of a universal (one world government) co-existence. The Lord Jesus said in Matthew 15:13,14, "Any plant not planted by the Father will be pulled up by its roots." Let's leave them alone. "They are blind men leading the blind; and if one of the blind men leads another, both will fall into a pit!" We should all know which abyss GOD refers to in that passage!

The Soviet Union must understand that the United States is indeed a plant in the Garden of GOD. They must be assured that His intentions for American blessings must continue for a short while longer, insuring our free tomorrows. They must realize that the power we receive from the Holy Spirit is far superior to their "gods of lust." The power of Jesus is "unlimited." Even if the Soviets do possess more firepower, or more missiles, or more technology, or even more technology than the U.S.; their allegiance with satan speeds their ultimate demise.

The world as we know it is in its final chapter. Most scholars of Biblical prophecy conclusively agree to that fact. But one need not be overly versed with scripture to confirm that Jesus is already at the door, waiting for His final volume of world history to play itself out. The time when He will separate the "wheat from the thistles" is here and few will recognize this surety.

Restoring the integrity and preserving our freedom has been the cause of GOD's wise Prophet, - Ronald Reagan. Reverend Jerry Falwell of the Moral Majority in Virginia confirms that Reagan has never pulled back or compromised on any moral issue. "He has not reneged on one single thing," explains Reverend Falwell. "With him in the White House for a second term, we would see some dramatic things take place in the cause of traditional values! We (Christians and caring Americans) are going to do everything we can to help him, and I'm sure that he will have the support from all religious conservatives everywhere."

Reverend Falwell is a further confirmation of GOD's tested good fruit! Jerry stands as firm as Saint Peter on the rock for an America with high ideals, especially if Reagan remains in office. Jerry Falwell, like Oral Roberts, Paul Crouch, Hal Lindsey, Billy James Hargis, Billy Graham, and countless others, is the epitome of what faith stands for in the country. Three cheers for such Americans; we need many more like them!

Regardless of Soviet inspired subversions, our President's plan is working. The liberals emphasize reducing our defense budget. That is displeasing and frustrating to Ronald Reagan, as he sees the movements of our evil adversary (Russia) in the Middle East as well as Central America. Many liberal democrats are critical of Reagan's policies, but in the same respect, they fail to propose alternative solutions. The fastest way to find out if someone is doing something positive and true in this country is to watch the reaction from the Soviet Union on any policy. Judging from that country's overt expressions...Go get 'em Ronnie, you're Okay in my book!

Just Who (or what) Are The Soviet Leaders We're Asked To Negotiate With?

Most Americans have no idea of what motivates Soviet aggression in the world. Many don't understand their views and know little of their perverted ideology. In America, the politicians' private lives are opened for public display. We vote for the candidate of our choice through free election. Such is not the same behind the Iron curtain! To fully appreciate President Reagan's firm position with the Soviets, you should initially understand what type of "people" the Soviet Hierarchy produces. I use the term "people" with kind and unwarranted reservations, what you will discover is that their leaders are brutal animals incapable of compassion.

Our leaders negotiate in good faith with Soviet Heads of State that have no known personal history. They deal with entities that are not cognizant to the pleas of humanity and could care less for any spiritual foundations we hold dear. The communist is raised as an unbeliever in the Deity and programmed that he should place his faith in the sciences of man's productivity.

The former General Secretary of the Communist Party in the Kremlin, Yuri Andropov, was a deceitful butcher in life and is currently a prize candidate for sentry duty on the gates of hell. Andropov was a man known only to a few Westerners. The Kremlin's propaganda made him out to be an individual with great compassion with a desire and devotion for justice. Just for the record, let's trace his worldly achievements!

In 1956, Andropov played an integral part in the Hungarian Revolution. When it seemed sure that the

Hungarians would achieve their independence from Soviet domain, Andropov deceived both the Hungarian cabinet and its new leaders into believing that the Soviets would give way to the new sovereignty. In the interim, Andropov sent for backup troops as reinforcements and was directly responsible for the deaths of the new Hungarian Defense Minister, Pal Maleter and Premier Imre Nagy. As an Ambassador to Hungary, Yuri Andropov invited the Prime Minister to his residence for a celebration dinner. While at the dinner, KGB agents busted in, dragged out Maleter and imprisoned him. Premier Nagy sought refuge in the Yugoslavian Embassy, but was coaxed out by Andropov with the ploy of amnesty. Both Nagy and Maleter were later executed and the revolution was curtailed.

After being promoted to the Chairman of the KGB (the Soviet secret police), Andropov was instrumental in installing further perversions against his own people when he assumed control of the mental institutions. Any dissidents against policy, or any pro-western attitude was considered "a lack of reality towards the Soviet cause" and the victim was committed for "an examination." The actual meaning of Soviet commitment to these mental facilities was for "torture."

As the Head of the KGB, he was instrumental in the escalation of international terrorism and espionage. In a complex outside of Moscow there exists a special terrorist training school called Balashikha. In this particular house of horror, Third World allies of the Soviet Union as well as their own crack-troops (KGB) receive special tutoring in the arts of terrorism. Many graduates who express the highest degrees of depravity are retained on their ledgers for future political assassinations world-wide. The Politburo, which is the official policy-making and executive committee of the communist party, orders strategic murders and they are carried out by these terrorists.

The KGB, under Andropov's vile leadership, was directly related to such assassinations as Georgi Markov (a political immigrant from Bulgaria) in England, Afghanistan's President Hafizullah Amin was shot prior to their invasion of that country, and there is substantial evidence implicating the KGB with the attempt on Pope John Paul's life in 1981. Mehmet Ali Agca was the terrorist pawn. Recently one of the Pope's messenger's daughter, a 15-year-old, was kidnapped by members of a communist conspiracy. Her life was offered for the release of Agca from prison.

Under Andropov's direct orders, a Korean (civilian) Jetliner with 269 innocent people aboard was shot down "near" Soviet airspace. Although it will never be confirmed by the Soviets, it has been generally accepted that the airliner was destroyed because two of its passengers were staunch opposition leaders against communist aggression. On the flight were U.S. Congressman Larry McDonald, an anti-communist leader of the John Birch Society, and Fillipino opposition leader Benigno Aguino, Jr., who fought to rid the Philippines of the communist element.

Upon the orders of Andropov, the inhumane use of chemical warfare was used against innocent civilians during the Russian invasion of Afghanistan. Currently there are over a half-million enslaved South Vietnamese and ten thousand Russian political prisoners working on the Soviet pipeline project. Both political and religious persecutions escalated in proportion during his brief stay as the party leader. Most westerners don't realize that there are many Russian people who worship Jesus daily and love their GOD in private for fear of becoming a marked man. Once these believers become known to the Kremlin, these individuals are subjected to unusual harrassments, arrests, torture at Balashikha, and many times long prison terms for their acknowledgement of GOD. Their Christian children in the Soviet schools face continued rejection and ridicule for their beliefs. In the Soviet Union, the first day of school marks the beginning of a systematic instruction in atheism and continues until their graduation.

These are the "great" principles of Marxian-Leninism. These are the ideals and practices of the residents of satansville. These standards are the same that will be forced upon your children in future generations unless you understand the significance today. You must associate radical and liberal reform in America with a sinister design by the Soviet Union to subjugate the American people through misinformation.

These same liberals (socialists) thrive on discord. They are perverting every decent standard in America with their disruptions of status quo and persuading our students that their protesting of government foreign aid is good for America. It is not true. President Reagan's program for aid to El Salvador is important to a continuing American lifestyle. If El Salvador falls from lack of U.S. support, Costa Rica will be next, then Mexico. The communists are on our doorstep and most citizens seem to care less. We have the tendency to avoid the pressing issues and fail to appreciate what we have until we no longer have it. We must wake up to the reality that the power of the people is lessening. Why else would the liberal "demon-rats" in the Senate vote against the people who put them there when they succeeded in keeping vocal prayer out of the public schools. Americans wanted the vocal prayer returned to the public school systems by an 84 percent popular census. Yes, we are losing our power to the clutches of socialism from within our country and the rest of their team (Soviets) are banging on our back door.

Recently a most radical bunch of heathens stormed the office of Senator Robert Stafford in Winooski, Vermont. They occupied his offices for three days before police bodily threw them out. The group (Vermont National Central America Week "Civil Disobedience Committee") originally demanded that Stafford end his support for U.S. aid to El Salvador, Guatemala, Honduras and to anti-government insurgents in Nicaragua. They reduced their demand a short while later and promised to vacate his offices if Stafford would hold a public forum on the issue before the end of April.

This "Civil Disobedience Committee" is nothing more than an arm of the new age movement aimed at stripping further liberties from our country. Without U.S. aid, those countries would have no resistance against the communist movement and don't think for a moment the leaders and instigators of that radical committee don't know it! Many of the students of the 60 or more protesters were innocently implicated into that socialist assault on American integrity. They are being swayed by false prophets into believing their actions are justifiable. They cannot know what they are demanding and still be Americans in every sense of its meaning.

What the misled students don't realize is that our nation's sovereignty depends immensely on our foreign air support of Central America. Those countries don't want a communist government...they want freedom, and although their beliefs are strong they need supplies to continue their resistance.

Because of our involvement with the United Nations, Cuba became communist. In 1962 President Kennedy challenged the Soviets and won. Subsequently the Soviets dismantled their missiles and removed them from Cuba. Twenty-two years later the missiles have been returned, but it didn't stop with just Cuba. They made an attempt to install their twisted government on Grenada, but Reagan was wise and the Soviets were stopped in their tracks.

According to Hal Lindsey (author of many pro-American books on Biblical prophecy), when the Soviets took over Nicaragua they captured a most strategic location. Most people don't realize it, but Nicaragua is one country where the terrain would allow a new canal from the Atlantic to the Pacific. With a new canal they would be in a sound military position to cut off U.S. supply routes into the Gulf of Mexico, where much of our commerce enters the United States. Oil from South America could be stifled and shipping from that region to the U.S. could be forcibly denied by the Soviets.

Soviet arms buildup in Nicaragua has multiplied since the takeover and from that location (which is a shorter distance to

Washington, D.C. than San Jose, California) their SS-20 missiles (long range) could encompass the entire United States with their range. Cuba is only 90 miles from the coast of Florida, and if the Soviet Union is allowed to succeed with their aggression in Central America, by the end of this decade, they will be in control of most of the southern region near the Gulf of Mexico allowing a major striking base, have additional ports for replenishment of supplies, and be in position for high-sea piracy of incoming cargo to the United States.

Americans...Wake up! I realize that it is difficult to have foresight of what is happening when many of you have never seen the injustices taking place in other countries of the world. Except for the continent of Australia, I have been on every other and I've seen much of the religious persecutions. I can guarantee you, Americans truly live in GOD's country...the United States of America. Does it take a bunch of radicals coming into your home and dictating what you will eat, how you will vote or what business you will undertake in life to get your concern? You must take your head out of the sand and be willing to fight for your freedom of choice...otherwise you'll lose it.

Between the Soviet Union's push for world communism and the international "New Age" movement, we are being assaulted by a vicious crossfire of untruths! Radicals own your daily newspaper that comes into your home. They control the Congress, the House of Representatives and the Supreme Court. There's only one way to fight them. This November you must retaliate against socialism with the only power you have left - your vote. If you have always left the vote to others and then complained when the politicians don't conform to your thinking, you are the guilty party. If you don't like what's going on in America you'd better be willing to get out of that easy chair, go register to vote and then follow through with your Christian Heritage and let's get rid of the festering liberal belief in America. Let us change the destiny of America by replacing the liberals in government with men who abide by and devote themselves to the principles of GOD. Test the candidates (spirits) and see if their proposals are aimed for future prosperity or designed towards evil outcome. This year, vote Christian - forget your party allegiance.

The Soviet plot is real and you must accept it as fact. You must also understand that they are no longer thousands of miles from our shores...they are within our very own society and stagnating the minds of our youth with misinformation. If you care for the souls of your children and the future of America, you must move forth into tomorrow as part of the united effort to awaken our sleeping giant.

The Bible is the greatest Book that has ever been written. Its text is made up of more than one-third prophecy both past, present and future. Of this one-third, two-thirds of these prophecies have already been fulfilled and that is fact. If you feel that the final third is unlikely to follow the same accurate path, you are not making a logical assessment of the truth.

The final chapter of the world is being played out in this very generation and rightfully so the people of this planet have no middle-of-the-road in choice. The forces of GOD far surpass those of His adversary the devil, but you must understand that this earth is not His Kingdom. This earth is the kingdom of satan. GOD created it, GOD placed man upon it and He loves every living thing on its surface, but GOD does not control the hearts of men. That, He gave to you when he allowed freedom of decision in the Garden of Eden. You may either go one of two ways with your thought. You can believe that mortal man has all the answers you will ever need or you can study the Word GOD has given us in the Bible and realize its truths. It's obvious that the intellectuals of this present age do not have the answers necessary for survival...let alone prosperity. GOD does have the solutions to man's problems. If you accept that fact and bolster the knowledge with the assurance you will receive from Biblical prophecy, you're on the right road. The most important decision you will ever make is when you accept the Lord Jesus Christ into your heart and acknowledge that He died on the cross for the sins of humanity. Believe it - it's true!

Although GOD loves us all, all will not attain the salvation of their eternal soul. If you want eternal life, it's yours for the asking! When you accept Jesus as your Saviour you become one of the elect, a member of His household. You will be granted special blessings and be shielded from impossible tasks. With GOD everything is possible, and you will soon come to understand it as a factual association. You must not follow the same path as does the world, because the world is speeding towards eternal damnation. What man gives grows stagnant because its origin is from the everlasting heartbreaker - satan. GOD gives you confidence where there was none and hope where there is disillusionment. Jesus said that He was not a king of the earth (JOHN 18:36,37), meaning that His Kingdom was with His Father in Heaven. If we are to follow Jesus into the Kingdom, we must first accept Him as dying for our salvation. Then we must spread this fellowship to others.

If you love this world and its material possessions, then you are of this Earth and rightfully belong to it. If you know Jesus personally, you can't like what you see manifested, or condone the passions of the flesh. Regardless of what the heathens are saying, there is 'little time' remaining until the time of the Gentiles is fulfilled. When that time comes, so will the Rapture, when Jesus calls His faithful to meet Him in the air.

The Earth is consumed in evil desire. Corruption is winning out over the good and all the true values of life are being distorted from reality. When we fail to recognize the need for GOD in this world, we slip a little deeper in despair. We see His absence in our schools, in our community, in our government and in our world when we see pornography polluting the minds of our fellow man. We see it festering in the liberalists that call themselves servants of the people. The lawmakers, the politicians and many church leaders are blind men leading our nation into corruption. The attempt by the World Council of Churches and the National Council of Churches for a one world religious system is a conspiracy devised and orchestrated by satan, originating in the depths of hell. Its aim is for socialism and that's not far from communism, which is atheism, which is ani-GOD.

I see the world as a huge vessel in rough seas, a thousand miles from the nearest shore with an irreparable leak in its hull. It's sinking but the passengers continue to enjoy its last fruits, assuming someone will come up with an answer for repairing the hull and saving the ship from capsizing. The skipper of the vessel (truth) has abandoned the ship and has left its demise to the uneducated. Confusion is rampant and all the scholarly aboard are spreading their expertise in areas they know nothing about. The passengers that are speaking the loudest, know the least and the wise men aboard have begun praying to their Father in Heaven for divine knowledge. They realize that it is only a matter of time before the ship will sink and all the souls without 'life preservers' will surely die. The passengers look to the coming storm on the horizon. The foolish say that it will blow itself out and go in the opposite direction, while the wise know the storm is an hour away. Repatching the hole in the vessel will only buy time until the storm hits, and when it does the fibers of the vessel will not be strong enough to withstand the fury it will entail. What are you going to do? Will you take the position that the unworthy passengers with illogical foresight can save your life, or can you understand that there is indeed an answer to the puzzlement that is in the capable hands of One not of human sort.

That vessel is an analogy of our world situation. It is true that the end is near. Only those who are wise enough to ask for the answers are receiving a Life Preserver! That Life Preserver is Jesus Christ. Through Him only is the way to life, a life that doesn't end when we draw our last gasp. But a life of new beginnings. I hope your life preserver has not been manufactured with mortal thread.

We must reach out to those without the life preserver and save them from their impending death. We must at least try to reach the unwise entity and show them that there 'is' a way to life other than those developed by man. Without means of support, they will perish. That support must come from GOD's people and through divine guidance.

When you look at a neighbor who is floundering, show him kindness and offer him the alternative. There are many who do not see the Truth. Some call themselves atheists but fail to understand the meaning. Many say there is no GOD or that heaven and hell are what man makes of this world. They say heaven and hell are here on earth and judging from their complaints, they are half right. WE must plant the Good Seed in our neighbor by following a lead from the Father and by obeying His laws. If our neighbor sees that we are peaceful, kind, generous and loving, he may also desire the same for his family.

Unfortunately we will also encounter the children of satan in our travels. These will be people who will not listen to sound advice and therefore will not learn the way to the Father. Jesus said, "Don't give pearls to swine! They will trample the pearls and turn and attack you! And don't give holy things to depraved men!" (Matthew 7:7)

We are also going to lose many of the good men in this world to the deceiving influence of satan. Many of these will be turned into the light and be saved. Look at your neighbor, but don't judge him! If you have prejudices towards him because of his color or his origin, you must repair your own heart before lending any support to others.

At one time in my life I felt that GOD had made people different colors and gave them different features to distinguish them into classes. Prejudice is a pre-conceived judgement towards another. It is an opinion and we all know opinions are highly susceptible to error when the heart is not blessed. I lay no claim to perfection. I have been wrong in earthly opinions many times in my life. I have been guilty of pre-judging others; GOD says that we will not judge them at all. GOD made people different so that it would be easier for Him to decipher a good heart from an evil one. Many who say they are not prejudiced continually practice evil gossip.

I can remember telling my oldest children when they were only babies, "When you grow up, make sure that you marry someone with the same color skin. Otherwise your children will not be the same color!" Yes, I lay no claim to perfection and by this action I am no better than the next bigot or racist. The only difference is that I realize my opinions have been in error. I tell you in all honesty, "I would rather have my daughters marry a good Christian, regardless of color, than to associate themselves with an evil-minded atheist!" I'm learning and so should every Christian. The skin means nothing; it is the heart and soul that should be examined more closely!

As I write this book, I feel the ever presence of the Holy Spirit. I was a believer in Christ before I started this book eight months ago, but I now understand the full meaning of Christianity. GOD has changed my ideals and in so doing, He has altered my ideas on life. My fallacy of judging others has changed like a current in a mighty river. I am now prejudiced of the atheists, the communists, the socialists and every evil liberal on the face of this Earth that have the perverted idea of deceiving others into their filthy darkness. I don't hate them; I feel sorry for them!

You will indeed be happy if you choose not to follow the teachings of the wicked, nor associate with their evil designs, or contribute to their demise. Follow the principles of GOD and learn to lead others to Him. A mind is a terrible thing to waste, but the human soul is much more important.

We are in fact in the final chapter of this horror story called mankind. Your future decisions are meaningless without Divine Intervention in your life. This chapter tells of the evils that are preventing any positive world accord. The only association you need in the remaining years is with Him who lives Forever! GOD is not the King of this world because man has taken over that authority. Because man continually defies His orders and believes in mystical, unworthy projects, they will find no solutions.

Understanding that faith comes from hearing and hearing from the Word of GOD, will bring blessings upon both you and yours. Our President has admirable intentions for our country and he truly cares that America will move forward in prosperity. There is no way he can negotiate with communism and keep our nation positive! This should not be requested of him. Don't force Reagan to deal with satan (the Soviet Union). It can only lead to the compromise of our standards and the loss of the preserving salt from our integrity.

The Soviet Union is the swine Jesus mentions in Matthew 7:7. They believe as strongly in subverting and subjugating the world in communism as we are against it. You can't make concessions with the devil. Appreciate Reagan's firm stance with the powers of evil and look for ways to assist him, while shelving your criticism of his policies. GOD recognizes His own and President Reagan is indeed one of His! He has brought integrity back to the White House and faith back to the hearts of our people. Reagan admits that his power comes from GOD.

That's enough to tell us we have the right man in our country's highest office. GOD bless him and may each of us support his leadership.

You must remember that it is easy to walk in the way of evil and in this age the hardest undertaking you will face is being a good Christian. The attacks on President Reagan are numerous. One such atheist sympathizer, Dick Meister, a former reporter for a liberal newspaper in San Francisco, wrote an article in the <u>Las Vegas Review Journal</u> entitled "Invoking GOD to Justify Our Policies." In his worthless opinion he mocked Ronald Reagan for his "constant public references to GOD in his national addresses." He made the unjustified attempt to tell the people that Reagan only refers to GOD in speech to attract the attention of the "95%" who believe in GOD in this country. Meister took exception to the fact that Americans fail to acknowledge the existence of the atheist factor in our society. "Praise the Lord!" I wouldn't want to let that filth be known either!

Meister went on to exault the efforts of an atheist girl who joined with three others in Livermore, California, to win a court order that banned as unconstitutional the recitation of the usual prayer at the beginning of the graduation ceremonies. Meister all but applauded her selfish motives and then even tried to justify her actions as righteous by explaining how her classmates jeered their disapproval upon her. He mentioned that the school district tried to overturn the decision and that the district failed to recognize and heed the words of religious leader, Dean Kelley of the, get this, "National Council of Churches." Kelley's words referring to the prayer being removed were, "Children's lives are not transformed by 'magical incantations' but by models set for them in the conduct of their elders." Can you believe that a supposed minister of GOD would refer to the "prayer" as a "magical incantation?" If you read on you'll find out more about the "National Council of Churches" and their regressive contribution to the preservation of the human soul. I thank the Lord that there's at least one school district that cares not to listen to rubbish.

Five-percenter Meister also found space to quote from his idol, Madalyn Murray O'Hair of the American Atheists (you remember her back in Chapter Three), who said, "There is a great amount of fear. Atheists are afraid of losing their jobs if their beliefs become known, afraid of angering their neighbors - even their wives or husbands." What these animals should be fearing is the "Wrath of GOD" and His swift and fair judgement! Repent, Madalyn, Repent!

Meister goes on to say, "Think how it would be if everyone took that clear promise of freedom as seriously as did the girl who caused the removal of ceremonial prayer." Meister has his information twisted. What he contends is that it's okay for someone of minority beliefs to cause a loss of the majority's freedom of expression, - "but don't take mine away." Dick ("do as I say and not as I do") Meister has his logic mixed up, but it's nothing a good baptism with the Holy Spirit couldn't remedy.

Allowing Meister the opportunity to air his dirty laundry through the media only substantiates the claim that the press is nothing higher than socialist propaganda. What they need to do is filter out the slime and allow the more positive flow a chance to breathe in our society. But I guess this world will never recognize the truth! Meister went on to slight Reagan for calling it "a tragedy that American women are allowed to choose whether to give birth." Isn't "mass murder" a tragedy, or is the annihilation of "developing human beings" acceptable because our liberal courts say so? For those journalists that know Dick Meister, tell him that I will contribute one ticket in his name for that banana boat heading south as mentioned in Chapter Fourteen.

Yes, brothers, people like Meister are the cause of our trouble in world alliance. If you have ever come in contact with them, you know what I'm saying. They live in the darkness of the outer world; they are the blind leading the blind, and satan is licking his chops, waiting for their passage into his realm of fire and brimstone.

You must realize that true men of GOD are not ashamed to involve Him in their every action; whether that be in the affairs of a country as Ronald Reagan has done, or, our every day routines. Meister is one of the pitiful because he is backing and bolstering the losing side and doesn't know it. He is going against all that is good in this world in favor of subversive elements.

We must pray for people like this...they are heading for eternal destruction and an afterlife of torment. These humanists wouldn't know something good if they stumbled over it...and that in itself is sad.

When you see the grouping of Democratic presidential candidates chastising the Reagan issues...you are witnessing a "satan versus GOD" scenario.

Placing the hearts of Mondale, Hart and Jackson in their proper perspective...you wouldn't come up with even a trace of the real love and compassion of President Reagan. They, too, attack everything that is good because evil minds know no better. May GOD have mercy on us all if anyone but Reagan is elected this Fall!

CHAPTER ELEVEN

"The Communist Manifesto!"

Why it represents a piece of

GARBAGE!

Based on the accounting of the 1983 World Almanac, the current population in our world is over 4.7 billion. Of this enormous multitude that makes up our planet Earth, only 25% believe in the salvation of the soul through Jesus Christ. That fact verifys what Jesus meant when he said "The road to hell is wide and many will take it, but the path to heaven is narrow and few will walk in the light!" There are more than twice the amount of people that do not believe in God, than those that do (2.17 billion non-believers) and another billion and a half that believe in different faiths such as, Islam, Hinduism, Buddhism, Confucianism, Shintoisism, Taoism, Judaism, or Zoroastrianism. All the combined faith of the earth's population in God comes to just better than 50% of every man, woman or child, and to me that is really sad.

The records clearly indicate (Guiness Book of Records) that Mao was the largest mass murderer in world history, but that record is destined to be broken in the near future. Mao was responsible for more than 50 million deaths of his fellow countrymen, however Karl Marx and Friedrich Engels, composer and assistant deviate of the Communist Manifesto, are the two most likely candidates for new titleholders.

The Communist Manifesto (wonder if we derive "infestation" from the word?) has been construed by many experts as the most deceitful, most heinous and the most humanly damaging collection of lies that has ever been contrived by any entity. It is purely and simply an advocate of the spirit of anti-christ and represents, to those who follow its principles, eternal damnation of the living soul.

Humanity's biggest mistake (Communist Manifesto) was contrived by Karl Marx in 1847. To this day, seasoned with a little deception from Engel and Lenin, it infests and debases mankind with its erroneous principles.

Karl Marx saw a trend of the capitalist society and twisted its principle; he saw progressive advancement of industry and tried to suppress it and he saw new beginnings for mankind and tried to write an end to the hopes of the free world. Karl Marx's work did accomplish much, but nothing worthy of imitation. His most important claims to history are the alienation of millions from eternal life and the presumption of his title as the "keeper of the gates of hell!"

The basic principles of communism result from his 'artistry' and since its infestation, the free world will never be the same. His work can be directly attributed to mass slavery of millions, persecution of many more millions through secularism, millions of deaths attributed to mass starvations, terrorism, negativism and mass stagnations of the human mind.

God's intentions for His creations was to go out into the world, to multiply and produce and be thankful to the Lord God for their harvests. Under the principles of communism there is no worship or credit given to the Almighty, there is no production in positive modes and its attribution towards the starvation of entire nations was not close to the purposes of humanity.

Marx would have you believe that he had great compassion for the lowest rung of civilization - the proletariat (the poor or a worker dependent on selling their labor) and continually promotes rebellion among workers toward their leaders. In other words he entertains that the working class should lash out at the only source of income the worker has for the preservation of his family, otherwise known as "biting the hand that feeds you!" Compassionate is a term that definitely does not describe the lazy, good-for-nothing known as Karl Marx. In a nutshell communism is not only un-American, but......anti-Christ, un-Godly and synonomous with slavery and famine.

Let's examine the pornography of communism:

Marx: Communism is the doctrine of the condition. that liberates the poor and distributes all goods equally.

FACT: Communism results in regressive human actions, is the prime cause of famine through less than maximum production and promotes rebellion, chaos and secularism.

Marx: Communism eliminates over-production and by distributing the goods equally results in plenty for everyone.

FACT: Communism surely eliminates over-production because it promotes laziness and non-productivity. Marx fails to mention that the goods are not distributed equally...only to those who are capable of producing. Those incapable are not mentioned.

Questions Posed To Friedrich Engel, and the truth!

Question: What will be the influence of communist society on the family?

Engel: It will transform the relations between the sexes into a private matter in which society has NO OCCASION TO INTERVENE! Children are educated on a communal basis, and in this way removes the two bases of traditional marriage, the dependence, rooted in private property, of the woman on the man and of the children on the parents.

FACT: It transforms the family into an uncaring entity, incapable of compassion and the privacy Engel speaks of is non-existent. Just ask one of the many defectors from the Soviet Union. Educating children communally alienates the child from the ability to love or respect parents or anyone, promotes racism, (communal means: collective ownership (slavery) based on racial or cultural grouping (segregation) and removes any free will. NOTE: To convince me you had better come up with better analogies, - I kind of like free will, my present family ties of love and affection, the dependence my family has with God and His blessings to me for the preservation of my family, and the freedom to pursue the religion and occupation of choice....By the way, with one party running the show, who's watching the party leader!

What is the attitude of communism on existing nationalities?

Engel: The attitude remains the same!

FACT: What does that mean? Does it remain to separate the different nationalities (description of communal) or could it refer to one of your friend Mark's idea of removing private property when he suggested the confiscation of all private property of immigrants and those that rebel against the majority? If he were alive, I would also ask him about where they place the

Jewish and Christians in the rung of the Soviet Union Ladder!

What is the attitude to existing religion?

Engel: No change!

FACT: Hah!!! Tell that to the persecuted in the Soviet bloc. Explain it to the thousands in Siberian concentration camps! Voice that opinion to the millions of souls that are lying in graves because of their preference to worship their God!

Communism is a festering evil in this world and proposes everything that God is against. They will bend your ear that when everyone gets their fair share, poverty is eliminated. One fallacy is that with communism everyone doesn't get their fair share. If you are lonely, poor or disheartened by your shortcomings in life – don't fret or give in to social communistic ways. Where God reigns supreme, therein will lie hope, love and kindness. You have the free will to go out and do something with your life in America. That freedom is non-existent in the Soviet Union. Cherish the moments you can spend with your children because if communism takes over this country you won't have that opportunity. Go outside and breathe the fresh air and thank God for it. With communism all the air is polluted. Thank God for the freedoms of choice because those liberties are being threatened by the day, and even the very minutes of the day.

The trouble with many Americans is that they take the blessings of freedom too lightly. Isn't it a fact that the things we appreciate most are the things that we have lost! We must appreciate what we have now and fight for the right to retain them in the future.

God doesn't give good things to those who wait lazily. He bestows the greatest treasures on those who ask for them and praise Him for their deliverance. Riches are not defined as material wealth that will rot in time. The riches I speak of can only be attained by the acceptance of the Lord Jesus Christ into your heart. The Communists will promise you an existence based on erroneous hopes and inaccurate forecasts. Christ offers you an eternity of peace and serenity if you accept His plan and follow its principles.

If it's communism you desire, go get it. In fact I'll see to it that your passage is prepaid on the next banana boat heading east. But if it is peace you are desiring, forget this nonsense called communism. Tell the next liberal you come in contact with to remove his clammy carcass to the center of hell and that you want no part of his impending destination, nor his idiocy of logic. He'll get the message that the garbage he proposes is not only unwelcome, but the object of scorn to those who love freedom everywhere. COMMUNISM DOES NOT WORK!

The Communist Man(infestation) not only misrepresents the meaning of human decency, it totally insults the presence of wit. In addition to formulating despair among its devotees, Karl Marx even outlines their plan for its implementation, including the promotion of rebellion.

Karl Marx's 10 Easy Ways To Overthrow The Government!

The methods of success will differ in various countries. Nevertheless in the most advanced countries (America) the following will be found pretty generally applicable.

I. Abolition of all private property and the application of all rents on land is to be paid to a central fund for public purposes.

Question #1:	Do you have free elections to determine who oversees the central fund or where the money will be spent or what you do with those who dissent on giving up that which they own?

2. You must then assess a heavy progressive or graduated income tax!

Question #2:	Isn't that what the liberal Democrats are already suggesting, much to Reagan's displeasure? In other words raise all taxes, throw the people out of their homes and GIVE THEIR HOMES TO WHOM?

3. Abolition of all right of inheritance!

Question #3:	Does this mean that our children have NO RIGHT to the possessions we attain in our lifetime of toil? How Swift!

4. You confiscate all property now owned by immigrants and rebels!

Question #4:	Which COMMIE determines who the rebels are?

American heritage is founded by immigrants so who determines which ones we begin with?

5. Centralize all credit in the hands of the State by means of a national bank with State Capital and an exclusive monoply!

Question #5: Aren't we moving closer to that procedure with the new limitations on banks...many going bankrupt as a result? Wonder whatever happened to the confidentiality of bank accounts?

6. Centralization of the means of communication and transport in the hands of the State!

Question #6: Who will determine who rides, who walks and WHO TALKS?

7. Extension of factories and instruments of production owned by the State, the bringing into cultivation of waste lands, and the improvement of the soil generally in accordance with a common plan!

Question #7: Will the outcome bring American production on a level with the productivity and agriculture in the Soviet Union? If so, NO THANKS FOR NOTHING!

8. Equal liability of ALL to labor! Establishment of Industrial armies, specially for agriculture!

Question #8: You say ALL are to labor, do you propose a retirement age or shall we endure to the end? If I am disabled, do you take me out and bury me alive, or do you shoot me first?

9. You combine agriculture with manufacturing industries. There will be a gradual distinction between town and country, by a more equitable distribution of population over the country!

Question #9: How do we combine agriculture and manufacturing? Is it sort of a highly productive GREENHOUSE that we produce the vegetables along side of new machinery? Who will determine which race and culture of people move to Oregon and which move to Florida? What do you suggest? Do you propose that we blow up the cities to make it all country with no distinction?

10. "Free" education for all children in public schools. Abolition of children's factory labor in its present form. Combination of education with industrial production, etc., etc.

Question #10: Whatever you mean by ETC., ETC. suggests to me that I shouldn't ask? Who will determine the course of study my children will learn? If he is a little slower than the next child, will he get special tutoring? Who will determine when my child is ready for the factories? Will he have the chance for EQUAL OPPORTUNITY if he is not the same race, or does not share the same religious belief as the Party Leader? The reason I ask this of your "LOWNESS", is due to the PRACTICE PRESENTLY EXISTING IN THE SOVIET UNION as well as in all countries under communist rule which contradicts every aspect of your ridiculous manifesto!

According to Mr. Karl "SATAN" Marx, in the course of this development, all class distinction will just disappear, all production will have been concentrated in the HANDS (Whose?) of a vast association of the whole nation and the public power will lose its political character.

Isn't that just a fine proposal? All class distinction will disappear just as it has in the SOVIET UNION! All production will be concentrated into the hands of a vast association of the whole nation. Who, but the precious few, will determine the capability of the (HANDS) in charge? Notice the inference to "THE PUBLIC POWER WILL LOSE" and you can stop right there! I am sick to my stomach! I have come to one conclusion in researching Marxism ideology. IT STINKS!

Is this "THE" government real Americans desire? I think not! I want to be able to exercise my brain power and give my children that same opportunity. If I want to move my family to Oregon, Florida or even the North Pole, I want to be able to make that decision without asking some "COMRADE!" If I want to take time out in my day's labor and give thanks to Almighty God for His blessings to me, I DO NOT WANT TO DO SO IN A CLOSET for fear that SOME COMRADE WILL EXPOSE ME to some General Secretary Chairman, whom I had no say in getting appointed! What I want, what I desire and WHAT I DEMAND is FREEDOM! For that liberty I am prepared to fight to the death for its preservation.

CHAPTER TWELVE

Decline Of American Integrity!

And when ye see Jerusalem compassed (surrounded) with armies, then know that the desolation thereof is nigh."
LUKE 21:20

America's earliest patriots would be rolling over in their graves if they were to see the present allegiance many so-called "Americans have for the Stars and Stripes." Even a quick glance at society tells you that we have been suffering from lost nerve and a weakening in our once prideful, once powerful backbone.

The fault lies not with our present Administration; the bloodletting is the result of a vicious conspiracy and comes from within our very boundaries. Some of the blame falls directly back on our own neglecting shoulders for our failure to exercise caution with the power of the vote. We have allowed communist sympathizers and outright socialists to dictate our internal affairs and foreign policies for more than two decades now. All this while many unconcerned citizens have clung to their false security blankets of peace at all cost. We've simply been passing the buck.

Because of our mass failure to exercise the proper insight to the future, our foreign allies are now viewing America with extreme distaste. We have allowed the wealthy industrialists a free hand in determining our foreign affairs (see Trilateral Commission at the end of chapter fourteen) and in so doing, given up our precious sovereignty for the greedy interests of the rich and powerful people who really govern this Country.

What we have failed to recognize is that war has always been necessary for the preservation of freedom. Without this acknowledgment, we are only slaves under the whip of a dictatorship...one that is so heartless that they have blatantly removed America's last outpost of hope from society...GOD! The more we view our changing world the more we understand that the real cause of this regression is due to our placing unwarranted faith in these illustrious, liberally minded pacifists. The controllers of this Country are not just found in the White House, in Congress, in the Senate or in the House of Representatives; the real "godfathers" of this nation sit on their golden thrones in places like Manhattan and in Hyannisport. They pull their strings and manipulate many of the very ones our votes have put in office. They control what you do, when you'll do it and how it shall be done. They set the price structure, they control the liberal elements and dictate both the internal domestic policies as well as most of the world economy. Because they control the production and distribution of food...they have the people under their thumb. By controlling the world's energy supplies, they dictate foreign policy with allied nations and because they control the monetary system, their objectives shall be attained.

ONE WORLD GOVERNMENT IS HERE!

The national media and most of the books have been rewritten in favor of their philosophy and theories and it's all just the begining of their selfish conspiracy to overthrow the basic principles of conservatism in America. The treasured standards of faith and allegiance have been shelved in favor of their social reform programs aimed at desensitizing the nation's life's blood. Because they have control of what goes in the national newspapers and magazines, they are reaching their objectives by misinformation and outright deceit.

These rich and powerful profligates despise the very ground Ronald Reagan walks on and will spare no avenues of untruths to insure that he will not be reelected this Fall. Reagan is one that has not given in to their pressures and because he hasn't...he's their prime target. You'll never hear anything good about Ronald Reagan from the national media; newspapers, the national networks or radio. Why is this you ask? The reason is that they control every facet of the national media from your network newscasts to the smallest radio station. They have been brainwashing the American people into believing that we must not be involved in war at any cost. Because they have rewritten the text books; they also control attitudes of the young new lions who are the future world puppets.

These same outlets will paint Ronald Reagan as a "monger of war" and discloud the real truths with praise for Mondale; a man who propagates "free choice in mass murder" (abortion), and that our GOD should not be allowed to be spoken to in our public school systems. Anyone who opposes their dictatorship is removed in favor of those that will. We may be able to place Reagan back in the presidency, but with "yes men" like Thomas "Tip" O'Neil attacking Reagan's every policy...they'll win out in the end. It's not only O'Neil; he's only protecting his own skin, but ask yourself why these liberals don't want America defending themselves against the spread of communism in the world. They know of the plan to convert American allegiance to one of global awareness, in lieu of sole American patriotism. They know it, I know it and now you know it. What can the American people do about it? Well, for one thing we can remain firm in our committment to GOD and Country and vote for GOD's people in the next election...foregoing any particular party affiliation. This can help greatly, but unfortunately most of this nation is made up of people who will believe their vicious lies about the true intentions of Ronald Reagan. If you want real information turn on your religious channels and believe in people who will give you real answers.

Yes, on a scale of 1-10 our nation's intestinal fortitude teeters on one and a half and is dipping. Whether this patriotic indicator is raised or lowered further, depends on how the American people will vote this November. Whatever pathway we choose we must understand that there is no avoiding a World War III...we can only stall the inevitable confrontation but the good news of it all is that most of the believers won't be here on Earth at the time of the worst war in history (see chapters twenty & twenty-one).

Americans have been relegated to accept and believe in anything the national media throws at them. The world is continually looking for a peace that can never be solidified through human achievement. For the most part, the liberal elements in America are spineless cowards who would rather "switch than fight" for liberty. As long as real Americans allow them their protests against well intended policy...they shall gain on their objectives of world subjugation to socialism. Therefore we should not complain when many of our grandchildren are speaking fluent Russian and calling us "comrade!"

WHEN IT ALL BEGAN!

Although the escalation of liberal protests began in the late fifties, the real damage manifested with the inception of the United Nations at the end of World War II. When America began associating directly with other nations through establishing interdependence, the downfall of proper allegiance followed accordingly.

The last two great American battles were won by the last remnant of true patriots in the 1940s. The great American warriors who gave up their liberty in those wars surely deserve better recognition than the present so-called Americans give today to our Country. We had won two great wars; neither started by American aggression, but both ended for the cause of righteousness. Since the formation of the

186

pro-communist United Nations, we have been misplacing the ideal goal of national sovereignty. We have surrendered to a global alliance who has never agreed with our motivations nor our policies of individual free enterprise. We stand back and have allowed this evil manifestation to organize on our very shores. They were allowed to mingle with our people and pollute the free will with evil doctrines of social welfare throughout the world.

I'm not saying that Americans shouldn't assist the nations less fortunate; I'm saying that this helping hand should be from our own free will and not by dictation. You must understand that socialism and communism are identical in meaning. Both forms of government are predicated on a dictatorship; both reduce the free will and spirit of the citizen to endure with full motivation. They both stagnate the American goal of capitalism.

Now, less than forty years after our last great feat of heroism on the battle fields of Western Europe and the South Pacific, we are witnessing a sickening occurrence in our Country. We have become the breeding ground of liberal thought and have thrown out our freedom while letting every communist inspired organization float freely throughout our communities.

The national media exaults the unrighteous and condemns those few with positive aspirations for the people. Because people hear it on the network television stations...they believe the lies and allegations. They attack our President with misinformation and degrade our GOD by omitting His importance in every area of society. GOD have mercy on the human race.

The following is a documented accounting of our liberal stance towards "peace at all cost!" It will give you an idea of how weak and uncaring we have become as a result of an allegiance to the devious attempt at one world global interdependence...the U.N.

On October 7, 1952, an American B-29 with a crew of eight vanished over Japanese territorial waters in the exact vicinity of the recent downing of a Korean civilian jetliner by the Soviets. The Russians later announced that the B-29 had flown over Yuri Island, in alleged "violations of Soviet frontiers" and was chased out over the sea. The U.S. believed the plane had been shot down and demanded reparations. The Soviets refused to pay and the matter was dropped by U.S. authorities.

Five weeks later, on November 13th, Soviet fighters shot down an American-made unarmed Swedish C-54 trainer over the Baltic Sea. Soviets authorities immediately denied the kill but admitted having "directed the aircraft away from Soviet frontier."

On March 10th, 1953, Communist Czechoslovakian jets shot down an American Thunderjet inside the U.S. occupied zone of West Germany. The U.S. warned the Czechs that "necessary countermeasures" would be taken if there were any repeats of such provocations!" A squadron of faster S-86 SabreJets was transferred from a U.S. base in England to Germany but there was no further incident. The matter was dropped by U.S. authorities.

Four days later that same week, a Soviet fighter fired on an American weather reconnaissance RB-50 Bomber off the Kamchatka coast in the same area where the Korean Airliner tragedy took place in September 1983. The American plane returned fire. Neither plane was hit.

On July 29, 1953, Soviet fighters shot down a U.S. Navy Neptune P-2V patrol plane 40 miles off the Siberian coast. American seaplanes rescued nine of the ten crew members and the other was presumed dead and never found. The Soviets claimed the plane had violated Russian air space and had fired first. The U.S. denied both claims and threatened to take the case before the "United Nations Security Council," but didn't, and the matter was eventually dropped by U.S. authorities.

Soviet fighters shot down an American RB-29 reconnaissance plane on November 7th, 1954, ten miles off the coast of the Kuriel Islands north of Japan. It crashed on the Japanese Island of Hokkaido. Both the U.S. and Soviets complained to each other about the incident. Senator William Knowland demanded that the U.S. break off diplomatic relations with the Soviets but nothing was done.

On June 22, 1955, Soviet fighters fired upon and damaged a U.S. Navy Neptune patrol plane over the Bering Straits between Alaska and Russia. The Soviets claimed the plane had been over their air space but offered to pay for half the damage inflicted on the aircraft. Nothing was ever paid.

On April 18, 1956, a U.S. Air Force RB-47 was shot down by Soviet fighters over the Kamchatka Penninsula in almost exactly the same location as the Korean Airline tragedy. All crewman on the Air Force plane were lost with no further accounting from the Soviets.

On September 10, 1956, a U.S. Air Force RB-50 was reported "lost" in a typhoon in the Sea of Japan. Some Air Force officers had believed the plane had been shot down by the Soviets but no investigation was ever made. The Soviets remained silent.

On June 27, 1958, an Air Force C-118 unarmed transport plane was shot down by Soviet fighters in Armenia after straying thirty miles into Soviet air space. The crewman survived. The U.S. expressed "regret" over the incident and the American flyers were released on July 7th.

On September 7, 1958, a U.S. C-30 reconnaissance plane crashed in Armenia 24 miles inside Soviet air space. The Soviets at first denied all knowledge of the incident (reminiscent of their handling of the Korean Airliner tragedy in its early stages), but later announced the plane had crashed and six crewman were dead. The Soviets denied having shot the plane down and made no mention of the eleven crewmen aboard. They have never been accounted for.

On November 7, 1958, a U.S. Plane was fired upon by Soviet fighters over the Baltic Sea but was not hit.

On May 1st, 1960, a Soviet missle downed a CIA U-2 Spy Plane piltoed by Lt. Francis Gary Powers deep inside the Soviet Union. Powers was convicted of espionage by a Soviet court but was later exchanged for the convicted spy Colonel Rudolph Abel.

On July 1, 1960, Soviet fighters shot down a U.S. Air Force RB-47 reconnaissance plane near the Kola Penninsula killing four crewmen. Nothing was done about the incident.

The Soviet Union will not hesitate to commit such crimes again...because they haven't been called on their other "acts of war." The way they see it is that America is weak and due to their overly liberal outlook for peace at all costs...they will never do anything to alter that stance...You know something...they're right!

The Soviets have interferred with numerous civilian airline flights over or near the Soviet Union. In at least one instance forcing an airliner to crash land inside Russia. Private aircraft flying to the Soviet Union must first land in

KOREAN AIRLINES
747

I have the Capitalists in sight. What do I do?
Shoot them! The US will do nothing!
USSR

Paris or Copenhagen to take on Soviet pilots for the trip inside Russia. There is one exception: American industrialist Armand Hammer's jet is allowed to fly directly into Moscow. Hammer is the communist's best friend in America because his father was the founder of the American Communist Party in the days of Lenin.

The State Department was instrumental in soft-pedaling the wanton killings of American airmen by Soviet fighters and time after time these incidents were finally dropped by the American government...quietly being swept under the rug.

Today, high flying satellites have taken over most spy, reconnaissance and weather missions formerly flown by U.S. aircraft. That is one reason that it was so preposterous that the Soviets could propose that the Korean Airliner was some kind of spy plane.

The temporary sanctions the United States placed on Soviet commercial airline traffic and the ineffective official outrage over the air-massacre of the 269 innocent passengers of the recent Korean Airliner can only be interpeted by the Kremlin as another "wrist-slapping," by the ever softening, ever retreating, ever accomodating, ever appeasing United States and its western allies.

It only concludes a sad state of affairs within our Country. It only contributes to the conclusion that the Soviets will not hesitate to commit such atrocities again.

(Source of information on Soviet aggression against American military planes supplied through the Christian Crusade Newspaper (November 1983 Issue) Billy James Hargis....much thanks..see chapter 17)

You must understand that the future problems facing America are indeed complex. Our patriotism appears to be past the point of reversal. There are no remaining, clear-cut human answers to the state of confusion that is our foreign relations. Because of this eminent fact, America is continually being left wide open for future communist aggression against our sovereignty and that of our allies abroad. Taking less than retaliatory actions against the Soviet Union has reinforced that Country's future aspirations and goals of subverting the entire free world with the evils of a dictatorship by the name of communism.

When we have a Country governed by wealthy profligates in search of one world global control by food, energy and a revised monetary system...you have set the stages for Biblical prophesy to become fulfilled. You have set the stages for one world government and a one world religious system which has no intentions of allowing our GOD His proper place of control.

The very next step Americans can expect is the announcement of the prophesied one world dictator. Biblical prophesy accurately assesses this man as the most cruel and vicious dictator of all that have come before. He shall bring the entire world to the precipice of total devastation (see chapters 20,21).   Do not look forward to any upsurge in the economy or any peaceful co-existence with the Soviet Union...it simply will not take place now...or in the immediate future...it's not designed that way and will not happen.

The "beast" known in the Bible as the antiChrist has long been in training in the eastern sector of the world and as you continue to see the economic collapse of this world...know that world catastrophes will continue to keep pace, ultimately bringing on this new world leader. This "beast" will come in with all the answers to all the world's problems; with great flatteries for many nations and by promoting world peace, he will destroy man in the process. He will turn the world against everything that is right and will deceive the entire globe into believing that Christianity is the real enemy of the world citizens .

Folks, this isn't a faerie tale that will all go away when you awaken from your slumber! It is a very real and vicious conspiracy, long in the planning and at the point of irreversibility. America is the only Country remaining in the world where GOD's message can still be preached without interruption. We represent the last outpost as a base in which to get the gospel to people throughout the world as a testimony to all nations...We are there, folks, and unless you can have this understanding...you may become one of the many who the Bible prophesied will be forever lost by deceit.

If you don't get up to bat now...the games going to be called on account of the most darkest darkness that will ever come over the world. God is commissioning His people to get this message out and you must not take it lightly. If you haven't accepted the Lord Jesus Christ as your personal Savior...it's high time you make your decision of which side of the fence you plan to be on.

All the really wise men of this age agree conclusively that the world is at the prophesied crossroads; a period of time that the Bible calls the "end times!" Never before in the history of humanity have personal preferences been more important...You will either accept Jesus Christ as the world's only answer of salvation...or, continue to accept the ways of mankind and be eternally lost in a wave of deception. Don't take my word for it...talk to your pastor (if you attend a Bible believing church) or call the prayer partners at Trinity Broadcasting Network in California, Toll Free 1-800-421-2221. They,too,won't mislead you!

AMERICA: Losing Our Grip On Reality!

Our national division is a cause for the greatest of alarm. Our once staunch foreign allies have swiftly been losing their confidence in our ability of committment for world freedom. We have continually been shirking our responsibility of the global peacekeeper and this fault widens in juxtaposition with the escalation of every liberal thought. We have too many pokers in the fire; some of the more inefficient must be withdrawn if liberty is to be given a chance to survive...or at least prolong and maintain a proper restraint against communism. America is being pressed by socialists to negotiate in good faith with demonic influence and it should have never even been asked for. It should never occur!

Recently France, Italy and Jordan have voiced their concern that the Soviet Union should be included in the Middle East situation. Can you believe the naivete of these nations? The Soviet Union and their communist bloc allies have been the root of the problem in the area since I don't know when, but now three rather naive countries want them to become involved!!! The Russians are the cog in the wheel of progress and the antagonizing promoter of terrorism in Lebanon (through their support of Syria) and these three countries now want them to become involved.

Since long before 1945, the Soviet Union has been the main supplier of technology to terrorist countries. They have pushed their evil plans on anyone that will listen and by direct and indirect force, they have participated in every terrorist bombing in the Middle East for the past thirty-years. They're involved all-right..up to their ears. If the Soviets really wanted to help...they'd keep their filthy nose out of the entire area and allow the peacekeeping of those countries to humanitarian effort.

King Hussein of Jordan indicated that Russia should be included in any effort to bring "peace" to the Middle East, "or else they will make their presence felt in the region!" This same king, who has been regarded in the past by the U.S. as friendly to the American cause, recently rejected President Reagan's proposal to fund a special contingent of approximately 8,000 Jordanian troops as a strike force in time of need. We offered to fund and train this operation...it was turned down...why? He explained that Jordan has been beefing up their own forces for any possible use in aiding other middle eastern countries if requested. You have to wonder how much assistance Israel would receive from Jordan when needed? I doubt that it would be available to the Jews!

The United States has been working with both Egypt and Jordan for a lasting peace in the Middle East, but until such time as these nations begin recognizing the State of Israel...nothing will be enhanced in this relationship. Don't count on these two nations ever accepting Israel...so, don't count on any lasting alliance to the United States from either Egypt or Jordan. If America makes any deal with these countries without their recognizing GOD's Country of Israel...look out and for believers...look UP, because Jesus will be calling!

The Arab Nations have publicly chastised Egypt for the treaty they signed in good faith with Israel. Their radical and Soviet inspired censorship of Egypt clearly indicates the Russian involvement in both policy and devious intentions which will lead to their future invasion of Israel in fulfillment of Biblical prophesy.

Our pullout from Lebanon was just another assurance to the Soviet Union and our allies that our future committment for the preservation of peace is non-existent. President Reagan was correct in his assessment on America's direct involvement in the crises. Again the liberal element in our Country forced our withdrawal. Now liberals like the Speaker of the House, "Tip" O'Neil, have tried to reverse the actual blame for this loss of integrity to our President, when all the time it was from the sources that keep him in the House...the liberal anarchy in their ivory towers of Manhattan. Sorry "Tip,"...real Americans aren't buying your propaganda!

Can you get the drift on America's socialist movement? Everytime we commit our armed forces to a cause of liberation...we are being backed off by liberal pressure.

We could have won both the Korean War and Vietnam in a matter of months were it not for this element of bureaucratic red-tape. If we would have given the reigns to the armed services and not allowed the wealthy in this country the opportunity to control the flow....Korea would have ended two years earlier and we would have boxed up North Vietnam's harbors and supply routes in no real time at all. The war would have been over quickly with no supply routes and 50,000 American boys would have been saved. I say if you are going to involve us in a war...play to win and leave the fighting to the military advisors...not to some rich godfather in New York who has the motivations of greed...and could care less for the bodies he leaves behind!

The Soviet Union is indeed involved up to their necks in the problems of the Middle East. Syria, Iran, South Yemen and Libya all have close ties to their communist cause and receive terrorist support directly from Moscow. All of these countries detest the presence of Israel and the United States, but they are not alone in their hatred. Although Italy and France have been considered American allies for years, they have recently been voicing stronger opposition to American involvement in many of the areas of the world. Why? Could it be that those Countries have their own communist elements taking over? Maybe!

ROME: The Holy City Devaluated!

Premier Bettino Craxi, the Socialist Head of State, recently signed a revised edition of the 1929 Concordat with the Vatican. According to Pope John Paul II, it had a significant importance between the church and the state. The new treaty stipulates that Roman Catholicism is no longer the official state religion and changes the status of Rome from "a sacred city" to a "city of particular significance" to Roman Catholics worldwide.

Italian public schools will still give religious instructions but NOW, only if parents request it for their children. Previously, Italians who did not want the instruction had to ask for an exemption. The Pope said he considers the pact "of significant importance as a judicial base for peaceful bilateral relations."

Fr. Lawrence Farrelly, Pastor of Saint Viator Catholic Church in Las Vegas, has acknowledged this change as indeed most signicant in that it will relieve the Vatican of certain political responsibilities it had assumed in the past. Monsignor Thomas Meger of the Chancery Office in Reno, Nevada, views the alteration as a very positive move. "It will free the Pope from the business of the state to concentrate on more humane matters facing the world," explains the Monsignor, "The Pope would not have signed anything that would adversely affect the church!"

I trust the sources I contacted on the matter and sincerely hope they are not being naive to what this transformation is all about. Our world is changing rapidly and any devaluation of power taken away from men of GOD is indeed significant, but possibly not in the manner the church admits to. I would feel much more at ease if the power in this world were left to men of GOD, rather than in its present control. In Revelation 17:9, it is explained that this anti-Christ will rise to power from the city of seven hills...anyway you slice it...that's ROME, and any positive or negative developement in that region has my utmost attention.

Understand the wording of the "revised Corcordat!" The treaty removes Roman Catholicism as the official state religion! It marks the END of the status of Rome as "THE SACRED

CITY!" The word <u>SACRED</u> means "holy" or SET APART for the worship of GOD! You may say that I am making a play on mere words or that the alteration means nothing at all...but what would be any advantage of lowering any standards of power or reversing 55-year-old church guidelines to compensate for a changing heart of mankind? Under the 1929 Lateran Concordat, marriages were indissolvable and compulsory religious education was "the basis and crowning element of public education." I view any change towards liberal practice, however slight it may seem, with keen acknowledgement.

Of late, terrorist activity in Italy has been escalating. We can acknowledge the attempt on Pope John Paul's life as originating within the confines of the Soviet Union...and more accurately...Moscow.

It has been assumed that Soviet KGB hit men recently assassinated the United Arab Republic's Emirates...Ambassador Khalifa Ahmed Aziz Al-mubarak. Al-mubarak, 36, was the Ambassador to France...the Arab nations did nothing about the incident leading to the belief that they knew of the plot ahead of time. Two days earlier, in France, "unidentified gunmen" murdered exiled Iranian General Gholam Ali Oveissi. This escalation of international violence and terrorism has its epicenter in the land of satan...Russia...the only place qualified for such a formal education is located at Balashika in Moscow. Coincidence? There's no doubt that it isn't!

In the remaining years of humanity, this terrorism will not only be limited to the Middle Eastern countries and those of the Mediterranean...they will branch out to the United States. We already know that the Soviets don't care that Americans have a President who truly cares...added caution should be exercised to protect this man of GOD. We don't want to give the liberals in this Country something to shout about!

Americans got a little taste of terrorism when the Ayatollah Ruholla Khomeini had our Embassy attacked by so-called "students." They were no more students than I'm the reincarnated Shah of Persia, but we did get a small taste of Iran's overt hatred for the United States and capitalism. We also saw what a country would do with a fanatic in control...Chernenko and Khomeini are related in satan worship and you can count on their allegiance against the U.S. and the State of Israel in the very near future.

Israel is presently encompassed by a hostile enemy on all borders and that brings to mind a scriptural warning from Our Lord Jesus Christ:

> "And when ye see Jerusalem compassed with armies, than know that the desolation thereof is nigh."   JESUS CHRIST Luke 21:20

If you care to do so, you'll have no problem tying it all together in a neat package. With the knowledge that the United States has lost immense international integrity (all attributed to the liberal element), Syria, Iran, South Yemen and the Soviet Union are presently on the border of Israel and threaten its desolation at this very moment. Lebanon, Jordan and Egypt have chosen to remain neutral and will offer absolutely no assistance when the invasion takes place. The PLO (Palestine Liberation Organization) and their leader Yassir Arafat await the further instructions from Moscow...their beloved partner in terrorism. Not a nice entanglement, but it surely represents a cause for foreign intrigue. It is a story with a predetermined conclusion and is totally chronicaléd in the Word of GOD...the Bible. The pending finish to the saga will take place by GOD's eternal will...all in His way and all left to HIS patience...His time will come and when it does it would be adviseable to acknowledge the winning side of the ledger ahead of time,and save the only thing you have worthy of treasuring....that, my brother and sister in Christ, is your eternal soul!

All the great world philosophers, all the learned scientists and all the intellectual minds of this generation with their carefully laid plans for the future of humanity will all go awry in the end. Their combined wit wouldn't make up the common sense of one baby Christian. Men so brilliant in the strategy of war; but ever so dense in the ways of GOD. The Bible says that these great humanists will have eyes, but fail to see. They will have ears and fail to listen.

There is no question that these INTERNATIONAL conspiracies are aimed at the destruction of GOD's Holy Country, and more specifically...Jerusalem.

The United States' committment to the preservation of GOD's Holy Land must be our nation's prime concern as we move into Planet Earth's final hoorah! Ronald Reagan understands the significance...Just so, America must also!

CHAPTER THIRTEEN

"Planet Earth's Final Alternative"
World Evangelizing a must. . .

"Your Heavenly Father knows what you need. Set your
hearts on His Kingdom first, and on His righteousness,
and all these things will be given to you as well."
(Matthew 6:33)

Regardless of wars and rumors of war, the glimmer of hope for world revival still flickers. Realistic dreams of peace among nations is not a fantasy of utopian expectation and mankind can reverse his impending ominous inclinations. Recognizing the obvious existence of our perplexities will enable us to seek out real solutions, but it is necessary that we follow certain guidelines if our search is to be considered fruitful. We must agree that the science of man in himself is not adequately equipped with the intellect to cope with the needs of humanity. As that is evident by past performance we can readily assume that the common denominators for world revival should not be left in the incompetent care of mortals. The Lord GOD Almighty endures as this planet's final alternative.

As it is a factual statistic that there are over one billion men, women and children that accept Jesus Christ as their saviour, it remains eminent that over 78 percent of the world does not. It is the hopeful task of these Christians to share the wealth with ones less fortunate people and bring them into the light. The one dubious problem we face in this movement is our own spiritual faith in Christ. Jesus said that we should not judge others. That "we should get the board out of our own eye before we should be worrying about the splinter in our neighbors!" How strongly do you believe in Christ? You cannot lead others into the light if you are still in the darkness yourself! This represents our stumbling block - a hurdle we must overcome with our reliance on the mighty

198

shoulders of GOD. I realize that it is difficult for any real Christian to understand the logic of those who do not believe in Jesus, but to successfully convert others it is the overt example we must establish. We must exhibit the existence of Jesus through our own actions. How we show our love for our neighbor will determine the ratio of souls that are ultimately saved.

To save the soul of another, you must first convince them that their lives will change for the better when they accept Jesus into their heart. You must inform them of your experience both with and without His saving graces. It is an impossibility for anyone to really know and believe in Jesus and at the same time look upon his neighbor without love and compassion for his needs.

Once you have acknowledged Jesus as Lord, He takes over your entire being, He brings love where there was hatred, compassion where there was denial and understanding where there was doubt. If you are experiencing financial difficulties, He will provide solutions and bring you subsistence when it would otherwise seem impossible. You see, with GOD anything is possible, but you must have faith in Him. I realize that to the non-believer, these are only words but what do you really have to lose in trying? I can say in all earnestness what you will lose if you hear the 'good news' and don't respond. You'll lose the eternal life that is promised to those who trust in GOD, you'll lose your desire for living and those things that you may cherish will be taken away. That's not a threatening statement, it's a promise from GOD. Jesus said, "If you love your life and cherish it, you will lose it!"

Trusting in GOD and following His demands cannot help but change your life forever. GOD's commandments (Chapter Six) represent His covenant with those that will keep them sacred. Think about it! Would the world be at war if His commandments were followed? Would man detest and hate his neighbor if both were walking the path He has set for our lives? If you are honest with yourself you know the answer already!

Did we have the problems with our youth when we had public school prayer? We may have had our crosses to bear, but it was never as burdensome as it proposes today. GOD didn't say that if we accept Jesus we would no longer have problems. He said if we accept Him, He would give us the solutions to these problems and take care of our tomorrows.

The intelligence in the world today is vastly advanced from what it was a hundred years ago, but in the same respect man is not closer in the knowledge of truth.

Man's accomplishments for the progression and preservation of the human race have taken on a most sinister trait. The brilliant minds that split the atom and that developed nuclear weaponry were deficient of common sense and lacked the proper insight for its potential future dangers to world peace.

Americans are not cognizant of the real dangers these nuclear weapons will cause the world nor are they able to perceive the reality that 'every form of weaponry ever devised in the history of warfare has ultimately been utilized!' All the destructive force used in World War II totalled but three megatons of TNT (3 million tons), and that included the deployment and use of the two atomic bombs on Nagasaki and Hiroshima. Today the aggregate total of the world's nuclear arsenals surpass that figure five thousand times over. The firepower of just one nuclear submarine is twice the destructive force used during the six years of World War II. One submarine! In the United States we have 19 such subs and 15 others with greater expectations of devastation. There are 16,000 megatons currently available for use in the world. Is this knowledge cause for alarm? You better believe it!

It proves beyond a shadow of a doubt that world leadership is not in control. The future of America and the world is in the hands of man, when it should be left to GOD! Man will not diffuse this eminent threat to world survival until it will be past that point of irreversability. Nuclear freeze is not the answer to security and it is certainly not advisable to limit our production without a similar accord with the Soviets. We have already established the fact that the Soviet Union cannot be trusted, so you may say, "what are the alternatives?" Well, we could show the Soviets our good intentions by disassembling our nuclear strength in the hopes that they would assume a like posture, but realistically that plan would open the door for aggressive nuclear blackmail. We could launch a massive thermonuclear attack on the Soviet Union (hoping to catch them by surprise) wiping out humanity in so doing, or we can enlist the assistance of the one hope we have left...GOD Almighty!

If we choose the latter alternative, we must devise a way to get this message to the atheists of the Soviet Union. They are as convinced that GOD doesn't exist as we are that He most certainly does. Because of these totally adverse beliefs it represents a human impossibility. What it comes down to is faith and prayer. Faith in GOD's intentions with the hopes that through His divine intercession He would convert the beliefs of our chief world adversary into a trust that can only be experienced when you truly know Him. And trust in GOD that that is indeed His ultimate plan for the preservation of His creation. As mankind is long passed that point of reason, we have no other practical alternative but GOD! It is the only logical reality!

The atheist says that the Christian's belief in God is blinding. Rephrased in meaning, they are absolutely accurate in their contention. A real Christian KNOWS that he will find the true light if he blinds out the evil influence in his life. A real Christian also realizes that perfect physical vision does not alter the fact that those who do not place their trust in GOD Almighty are walking in the deepest form of darkness that could ever be experienced. The atheist is the one that is blind.

As God grants knowledge and insight to those who love Him, let's look closely at the current trends the world has adopted. Let us not be that naive to expect our GOD to work miracles with Soviet ideology or convert the world's 2.4 billion non-believers just because we have a Christian desire for peaceful utopia. GOD's plan for this world is unchanging and justified. His designs are pure and simple and He does not compromise on His word. GOD has given man a covenant that, if followed, will result in eternal fellowship...if broken it will certainly cause many unhappy endings and horror.

When GOD came to Earth in the form of a mortal (Jesus), He witnessed all temptations of the human will. He knows that man is sinful and because of His love for humanity He gave up the life of His innocent Son so that we would not only be forgiven for our iniquities, but share in His promise for eternal life. Unless we understand this surety, there exists no hope for that divine fellowship.

As you can see the destiny of humanity is contingent on GOD's demands. You can either accept His principles and live, or denounce them and die! What is life and death? Life to the atheist is all materially minded. Your heaven and hell are right here on earth according to their narrow mind and when you die you just cease to exist! If that were the case, GOD would have said so...but He didn't!

<u>Who do you choose to believe</u>? Do you believe the unsubstantiated views of the atheist that represent all that is evil, all that is negative and of those that dwell on the aspects of Satanic culture? Or are you to believe in the power of the living GOD, in His many blessings, in the truth and wisdom he generates and the positive expectations you will surely receive if you believe? Hard decision - huh?

To GOD, life in meaning is not of this world. Life is a spiritual existence that transcends death and transposes the soul to an infinite splendor. Death is not the end of life, but the beginning of a new and glorious fellowship with the Creator. Jesus (GOD) said that He is the Messiah, He is the resurrection and He is the bread of life! If you believe in Him and obey Him, you will receive this eternal life! Don't be mislead by the deception that is Satan.

When you accept Jesus into your life you become whole, blessed with the power of the Holy Spirit. As long as you have Jesus within your being, none of Satan's influence can have effect on your soul. Your earthly deeds will be refined because you will acknowledge no other way. As long as you endure in the Lord, He will endure with you and make your seed multiply to the ends of the earth. When you stumble or falter along the path of life, you will be able to recover because you will be walking in the Light. If you have the blessings of Almighty GOD, you will need nothing else!

As Christians, we must try to be like Jesus each day of our life. You must transfer your effervescence to everyone you meet, regardless of how they will treat you. When you give love and compassion to your fellow man, you are being like Jesus! When you show understanding to others, you are being like Jesus! When you show mercy, kindness and strive for truth, you are indeed like Jesus and will be rewarded for these deeds.

Although this Earth was made by GOD Almighty it is also representative of the devil's playground. GOD did not intend it that way when He created the heavens and the earth, but Adam and Eve chose that destiny by trusting Satan and denying GOD's wishes. Since that time GOD has shown man His Wrath for denying His will. GOD saw the evil that existed in the days of Noah and destroyed the earth with a great flood. He saw man's evil in the days of Nimrod and destroyed the Tower of Babel, scattering the people to many lands with different tongues. GOD saw the evil in Sodom and Gomorrah and destroyed the cities and all that remained within. The Babylonian Empire, the Medio-Persian, the Greek and the Roman Empire all met with similar fates because of satanic idol worship and corruption. What makes man feel that the same destiny will not befall our current generation?

The Bible is a pure testimony to the fact that history repeats itself at every interval when the deeds of mankind have regressed to despicable levels. The parable of the fig tree seems to indicate that that time is overdue. The integrity of the world is today at its lowest level since the fall of the Roman Empire. Most men no longer look to God for guidance and to many He is non-existent. Homosexuals are actually being accepted by a vast majority; mass murder of millions (abortion) is being condoned and promoted by our own legislature and in many factions of the church; GOD has been banned from the public schools; astrology and witchcraft are in vogue and practiced by multitudes; drug and alcohol abuses are at epidemic stages; rape and other sexual deviations are limited only to the twisted perversions of the mind and un-Godly; anti-Christian organizations are allowed to thrive in our communities. If that isn't an exact Biblical description of the 'end times' mentioned by the prophets of God, I don't know what is!

The only chance the world has left is also an avenue traveled by few. Those who have knowledge of the scriptures have cause to be ECSTATIC! The intensity of spreading the Gospel throughout the world has increased and many are being brought into the Light, but these figures are being dwarfed by the many who still deny the truth. GOD said that it would happen this way and the human race is right on course.

GOD's Prophets were not limited to the Bible. There are many GOD-fearing Prophets of our present generation that are unrelenting in their quest at spreading the "good news of the Kingdom." Men like Paul Crouch, Pat Robinson, Billy Graham Billy James Hargis, Oral Roberts, Jimmy Swaggart, Hal Lindsey and many thousands of others, less known but equally important, are contributing greatly to evangelizing the millions that come to Christ each year. It's just not enough to save the world!

Humanity is progressing at a fever-pitch towards devastation. The unfortunate part of this fact is that man will not recognize the dilemma. "This 'GOOD NEWS' of the Kingdom will be proclaimed to the whole world as a witness to all nations. And then the end will come!" (Matthew 24:14)

If you have eyes, ears and logic, you will understand that this parable from the mouth of GOD, is happening at the very moment you read this book. No other time is more appropriate than the present for its reality.

We who know and love God also realize that He is fair and just. He is our Heavenly Father and cares greatly for this world and all its people, but if history is to tell us just one thing other than its constant repetition of events, it would have to be the fact that every world disaster has had many warning signs.

The current warning sign GOD is giving us is the Bible and its prophesy, but there are others. He gave us wisdom to decipher good from evil and the ability to know the difference. The unwise say the world situation is a passing trend. They will say, "History has always had wars and always will." In America they are saying, "Who cares what happens in the Middle East so long as they keep the war there." While still others are saying as Jesus prophesized they would, "The end of the world isn't coming. Humanity is basically 'reasonable' and we will get by, - we always have!" Well I say this! Humanity is anything but reasonable. Man's ideas today are barbaric and most all technology is being used towards negative expectation. The crisis in the Middle East is indeed a major problem for both the United States and the world. The

GO YE INTO ALL THE WORLD, AND PREACH
THE GOSPEL TO EVERY CREATURE. HE THAT
BELIEVETH AND IS BAPTISED SHALL BE SAVED;
BUT HE THAT BELIEVETH NOT SHALL BE DAMNED.

MARK 16:15,16

end time stages are set in exactly the location the Bible has prophesied, with the exact predicted cast of characters. Anyone that even hints that God is only a figment of man's imagery or that the parable of the fig tree is coincidence is obviously not operating on all cylinders.

God is the only reasonable solution but man opts to go it alone. We are at a precipice of world confrontation with many unholy men at the helm. Man has not shown any inclination to seek the answers that only GOD has. Because of this lack of proper dependence, we will find no reasonable solution. Because of this gross neglect of human standards, the world will soon experience a horror like nothing else that has ever been before. And we deserve what will come about!

At the beginning of this chapter I mentioned that the world has only a glimmer of hope for reversing that devastation we surely face, but that expectation of desire has only one alternative. There are only a little better than one in five that trust Jesus Christ as their Saviour, and although that figure would indicate over one billion the ratio is far too low. There are many potentially good people that still walk in darkness and must be brought into the light. Could this one in five also be indicative of the parable that mentions that "the gateway to hell is wide and many will follow it to their destruction?"

Other indicators of the 'end times,' also prophesied by GOD, are the numerous earthquakes that are occuring worldwide. In Mark 13:8 Jesus said, "For nation will fight against nation, and kingdom against kingdom. There will be 'earthquakes here and there' and there will be famines. This is the beginning of the birth pangs!"

"Earthquakes here and there" can easily be construed as 'everywhere' and I would feel safe in so stating. Earthquakes are considered by most as 'an act of GOD' and they occur as a result of a release of stress and strain from within the earth's crust. In the year ending on December 31st, 1983, according to Carl von Hake, a geophysicist from the National Geophysical Data Center in Boulder, Colorado, there were more than 70 major (significant) earthquakes in the world. A significant earthquake is considered one that surpasses 6 on the Richter Scale, but is generally 6.5 or greater. Hake commented that there is constant action going on all the time and possibly more than a million smaller quakes occurred last year. Some of the more devastating quakes are listed here.

In the United States, on May 2nd, 1983 in the town of Coalinga (southeast of Fresno in Central California) a quake registering 6.7 on the Richter Scale left 500 homeless, caused $31 million in damage and injured 45 people. On July 12th in Valdez, Alaska a 6.4; in Challis, Oregon on October 28, a mammoth quake registering 7.3 caused considerable damage including 2 deaths; and in Hilo, Hawaii a while later a 6.6 shook the Island causing some damage.

On the world front, more than 1,350 people lost their lives in Erzurum and Kars, Turkey, when an earthquake of 6.9 demolished more than 50 small villages leaving 25,000 homeless on October 30th. In Damavand-Amol, Iran, on March 25, 30 were killed and the shock was felt in Tehran, considerable damage with many homeless. Two hundred and fifty people were killed on March 31st in Popayan, Colombia, with a 6.7 quake and on May 26th a 7.7, centered off the coast of Akita, Japan, killed 104, causing extensive devastation to dwellings, roads and vessels as a result of the seismic sea waves that ensued on the Oga Peninsula.

Sixteen were killed when a 6.5 quake hit Luzon in the Philippines, 443 were killed and over 150 others were injured in the country of Guinea in north-west Africa on December 22, 12 quake deaths were reported in Skopte, Yugoslavia, in February. These are only a few of the quakes that were reported to or registered by the Center. One of the largest quakes in history occurred at Tangshan, in mainland China in 1976, when they were hit with a quake of 8.0 on the Richter. It was originally estimated at killing 650,000, but that figure was later adjusted to 240,000 fatalities.

You would be surprised at how many people still contend that these acts of GOD and the wars and 'rumors of war' are all coincidence. Many more fail to understand the correlation between world current events and Biblical prophecy. Jesus said that the world would be warned but would not listen. We are being warned and we are failing to listen!

We acknowledge that it is an impossibility to either think like GOD or understand His infinite love for us. Hypothetically speaking let's make a feeble attempt, if only for human logic reason.

We know how much we love our children, often going without personal luxuries to make them secure and happy. We hope that they will return this affection by obeying our wishes, which are intended for their betterment. When our children disobey our regulations we feel an immense hurt and many times display our displeasure with anger and discipline. Most parents will issue warnings far ahead of this disciplinary action. As GOD made man in His image, wouldn't our Father in Heaven also show these same frustratons, anger and discipline to those HE loves far greater than the love we have for our offspring? I feel GOD punishes those He loves with justified discipline and divine compassion. Mankind is the sum of all GOD's offspring, He loves us all infinitely and surely far greater than the comprehension of human thought. As we discipline our children fairly and distribute our gentle wrath according to the disobedience of the child involved, isn't it fair to assume that GOD Almighty also distributes selective punishment according to the offense against His grace? I feel that this last paragraph is as close an understanding of GOD's feelings as humanly possible to comprehend. What do you think?

Don't we deliberately defy His wishes quite often? Although minutely similar in context, didn't we defy our parental advice from time to time and don't our children defy us also? Understanding GOD and His infinite wisdom is an impossibility if you do not know Him. Even those that love Him and try to obey His principles fall short of this knowledge. The reason is simple. He did not intend that the mind of His subordinate would attain such wisdom. So when we try to understand His logic and reasoning for any of His Divine Action, we liken it to what a mortal would do in a given instance. When we question GOD for His actions, as many of us do and shouldn't, He will only give us an answer if He so desires. That is something most people fail to recognize. You do not question His divine wisdom and authority! You didn't when you were in the armed forces with superiors and they were mere humans. Don't question the authority of GOD and maybe He'll change your life to such a degree that HE WON'T HAVE CAUSE TO QUESTION YOUR ACTIONS!

We know that Jesus Christ is the representative of all that is good in this world. Even those that do not know Him cannot find fault in that statement. We also know that Satan is synonymous with evil. Why is it such a difficult undertaking for the human to do what is right, follow GOD's plan and live in peace? I guess the answer is so simple many feel there must be some great secret veil attached to his design. I feel totally justified and inspired in stating that "THERE IS NO SECRET THAT MAN NEEDS TO KNOW THAT GOD WILL NOT REVEAL TO HIM!"

Our Father has given us ample warning of what 'will' take place. Only He knows that time when His patience will run out. When it does, there should be absolutely no excuses from anyone. You can make your commitment to Jesus now and live for Him only, or you may choose the side of brimstone and allow Satan his evil liberties. To me it is an easy decision, the only choice and humanity's only alternative. Choose wisely!

CHAPTER FOURTEEN

Discernment: Voting for GOD & Country . . .NOT the Party

"He that is not with Me is against Me,
and he that gathereth not with Me scattereth!"
JESUS CHRIST (Luke 11:23)

As you should be quite aware by now, the Bible was surely one of GOD's greatest gifts to humanity. What Jesus meant by the above is that any man who deliberately goes against His cause is against His principles and is NOT WITH HIM!

Considering this valuable understanding, we can rephrase it in the same context. "Any person who stands firm against the teachings of Jesus Christ (GOD), is an anti-Christ!"

In Matthew 12:33, Jesus tells us more on discerning between the good and evil people. He says:

"Either make the tree good and his fruit good,
or make the tree corrupt and his fruit corrupt:
For a tree is known by his fruit!"

What God means here is that "any man doing good by his actions...is a good man and pro-God. Anyone that does not do good and finds ways to go against GOD, is a bad man and anti-GOD!" If you notice one key point, Jesus has mentioned a "tree," in His parable, but He is talking about men because of the word "his," in reference to the tree.

We all should acknowledge that the knowledge that comes from GOD is supreme wisdom, not just words. What we must do as believing Christians this Election Year is weed out the bad politicians (ones that are outwardly opposing God's principles) with our voting privilege and replace them with those who openly back the Godly principles. For as man is the product of "his good or evil works," we must discern between the two. Based on just two important issues this very year...voting this Fall should be quite easy.

The Presidential Candidates

If Americans were to believe what is written in the (socialist) presses and hear what they are saying about Ronald Reagan, we would be overlooking the only good apple in the bunch!

More important than that, we would then be failing to comprehend the principles of GOD. Discern the spirit of each man by his works. By acknowledging Reagan's accomplishments, we find the real truth about this candidate (not the liberal medias' version of clouding the truth). If you listen to all of Reagan's speeches, you won't hear a one where he hasn't mentioned our GOD. Ronald Reagan is indeed a man sent to us by God in these critical times. The media in this Country allows any atheist to put forth their filthy lies. They allow them to slander our Father in heaven and attack every thing that is good for America...To find something positive about Ronald Reagan in the papers is almost an impossibility.

Every time Reagan mentions our GOD, some seamy and shoddy journalist says he is doing it only for the Christian vote. Why most publishers allow atheistic liars and liberal writers (same thing) to put their "smut" on the front pages can only be explained by understanding that the newspapers are just the right arm of the Soviet Union! It would be refreshing to hear all the Godly doings for a change, instead of all the slander of the righteous.

I tell you this: "In this age or any period of our history, WISE MEN STILL SEEK GOD for assistance!"

What About Reagan's Opposition? (What about'em)

The current leader in primary delegates is Walter Mondale. As of May, 1984, Mondale has a comfortable lead over Gary Hart for the Democratic presidential nomination. If the Christians have a say in it, they could be the only nominees and both would still lose.

By discerning the "good men from the bad," Mondale, in the eyes of GOD and those who love GOD, hasn't a wisp of a chance to become our next president...regardless of the misinformation he is smearing on Reagan.

If Mondale was the only apple tree in America, you'd have to find something else to eat...there'd be NO FRUIT!

Walter has gone against the Word of GOD and taken the gray area on the abortion issue. It's plain and simple, "if your not for GOD, you're AGAINST HIM!" Mondale took the middle of the road to try to escape riling anyone. I tell you this...he riles this Christian.

Checking Mondales "record" a little deeper,......we find that he is against vocal public school prayer. Evidently Mondale hasn't noticed how our education system has deteriorated since GOD was banned. He is for silent (transendental meditation) prayer though. Next they'll be telling us to worship any god we want, and believe me...that "IS" the next step.

VOTE FOR FREE AMERICA
REAGAN

Walter says that it's okay to have silent prayer in our schools, so, if that's what we need, it's quite evident what we don't need...and that's Walter Mondale as our next comrade.

The next leading candidate for the demoncratic presidential nomination is the illustrious senator from the great State of Colorado, Gary Hart. He is another that continually evades the real issues.

Hart, like Mondale and Jackson, feels God shouldn't have the "choice to decide whether developing human beings should or shouldn't live." BOY, this is going to be the easiest year we've ever had to get the right candidates elected!

As Hart is for "pro choice" in "mass murder" (abortion), and another who is AGAINST GOD in our public schools, He's also another anti-Christ and WE DON'T NEED any more anti-Christs in America than we already have. Sorry Gary, try another Country!

Christians everywhere were treated to how Gary Hart feels about GOD when he was one of the dissenting votes against Senate Joint Resolution #73 on March 20, 1984! Because of eleven (11) votes like the one Hart cast against GOD, our children can't speak openly to the Father in heaven in the public schools.

The next candidate, Jesse Jackson, at first gave me some mixed emotions. Jackson is a Baptist minister and trails Mondale and Hart by a wide,but narrowing margin.

Many, including myself, cheered Jackson when he went to Syria and returned home with our pilot who was shot down behind enemy lines. Supposedly through great diplomacy, Jackson persuaded Assad, (the Syrian leader) to release the pilot as a good will jesture. I wonder if we'll ever find out why Assad really released the prisoner?

Discerning Jackson tells us that with him in the White House, it could be even a bigger mistake than the previous liberal agents for "democracy." Let's see why!

First off, Jackson is for "pro-choice" in abortion and against vocal public school prayer. Usually it takes three strikes to dispose of a batter...Jesse gets four...but he's still not qualified for our nation's highest office.

Not only is Jackson "pro choice in mass murder(abortion) and against GOD in the public schools," he also has ties to Louis Farrakhan, the radical leader of the Nation of Islam. It was Farrakhan who threatened a Washington Post reporter, Milton Coleman (also a black), with quote "punishment" for attacking Jackson for referring to the Jewish race as "Hymies!"

It was Farrakhan that made the public statement after his threat that "I don't want you "religious sissies" to come telling me about the forgiveness of Jesus Christ. I know all about Jesus

Christ...but I know one thing about Jesus, he "HATES" cowards and He "HATES" turncoats and traitors and I'm with Jesus to punish traitors!"

I don't think the Christ Farrakhan speaks of is the same one I know. He must be speaking of the anti-Christ, because my Lord Jesus doesn't "HATE" anyone. It's evident that his god and the Christian GOD are altogether different. If Farrakhan was truly pro-Christ, he wouldn't blaspheme our Lord by placing himself on the same level..."I'm with Jesus to punish traitors!" Only GOD has the right to judge others and gives His right to no mortal...Who gives Farrakhan any rights to punish anyone?

Just for the record, I am not a racist. I love my black brothers as much as I do my white, yellow and red brothers. If Jackson was right for the presidency, I'd be the first in line to vote him in...but he certainly isn't!

Although Farrakhan did accompany Jackson to Syria, it would be unfair to condemn Jesse for the ill-advised connection, but I would surely like to know the "real" meaning of why he calls his campaign "THE RAINBOW EXPRESS!"

In Chapter Nineteen, Constance Cumbey (author of best-seller, "Hidden Dangers of the Rainbow!) writes on an organization which is on the verge of "taking over the world picture," and when they do their first plan is to eliminate Christians and Jews. One of their "secret signs" is the rainbow, and they use it on their vehicles and in their conservations to identify themselves to other "NEW AGERS!"

I wonder if it's only a coincidence when Jackson was being publicized in the local papers about spending the weekend with Reverend Willie White in New York. The campaign issue was supposed to be detailing the nutritional needs of the poor in America, but the article closed with Jackson's statement, "Hey, look at this," (referring to the red, yellow, blue and green pillow case on his bed) "RAINBOW!" Could that have been a message to "NEW AGERS" that things are fine with the movement? We'll know soon enough, but in my opinion, he isn't the man for the job either!

By Jackson's referring to the Jewish race as "hymies," discernment of his spirit reminds me that another leader "Hitler" also used that term during the extermination of six million Jews in World War II.

A man like Jackson could be a great American leader if he had his preferences in their proper order and watched his associations. A man of his stature could be considered a "deliverer." I pray that Jackson's future motivations will be only concerned with delivering people to the Lord Jesus Christ...and no one else!

"He that ruleth over men must be just, ruling in the fear of GOD."

...King David (Samuel 23:3)

Being completely fair with all candidates, we have discerned each one's spirit based on their ideas and proposals. If America wants the chance to clean up our Country of the pornography, the sexual deviates, the criminals, the atheists and politicians that could care less for the principles of GOD, we have only one man that stands head and heals above the rest. He is THE man who will bring America out from 'down under' and the only person capable of understanding the needs of our countrymen...that need is GOD! That man is RONALD REAGAN! God bless him and may He govern over America till Jesus comes to take us home!

Let's Get Rid of The Anti-Christs In The Senate!

Many of the U.S. Senators are coming up for reelection this November (1984) and it's time all GOD fearing Americans began remembering like the good ole elephant. We must discern the ones who have GOD foremost in their hearts and those that are against GOD.

To have a better Country, we also have to have more Christian leaders in high offices. Knowing who to VOTE FOR is just as important as knowing WHO NOT TO VOTE FOR! I say VOTE FOR GOD and forget your loyalty to any party. It was quite evident that fourty-four senators had no loyalty to America or GOD when they voted on March 20th, 1984, to make sure GOD didn't get back into the public schools. It is the duty of every true Christian and Jew to make sure these senators DO NOT remain in office and continue infesting our Country.

Remember with all your heart the senators who are anti-Christ and shelve them this November!

How The Senators Voted On Senate Joint Proposal 73. . .Vocal Public School Prayer Ammendment!

STATE	VOTE FOR CHRIST	Vote Against anti-Christs
Alabama	DENTON	
	HEFLIN	
Alaska	STEVENS	
	MURKOWSKI	
Arizona		goldwater
		deconcini
Arkansas	PRYOR	bumpers
California	WILSON	cranston

How the Senators Voted on SJR #73...continued

State	FOR CHRIST	anti-Christ
Colorado	ARMSTRONG	hart*
Connecticut		weicker**
		dodd
Delaware	ROTH	biden
Florida	HAWKINS	
	CHILES	
Georgia	MATTINGLY	
	NUNN	
Hawaii		matsunaga
		inouve
Idaho	McCLURE	
	SYMMS	
Illinois	PERCY	dixon
Indiana	LUGAR	
	QUAYLE	
Iowa	GRASSLEY	
	JEPSEN	
Kansas	DOLE	kassenbaum
Kentucky	FORD	
	HUDDLESTON	
Louisiana	JOHNSTON	
	LONG	
Maine		cohen
		mitchell
Maryland		mathias
		sarbanes
Massachusetts		tsongas
		kennedy
Michigan		reigle
		levin
Minnesota		boschwitz
		durenberger
Mississippi	COCHRAN	
	STENNIS	
Missouri		danforth
		eagleton
Montana	MELCHER	baucus
Nebraska	EXON	
	ZORINSKY	

* candidate for the Democratic Presidential Nomination
** main anti-Christian leader in the Senate

State	FOR CHRIST	anti-Christ
Nevada	LAXALT	
	HECHT	
New Hampshire	HUMPHREY	rudman
New Jersey		bradley
		lautenberg
New Mexico	DOMENICI	bingaman
New York	D'AMATO	moynihan
North Carolina	EAST	
	HELMS	
North Dakota		andrews
		burdick
Ohio		glenn°
		metzenbaum
Oklahoma	NICKLES	
	BOREN	
Oregon		hatfield
		packwood
Pennsylvania		heinz
		specter
Rhode Island		chafee
		pell
South Carolina	THURMOND	
	HOLLINS	
South Dakota	ABDNOR	
	PRESSLER	
Tennessee	BAKER°°	
	SASSER	
Texas	TOWER	
	BENTSEN	
Utah	HATCH	
	GARN	
Vermont		stafford
		leahy
Virginia	TRIBLE	
	WARNER	
Washington		evans
		gordon
West Virginia	BYRD	
	RANDOLPH	
Wisconsin	KASTEN	
	PROXMIRE	
Wyoming	WALLOP	
	SIMPSON	

°Democratic candidate for presidential nomination (withdrew)
°°PRO CHRIST LEADER in the Senate!!!!!!!

There you have the complete public listing of how our U.S. Senators voted on Senate Joint Resolution #73...Vocal Public School Prayer.

As our Lord Jesus Christ has said, "He that is not with me is against me and he that gathereth not with Me scattereth!" He also said that "either make the tree good and his fruit good, or make the tree corrupt and his fruit corrupt: For a tree (man) is known by his fruit (good works).

In no manner do I indicate to you that everyone who voted for vocal public school prayer is the right person for the job, however, those senators who voted AGAINST GOD are definitely NOT THE RIGHT PEOPLE for America government. There is no acceptable explanation from any of the dissenters that can be logical. Many will say that they voted against the "spoken prayer" because "someone may be offended by listening to the principles of GOD!" Isn't that a shame! Learned Senators who are supposed to be leaders using such a poor excuse to cover their dastardly deeds.

NO TRUE CHRISTIAN COULD POSSIBLY VOTE FOR ANYONE THAT IS ANTI-CHRIST...REGARDLESS OF THEIR EXPLANATION!!!

It is quite obvious that the 44 dissenting senators didn't vote on the ammendment the way the people wanted. 84% of the voters in America wanted "spoken public school prayer." You tell me these 44 anti-Christs are duly serving the people of this Country and I'll show you someone who has their head in the sand.

Senators, or any public servant for that matter, are ethically required to vote with the majority. This they DID NOT DO! All we needed to pass the ammendment was 67 votes from the 100 senators. Most people I talked to called or wrote their senators and told them they wanted the prayer restored...Tell me there isn't a gross failure to communicate between these unGodly senators and the ones who placed them in office.

When you have governmental officials who fail to do their obligation, there is only one thing to do...YOU GET RID OF THEM - RIGHT PRONTO!!!!!!!

The Senate rejected SJR #73 by a vote of 56 FOR GOD and 44 anti-GOD. There is only one thing you can do this November...you MUST GET OFF YOUR DUFF and...

GET OUT AND VOTE

This is an election year. Christians and Jews everywhere must stand up for GOD and Country before it's too late. It seems like the POWER of the VOTE is the only real right you have left. Go get registered and let's show these "liberal anti-Christs" THE DOOR! If you truly love our Country, unamericanism can not be tolerated. The senators who voted against GOD are many of the same who also are for legalized abortion (mass murder of developing human beings). That should tell you what life form of individuals have filtered into our society in the last 25 years.

WEICKER... A Modern Day Herod!

The rejection of GOD followed two weeks of heated debate and intense lobbying by our president. Ronald Reagan did everything he could to persuade the senators who were undecided prior to the vote. He even personally invited over thirty senators to the White House and of these only six had the courtesy to respond.

"This has been an important debate revealing the extent to which the freedom of religious speech has been abridged in our nation's public schools," pleaded Reagan, in a written statement, "the issue of free religious speech is not dead as a result of this vote. We have suffered a setback, but we have not been defeated. Our struggle will go on!"

Those are the words of a person who truly cares for the revival of standards in America...They represent THE MAN who should, by the graces of GOD, retain the Presidency this Fall! We can not lose Ronald Reagan and remain a strong Country, especially with the Democratic "material" we would have to work with in the remote case of either Mondale, Hart or Jackson being elected.

Senate Majority Leader, Howard H. Baker, Jr., (R - Tennessee) said as the debate drew to a close. "We will either restore the neutrality of the state in respect to religion, or, we will officially affirm an "anti-religious" (anti-Christian) bias in our schools." He goes on, "This ammendment simply restores the neutrality that ought always to have been in the exercise of religion." In other words, Senator Baker meant PUT GOD BACK IN THE CLASSROOM WHERE HE OUGHT TO BE!

The major anti-Christ in the Senate was the leader of the opposition to keep GOD out of the classrooms, "LOWELL WEICKER," R-Connecticut. Take the time to jot it down and remember the name!

Weicker said, "the proposal would have us forfeit our birthright of religious liberty for a mess of political pottage."

I would surely like to know who Weicker referred to when he says "us" and "our heritage?" He doesn't represent "us" and who's birthright is he clamoring about? If he was referring to "our heritage here in the United States of America," he's wrong! Someone ought to inform Weicker that eighty-four percent of all Americans wanted GOD and His influence restored to our public schools. Without this preserving element over the past 21 years, we have witnessed grave losses of proper allegiance that have lead to mass declinations in both moral ethics and spiritual values.

Someone ought to drill it into Weicker's head that America receives its power directly from our GOD Almighty and when you remove the "Source".......you also eliminate the energy! Our BIRTHRIGHT in America is GOD!

Weicker went on to say, "We (there he goes again talking for all) cannot bring "our" children closer to GOD by blaring a formula over the public address systems of our schools. This is not a political issue. If anyone makes it so, (GET THIS) I hope it will be the cause of their defeat...republican or democrat!"

I'll tell you this Weicker, "You don't speak as a representative of all God-fearing "real" Americans, who make up over 84% of this Nation...And you are not qualified with the intellect to speak for my children - who are God's children first and last! As far as religion being a "mess of political pottage," those are your words...don't use them and at the same time say you represent "us!" You don't know the meaning of religion...nor are you aware of the influence of our GOD!

My human rage surfaces when I think of "men" such as Weicker. It is apparent when I say that "Weicker and his 44 dissenting "comrades" ought to be set adrift on a banana boat heading south with a slow leak in its hull. As their captain they could recruit the "head anti-Christ in America," Madalyn Murray O'Hair. They could whistle aboard as first mates both "Tip" O'Neil and Edward Kennedy and as their crew, every subversive protester in America. With such illustrious leaders, they'll get to 'hell' that much faster!"

That's my earthly rage coming out! But of this earthly kingdom I lay no claim. I forgive you Lowell Weicker, "Tip" O'Neil, Edward Kennedy and Madalyn Murray O'Hair as do I pray that our Lord will also. For you are of this earth and all that it holds dear to heart. You give as the world gives in this domain of satan. I forgive you for your blindness, for you know not what you are doing. You are the modern day Herods and are the blind leading the blind!

It's evident that you are not familiar with the scriptures where our GOD says:

"He that is not with Me is against Me,
and he that gathereth not with me scattereth..!"

I pray that each one of you fourty-four dissenters are forgiven for this misplacement of proper recognition...for what you have done is to blaspheme the Holy Spirit of GOD!

Thank God for men like Ronald Reagan, Senator Jesse Helms, Senator Howard Baker, Senator Paul Laxalt and the 53 other great Americans who saw the necessity for GOD in our classrooms and acted affirmatively.

Senator Jesse Helms, the good Senator from North Carolina, said, "We have just begun to fight. As long as I am in the U.S. Senate, there will be other rounds!"

I say to all true Christian and Jewish Americans, "a vote this November for REAGAN, BAKER, HELMS, LAXALT and the other AMERICANS is not only a vote for the United States of America.......Moreover, it is your commitment and covenant to GOD!

In further disrespect and blatant failure to vote for the majority's wishes, Weicker told reporters smuggly after the ammendment was defeated, "I don't think this particular battle will be fought again this year!"

Listen to what one writer says in a release through the Associated Press, "Reagan promised his constituency a vote...and he delivered it. He has been unable to deliver congressional passage on any of his issues...prohibitions against forced busing, abortion, an effort to limit the authority of federal judges and a balanced budget." Isn't that nice! With all the liberals in the Senate, the Congress and the House of Representatives...I WONDER WHY!

The liberal Press even attack Reagan for his efforts in persuading the undecided Senators and are laughing at the fact that only six had the decency and respect to show up to his invitation to the White House.

Senator Howard Baker defended the President saying, "It is a leadership prerogative of the President and it's even more important when it's a morally sensitive issue like vocal school prayer."

Weicker called the President's lobbying "tasteless" and said, "This is not the type of issue you can lobby on. It is a matter of deeply held beliefs, not like a missile system." One must really wonder just "how deep" Weicker's beliefs really are?

CONCLUSION

Real Christians everywhere must realize that there is a vicious conspiracy taking place in America...one that will escalate apostasy in the churches and in our heartland. It is the liberal elements that tear us apart. GET OUT AND VOTE THIS NOVEMBER...Let's VOTE FOR GOD and forget the party affiliation. GOD BLESS YOU!

Prelude to The Power Of Your 1984 Vote!
The Trilateral Commission

Before you go to the polls this November, I believe there is a little information each one should be aware of. If you have ever had the opinion that the American people have control over policy making through their voting power...you're being very naive. I'm not saying that your vote doesn't mean anything...they all count. What I am saying is that our Country IS NOT A DEMOCRACY and the voters are all in a general category...unfortunately they are for the most part uninformed and naive to who controls our foreign policy and our internal economics. The American people do not control either.

There is an organization in our Country called the Trilateral Commission. It is the brainchild of one of the weathiest families in the world and its founder was David Rockerfeller. This organization was formed in 1973 and is made up of 65 people who have been carefully selected throughout the United States. Not just anyone can join this group...they are SELECTED.

The grandfather organization of this group of superrich and powerful individuals is another organization called the Council on Foreign Development. This organization has 1600 members and was organized in 1922. The ironic part that links these two organizations is 1)...They both have the same Chairman - David Rockerfeller, 2.) They both have the identical professed aim, 3.)Most of the 65 members of the Trilateral Commission are also members of the CFR and 4.) their members are all wealthy members of society from Heads of the multinational corporations to the important people in the national media and also our children's educators.

Trilateral's Professed Aim!

According to possibly the second most powerful member in the Commission, Henry Kissinger, the professed aim of the organization is a one world (or at least a limited one world) government which controls the food production, the energy supplies (namely oil) and the monetary system...

Kissinger is quoted as stating truthfully, "If an organization can control food...they can control people. If they can control the energy supplies - they can control nations. You all know that those who control the monetary system have the control over the world.

The Trilateral Commission is made up of very sophisticated individuals talented in finance and world economics. Their Chairman, David Rockerfeller oversees this organization and the three separate areas of concern are Western Europe, North America and Japan. The first 35 members are also members of the CFR and include very high ranking officials in the government.

According to Alan Cranston (a former member who took his name off the committee...there's a difference between taking your name off the committee and resigning) has been quoted as saying that "world government does not give up your sovereignty. What it does is shift your allegiance to the world picture, rather than just the United States."

One former member, Admiral Chester Ward says, "The Council for Foreign Relations' goal has not been altered in more than 50 years, and that is their professed aim to abolish nationality and place all emphasis on interdependence which is the same as one world government or global government-they're all the same."

But Why Abolish Our Nationality?

Anyone knows that this group could not get their way if the American people remained allegiant to the sovereignty of the United States. Patriots would never accept such a plan. So, according to Kingman Brewster,Jr., the council wants the people to look upon themselves as world citizens instead of U.S. citizens and place their interest on the world scene as a result of shifted allegiance.

I'm not dictating to anyone which is right or wrong. To me it is wrong and I'm against anything that removes patriotism to our GOD, our Country or our families. This would do just that!

David Rockerfeller has always believed that "Free enterprise" is a sin, and has never been for it...Sounds peculiar coming from someone so rich...but let's look at the power of this gentleman and understand why a monopoly would suit his needs more.

First, Rockerfeller is the Chairman of the North American Chapter of the Trilateral Commission, the Chairman of the Council for Foreign Relations, until recently he was the Chairman of the Chase Manhattan Bank. He is the head of a family that owns, controls or has substantial security holdings in many of the major corporations in America.

The largest bank in the United States is the Bank of America...its chairman of the board is a member of the CFR.

The 300 member family of David Rockerfeller has security holdings in three of the five largest banks in the world, including the world's most powerful bank, Chase Manhattan. The Chase Manhattan Bank has over 50,000 affiliate banks, each with an average of more than 20 million in assets.

That tells you that one bank controls more than one trillion dollars.

The Rockerfellers have vested interests in the control of Exon,...Standard Oil, Eastman Kodak, Texas Instruments, Minnesota Mining, IBM, Mobil Oil, Quaker Oats, Xerox, ITT, Westinghouse, Texaco, Sperry Rand, Kaiser, Penn Central, Chrysler, Boeing, Consolidated Freightways and more large corporations than can be listed for lack of space. The Rockerfeller Foundation controls 25% of all world banking and 30% of all insurance companies including three of the top four in the country, and 9 of the top 20 transportation corporations and 37 of the top 100 industrials.

I'm not even indicating anything against this family. It is evident that they are shrewd businessmen. But when people are so rich that they can control the very decisions of a country, let alone many countries in the world...something isn't quite like it was intended by GOD. A democracy is the people, or so its supposed to be. The influence the Rockerfellers have in the world controls the way most of the people think...that's not a democracy...it's a monopoly if not in true meaning.

Shortly after the United States was shocked by the Watergate scandal, a fellow by the name of Jimmy Carter was interviewed by David Rockerfeller. What the Council for Foreign Relations needed was a president who was not known well - a man who talked of family life and religion. Shortly after this interview, Carter was announced as a candidate for the presidency. As you well know this relatively unknown went on to win our nation's highest office in 1976. The word was that Carter was going to sweep "clean" the country's Congress, Senate, House of Representatives and the Judiciary branch. Carter was going to make a new America.

As soon as he was elected, he placed 18 CFR members into controlling positions in government. Walter Mondale was the Vice President, the Secretary of State was Vance, Secretary of Defense Brown, National Security Advisor Andrew Bruzinski and fourteen others were appointed. So, of the 65 original Trilateral members, 18 were appointed to high cabinet posts.

World government doesn't sound too bad the way they put it, but the problems surface when you shift your patriotism to the United Nations...or the world picture. The city of Milwaukee, Wisconsin, already consider themselves as citizens of the world and the State of Illinois has already made this issue a resolution. Is that to say they are bad? No! But do they really know what they are becoming involved in? I don't think so!

According to Biblical prophesy, it is a widely known fact that in the end times of the world the people on this earth are going to be forced into a one world governmental system. This will be the exact catalyst which will bring on the most cruel dictator the world has ever known...the antiChrist. Eventually that will lead to the persecution and murder of all Christians and believing Jews alike.

If we submit to this one world government, in essence we are surrendering our total freedom to nations like the Soviet Union and China and every other communist country. But let's just say that this goal of the Trilateral Commission is good for America. If that's the case,...(and it isn't) why are these business magnates keeping the knowledge in wraps? If it's good, tell the American people and let's vote on it! I'll tell you why these industrial wizards won't mention the Council of Foreign Relations or the Trilateral. They know full well that there are still patriots in this Country that love liberty dearly and are willing to fight for their rights. Yes, uncommon to popular belief...they're still around, and you can bet your boots, or anything else you have...these patriots are mostly believers in GOD! There's the stale note that keeps this in the closet!

These Commissions and Councils control the national media, the education and the economy of the United States, but the Constitution has kept them from a total dictatorship up to now. But, the patriots are dwindling rapidly as are many of the borderline Christians and Jews.

At the end of World War II, America was prideful of winning the wars on two separate theatres (see chapter ten). Everyone, well almost everyone was a patriot. GOD was in the schools and children were being raised to believe that America could do anything under the leadership of GOD-fearing people. That's changed. GOD has been removed by a total conspiracy and since, the moral and spiritual values in America have plummeted to record low levels. Morality is non-existent in most areas of our nation and spirituality has followed suit.

Since the end of World War II, the United Nations and the Council for Foreign Relations have become firm partners. Now the pressure is being placed on society to transform liberty and free enterprise into unholy alliances with communists and overt socialist concerns.

Is that to say that these organizations are unGodly? I don't know the answer but it does bring to mind a scripture: "There is nothing from without a man, that entering into him can defile: but the things which come out of him, those are they that defile the man." (Mark 7:15)

Once we submit to one world or global government...our loyalty definitely goes down the drain. If we divert our total attention to the United Nations...what form of government do you think we shall have? I'll tell you one thing...it won't be a republic! If you say socialism you're half right. What we would be inviting is overt communism, or a totalitarian government known as a dictatorship! With any world government, there has to be one person with more control than others and that will become in GOD's time, the lawless one...the anti-Christ!

It's bad enough that America has to be controlled by the elite few wealthy at a time when our nation teaches a two-party system, but they are now asking us to submit to relinquishing the few freedoms we have left.

With a one world government, would the next thing become a one world religious system which could make it easier to control all of us "fanatics?" You hit it right on the head again!

On February 17, 1950, James Woberg, speaking to a group of elected Senators is on congressional record as saying, "we shall have one world government whether you like it or not by conquest or consent!" That's on the record and cannot be misinterpeted.

There is no earthly advantage for free America to become a part of any one world system. That is unless you believe what these organizations are saying that it will reduce a chance for a global world war III. "Peace at all costs!" I don't buy it, but make your own decision.

What Is Interdependence?

We are already in a most disastrous world predicament. We are no longer a nation that can be dependent on our own resources whereas we ARE dependent on other countries for both natural resources and other necessities of life. We look to the oil-laden Middle East for our energy, the Caribbean for our sugar and other spices, and Japan for their advanced technology of electronics and clothing.

Because of these associations, the world has moved closer than ever before to this global alliance. If this Trilateral Commission was intended to promote good will, why can't you find the information about them in any encyclopedia or other history books, either at the graduate or undergraduate level? Would you believe that this Council for Foreign Relations also controls who writes the books on education? It's true! In a book by Henry Kissinger on nuclear warfare, published by the CFR (and they're not a publisher) in the preface, the aim of the Council is clearly outlined...Their intent is to rewrite the college level text books at both the graduate and undergraduate levels. One book published in 1954, "Major Problems of U.S. Foreign Policy," on the second page the intent is again clearly indicated. They intend to write the college text books on economic and foreign affairs. You cannot find a college text book today that teaches any other theory than the one that is adopted by the Council for Foreign Relations.

The Trilateral Commission intends to control all food, all energy and all monetary systems, convert all countries of the world into a one world order and the sad part of it all is...they'll do it! We don't have a choice any more but to take what the "controllers" dish out. One thing they can't control with the world's people and that's the desire of the human heart. They can not change the relationship Christians and believing Jews have with Jesus Christ, regardless of any persecution. Our GOD must really be laughing at the common sense of the world's intelligence. His Plan is coming into fruition and many of these supposed higher intellectuals are falling away from known truths...just like GOD said they would.

With control of the world's food supply they will control many people. By controlling the energy sources they will control many nations of the world and by controlling the monetary system they will ultimately be doing all Christians and believing Jews a big favor...GOD will be coming for His people real soon!

When I saw some of the names of the Senators who voted against vocal public school prayer I was initially shocked. The Kennedy Family are devout Catholics...why would Ted Kennedy vote against GOD in our schools? Why would anyone who professes to love this Country vote Him out of His rightful place, if they weren't part of the Commission too. My guess is that Kennedy is one of these elite members, but as I said, it's a personal opinion.

When the Trilateral Commission was revealed, many of their members withdrew their memberships, only a few resigned. Because of the obvious political disadvantages to become known as a one world advocate...many have, at least temporarily, left the organization, but you can bet on it...they haven't totally severed their relationship with some of the most powerful men in the world. Nor have they given up with their goals for America. GOD said in the end times that many who profess to be religious people, do so only on the surface. I recommend that everyone write the Trilateral Commission for a list of their members. Find out who they are and also who they have been...do it for your own benefit...then vote your conscience in this coming election.

CHAPTER FIFTEEN

Desensitising the Children of God

"Verily I say unto you, Except ye be converted, and become as little children, ye shall not enter into the Kingdom of heaven."

Matthew 18:3

As all real believers will attest to, this generation is the product of misconception and savagery. No longer are eternal values held sacred...no longer are the righteous applauded...no more is honesty and integrity the backbone of real beliefs...and no longer do people of this earth seek the face of GOD in their lives!

My heart and soul cry out to the inhabitants of this world to repent and thusly alter their ominous destination. Why can't man see the truth? Why have they become infested with false ideologies? Why won't they read the Word of GOD and understand that His Plan for mankind is reaching the precipice of fulfillment.

When our little children cannot ever bring their Bibles to school and worship the Almighty...it's time to awaken! When the false-Christs are teaching differing doctrine and mislead the Body of Christ...it's time to awaken! When nursery school leaders in charge of our babies begin molesting this innocence and selling for profit nude pictures for perversions...it's past the time to awaken!

Homosexuals infest this country. When you have a good, God-fearing woman like Anita Bryant attacked for trying to rid society of this phlegm, you have deep moral and spiritual problems. When you live in a country that upholds that GOD should not be allowed in our schools, or see our females get raped on pool tables while "men" sit around and laugh about it, then when they get mild sentences from the liberal courts, tens of thousands protest in the streets...you have a land that is controlled by satan.

When you have preachers like Jim Wallis (Editor of Sojourners Magazine) say "It took this nation many years to convert from slavery. Now we are trying to convert from nuclear weapons," you have the begining of apostasy and that's been prophesied more than 2500 years ago. Their authority to protest against the government and nuclear weaponry doesn't come from GOD! Who then gives them their authority other than other humanists.

In the United States there are over 450,000 cases of family violence each year according to the Bureau of Justice Statistics. There were 4.1 million cases of family violence in the nine years from 1973 to 1981...and that's only those that have been reported!

On our Universities our children can "play house" in the dormitories and it's been accepted now since 1970. Fornication is okay...have fun, but be safe is the outcry of sinners everywhere.

Many parents "don't care if their sons and daughter have their boy and girl friends over to spend the night in carnal love-making." It's okay...but be safe! If they become impregnated, many will pay to murder the child and if they get the little developing human being before the sixth week...no problem! They don't care if the little heart begins beating ten days after conception...Why should they, man can do anything they want because our court system is made up of atheists and secular humanists.

"Homosexuality is okay if that's your thing, right?" After that why not try sadism or perhaps it's masochism that turns you on? If abortion is okay because the courts say so, let's up the age and do away with three and four-year-olds if we get tired of supporting them.......okay? May GOD have mercy...satan is alive and well on Planet Earth!

In our House of Representatives we have a Speaker of the House that twists every word of truth that comes from the mouth of the righteous men in America. Thomas "Tip" O'Neil has attacked and ridiculed our President on every occasion. He claims that the pullout of American troops from Lebanon was due to Reagan's miscalculations in government, but fails to mention that his very own liberal representatives and congressmen were indeed the ones who put on the pressure.

"The truth (O'Neil wouldn't know the truth if it jumped up and hit him in the keister) of the matter is his policy failed. The ineptitude on their (administration) part, they miscalculated...The deaths of the U.S. Marines are the responsibility of the president of the United States. He acted against the wishes of "our" top military advisors in this country. And now he is looking for a scapegoat."

I tell you this...Judge and test the spirit of "Tip" O'Neil and you come up wanting a breath of fresh air. He has gone out of his way to endorse a man (Walter Mondale) who believes that GOD shouldn't be in the public schools, a man after his own (black) heart. He endorses Mondale for the nation's highest office after Mondale agrees that women should have the power of GOD to determine who lives and who doesn't.

When you have Superior Court Judges like Sheridan Reed in San Diego, California, who rule in favor of a known deviate (homosexual) to have legal custody over a God-fearing Christian woman, Betty Lou Bately...you have gross ethical violations and incompetant men in our judicial system.

"Forcing a child to live in an abominable environment such as overt homosexuality is de facto child abuse," said Reverend Maurice Gordon, pastor of the Lovingway United Pentacostal Church of Denver, Colorado, who had helped Mrs. Bately during the time she was hiding with Brian (the son). Mrs. Bately had custody of Brian when the couple was divorced in 1976. In September, 1982, Superior Court "Judge" Sheridan Reed switched custody to the homosexual father on the grounds he had been denied visitation rights. Mrs. Bately and her son, Brian, age 12, hid in Colorado to avoid sending Brian back to a world of perversion......Tell me that's justice?

The father, Frank Bately, said, "I'm a responsible, loving parent and I'm not promoting any lifestyle or anything like that." Whether he is loving or not, he doesn't promote a healthy, Christian lifestyle by subjecting his son to such a debasing and immoral atmosphere.

Yes, we are indeed in "bad times on planet Earth" when we have such gross injustices in our Country and in our communities.

When you have men like James Cracraft, a history professor at the University of Chicago (also a fellow of the Russian Research Center at Harvard and Senior Editor of the Bulletin of Atomic Scientists), overtly indicates false truths that President Reagan's intentions for America are incompetant (January 1984 issue of the Bulletin of Atomic Scientists) and clearly applauds the actions of the Soviet Union...you have a grave situation brewing in America.

In fact, the Bulletin of Atomic Scientists is jam packed with communist sympathizers and liberal promoters.

Cracraft says, "No president of the United States has villified the Soviet Union, both leadership and people, as frequently and as thoroughly as has President Reagan - or as stupidly, referring to both the content of the insults and their effect on world opinion." His remarks (Cracraft's) remind me of what our GOD has told us, that the more they profess to be philosophers, the more stupid they become! Cracraft is also the editor of THE SOVIET UNION TODAY! From reading his article it becomes evident that Cracraft's allegiance isn't for the good of America. He professes that the Soviet Union is a Country worthy of trust......Maybe he believes that, but Americans aren't that STUPID!

These "scientists" propagate that America should disarm

at a time when the Soviets are stockpiling nuclear weaponry and ultimately preparing for an all-out assault on the free world. It doesn't require a genius to see through this faction's veil of illogical pretense, nor do true Americans have any trouble deciphering that the Soviet Union is not just an adversary...they are the ENEMY of freedom!

I wonder if the Soviet Union would allow the existence of a Pro-American magazine in their midst???

Some of the previous instances and happenings are indeed a detrimental example for our youth to be exposed to, but there is a far greater deceit being conceived and its aim is directly at our young children. Believe it or not, it begins with the toy manufacturers of America!

"Harmless "IMAGES" of the Beast!"

How many of you believers in GOD have noticed the appearance of the newest lines of "toys" that are being made available to our children? If you haven't, pay real close attention to this section!

Most of us have seen the movie "STAR WARS." Few of us realized just what the "force" was referring to when the movie was grossing millions across the United States...that is until you completely analyse the deception. The "force" in that movie was never referred to as GOD. They were referring to an invisible thought process which enabled the JEDI warriors to overcome the forces of evil (Darth Vader). Although they clearly indicated this force to be "good," the "human thought process" gives overt, divine acknowledgement to the power of man...a power that is non-existent in reality! What the JEDI had to do to receive this "power," was to BELIEVE IN THEIR SENSES. Who was the god of the movie who trained Luke Skywalker? None other than a "demon-like" creature by the name of YODA!

My children saw the movie four or five times and I TOOK THEM...Have mercy! But that's not all...Not only has GOD been thrown out of every facet of human thought in that movie, look at the inspirational movie "E.T." which attracted multi-millions! They gave a "lovable" creature from outer space the credit for having powers of "healing" and the little beast appealed to almost everyone with compassion. If I was so touched by the ending...how do you feel it effects our small children?

We remember when we were young. We would see a Tom Mix, Roy Rogers or Gene Autry movie and on the way home we would reenact the parts of the heroes and villains when we would play cowboys and Indians. Didn't we??? Now the toymakers are recreating the figures of the "good demons" and the bad demons. They are making "innocent" replicas (images) of the unGodly beasts in those movies. THEY ARE EXACT IMAGES OF SATANIC CREATIONS (see sample pictures of the toys). The toy makers are recreating people with monster heads, snake heads and miniature demons and our children desire them as toys because they saw them in the movies and want to use their imaginations to play out their fantasies.

I want to tell you this! A child's fantasy to them is a reality! When we were children, if we were to see such creatures in our dreams...we would awaken with a start and call for mother. It was such a frightening experience to us that we thought about it for long periods of time.....Didn't we?   That seldom occurs with our children today because of the toy masks, comic books, and miniature replicas of the beast (satan). He is succeeding to desensitize our babies with "satanic and horrifying beasts," and the whole Country has fallen prey to his sinister desires.

We must realize that our children are "the Kingdom of heaven!" Desensitize them as children and they will be lost!

We must understand that these little toy creatures in our homes are softening our children to readily accept the inevitable myths that SATAN ISN'T BAD AT ALL!

I fell for it too. I was watching the Trinity Broadcasting Network one morning and Paul and Jan Crouch (the founders of the PRAISE THE LORD program) were talking about the deceits of lucifer...how evil he is and to what extent he won't spare to corrupt the good in society. My eyes caught sight of some of my children's toys on the floor and went over to survey their appearance...I was shocked to a most grave understanding...the little figures were exact duplicates of the image of the beast (satan - see #3)

What I did next was to completely inventory their entire toy box and other hiding places where they keep their toys. To my surprise, almost fourty-percent of their current toys were demonic in appearance. I immediately dispensed with every toy that even hinted of satanic influence. After my onslaught against the kingdom of satan...utter fear came over me...what would I tell the children when they returned from Grammy's? I then got on my knees and had a very intimate conversation with our GOD.

> Dear GOD, I know You approve of
> my actions in removing these images
> of the beast but I request that the kids
> understand also. I ask you to speak
> to them and explain why their Daddy
> threw away their playthings. I ask

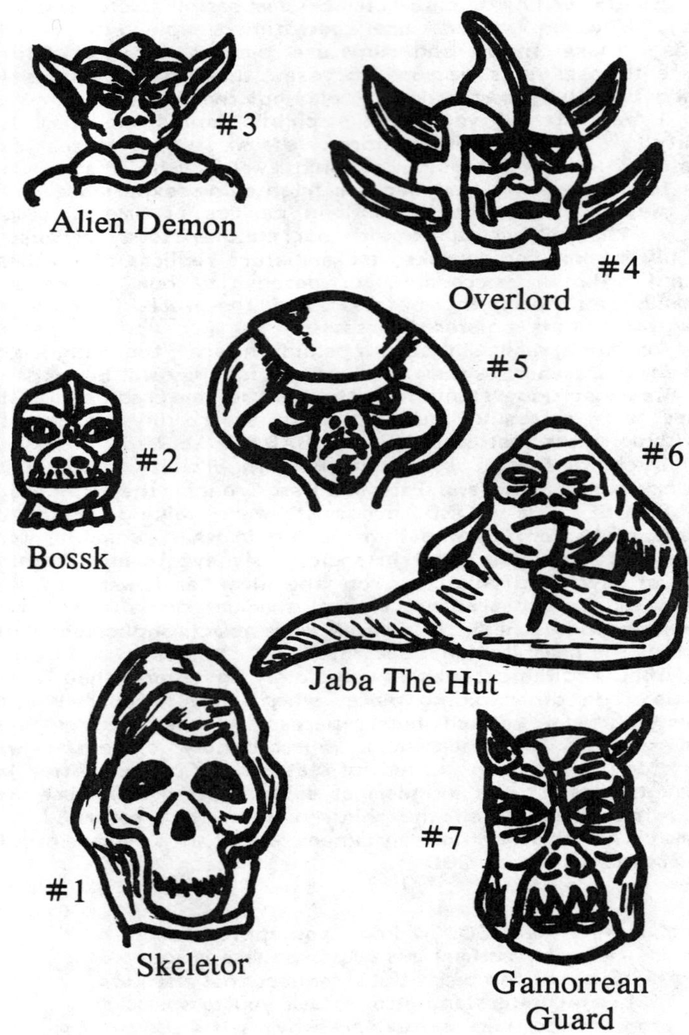

#3
Alien Demon
#4
Overlord
#5
#2
Bossk
#6
Jaba The Hut
#1
Skeletor
#7
Gamorrean
Guard

You to speak to them and give
them knowledge and reason beyond
their tender years on this matter.
You know I always ask you to protect my family and me from all evil;
please tell them in their hearts and
minds that those toys were evil! I
ask You these things in the Name
of Jesus. Amen and Amen!

What do you think happened? You guessed it, believer...God answered the prayer...I received absolutely no recourse and disapproval from the children whatsoever.

GOD spoke to Andrew and Nicholas (the baby, Natalie, was too young) and told them that what Daddy did was for their best. He told them that their souls would be brighter without that evil influence. God told them not to be mad at Daddy and even told them to thank me for removing them. You know something...Andrew, my seven-year-old, found some that I had somehow missed and brought them to me saying, "Daddy, get rid of these, too!"

I tell you this...For those who don't feel GOD listens to all our requests in promotion of His Kingdom...you haven't tried communicating with Him. Any action or request you ask in the name of Jesus in glorification of His name...He grants. GOD IS REAL, BELIEVE IT!

We know that television is a great influence on our children and this area, like the theatre, can be most damaging. Next Saturday morning, take a look at what your children are watching on the tube. You'll see every satanic creature imaginable, including witches, demons, goblins and wizardry.

If you are a caring parent, there is no way you will allow your children's minds to become polluted with the network garbage. Turn on the Disney channel or let them watch the Christian Children game shows on TBN or "Super Book" on CBN. Children don't know what's good for themselves...you dictate the information that goes through their imaginations.

For our older children, the teenagers, the record makers are having a direct demonic effect on them too...and much more carnally! Many of the "rock groups"(punk and otherwise) have been "backward masking " evil messages to our children...evil thoughts that can only be picked up by the subliminal consciousness of the mind. If you reverse the tapes or play the records backwards, you will hear messages like "satan is god," kill, kill, kill: satan asks this of you, rebell against authority, sleep with the dead, I love satan, and many other messages that will awaken America and the world to the ever presence of satanic worship among rock "musicians." (See Chapter Nine)

Our children are both "Gifts from GOD" and "Children of GOD." They must not be allowed to be infested with the vile and degrading spirit of satan. If your child has already been possessed...pray this prayer and you, as a child of GOD, will be able to "cast out these demons in the name of Jesus."

"...And those who BELIEVE
shall have My authority to cast out
demons and they shall speak new
languages.."   Mark 16:17

"The graven images of their gods shall ye burn with fire: thou shalt not desire the silver or gold that is in them, nor take it unto thee, lest thou be snared therein: for it is an abomination to the Lord thy GOD.
Neither shalt thou bring an abomination into thine house, lest thou be a cursed thing like it: but thou shalt utterly detest it, and thou shalt utterly abhor it; for it is a cursed thing.
DEUTERONOMY 7:25,26

Beware of the Game; "Dungeons & Dragons!"

There is another evil influence in our land by the name of "Dungeons and Dragons." The name alone should give you a hint as to its original deceit. This game is popular among many teenagers and even has been seen in the leisure times in churches. This game has certain plateaus in which the player assumes the identity of one of the characters in the game. These characters are outlined as both good and evil. They are witches (good and bad...if there is a difference), warlocks, slave masters, demons, goblins, wizards and a variation of "gods," all with special powers and limitations.

The participants, by use of directions provided, learn the "powers" of these minature beasts, and in actuality, can be possessed with their influence by imagination. The weaker the individual, the more likely the person is to become possessed (weaker meaning spiritually and morally).

These players graduate and aspire to grand wizards and accomplished assassins. They cast spells and actually learn how to praise these demons. In one of the illustrations, a naked man is bound spread-eagle on a sacrifical table while a woman in black inflicts certain rituals on him. The regulations of the game allow the participant to "aspire" to great heights of perversion. They are thoroughly trained to rob, rape, murder, cast spells and every other debasing trait of satan worship...all in the name of good clean fun! Find out what your children are doing...before it's too late.

You must understand that all this is happening in our world! The upgrading of sexual perversions and violence on television has grown to epic proportions and there is no end in sight. It is not being produced for positive design and the effects on the children will have disastrous effects if left unattended.

What these influences are doing is desensitising American youth and corrupting the highly vulnerable minds of our future leaders. America, WAKE UP TO REALITY!!!

When the anti-Christ, that has been prophesied in the Bible, comes on the scene in the not too distant future...these children will be susceptible to all his evil and perverted commands. Don't be foolish and fail to recognize the truth I am writing about. The truth of it all is that it is VERY REAL, and not the product of an alarmist.

DO NOT place this book on the shelf or in a corner and forget its message. I beg your compliance. Give it to a friend and allow them to awaken to the real facts. The Bible prophesies that many will not understand the evils when they take place because they will be blinded by lust. WAKE UP...

GOD is asking you to understand all that is in this book and act upon the advice. If you don't want to believe me, ask your preacher of its message.

GOD is pleading with you through the Holy Spirit to arise from your chair and destroy all the evil images in your home.

GOD is asking you to remove all images of the beast that your children are playing with and upon compliance...you will see the relief in your children...PRAY ABOUT IT! He is listening right now!

After you have prayed the prayer on the preceeding page, call one of the prayer lines listed in this book and share your story. If you can't get through, call me personally at Hall Publishing...I know what you are going through...I understand that satan is alive and thriving on planet Earth.

In Proverbs 2, GOD explains what He will do for you if you really seek His knowledge sincerely:

> "My son, if thou wilt receive My words, and hide My commandments with thee; So that thou incline thine ear unto wisdom, and apply thine heart to understanding;
>
> If thou seekest her as silver, and searchest for her as for hid treasures;Then shalt thou understand the fear of the Lord, and FIND THE KNOWLEDGE of GOD.
>
> For the Lord giveth wisdom: out of His mouth cometh knowledge and understanding."

PROVERBS 2:1-6

In reference to the making of this book, many possibly have not as yet received the inner message that it was not assembled sans divine assistance. Let me say this. Look around you and see the utter chaos as it occurs. How many of your neighbors greet you with a warm smile and friendly words of kind wishes? How many do you see with big smiles on their faces and twinkles in their eyes? When you have seen these rare individuals, how many of you have said, "Something must surely be wrong with them?" The world is rapidly changing and, unfortunately for those who lay claim to this world,...not for the better.

In reality, can't you understand what is missing from our society? If you say love...you're partially accurate in your assessment. What is really missing is the analogy of LOVE...and that is GOD!

Because of His absence in this world man has become selfrighteous. He is heartless and uncaring, grasping, boastful, arrogant and rude; children are disobedient to their parents and ungratefully unappeasing Man has become irreligious. They slander, they are profligates, savages and against everything that is good; they are treacherous, reckless and demented with pride and prefer their own pleasures of the flesh over the love that comes only from a relationship to our GOD!

Many keep up the outward appearance of religion but are rejecting the power within. Doesn't that really sum up the world around you? GOD bestowed His divine knowledge on His Prophets of yesteryear and this current generation (described in the previous paragraph) is most accurately described in II Timothy 3:1-5 respectfully. Those who say that the Bible should not be taken 100% literally are in actuality...blinded with a false sense of trust in the shaky accomplishments of man. They are the professors of human knowledge who are deficient of real understanding...They lack the gift of common sense and are so intellectual in earthen affairs and humanistic endeavors that they fail to acknowledge the presence of divine wisdom, nor do they take the time to seek the One of its origin.

"Wherefore, behold, I send unto you prophets, and wise men and scribes: and some of them ye shall kill and crucify; and some of them shall ye scourge in your synagogues, and persecute them from city to city."
Matthew 23:34

That previous scripture is from the mouth of GOD concerning His prophesy for the world. This prophesy is fulfilled in our very generation. If you have the proper wisdom you will see the present day men "who are gifted with more than ordinary spiritual and moral insight (prophets)." They are the Oral Roberts, the Billy James Hargises, the Hal Lindseys, the Dwight Thompsons, the Jimmy Swaggarts, the Kenneth Hagins, the Charles Stanleys, the Gary Greenwalds, the Doug Clarks and the thousands of other men of GOD who have this gift.

If you have eyes to see and ears to listen, you will understand that GOD has already sent the wise men into this generation. Men like Paul Crouch who founded the Trinity Broadcasting Network (TBN) and Pat Robinson, founder of the Christian Broadcasting Network (CBN). They are "wise men" of GOD who have heard His calling to spread the Gospel of the kingdom in all the world as a witness unto all nations (Matthew 24:14). What better way in this current generation to get "the Word" out, than by satellite television. Other wise men of this generation include the Billy Grahams, the John Wesley Fletchers, the Demos Shakarians, the C.W. Wards, the R.W. Shambachs, the Arthur Blessits, the Kenneth Copelands, the Robert Schullers and the thousands of others who exercise sound judgment in the knowledge of GOD.

He has sent His authors and journalists (scribes) out with divine information to insure that His very elect will not be deceived by the many false prophets and false Christs that satan is pouring into this world (Matthew 24:24). People like Constance Cumbey (Hidden Dangers of the Rainbow), Hal Lindsey (Late Great Planet Earth, Satan is Alive and Well on Planet Earth and the Rapture), Pat Robinson (The Secret Kingdom), Oral Roberts (GOD Still Heals Today) and many other GOD-gifted writers who have heard His calling to get His "final warning" to the many who remain in spiritual darkness.

Those who truly acknowledge the workings of GOD will testify with extreme assurance that "Ominous Portents of the Parousia of Christ" (Revelations of Brimstone) is also a book of divine fiducial knowledge from GOD. Discern the spirit on which this book has been assembled and you'll come to no other explanation.

Another book of inspiration and knowledge is "Adventure in Adversity" by Paul Billheimer, who went home to Jesus last year. Copies may be obtained through Trinity Broadcasting Network ; P.O. Box A ; Santa Ana, California 92711. Enclose a love offering to further assist the Crouches of TBN with their heavy financial burden of getting GOD's message to our world.

In the following chapters of this book, some of you may become offended...others will be shocked. None will say in all honesty, that,what is said is not the truth.

Our GOD yearns for a close spiritual relationship with you and you will see how His eternal "Plan" for mankind is swiftly unfolding. Humans are not adhering to His commandments, His covenants or His divine hopes. He gave mankind a "freedom of choice," and man has chosen the pleasures of the flesh over proper restraint and eternal fellowship with their Maker.

In the following chapters you will come to acknowledge the "Power that IS," and hopefully change your course as a result of your added knowledge.

We are living in a time of joyous expectation for all believing Christians...a time in which we will witness the return of Jesus Christ to spare believers the horrors of the Tribulation period (The Rapture). If you don't know or believe in the Lord Jesus Christ, you don't know what you are missing. By accepting Jesus right now, you will be able to read the closing chapters of this book with extreme assurance that you will not be left behind to face the nearing Wrath of GOD on non-believers...Get on your knees, humble yourselves and say this prayer:

> Dear GOD, I have sinned against
> you and my fellow man. I ask you to
> forgive me. I accept that my Lord
> Jesus died on the cross for my sins
> and that by His Blood, my sins have
> been washed clean. I accept Him into
> my heart in the name of Jesus. Amen
> and Amen!

I WELCOME HOME all you new brothers and sisters in Christ.... Now read on with the knowledge that Jesus comes for us soon!

And Jesus said unto him, "VERILY I SAY UNTO THEE, TO-DAY SHALT THOU BE WITH ME IN PARADISE."

LUKE 23:43

CHAPTER SIXTEEN

Will Man Destroy Mankind By Nuclear War?
By Evangelist Oral Roberts

"But as in the days of Noe were, so shall also the coming of the Son of man be. For as in the days that were before the flood they were eating and drinking, marrying and giving in marriage, until the day that Noe entered into the ark, And knew not until the flood came, and took them away; so shall also the coming of the Son of man be."

JESUS CHRIST Matthew 24:37-39

People across the nation are talking about nuclear weapons...the possibility of world-wide war...the possibility that man might destroy himself from the face of the earth. MANY are fearful.

But...

I've got GOOD NEWS for you today. The Bible does not teach that man will annihilate the human race. The devil does not have the absolute power to destroy all of God's creation and wipe away mankind.

The Bible gives us a different message. It tells us that God is in control...that prayer works...That God has a plan that's different from man's plan.

This word from God is for 'today,' this very hour, and it's one of the most important messages I've ever shared with you.

You "can" escape the coming nuclear holocaust. You have the time if you act now. I am expecting this from you.

Let's begin with...

THE DAY AFTER

In November 1983, the American Broadcasting Company (ABC) aired a movie on television called "the Day After." The movie depicted a nuclear war between the United States and Russia in which each nation launched nuclear missles against the other.

The movie showed the people in Lawrence, Kansas, running and screaming in absolute panic as the nuclear weapons were seen rising from nearby silos. We saw the people scramble for food and supplies, trying to find a place to hide as they faced the final minutes before the bombs hit their own city. We saw the skin melt from their bodies as the bombs exploded.

Evelyn and I watched that movie and also the discussion that followed it.

After a while, a pattern began to emerge and this message began to form in my spirit from the word of God.

What Was Missing In The Day After?

I said to Evelyn, "Honey, do you notice what is absent from this film?"

"What?" she asked.

"Nobody's praying," I said. "The polls say that 80 percent of Americans believe in God. These people in the movie are supposedly facing great devastation and possibly the end of their lives, and not a single person is shown praying or calling on God. If people knew there was a nuclear strike, they'd be on their knees! They would be calling out to God as never before. This movie is not reality - it's a farce!"

As we watched the distinguished panelists discuss the movie, I waited to hear just one of them mention the name of God or encourage the people to pray that such a war might never happen. Not a word was said about the Bible's description of the end-time drama which includes the Second Coming of Christ.

The Bible Does NOT Teach Worldwide Nuclear Holocaust

The Bible does not teach that man will utterly destroy himself. This does not mean that we may not see an isolated nuclear explosion on earth. But the type of 'total' nuclear holocaust depicted in this movie is not prophesied in the Bible.

God has not given that power to man. Man does not have the authority from God to wipe out mankind. You need to know this!

The great war described in the Bible is not a war which man is fighting against man. The great war that will annihilate the unregenerated human race is not set off by human beings. That war will be a war between the antichrist and Jesus Christ, and it will happen at the Second Coming of Christ in the Battle of Armageddon (See Revelations 16:16).

I can tell you on the authority of the Bible that you can sleep tonight without worrying that America will be destroyed by Russia or that Russia will be destroyed by America.

Jesus said that there would be wars and rumors of wars and that nations would rise up against nations.   (See Matthew

24:6,7). But Jesus did not teach that the nations would cease to be or that one people would extinguish another from the earth.

As I write to you today, I am told that more than 40 wars are going on right now in this earth - more than 40 groups and nations have risen up against one another. But they're not going to annihilate themselves or the entire human race.

God has entrusted that power to Himself and to His believers. The Bible gives us four great reasons why the devil will not destroy this earth.

1. The Preaching of the Gospel to All Nations Will Bring About the End of This Age - NOT a Nuclear Holocaust

Turn in your Bible to Matthew 24:14 and underline this verse. It says:

"And this gospel of the kingdom shall be preached in all the world for a witness unto all nations; and then shall the end come."

Friend, let this verse sink into your spirit. Jesus himself said that the gospel takes precedence over everything else. It 'shall' be preached whether the devil is for or against it, whether mankind is for or against it.

The preaching of the gospel will precede the end - not a nuclear holocaust, not an act of man against man. The unleashing of the Word of God, not the unleashing of man-made missles, will bring about the Second Coming of Jesus.

Today, young men and women across this nation and around the world are hearing the call to preach the gospel. That's the very reason Oral Roberts University was called into being. God told me to "raise up your students to hear My voice and to go where My voice is heard small, My light is seen dim, and My power is not known - even to the uttermost bounds of the earth. Their work will exceed yours. And in that I'm well pleased."

Right now, the sun does not set on any continent where there's not an Oral Roberts University student or graduate preaching and teaching the gospel and healing the sick. And we're just one part of the Body of Christ.

Jesus said the gospel would be preached to all nations for a witness. He didn't say that everybody in the world would be converted. The Bible doesn't say that all the nations will be saved. But I believe all will be given an 'opportunity' to accept Christ. The gospel will have an impact on every nation - a remnant from every nation will be saved - and then shall the end come.

No, the devil does not have the power to start the end-time drama. We who are the believers hold that power because it is up to the Christians to preach the gospel and not stop until they preach it to all nations.

2. The End of the Age Will Be Similar to the Times of Noah – NOT Similar to a Nuclear War

In Matthew 24:37-39, Jesus gives us a second reason why the devil will not destroy the earth by nuclear war. This passage of the scripture says:

"But as the days of Noe were, so shall also the coming of the Son of man be. For as in the days that were before the flood they were eating and drinking, marrying and giving in marriage, until the day that Noe entered into the ark, And knew not until the flood came, and took them away; so shall also the coming of the Son of man be."

When Jesus describes the time right before His Second Coming, He does not describe a scene of devastation. He describes a world in which everybody is just going about normal routine business. Working, eating, marrying, giving birth...it's just the same old everyday world.

Let me tell you, if the two superpowers of this world were preparing for an all-out war, things wouldn't be normal. If nuclear missiles were launched, things wouldn't be normal. If nuclear bombs were exploded, there wouldn't be a lot of folks left to marry and there wouldn't be an 'attitude' that everything was all right.

In Luke 12:39,40, Jesus said that the end of the age would be like a thief coming in the night. People won't have time to stall, stock up or dig a bomb shelter. When God puts into motion the end-time events, the wicked forces of this earth will have no time to prepare, to pray or to repent.

Now if the leader of the United States or the leader of the Soviet Union pushed the buttons to release the warheads that would destroy the earth, we would have time to know about it. We would not be caught totally unaware. But that wouldn't be the case at the time of the rapture. The coming of the Lord will be sudden and unexpected by the world at large.

Where do we stand today then? I believe there's a stalemate. I want to remind you for a moment of World War II. If Japan had possessed an equal number of atomic bombs to those held by America, do you think America would have dropped the bombs on Hiroshima and Nagasaki? No way in the world.

Today we're told that America and Russia 'each' have 20,000 powerful warheads. There's a stalemate. The mind of man has created something out of its natural order, but God has decreed that man will not have the power to use such weapons to completely destroy mankind, the masterpiece of His creation.

Now we can be concerned. We can work so that the number of these awesome weapons will be reduced on all sides. We can work to make sure that others don't get them. We can keep the stalemate in place. But we should NOT be cowering with fear so that we can hardly move! Not if we have Jesus Christ as the center of our lives.

3. Those Who Believe in Jesus Christ Will NOT Suffer God's Wrath

The final Battle of Armageddon that is described beginning in the fifteenth chapter of the Book of Revelation will be between Jesus Christ and the antiChrist. Prior to that great battle, much of the earth will be destroyed as the angels pour out the vials of God's wrath on 'unrepentant' man. (See Revelation 16 & 17)

The antiChrist and his cohort, the false prophet, will dupe the world and bring devastating economic, political, military and moral chaos on earth. Unrepentant man will writhe in agony under their reign. (See Revelation 13)

But I want you to pay special attention in the Book of Revelation to the word 'unrepentant' - or sinful, wicked, rebellious.

The wrath of God and the wrath of evil man will fall upon those who blaspheme God - who totally and eternally reject God's plan for their salvation. The people of God will NOT suffer God's wrath. They are the recipients of God's mercy.

Turn again in your Bible to Matthew 24:40,41. Jesus describes what will happen to those who trust Him:

"Then shall two be in the field; the one shall be taken, and the other left. Two women shall be grinding at the mill; the one shall be taken, and the other left."

In Luke 17:34, we read where two will be in bed - one shall be taken, and the other left.

These scriptures speak of the catching away of the Bride of Christ, of the real believers. We call this the 'Rapture.' First Thessalonians 4:16-18 describes this great event in more detail:

"FOR THE LORD HIMSELF SHALL DESCEND FROM HEAVEN WITH A SHOUT............."
I THESSALONIANS 4:16-18

"For the Lord Himself shall descend from heaven with a shout, with the voice of the archangel, and with the trump of God: and the dead in Christ will rise first: Then we which are alive and remain shall be caught up together with them in the clouds to meet the Lord in the air: and so shall we ever be with the Lord. Wherefore comfort one another with these words."

I want you to pay special attention to three things in these passages from the Bible.

First, we who believe in Jesus Christ are going to be WITH Christ when God pours out His vengeance upon the earth.

When Jesus calls for us with a shout, gravitation is going to loose its grip and we'll rise to be with the Lord.

Up until that moment, we'll be working and sleeping as usual. The Bible does not teach that Christians will be hole up somewhere in a bomb shelter or suffering under the torture of nuclear fallout or running in panic through the streets. The Bible says that two will be working in the fields, two will be grinding grain, two will be asleep.

Now if people knew that a nuclear holocaust were coming, they wouldn't be sleeping peacefully or working normally!

Jesus taught in a parable that we are to "occupy" until He comes. (See Luke 19:13.) And, friend, that's what we should be concentrating on...that's what we should be doing. We are to be about the work of the Lord right until the split second when He calls for us with a heavenly shout!

Second, the Bible teaches in these verses that JESUS HIMSELF will bring about the culmination of the end time.

Jesus Himself sounds the final battle cry. Not America. Not Russia. Not the devil. Not the forces of the antiChrist. Jesus brings about the end of this age.

In Matthew 24:36 Jesus says, "But of that day or hour knoweth no man, no, not the angels of heaven, but My Father only." God and God alone is in control of the eternal timetable! He alone sets the time!

We are to do everything possible to preach the gospel to all nations for a witness and to set the stage. That's our calling, our commission. But God alone raises the curtain to begin the final act of history.

Third, the Bible teaches in these passages that we are to COMFORT ONE ANOTHER with these words.

Let me assure you, there would be no comfort if we experienced a worldwide nuclear holocaust. But that isn't God's plan. His plan is for us Christians - those who truly believe in Jesus Christ as the Lord and Savior of our lives - to be with the Lord and protected from God's wrath.

4. The Bible Teaches That Judgement Begins in the House of God - NOT in Military Planning Rooms

The Bible says in I Peter 4:17:

> "For the time has come that judgment must begin at the House of God: and if it first begin at us, what shall the end be of them that obey not the gospel of God?"

The judgement begins with us. It begins as we preach the gospel throughout the earth for a witness to all nations.

The gospel cuts and divides the believer from the unbeliever. It separates the righteous from the unrighteous. It's the sole dividing line. When God judges us before His throne in eternity, it will be on the basis of what we have done with the gospel. (See Revelation 20:10-15)

Judgement does not begin in Moscow, in Washington, D.C., or in the other halls of government on this earth. Judgement begins with us Christians and with our efforts to preach the gospel in all nations. Are you hearing this?

GOD Has a Plan That Is Different From Man's Plan

God does have a plan for the end of the earth as we know it. God's plan includes worldwide war. It includes utter devastation of the oceans, waterways, land and air as they exist today. (Again see Revelation 15)

God's plan is an absolute black and white plan. Sin 'will' be wiped out. Those who fail to believe in Jesus Christ 'will' choose to follow the devil and 'will' be destroyed.

What is the plan of God for man?

Where do we stand in the unfolding of that plan today?

How can we be fully prepared for the future?

These are the questions I want to answer with you next from the Word of God.

God Has A Victory Plan

God does have a plan. He has a way for us to live in VICTORY. That victory begins the moment we accept Jesus Christ as the Lord and Savior of our lives and it NEVER ENDS. It lasts throughout all eternity because it's a victory in our souls. It's a victory that can survive any outside circumstance - any event, any problem, any difficulty, including death itself.

First, it is GOD'S Plan That People Should Repent of Their Sins, Be Baptized, and Be Filled With the Power of the Holy Spirit

In John 7:37-39, Jesus said,

> "If any man thirst, let him come unto Me, and drink. He that believeth on Me, as the scripture hath said, out of his belly shall flow rivers of living water. (But this spake he of the Spirit...)"

I want you to notice that Jesus said, "If any man 'thirst'." You know we can do without food for a long time, but a person must have water to live. Jesus is speaking here of life - of the great desire to have eternal life, abundant life, life that is full and fulfilling.

He said that when you believe on Him, something is going to happen in our belly area. Now that's not the stomach. It's the "pit of the stomach" or the solar plexus area where we feel our deepest emotions. It's where we feel extreme joy and, at times, gripping fear. Jesus said that when we believe on Him, we will feel the power of the Holy Spirit and it will come up in our inner being as a rising tide. It will be a stream of new life flowing in us out of our belly area.

Turn to Acts 2:38 and you'll read where Peter was preaching on the Day of Pentecost.

Jesus had been crucified, resurrected and had ascended to heaven. He had sent the Holy Spirit to 120 faithful men and women in an upper room where they were meeting in Jerusalem. The people had been filled with the Holy Spirit as Jesus had described, and they were praising God in "other tongues." A crowd gathered to see what was happening. And Peter used that opportunity to preach a sermon that won 3,000 souls to Christ in one afternoon. Here is his final plea:

> "Repent, and be baptized every one of you in the name of Jesus Christ for the remission of sins, and ye shall receive the gift of the Holy Ghost." (Acts 2:38)

Note that it says you 'shall' receive the Holy Ghost. No 'ifs', 'hope so,' or 'maybes'. It's the same as John 7:38, "Out of his belly 'shall' flow rivers of living water." (which is the Holy Spirit)

It is God's plan that those who repent and believe on

Jesus Christ 'shall' receive the Holy Spirit. That means you go immediately into the "rivers" of the Holy Spirit flowing up within you.

The Prayer Language of the Holy Spirit Connects You Directly With God

A man from California traveled to see me recently. I was preaching in chapel at Oral Roberts University and he happened to be there and asked for prayer. After the service I prayed for him.

He had his head down and the tears were streaming down his cheeks and dropping onto the carpet. He said, Brother Roberts, I've cheated on my wife for years and she finally left me. She's not coming back." Then he told me he had invested over a million dollars in the oil fields of Oklahoma and Texas and his million dollars had gone down the drain.

I asked him if he had a relationship with Jesus Christ.

"I was born again about three months ago," he said, "when my daughter prayed with me."

I was thinking to myself, this is certainly a strange born-again Christian, and then he blurted out, "The truth is, I don't have a connection with Him. I've come 1,500 miles to see you because I feel Oral Roberts can connect me with God. It's only God who can bring my wife back to me now."

This man told me that he had never 'felt' the presence of God in his life and I said to him, "If you had ever felt it, you would know it. If you haven't, you don't know it. The Holy Spirit has either entered your being and risen up inside you like rivers of flowing water, or He hasn't."

"I want to be connected to God," he said, "I really want to know Him."

"Then let's pray."

I led this man in a sinner's prayer, and if you have never prayed a prayer like this and you want Jesus Christ to be alive in your life, I invite you to pray it out loud today:

"Oh, GOD, be merciful to me, a sinner. Be merciful to me - a sinner. Oh, GOD, I have not put you first in my life. I've put myself first. Jesus, I believe you are the Son of GOD. I believe you died for me. I believe you rose from the dead for me. I believe You are coming into my life and I receive You as my personal Savior right 'now' in the name of Jesus Christ of Nazareth. Amen and amen."

248

This man finally got serious about it. He 'really' began to pray and call upon GOD. He believed like he never believed before. Finally he looked up with a glow in his face and he said excitedly, "I've believed! I've believed!"

"How do you know?" I said.

"Because it's coming up right in the pit of my stomach."

"That's the Holy Spirit," I said, "Begin speaking right NOW by the Spirit in your prayer language."

I began to pray in my prayer language and then I stopped and said to him, "You are a spirit first and foremost. You live in a body, but you aren't just physical. You have a mind to think through, but you aren't just mental. You are a spirit and GOD is a Spirit. Begin to pray out of your spirit to Him."

And this man released his prayer language right then and there.

Since he returned home he has begun writing me. He says he's really putting GOD first in his life and trusting GOD as his source. He has become a partner with me.

Now let me say this to you:

If 'you' have never released your prayer language and you have believed on Jesus Christ, you 'can' release your prayer language. You can speak out of your spirit. It's GOD's plan for you to do that. You will be strengthened enormously in your inner self by doing it.

Second, It is GOD's Plan That We Interpret Our Prayer Language Back to Our Minds So We Can Have Daily Direction in Our Lives

When GOD created Adam, He made him in such a way that his spirit was over his mind. But when Adam rebelled against God, his mind rose up over his spirit. He began to try to reason things out for himself. He lost his language of spiritual communication 'directly' to GOD.

It's like that for us today. We have our minds as the guiding, dominant force in our lives. Our spirits are suppressed. When we believe on Jesus Christ and He sends the Holy Spirit flowing up like rivers into our innermost being, our spirit is elevated back to its supreme position. Our ability of communicating directly with GOD is restored to us.

I repeat: When you really believe on Jesus, He immediately causes the Holy Spirit to 'erupt' in your innermost belly and the Spirit of GOD to come rising up. As you speak out the syllables of your spiritual language to GOD, I believe you're speaking to GOD in the same way that Adam had spoken to GOD 'directly.' You're talking personally to GOD. You're speaking from the deep recesses of your inner man. It's your own unique 'prayer' language. (See I Corinthians 14:2, 13-15)

Now I want to make one point very clear to you...

Your own personal prayer language is different from the "gift of tongues" as described in I Corinthians 12:10. (It is one of the nine major gifts of the Holy Spirit that is listed in the twelfth chapter of I Corinthians.)

The gifts of the Holy Spirit are given by the Holy Spirit as He 'wills' it to allow us to minister to other people. The gift listed as "utterance of an unknown tongue" is always to be accompanied by the interpretation of that tongue in your own language. (See I Corinthians 14:27,28.) The gift is NOT for the person doing the speaking. It's for the person who is hearing the message and the interpretation. In other words, you are the 'deliverer' of a word from GOD to others. You are the instrument and others are the receiver.

Your own personal prayer language of the Spirit, on the other hand, is your personal language "in the Spirit." It's a language you 'will' to speak to GOD as the Holy Spirit rises up within you to give you utterance. A gift of the tongues comes to you as a believer by the 'will' of the Holy Spirit...but your personal language comes out of 'your will' as need arises.

When this man came to me from California and had repented and believed on the Lord Jesus, he immediately experienced the divine rivers flowing up and began to speak in a beautiful language. By his will, the Holy Spirit language within him came up over his tongue and rolled out of his mouth until I said, "Now stop and immediately pray in English."

He did. And when he finished, he looked at me in amazement and said, "I never prayed a prayer like that before."

His prayer in English was spontaneous. He didn't have to labor in his mind for the right words to use. His prayer was natural and easy flowing. It was 'inspired.' He spoke it out because he 'willed' to do it.

Several years ago when my daughter and son-in-law were killed in a plane crash, Evelyn and I hurt so much we didn't know what to pray. We didn't even feel like praying. One night Evelyn came to me and said, "Honey, hold me. Pray for me. I don't think I can make it through the night."

As we held each other, we began to pray and then to pray in our prayer languages. Let me tell you friend, the Holy Spirit takes up the praying. He intercedes for us with groanings in our hearts that we cannot utter. There's no equal for that kind of pain in human language alone.

We prayed in our prayer languages and then stopped, and I began to pray in English. And out of that GOD gave me an interpretation that released us from the horror of our daughter's death. We caught a glimpse of our daughter and son-in-law in heaven!

Out of that experience God gave us the strength to begin to understand and to go on with our lives. And right after that, GOD gave us the plan for the "City of Faith Medical and Research Center" which is helping thousands in every State in the Union and all over the world!

Friend, GOD took our pain and gave us joy in return. He took our confusion and gave us understanding in what to do. I can tell you this helps.

That's what praying in the Spirit and interpreting back can do in your life. It can give you the boost of power you need to get over the hurt. It can give you the direction you need to turn your circumstances into something good.

Yes, GOD's plan is for us to live out of our 'spirits' – to pray out of our spirits – and to interpret GOD's messages back to our own minds so that we might have better direction in our everyday lives.

****

Evangelist Oral Roberts is known around the world as one of the outstanding men of GOD in this generation. He has been in the healing and deliverance ministry for over 36 years. Since 1947, he has conducted over 300 healing crusades on 5 continents and written more than 50 books, including "Miracles of Seed Faith" which has found its way into the hands of nearly 8 million people.

Oral Roberts is the founder of Oral Roberts University and the City of Faith Medical and Research Center, located in Tulsa, Oklahoma.

Oral Roberts is a man blessed by GOD who truly cares for people and reaches out to them with the healing power of GOD's love.

His input to the making of this book is highly appreciated. Oral took the time out of his busy schedule to personally respond to my request. I love this brother. Write him for a FREE booklet on his ministry and information on his many books inspired by Almighty GOD.

Evangelist Oral Roberts
Tulsa, Oklahoma 74171

Pray for him and the great work he's doing in the name of Jesus Christ! Become one of his "FAITH PARTNERS" by enclosing a 'love gift' to further assist him in preaching the Gospel of the Lord to all the world!

"DAUGHTERS OF JERUSALEM, WEEP NOT
NOT FOR ME, BUT WEEP FOR YOURSELVES,
AND FOR YOUR CHILDREN.
FOR, BEHOLD, THE DAYS ARE COMING
IN THE WHICH THEY SHALL SAY,
BLESSED ARE THE BARREN, AND
THE WOMBS THAT NEVER BARE,
AND THE PAPS THAT NEVER GAVE
SUCK.
THEN SHALL THEY BEGIN TO
SAY TO THE MOUNTAINS,
FALL ON US; AND TO THE
HILLS, COVER US.
FOR IF THEY DO
THESE THINGS IN
A GREEN TREE,
WHAT SHALL BE
BE DONE IN
THE DRY?"

(Luke 23:28-31)

CHAPTER SEVENTEEN

Beware When They Say...''Peace & Safety!''
By Evangelist Billy James Hargis

> "For when they shall say, Peace and Safety; then sudden destruction cometh upon them, as travail upon a woman with child; and they shall not escape." I Thessalonians 5:3

As Christians, we have all heard sermons on the "signs of the times." Some of the first sermons I ever heard on Biblical prophesy were on the "signs of the times" that would be fulfilled before the Second Coming of Christ. Some of these signs included religious apostasy (falling away from known teachings of Christ); the rise in sexual perversion; an increase of promiscuity and/or pre-marital and extra-marital sex and divorce; wars and rumors of wars, etc.

But, few of the old timers ever preached on I Thessalonians 5:1-4, yet, this particular prophesy that is to be fulfilled before the Second Coming of Jesus Christ, is one of the clearest and most detailed "signs of the times" in the Bible.

The Apostle Paul makes it very clear that he is talking about the Second Coming of Christ..."The day of the Lord cometh as a thief in the night." (verse 2) Then, he says, "For when they shall say, Peace and Safety, then sudden destruction cometh upon them, as travail upon a woman with child; and they shall not escape."

In other words, when the religious world is so pre-occupied with "peace on earth," efforts by compromise, political negotiations, i.e., by man's schemes for peace and safety, "then sudden destruction will come upon them...they shall not escape, so then, beware, lest that day should overtake you as a thief." (verses 3 & 4)

I forecast a greater division in the Body of Christ (church) in the immediate days ahead than the historical Catholic versus Protestant schism or the "liberal versus fundamentalist" controversy. This division will be between the Bible-believing Christians on the subject of unilateral disarmament.

Already there is a hue and cry in the nation to disarm...peace at any price...unilateral disarmament. Man can not bring about peace on earth. It will only come with the Second Coming of Christ. But when evangelical and charismatic

Christians and some fundamentalist Christians get involved in promoting "nuclear freeze," "negotiated political peace" with anti-Christ communists and "unilateral disarmament," it will inevitably produce a split in the Body of Christ. But more important to the lover of Bible prophecy, this is proof that the coming of Christ is near.

Traditionally, only the liberal church leaders who deny the inspiration of the Bible and the Deity of Christ would have promoted the nuclear freeze, unilateral disarmament and negotiated peace with the communists. The true Bible-believing Christian always stood pat against these things that can only aid the cause of international communism, but now even evangelicals, who held opposite views traditionally, are making strange noises about unilateral disarmament, nuclear freeze, etc., which will, beyond any shadow of a doubt, cause a division in the Body of Christ among the believers which consist of charismatics, evangelicals, the orthodox and fundamentalists.

The REAL Peace Movement in America

The phoney "peace" and "disarmament" and "nuclear freeze" movements now going on in America and the rest of the world, are in fact inspired by Soviet agents and propaganda and new media manipulation to weaken American defense.

Let me tell you about the REAL peace movement in America, the story the conventional news media won't report. In 1959, it was America that initiated the Antarctic Treaty banning nuclear weapons and military forces on the great icecap of the South Pole known as the Antarctic Continent.

In 1963, it was America that initiated the Partial Test Ban Treaty with the Soviet Union, one of the many they have secretly tried to break by illegal testing.

In 1967, it was America that initiated the Outer Space Treaty, banning nuclear weapons in outer space and pledging space for peaceful, not military, purposes.

In the same year, 1967, it was America that initiated the Treaty of Tlateloco, banning nuclear weapons in Latin America.

In 1970, again it was America that initiated the Treaty of Non-Proliferation of Nuclear Weapons, another one broken by the Soviets.

This phoney "peace" movement initiated by the Soviets here in the 1980s is nothing more than a propaganda ploy and a ploy designed to stop the placement of missiles in NATO countries, missiles that would balance those of the Soviet Union that are already in place threatening Western Europe. It also is designed to stop deployment of the neutron artillery shell warhead...mistakenly called the neutron bomb by the news media...that would overcome the Soviet advantage of tanks in Europe...tanks that have increased in number from 20,000 to 40,000, while the Soviets have been promoting the so-called "peace" campaign.

Hand in hand with the disarmament and peace movement, has come the nuclear freeze movement. Nuclear weapons have deterred the Soviet Union from using its overwhelming conventional military forces from overrunning Western Europe and launching World War III for 30 years. The way the Soviets see it, if they could just persuade enough Americans to come out politically against nuclear weapons...the way they came out against the Vietnam War that the communists won...then that 30-year deterrent against their conventional military force could be removed and the way would be opened for the conquest of Western Europe and who knows how much else of the world.

There are a half-dozen United States Senators running around all over the country and parts of the world making speeches against the U.S. nuclear defense and demanding a "nuclear freeze." Senator Ted Kennedy is one of the most prominent of these peace-disarmament-nuclear freeze senators.

There are a half-dozen liberal entertainers in Hollywood I could name who are among the major mouthpieces and financial supporters of this Soviet-inspired nuclear freeze movement. They have either been duped by the communists or know nothing about communism and what they are doing...how they are being used...to weaken American defense and resolve our political will to resist godless communism...I could name...I WILL name them:

Goldie Hawn, Henry Winkler, Olivia Newton-John, Dinah Shore, Robert Wagner, James Garner, Ron Howard, Jean Stapleton, Mary Tyler Moore, Jane Fonda and many others who find it fashionable to support what they consider to be liberal causes such as the nuclear freeze. If they ever took time to think it through, they would realize they are supporting a communist cause that is more reactionary, more tyrannical, more un-democratic and un-liberal than Hitler or Attila the Hun because communism is a strict dictatorship.

These entertainers would be among the first suppressed if the communists ever came to power in America because it is known they dissent against the government. In America, we consider that to be their right, even if we think they are wrong. But under communism they would not be given such an opportunity again.

Soviet-front organizations dominate this phoney peace and nuclear freeze movement. I've named them before on my program...for the benefit of the readers of this book, I'll name just a few right quickly...organizations with either definite anti-American policies or outright connections with the Soviet Union, all with offices in the United States, mostly in Washington:

The World Peace Council...the United States Peace Council...the Institute for the United States and Canada...the American Committee on East-West Accord...the American Friends Service Committee...the Arms Control Association...the Center for Defense Information...and the Center for Development Policy.

All of their titles seem innocent enough, but every one of them is busy at work turning out literally tons of propaganda designed to weaken America's defense.

The real peace movement is not the one being led by these Red-fronts, communist agents, the sympathizers and the dupes. The real peace movement has existed a long time in America's efforts to keep the peace through solemn treaties. And the real peace movement is led by Christians in America who are not fooled by godless communism. The ones who have a strong faith in Christ Jesus as their Saviour and stand ready to defend their country...our Christian America...against the godless forces of evil that would destroy it.

Confirmed: The Communist World Council of Churches!

The big world meeting of the World Council of Churches in Vancouver, British Columbia, was held in 1983. The main thing that was achieved was the confirmation that this organization is indeed an agent for communism.

After 18 days of phoney-baloney talk about how church people can be both Christians and marxists or other nonsense, the World Council of Churches finally got to its big gun, its final dramatic play, the real reason why the meeting was set up in the first place...<u>DISARMAMENT</u>.

And by disarmament, the communist World Council of Churches meant unilateral and immediate disarmament by the United States, never mind the Soviet's increasing stockpile of nuclear weaponry.

In the 'big' final statement aimed at Christian Americans, the Council called for a "complete halt" in not only nuclear weapons research and production, but urged Christians to refuse to work in nuclear weapons plants or in any capacity related to nuclear warfare, presumably that includes the armed forces.

And to emphasize that the call for disarmament was unilateral and meant for the United States only, the World Council of Churches stated that: "Such a position supports the struggle to cause 'one's own nation' to commit itself never to own or use nuclear weapons, despite this period of nuclear vulnerability."

The Council also rejected the idea of nuclear deterrence...that is, keeping peace in the world by armed strength, which has been the American and Western Allies policy since the end of World War II..as "morally unacceptable" and incapable of safeguarding peace in the long run.

I don't know what the World Council of Churches thinks the "long run" is if it isn't nearly 40 years since the end of World War II without the emergence of World War III on a major nuclear scale. The only reason it hasn't is because of America's nuclear deterrence, the very thing that upsets Moscow and the World Council of Churches the most.

As for Christians not defending their country, that's straight communist propaganda. Christian Americans, as well as Americans of other religious faiths, have been defending this country for more than 200 years, thank you, and doing a fine job of it. The prayers of Christian Americans for this country, for the men in our armed forces and for the safety of our country have been a major reason why America still exists.

For the World Council to come along and say that it is 'morally unacceptable' for Christian Americans to defend their country and to say that nuclear deterrence cannot safeguard peace in the long run is not only contrary to historical facts, but confirms again that, to me at least, the World Council of Churches...and its American affiliate, the National Council of Churches, with whom it shares offices in New York City, are nothing more than propaganda agencies for world communism.

Only state-controlled religions are tolerated in the Soviet Union. That's not Chrisianity. The true Christian churches in the Soviet Union meet secretly to avoid persecution and even taking these precautions, they are sometimes raided and the leaders imprisoned and exiled. So the phoney-baloney preaching of the World Council of Churches to Christians is aimed exclusively at Christian Americans.

I can't speak for all Christian Americans, but I can speak for one, myself. And here is my answer to the World Council of Churches and the National Council of Churches: I totally reject your suggestions concerning disarmament and nuclear deterrence policies. Wrap them up and send them back to Moscow where they came from.

American Bishops and Communist Party Line

The designers of communist propaganda in Moscow cheer the nuclear position, also championed by the National Council of Catholic Bishops.

The American bishops have swallowed the communist nuclear freeze line completely, along with the hook and sinker. Using liberal pacifists as "experts" in their 'freeze report,' the bishops say it is time to raise the "moral, human and religious dimensions" of the nuclear threat. That's what makes the communists cheer,...and laugh. The communists are not interested in moral, human or religious dimensions, they are only interested in imposing communism on the entire world at any price.

Can't these bishops understand that communism is godless, atheistic and anti-Christ by its own manifesto and other policy documents? Can't the bishops understand that the enemy is not the nuclear bomb or the U.S. Defense Department, but the enemy is godless communism that is already prepared to strike America first with a nuclear bomb rain if their plan of encirclement of America were to fail, which it isn't.

These Catholic bishops don't understand communism or its goals. They haven't learned anything about the international communist revolution still going on today and the international communist conspiracy that the revolution fosters and supports. These bishops have taken each other and their followers by the hand, like the blind leading the blind, and are going for a walk in the midst of ravenous wolves. Christians are the communists' number one enemy. They are always the first to be persecuted or eliminated when the communists take over a country. But listen to what the National Conference of Catholic Bishops say in their 66-page draft recommending a nuclear freeze:

"If nuclear weapons may be used at all, they may be used only after they have been used against us or our allies, and, even then, only in an extremely limited, discriminating manner against military targets." (That's an open invitation for the Soviets to bomb us first.)

And it's a promise that if the Soviets place their nuclear launch sites in the midst of a civilian population...like the PLO did, using civilians as shields in Beirut...then we won't strike back for fear of killing civilians.

No wonder the Kremlin propagandists are cheering and laughing at Americans. The bishops are laughable in thinking that a nuclear freeze on our part will have the slightest effect on Russian plans to nuke us into submission whenever they feel they won't get blasted in return.

The Soviets don't plan to "freeze" or disarm anything on their side. The whole nuclear freeze and disarmament campaign was hatched in the Kremlin and aimed only at the United States. The so-called "peace" demonstrations and "nuclear freeze" marches that began in Europe earlier this year (1984) and spread to the United States just didn't happen...they were carefully planned and orchestrated by communist agents upon orders from Moscow. They are the response to the American plans to deploy Pershing and Cruise missiles in Europe.

We are deploying missiles to counteract the Soviet deployment of missiles and Backfire Bombers in new positions threatening Western Europe...our NATO allies we pledged by solemn treaty to defend. There have been no "grass root" marches or demonstrations. They have all been planned and promoted by communists, Soviet agents, sympathizers and dupes who have used the leftist, liberal news media as a means of publicity.

The communist campaign to disarm America is not new. It is led by many of the same people who captained the Red propaganda campaign during the Vietnam War...a disaster for South Vietnam, our betrayed ally, more so than a disaster for us.

The national news media has failed in its duty...if that's the word for whatever they do...as journalists, by not telling the American people the truth about these phoney peace and nuclear freeze demonstrations and associations. Have you heard the media talking about the World Peace Council? That's the communist front in America to promote disarmament and nuclear freeze. In Europe, it's an organization
called Socialists International. Where is "60 Minutes" with an expose on these Red fronts? Television film of people marching provides the alleged "action" TV news needs, but who put them up to it? What is the origin? If TV did its job, they would dig into the World Peace Council and Socialist International. They would give all the facts about this Kremlin nuclear freeze campaign instead of serving them by making Americans think that it all started in a pacifist grass-roots of our country.

As for the bishops, I can only say that they should know better. They should do their homework on communism before they play into communist hands by issuing a nuclear freeze resolution.

Anti-American Propaganda in the Public Schools

As if our public schools weren't in enough trouble, along comes the National Education Association with one of the most blatant pieces of communist propaganda yet for the consumption of our children.

It was NEA's parting shot to American youngsters just prior to Summer vacation in 1983. It was a pamphlet called

"Choices: A Unit on Conflict and Nuclear War," but it didn't offer any choices...It was an out and out allegation for unilateral disarmament by the United States, which is the number one propaganda goal of Moscow today.

The only "choice" the NEA offers youngsters is for the option of nuclear freeze by the United States. The NEA takes the debatable position that the U.S. is so far ahead of the Soviet Union in the nuclear arms category that we can afford to freeze our program, whether Moscow does or not.

The pamphlet is not only one-sided, it is incorrect in many instances. It claims that our national defense budget is larger than social spending when in fact the defense budget gets approximately 29 percent of the federal expenditures while 42 percent goes to social welfare on a national basis and II percent to the States for various local social programs.

The main trouble with these leftist allegations being distributed in our public school systems is that it doesn't explain why the United States must continue to spend these amounts on national defense. It doesn't inform the students of the Soviet military buildup, the Soviet missile threat to Europe, the Soviet history or their programs of military aggression. It says nothing of the Soviet Union's conquests of Afghanistan or Central America.

It's bad enough that the public schools are failing in their objectives to properly educate the youth of America...turning out millions who the National Commission on Excellence in Education refers to as "functional illiterates." Now the National Education Association, which spends most of its time and capital as a super-union devoted to higher salaries for teachers, has become an additional outlet for communist propaganda.

The NEA turned to the Union of Concerned Scientists for the technical help in preparing the manual. The Union of Concerned Scientists is a leftist, liberal organization that has yet to take one conservative stand on anything from atomic energy plants to Darwin's theory on evolution and zoology. It has become a convenient vehicle for just this sort of communist idiocy.

This display is a perfect example that explains why the public schools in America have become a laughingstock. They are more interested in fictitious allegory and untruths than they are in education. They have allowed prayer and Bible reading out of the public school in favor of secular humanism propaganda. They have tossed out the truth of GOD's creation in favor of Darwin's misrepresentation on evolution. They dispense with the teaching of our free enterprise system in favor of socialist related ideology and are allowing morality to stagnate while they promote sexual awareness in the classrooms.

Now they bring in this unbalanced, biased and ludicrous piece of communist trash about our need for a nuclear freeze and foist it off on unsuspecting and worldly naive junior high school students as factual information when it represents nothing but communist subversive slime.

Any time we think our public schools can't get any lower in ideals, they discover an innovation to prove us in error.

Why We Can't Afford A Nuclear Freeze!

There are several reasons why the U.S. cannot afford to tarry with the arms race...the most obvious is that it would compromise our national security and expose our nation to overt nuclear blackmail by the Soviet Union.

A more important reason, many times overlooked by either the opponents or proponents of the nuclear freeze debate, is this: The Soviet weapons systems...the missiles that would deliver the nukes...have been consistently improved over the past twenty years while ours have been rotting in their silos.

In the twenty years since the Cuban Missile Crisis showdown between Kennedy and Khrushchev, the Soviets have played an effective game aimed at nuclear superiority. They now have become so mighty that the U.S. is forced to reevaluate our position as the strongest force on planet Earth. That is now a subject of great conjecture and debate.

Had there been any question about our vast superiority in technology twenty years ago, Khrushchev would have never been backed down by Kennedy. We were the strongest then. Such is not the case now.

If a nuclear freeze is to come about now and we are locked into our present nuclear status, we will be accepting a permanent vulnerability, a policy that would expose our national defense as weak and be agreeing to a self-imposed program of appeasement that could ultimately invite our own destruction.

You can freeze the manufacturing and deployment of nuclear weaponry, but you cannot place a halt on the natural aging process that results in the deterioration of these technologically complex machines.

Simply stated, our weaponry is already much older and less sophisticated than those of the Soviet Union. If we were to make any unilateral agreement with the Soviet Union concerning a nuclear freeze today, the fact remains that these missiles would become obsolete before one speck of paint would peel from the Soviet stockpile of thermonuclear weaponry. That's the present Russian advantage.

Certainly we should be concerned when it comes to nuclear powered devices of destruction. Millions of Americans are living in constant fear of a possible future exchange, but they become misinformed when they assume the stance that the way to remove the threat is by disarmament or joining the peace movements or even so little as a nuclear freeze which would render the United States at the door of submission to a communist dictator.

Before anyone gets carried away with the terror of such warfare, view the prospects from our adversary's vantage point. Their ideology may be godless and their dedication may be aimed at world conquest, but at least on the surface they appear to be of human species, capable of logical reason in respect to the ramifications of any future nuclear exhibition. Yes, even totalitarians are not immune to the fear that such an exchange would propose to their homeland. They are not as foolish as they sometimes appear.

So, if we freeze our already antiquated system of determent and make an avowal of never using our weaponry, the Kremlin no longer would have cause to fear our retaliation. In other words we would lose possibly the only real deterrent we now possess...one that has protected our country in the past twenty years from Soviet missile deployment. If we say to the Kremlin, "We'll freeze, you do the same," we would be placing false hopes and trust in an alliance with a ruthless band of gangsters. Would they really keep up their part of such a treaty? Don't count on it! It's a gamble that the United States need not entertain, at least not with the prospect of our future freedom in mind.

We do not want to use nuclear weapons and in retrospect we don't want to participate in the expensive arms race, but in relation to the historical evidence of sincerity, the Soviets simply are not trustworthy and could not be relied upon to adhere to any positive arms bans or positive treaties. If we do not assume this position with these irrational entities, we will ultimately lose any advantage we now possess, if any.

The United States is not going to be the cause of a World War III. If that wasn't the case, we could have exercised our superior options at the end of World War II, when we were the only nation with nuclear weapons. We used the bomb to end the war, a war we didn't start. Now we must use the presence of these weapons to prevent a war...not to invite one.

Modern Pulpiteers Lean Left

If you've been wondering why the modern pulpit is in essence preaching Marxism, secular humanism and a social gospel, you must acknowledge the fact that most have been educated and are graduates of schools where liberalism runs rampant.

WHO IS A LIAR BUT HE THAT
DENIETH THAT JESUS IS THE
CHRIST....(I John 2:22)

LET NO MAN DECEIVE YOU BY ANY MEANS: FOR
THAT DAY SHALL NOT COME, EXCEPT THERE
COME A "FALLING AWAY FIRST,.."
(I THESSALONIANS 2:3)

These modernists, and I'm talking about many of the preachers of the last twenty years, are the ones who are mostly affiliated with the National Council of Churches and the World Council of Churches...the very same entities who are dedicated to the merger of all denominations into a one world church to conform to their hopes for one world government.

The many mainline denominations that employ these 'preachers,' also support the seminaries that educate them in these new liberal beliefs apart from Jesus Christ. These preachers, many of whom are the leading liberal writers and philosophers of religious doctrine of this age, are the very same who are casting doubt upon the deity of Christ, His virgin birth, His resurrection, His miracles, His teachings and His very being.

A New York based foundation, the Institute for Educational Affairs, asked 200 questions of more than 1,000 randomly-sampled faculty members at seminaries and theological schools to query their thought about America and its stand against communism.

Asked whether they thought that America was a good country with positive projections for the world scene, only a little over half responded affirmatively.

Twenty-seven percent of the Episcopal seminary faculty; 50 percent of the Methodists; 59 percent of the Roman Catholics; and overall only 57 percent of those queried felt America was a positive influence on the world.

These, my brothers in Christ, are the brain trusts in the facilities who educate our new religious leaders. They are misleading a 'whole generation' of young preachers at war against their own country.

Seven out of ten theologians felt that the U.S. treated the "Third World" unfairly. The Third World, being those countries in Africa, Asia and Latin America that have received more foreign aid from America than from anyone else in the world...but are still too cowardly to side with us in the United Nations. These are the exact same countries that are playing us against the Soviet Union in their bids to get more from each side. Had they polled me, they would have found out that "the Third World has treated the United States unfairly!"

Half of these leftist, liberal theology teachers claimed that the U.S. and what they called "repressive regimes" supported by the U.S., are a greater threat to the world than "communist expansion." I suppose by that they mean that the Shah of Iran was more radical than the Ayatollah Khomeini. Could they also be contemplating that Somoza was worse than the Marxists who now control Nicaragua and are persecuting believers in that region? They possibly contend that in Rhodesia, Ian Smith was far worse than the mass-murderer known as Robert Mugabe. I say "hogwash," those 'teachers' know nothing of history nor of current world affairs...in fact, they don't know what they are talking about.

And understand this: An astonishing percentage of mainline Protestant religous leaders believe that the United States would be better off if we altered our beliefs on socialism and conformed to it! Forty-nine percent of the Methodist leaders, 45 percent of the Presbyterians, 45 percent of the Roman Catholics, 41 percent of the Lutherans, 49 percent of the Episcopalians, 41 percent of American Baptists and even 23 percent...nearly one of every four...of the traditionally conservative Southern Baptists agree that socialism is our current answer to the problems we face in America and the world.

You can see the inroads the liberals, the leftists, the Marxists and the communists and other free-thinkers of every stripe are making into American religion. They are not attacking the churches head on, that's not their standard operational procedure, they are subverting the religious by converting the seminaries into centers for liberalism and socialist education. And here's the capper. Asked if a person could be a good denominational church member and at the same time be a Marxist, 68 percent of the Episcopal faculty members, 53 percent of the Lutherans, 49 percent of the Presbyterians, 49 percent of the Methodists and 31 percent of the Roman Catholics...nearly one-third...said "YES!" That many teachers could believe that godless Marxists, believers in the doctrines of communism, who are against the Lord Jesus Christ, can also be believers in Christianity is blasphemy, hypocrisy and sacrilegious.

If I, Billy James Hargis, have ever stood for anything, it has been for Christ and against godless communism. The two are highly incompatible. They cannot be meshed together in any way...not in the tiniest fabric. In fact, Marx and the Communist Manifesto declared war on Christ, on his believers and on religion more than a hundred years ago and the power of the Soviet Union today shows us how successful that war has been.

I say this to you believers in Christ Jesus: Communism will continue to grow and be successful as long as mainline religions allow these liberals, these left wing radicals, the Marxists, the communists and their sympathizers, to take over their pulpits, their churches and their denominations. Communism must conquer Christ and His people to win. We know Jesus Christ is going to be victorious, but we are trying to keep His people from falling away and backsliding until He returns to earth to gather His believers.

The fact is that their plan is not the product of

coincidence, it's the manifestation of a sinister design to mislead the Body of Christ (the church) away from the intentions of GOD, and His plan. Many have been choosing the left road in the training of our future religious leaders, the preachers and priests of this nation. Christ's people must regroup and come away from these wolves in sheep's clothing...or as I once called them in one of my books, "the Red Bears in clerical collars."

****

EDITOR'S NOTE: Evangelist Billy James Hargis publishes an informative and inspirational monthly newspaper...the Christian Crusade Newspaper. His well researched material and writings on the "sign of the times," fill each issue. For decades now, Billy has been a loyal servant to the witness of Jesus Christ and an advocate against the principles and doctrines of the Soviet Union, atheism, Marxism, communism and un-American activity. In a time when America and the world flounder on the truthful principles of Christ Jesus, we need more Americans with the gumption to fight back and restore the basic principles we so lack in this current age. Write Reverend Hargis and tell this brother in Christ that you love him...and to keep up the good work of our Lord:

Evangelist Billy James Hargis
Christian Crusade Newspaper
Post Office Box 977
Tulsa, Oklahoma 74102

Ask for a "FREE" one-year subscription to his "for Christ and against Communism" newspaper. The work of the Lord in these times is expensive, so if GOD tells you to tuck in a love gift, do so with the confidence that you are assisting Him in the fulfillment of the scripture that says:

"And this gospel of the Kingdom shall be preached in all the world for a witness unto all nations; and then the end shall come!" (Matthew 24:14)

CHAPTER EIGHTEEN

Infant Baptism: Is It Really Necessary?
By Evangelist Jimmy Swaggart

> "Sirs, what must I do to be saved? asked a Philippian jailer.
> Paul answered unto him saying, "Believe on the Lord Jesus
> Christ, and thou shalt be saved!!!"
> ACTS 16:30,31

Recently, one of GOD's great servants has come under severe attack by many apostates across this United States. It was prophesized long ago that it would happen and our present generation is now seeing its fruition in our Country and around the world. Apostasy (falling away from known spiritual truths) is HERE and is thriving within many of this land's churches.

Many churches no longer preach that Jesus Christ was GOD...they hedge that He was only a great prophet. These humanist preachers are saying that man controls his own destiny and that the probability of a "virgin birth of our Lord Jesus" is, at best, a remote figment of thought. They no longer preach from the Word of GOD, opting instead for humanly acceptable doctrines of untruths and misinformations.

Now they attack the present-day Prophets of GOD who are getting the truth out to the people of the world. Evangelist Jimmy Swaggart has long been one of these servants of which I speak. Recently many liberals (or shall I say communists) have been spreading false information about the Swaggart Children's Fund (the largest fund of its kind in the world; building schools and caring for the world's children in GOD's graces). Many "churches" are degrading the Swaggart Ministries' efforts in service of GOD and blaspheme GOD with their vicious lies. Nothing could be further from the truth.

Jimmy Swaggart is a brother in dire need of prayers and support to continue these worthy projects. You who are the "believers in our Jesus Christ" must see through these evil contentions and allegories. Seek the "face of GOD" for the truth, and you will discover that these vile liars, many who are giving the impression of coming in the name of religion, are nothing more than disciples of satan!

R. HENRY HALL

For the glory of GOD and the benefit of the readers' many questions on salvation, I am including Brother Swaggart's views on the subject of receiving eternal salvation. I also include a personal letter from Evangelist Swaggart and information of his worthy projects in the glorification of GOD.

"A TESTIMONY of SALVATION!"

IS INFANT BAPTISM A SCRIPTUAL DOCTRINE?

No, infant baptism is not a scriptual doctrine; and more probably, infant baptism is responsible for sending more people to hell than perhaps any other doctrine or religious error.

It's a terrible thing when a person has been led to believe that his being baptised as a baby constitutes his salvation, and consequently he is on his way to heaven.

JESUS and the CHILDREN

The fact that Jesus loves children very much was evidenced when He made the statement, "Suffer little children, and forbid them not, to come unto me" (Matthew 19:14). As we've said so many times, we believe all babies and children below the age of accountability are protected by the Lord respecting their eternal souls. In other words, I do not believe any child below the age of accountability has ever gone to hell. Of course there is no differentiating between those who were baptized as infants and those who were not.

HISTORY of INFANT BAPTISM

Infant baptism appears in church history about the year 370 A.D. It came about as a result of the doctrine of baptismal regeneration – the teaching that baptism is essential to salvation, or if you want to turn it around, that water baptism saves the soul (or at least is a part of one's salvation). So consequently as the teaching of baptismal regeneration started being propagated, it was natural for those holding to this doctrine to believe that everyone should be baptized as soon as possible. Thus, baptism of infants still in the innocent state (and as yet unaccountable for their actions) came into vogue among many of the churches. Once again I state: these two grievous errors – baptismal regeneration and infant baptism – have probably caused more people to go to hell than any other doctrine.

MORE HISTORY

The professed conversion of Emperor Constantine in 313 A.D. was looked upon by many as a great triumph for Christianity. However, it more than likely was the greatest tragedy in church history because it resulted in the union of church and state and the establishment of a hierarchy which ultimately developed into the Roman Catholic system. There is great question that Constantine was ever truly converted. At the time of his "supposed" vision of the sign of the cross, he "promised" to become a Christian. But he was not baptized in water until near death, having postponed the act in the belief that baptism washed away all past sins, and he wanted all his sins to be in the past tense before he was baptized. In other words, he wanted the freedom to sin as much as he wanted and then when he was too old or too sick to care, he would have them all washed away by the act of baptism.

In the year 416 A.D., infant baptism was made compulsory throughout the Roman Empire. Naturally this filled the churches with unconverted members who had only been "baptized into favor." So whatever power the church had in the past relative to actual conversions was now null and void. The world consequently was plunged into the Dark Ages which endured for more than twelve centuries – until the reformation.

During this time GOD had a remnant who remained faithful to Him; they never consented to the union of church and state, or to baptismal regeneration, or to infant baptism. These people were called by various names, but probably could be summed up by their generic name, "Anabaptists," meaning rebaptizers. These people ignored infant baptism and rebaptized those who had been saved through personal faith. They also had a generic name for themselves – Antipedobaptists, meaning opponents of infant baptism.

NOW THIS IS STRANGE

The strange thing about these two diabolical doctrines of baptismal regeneration and infant baptism is that the great reformers (Martin Luther, for one) brought with them out of Rome these two dreaded errors – the union of church and state and infant baptism. Strangely enough, in those days not only did the Roman Catholic church persecute those who would not conform to its ways, but after the Lutheran church became the established church of Germany, it persecuted the non-conformists as well - of course, not as stringently so and not in such numbers as those before them.

John Calvin, as well as Cromwell in England and John Knox in Scotland, all stuck to the union of church and state and infant baptism and used their power, when they had power, to seek to force others to conform to their own views.

Unaware to a lot of people, this thing came to the Americas well in the early days of this republic. Before the Massachusetts Bay Colony was twenty years old, it was decreed by statute that, "if any person or persons within this jurisdiction shall either openly condemn or oppose the baptizing of infants, or go about secretly to seduce others from the approbation or use thereof, or shall purposely depart from the congregation at the administration of the ordinance – after due time and means of conviction – every such person shall be subject to banishment."

Religious persecution existed even in the early days of the United States of America. Roger Williams and others were banished – when banishment meant to go and live with the Indians – because they would not submit to the doctrine of baptismal regeneration or the baptizing of infants.

However, it was in the constitution of the Rhode Island Colony – founded by Roger Williams, John Clark and others – that religious liberty was established by law for the first time in thirteen-hundred years (over the world). Thus it was that Rhode Island, established by a small group of believers, was the first spot on earth where religious liberty became the law of the land. The settlement was made in 1638 and the Colony was legally established in 1663. Virginia followed, to be the second, in 1786.

As you can see, the doctrine of infant baptism has a long and bloody history, and it has been one of satan's chief weapons to condemn untold millions to hell.

Let Me Try To Explain It A Little Further

To the many who would ask, "What does the above have to do with us today?" I will say this: A LOT!

You see, the union of church and state continues today in most countries of the world. In these "state churches" they christen babies – which means "they make them Christians" by baptizing them; thus the person having been christened as a baby believes he is on his way to heaven simply because he was christened (or baptized) in infancy. Having been taught all his life that this saved him, he naturally considers himself saved by the act of infant baptism. The Roman Catholic church teaches baptismal regeneration and practices infant baptism. Its statement of doctrine says, The sacrament of baptism is administered on adults by the pouring of water and the pronouncement of the proper words, and cleanses from original sin."

The Reformed church says, "Children are baptized as heirs of the Kingdom of God and of His covenant."

The Lutheran church teaches that baptism, whether of infants or adults, is a means of regeneration.

Due to the following phrase, I believe the Episcopal church plainly teaches that salvation comes through infant baptism. In his confirmation, the catechist answers a question about his baptism in infancy by saying, "In my baptism, wherein I was made a member of Christ, a child of God, and an inheritor of the kingdom of God." (This is printed in the prayer book and can be read there by anyone interested enough to look for it.)

The fact is that most people who practice infant baptism believe the ceremony has something to do with the salvation of the child. These are traditions of men, and we can follow the commandments of GOD or follow after the traditions of men; it is up to us.

The Clear Bible Teaching Of Salvation

I believe the Word of God is totally clear regarding the matter of salvation. Jesus said in Saint John 3:36, "He that believeth on the Son hath everlasting life: and he that believeth not the Son shall not see life; but the wrath of God abideth on Him." In John 3:18 He said, "He that believeth on him is not condemned: but he that believeth not is condemned already, because he hath not believed in the name of the only begotten Son of God."

Basically this tells us there are two groups of people in the world today – those who do believe on the Son and those who do not. Those who believe are not condemned; they have everlasting life (whatever the church they may belong to). Those who believe not on the Son are condemned already, and they shall not see life, but the wrath of God abides on them.

I believe this is the clear, unmistakable teaching and language of the Bible.

If you will notice, the Word of God never says simply believe and be saved; rather, it seeks always to identify the object of faith – which is the Lord Jesus Christ Himself. John 3:16 tells us, "For God so loved the world, that he gave his only begotten Son, that whosoever believeth on him should not perish, but have everlasting life." It is not enough to just believe; one must believe on Him.

When the Philippian jailer asked (in Acts 16:30),"Sirs, what must I do to be saved?" Paul answered (in verse 31), "Believe on the Lord Jesus Christ, and thou shalt be saved."

And when Jesus had cried with a loud voice, he said, "FATHER, INTO THY HANDS I COMMEND MY SPIRIT:" and having said thus, He gave up the Ghost.

LUKE 23:46

It wasn't enough simply to believe; that belief, that trust, that dependence had to be in the Lord Jesus Christ.

If one is trusting baptism for salvation, he cannot be trusting Christ. Christ is not one way of salvation; He is the only way of salvation. There is no promise in the Word of God to those who believe partially on Christ. In other words, one cannot trust the Lord Jesus Christ ninety percent and baptism ten percent, or Jesus fifty percent and baptism fifty percent, or Jesus ninety-five percent and some church five percent, et cetera. As a matter of fact, there is really no such thing as partially trusting Christ. The man who is partially trusting is not trusting at all. And the sad fact is, the majority of people in churches in the United States and the world today are not trusting Christ at all - they believe they are trusting Him partially.

It's even sadder to realize that more people are going to hell through religious organizations than any other way. That's a shocking, startling statement, but it is true. In Matthew 7:22-23 Jesus said, "Many will say to me in that day, Lord, Lord, have we not prophesied in thy name? and in thy name have cast out devils: and in thy name done many wonderful works? And then will I profess unto them, I never knew you: depart from me, ye that work iniquity."

You see, any works offered to Christ for salvation are called by Jesus Himself, "works of iniquity."

There is an old song that expresses my feelings totally. It says:

My hope is built on nothing less,
   than Jesus' blood and
   righteousness;
I dare not trust the sweetest frame,
   but wholly lean on Jesus' name.

Portions of source material for this article were derived from a message by the late Dr. William Pettingill, entitled "Infant Baptism."

Dear Brothers & Sisters in Christ,

Jimmy Swaggart Ministries needs your tax-deductible assistance to continue with an uncompromising message from GOD. Won't you help him with your gift? Mail it to:

JIMMY SWAGGART MINISTRIES
P.O. Box 2550
Baton Rouge, Louisiana 70821-9943

From Jimmy Swaggart To You

March 15th will be my birthday. As I turn 49 years old, I feel like I'm at the most productive time of my life, and yet it seems like only yesterday when Frances and I first started in the ministry. Donnie was just a little boy about 2 or 3 years old, if I remember correctly. It seems like an eternity has passed, and yet it seems like it passed only yesterday. So much has happened.

I can remember some of the first sermons I ever preached. I recall one night, for instance, preaching in a little town called Crowville, Louisiana. There were about five or six people there. I remember asking one of the men if we should just dismiss the service because so few were there. He looked around and said, "No; why don't you go ahead and preach. We've come and we'd like to hear it." I preached that night. I still remember the text; it was on "More Abundant Life," and how God moved! It was like a wind of glory swept over that place. I forgot there were only five or six people there; it seemed as if that little church was packed to capacity.

Years later, I met this brother again, to whom I had posed the question on that memorable night. He said, "Brother Swaggart, that was one of the best messages I've ever heard and it strengthened me so greatly." I don't know how good the message was, but I do know that God blessed abundantly. Days like that are somehow never forgotten.

Many people ask me the question, "Did you ever dream God would use this Ministry in the way He has?" Well, if I know anything about humility - (I say it in this context, realizing that every blessing comes from God, every good thing has been from Him. I have done nothing good and I have deserved nothing good, it's all of Christ) - my answer would have to be, "No, I never dreamed that God would do what He has done." But to be honest with you, I am expecting Him to do even greater things.

I feel that God bestows blessings, not in response to meritorious deeds, but in response to commitment and willingness to serve. Everything I've ever done has always been with the feeling that I was in the will of God, and I've tried to do each thing to the best of my ability. I've tried to look at every undertaking as being exactly what God wanted done and as requiring all of my attention and all of my abilities. I never looked at any God-called task as a small thing. I never looked at any God-given direction as a little thing. When Frances and I were in churches that were very small by the high standards of today, that to me was really important; it still is now. And I did the best I knew how - I can honestly say before God that on no occasion have I ever stepped behind a pulpit without doing my very best. Sometimes it didn't turn out well (I thought), and sometimes the crowds were small, but ministering to people has always been of supreme importance to me - each message, each effort, each time, by God Almighty.

GREAT THINGS AHEAD

As I write these words, I'm anticipating great things ahead. I feel there's absolutely no limit to what God can do, and I also feel that, along with other ministries, God has laid His hands on this Ministry. I believe He's going to use it in these end-time days to touch millions of people, even over and beyond that which we are seeing.

I am witnessing things now I never dreamed would happen. Last year (1983) we were able to build, by the help and grace of God, some $8,000,000 worth of churches, Bible Schools, and schools for children, plus maintain radio and television programming in foreign countries as well as literature distribution and care for missionaries. This is a larger amount than was spent by ninety percent of the denominations in the United States of America. Now I want you to think of that. We thank God for the privilege and we feel that, as we continue to rely upon Him, we're going to be able to do even more. It's our goal that every single city, town, and village in this world hear the Gospel of Jesus Christ at least once.

There Is Something I Must Tell you

A short time ago we started crying out against the weakening of the great Methodist Church respecting the ordination of homosexuals. It was not an easy thing to do, but I love the Methodist people dearly and in view of that love, I felt I had to try to warn them.

Methodist conferences all over the nation are now issuing statements of faith, proclaiming their belief in the Word of God and declaring that they will not approve of these individuals in any type of ministry, but will pray for their deliverance. Oh, I'm not saying this is revival, but I am saying it is a start. And I would like to believe this Ministry had a little part to play in this great stand that is being taken by good Methodist preachers all across the nation who love the Word of God and the ways of God. Admittedly, it is just a beginning, but wouldn't it be wonderful if the great Methodist Church that once shook this nation from pillar to post by the power of Almighty God would come back to an old-fashioned, Holy Ghost revival? Remember, with God all things are possible.

The Furor In The Press

By now I'm certain you've heard of the tremendous furor in the Press and over television concerning our Ministry. I've been called, I think, just about every name in the book. I've been labeled a bigot, a racist, anti-Jewish, and anti-Catholic; and the sad thing about it is, I think I'm about as totally opposite of all those things as any human could ever be.

True, I have had to preach some things to the beloved Catholic people that I have not enjoyed preaching, but I want to make it very clear - I am not anti-Catholic. To be honest with you, I am not anti anybody. I am, however, anti-Satan, anti-sin, anti-wickedness, and anti-unrighteousness. To be sure, I stand tall and speak loud in my opposition to these things, and it has aroused the ardor of Satan simply because he has been uncovered (and if there's one thing that hell does not enjoy, it's being uncovered).

Let me say this - I do not oppose any people in general whatsoever. I admire and respect the Catholic priests and nuns very much for the sacrifices they make for their church. I do not, however, agree with the role of the priest, feeling that it is totally unscriptural. At the same time, I admire their sacrifices. But as to my being anti-Catholic (and the strict, legal definition of "anti-" would mean being opposed to a person because he is of a particular persuasion, irrespective of who that person may be), it is ridiculous for anyone to even think I am such a thing. I love the Catholic people, and because I love them, I've tried to tell them the truth. It's not a popular stand to take, and to be honest with you, not only are the Catholic priests opposed to me, but it would seem many of our Protestant friends are as well. But everything we've said and everything we've done has been for the sake of souls.

One day I'll have to stand before God, and because of the voice He has given us, there is much to give account for. The thought of people, maybe millions, pointing a finger at us and saying, "No one told me; no one said anything about the Word of God concerning salvation, and you had the opportunity and didn't do it" - well, I couldn't bear to face that. I may have done it well; I may not have done it well at all; but I can say that I've done the best I could do and that I've done it with love.

The College Is Coming Out Of The Ground

That's a peculiar statement, but of course I'm speaking of the dormitories, the classrooms, et cetera. We are anticipating a tremendous move of God respecting the College. It will be another tool in church growth and world evangelism. It's our business to see to it that young people have the opportunity to develop their ministry, whether they have a definite call from God or simply want to do something for the Lord. We want to be of service and we believe we can.

We believe that every person who has accepted Jesus as his Saviour - irrespective of whom he may be - has a call of God upon his life. It certainly may not be to stand behind a pulpit as a pastor or an evangelist, or to go to a foreign field as a missionary, et ceterea, but that call is there and he can be of some kind of service to the Kingdom of God. We want this Bible College to supply the means whereby that service can be developed in the hearts and lives of all people, regardless of whether their calls are to specific ministries or not. This call of God is certainly something that every Christian should sense because it is there.

Pray for the College. Pray that God will give us direction and that He will help us to do the things that we should do. Doctor Gray is working feverishly to put together a faculty that will be of service to the Kingdom of God. It is a monumental task, but the work is the Lord's and we know He will help us.

THANK YOU SO VERY MUCH

Thank you for your prayers, your support, your financial help, and all that you've meant to this Ministry. Some of you have given when you didn't have it to give; others of you have been able to give in abundance. May God bless all of you richly for your kindness and generosity.

Please pray for this evangelist; I've never sensed more victory in my life, and at the same time, I've never sensed more pressure. But despite Satan's opposition, the Gospel of Jesus Christ must be proclaimed - the great message of salvation must go forth. I know that as we continue to be faithful to this calling, God will enable us to overcome all of the forces of darkness. He will give total and complete victory because we have this testimony - everything we do, we do for souls.

CHAPTER NINETEEN

A PLANNED DECEPTION!
By Constance Cumbey

"Their script is now written, subject only to last minute editing and stage directions. The stage itself, albeit as yet in darkness, is almost ready. Down in the pit, the subterranean orchestra is already tuning up. The last-minute, walk on parts are even now being filled. Most of the main actors, one suspects, have already taken up their roles. Soon it will be time for them to come on stage, ready for the curtain to rise.
THE TIME FOR ACTION WILL HAVE COME."

(From THE ARMAGEDDON SCRIPT, by Peter LeMesurier, St. Martin's Press, 1982: NewYork)

One could easily think the above paragraph came from a Hal Lindsey book warning Christians of the evil that is to come. Incredibly, such is not the case. The above quote is the summation of "The Armageddon Script" by Peter LeMesurier, a noted occultist/pyramidologist with extensive Findhorn Foundation links. THE ARMAGEDDON SCRIPT is a how-to manual for New Agers and intellectuals interested in staging a simulated second coming of Christ. The deception they plan, if successful, could literally fool the Elect, "if it were possible." (1)

It is logical and proper to question just how on earth would one expect the average person of intellect in our world in general and nation in particular to support such a preposterous proposition. To the contrary, it is the intellectual whose support is being sought and won for such an undertaking. It is based upon popular theories on the intelligentsia and they are being courted by flatteries.

The theme employed to win intellectual support is a familiar one to someone trained in psychology or psychiatric theories. Rare, too, is the layman who has failed to hear of "Jungian archetypes." The theory employed is that we have all these Jungian archetypes in the form of unfulfilled prophesy cluttering up our collective psyche. Consequently, we fail to make human progress as long as we believe this prophetic fulfillment to be imminent. Therefore, the line of logic runs, we must take steps to exercise these prophesies which hang over us like a "sword of Damocles ready to reek mischief at any time." The author notes that "since there is no likelihood of their fulfillment, we must stage an enactment." Steps are then laid out in great detail for this enactment.

The Bible well noted that in the last days "evil men and seducers shall wax worse and worse, deceiving and being deceived." (2) Truly the author of THE ARMAGEDDON SCRIPT shows evidence of strong delusion when he proclaims "there is no likelihood that these prophesies will be fulfilled." He forgets his own role in bringing about the fulfillment!

LeMesurier is a man with strong New Age connections, including a publishing relationship with the Findhorn Foundation in Northern Scotland. His books are widely promoted and sold in New Age bookstores. His book shows that he strongly supports and promotes the New Age philosophies, including those of New Age favorites Trungpa Rampa, Edgar Cayce, Hugh Schonfield, Teilhard de Chardin and David Spangler. He cites the "Aquarian Gospel of Jesus the Christ" as well. From these works he has prepared a startling agenda of proposed world-wide deception. It is further obvious that this New Ager studied the Bible as well in order to present a scenario that might deceive less than well-informed Christians.

If his proposed deliberate deception were executed as written, it would be enough as Jesus said, "If it were possible, they shall deceive the very elect." (3)

Subterranean Orchestra's Agenda

What is the proposed agenda that the "subterranean orchestra" is tuning up for "down in the pit?" It is a truly startling one.

It calls for having their new 'messiah' in the Holy land by 1985 or no later than the arrival of Haley's Comet in early 1986. (5) The new leader is to carefully prepare for his role by studying scriptures and Dead Sea Scrolls, current Jewish messanic expectations, familiarizing himself with the prophesies of other major world religions and "the best in New Age religious thoughts." (6)

The science of earthquake prediction would then be employed for the remainder of the initial scenario. (7) LeMesurier coolly details some of them as follows:

"(a) The restored Messiah must reappear on Jerusalem's Mount of Olives at the time of a great earthquake.
(b) He must enter Jerusalem from the east, escorted by a procession of rejoicing followers

dressed in shining white.

(c) Visiting the tomb of his spiritual ancestor, King David, he must emerge in suitably-perfumed robes as the great monarch returned.

(d) Supported by a popular rising, he must proceed with his followers to the Temple Mount, there to be enthroned, anointed and crowned King of the New Israel." (8)

But, I can hear you arguing, surely no person of intelligence would expect such a program to succeed, what with the large number of opposed Catholics, Protestants and skeptical Jewish observers. To the contrary, this opposition has been calculated as a <u>part</u> of the scenario. LeMesurier warns that the opposition does not need to be considered, "because they will destroy each other!"

> "The massed forces of the Old Age, however, will be unable to check their headlong onrush. In large measure they will go on to destroy each other in a massive, mutual venting of long pent-up aggression....." (9)

What sort of a program would be offered to satisfy the spiritual needs of those living under this regime? As expected, LeMesurier rightly notes that it will <u>not</u> be the traditional Christian ones:

> "The new mission of the youth of the world, then, will be an international movement dedicated to spreading the already developing ideas and values upon which the New Age is to be founded. Those ideas and values will not necessarily be the traditional Christian ones.
> .....For the wisdoms of all ages and cultures will be called upon to surrender their most precious secrets, and the collective human psyche will add to it yet further wisdoms that have so far never even been expressed.....It is for the soul of man that the New David will have to fight..." (10)

LeMesurier may well be right for the wrong reasons. Yes, the "wisdoms of all ages and cultures will be called upon to surrender their most precious secrets." The Apostle John was clearly shown this by the Lord in the course of his Patmos Island vision:

> "And after these things I saw another angel come

down from heaven, having great power; and the earth was lightened with his glory. And he cried mightily with a strong voice, saying, Babylon the great has fallen, is fallen, and is come the habitation of devils, and the hold of every foul spirit, and a cage of every unclean and hateful bird. For all nations have drunk of the wine of her fornication, and the kings of the earth have committed fornication with her, and the merchants of the earth are waxed rich through the abundance of her delicacies."

REVELATION 18:1-3, KJV

Lest anyone think LeMesurier offered an unsupported piece of opinion, let the reader note the following. LeMesurier's books have received the benefit of major publisher support both at home and in England. New Age conferences have been held on this very topic. One such conference was reported in September, 1983, NEW AGE JOURNAL. (11) The Conference, approximately entitled "Facing Apocalypse" was attended by 125 activists of Jungian persuasion. It was organized by Robert Boznak, a Jungian analyst from Sudbury, Massachusetts. Its premise was that the vision of a cataclysmic ending of the world is itself a menace. The conference itself was held in an incredibly elegant hall that formerly served as a millionaire's mansion at Salve Regina College in Newport, Rhode Island. Some of the better known in attendance included Dr. Robert Jay Lifton of Yale University; James Hillman, considered the Country's leading Jungian scholar/analyst; Psychologist Mary M. Watkins of Clark University; Sicilian poet and anti-mafia leader, Danilo Dolci; Wolfgang Giegerich of the Jung Institute in Stuttgart, Germany, and theologian David Miller of Syracuse University.

The reader should be reminded as well, that the infamous HUMANIST MANIFESTO in effect carries this very theme. In the preface to HUMANIST MANIFESTO II, the author stated:

"As in 1933, humanists still believe that traditional theism, especially faith in the prayer-hearing GOD, assumed to love and care for persons, to hear and understand their prayers, and to be able to do something about them, is an unproved and outmoded faith. Salvation, based on mere affirmation, still appears as harmful, diverting people with false hopes of heaven hereafter. Reasonable minds look to other means for survival." (12)

This was reinforced within the body of the Manifesto itself:

> "Promises of immortal salvation or fear of eternal damnation are both illusory and harmful. They distract humans from present concerns, from self-actualization and from rectifying social injustices." (13)

One can easily see where the area of Jungian archetypes and acting out an end-time drama is an area in which occultists, atheists and agnostic humanists can find common ground. The occultists of all New Age persuasions could easily support such a figure because they believe it is their Christ as they define it. The atheist could participate because he would feel it would contribute to the furthering of human progress on the planet, with people being discharged of their ideas of a coming deity for once and for all. The humanist could participate because it would further the aims of their manifestos. In fact, maybe the humanists and New Agers are really not so far apart at that. Didn't the 1973 HUMANIST MANIFESTO II, read, "we stand at the dawn of the new age?" (14) Many recognizable New Agers and occultists appear as signers of that 1973 document including Isaac Asimov; Archie Bahm; and Lester R. Brown of the World Watch Institute. (15)

The Book of Daniel warned that the coming world dictator would not come in initially with guns. The angel warned him that:

> "And in his estate shall stand up a vile person, to whom they shall not give the honor of the kingdom: but he shall come in peaceably, and obtain the kingdom by flatteries." (16)

The real question is not whether there will be flatteries or not, but what form will these flatteries take? I believe the central flattery the anti-Christ will bring is one commonly used by satan in the past: "Thou shalt be as gods." However, it is also evident that he has been courting the intelligentsia by flattering themselves into thinking they can change the course of history by concerted play-acting a false messiah in his domain. Daniel was further warned that:

> "And such as do wickedly against the covenant shall corrupt by flatteries: but the people that do know their GOD shall be strong, and do exploits." (17)

It is evident from the context of the passage here that

while satan is busy inspiring his forces, likewise, GOD will give strength to His people.

A Proper Response To The Script

An important chapter for end-time Christians is found in Isaiah, chapter 8. First, it tells us whom we should fear:

> "Associate yourselves, O ye people, and ye shall be broken in pieces; and give ear, all ye of far countries: gird yourselves, and ye shall be broken in pieces; gird yourselves, and ye shall be broken in pieces. Take councel together, and it shall come to nought; speak the word, and it shall not stand: for GOD is with us. For the Lord spake thus to me with a strong hand, and instructed me that I should not walk in the way of this people, saying, Say ye not, A confederacy, to all them to whom this people shall say, A confederacy; neither fear ye their fear, nor be afraid. Sanctify the Lord of Hosts Himself; and let Him be your fear, and let Him be your dread."
>
> ISAIAH 8:9-13

One can quickly observe that the planned deception is of such magnitude that the elect might be deceived, if possible. One way that the elect might prevent themselves from falling for such deception is to remind themselves always that no matter how impressive the show, or the people calling for our acceptance of the new "messiah," if we are standing on the ground, he is a clear-cut phoney. We will behold Jesus Christ coming in the air and we shall meet Him in the air----NOT on a television set in our front rooms. I have recently been startled at how many Christians have expressed the belief to me that when the Bible said "every eye shall see Him," that it meant "on television." It is important too that we know where to place both our fear and our trust. We fear not "them that can slay the body, but are not able to kill the soul: but rather fear Him which is able to destroy both the soul and body in hell."

Chapter Notes

(1) Matthew 24:24 KJV (2) II Timothy 3:13 KJV (3) Matthew 24:24, (4) LeMesurier, Peter; THE ARMAGEDDON SCRIPT. New York: St. Martin's Press. 1981, citing pages 232-233. (5) Ibid., page 233. (6) Ibid.,232, (7) Ibid.,231, (8) Ibid.,237, (9) Ibid.,page 237, (10) Oglesby, Carl; "Life at the End of

the Road: Jungians at the Apocalypse." NEW AGE JOURNAL Volume 9, Number 2, September, 1983., (II) Kurtz, Paul (Editor); HUMANIST MANIFESTO i & II, Buffalo, New York: Prometheus Book, 1973, page 13. (12) Ibid., pages 16-17., (13) Ibid., page 14., (14) Ibid., pages 24-31., (15) Daniel II:21 (KJV), (16) Daniel II:32 (KJV), (17) Matthew 10:28 (KJV).

Constance Cumbey is a Christian Lawyer from Detroit, Michigan. She's married, with one child, Steven, age 16. She has been an Attorney since 1975 and is a graduate of the Detroit College of Law (Juris Doctor) with undergraduate studies at Wayne State University and Michigan State University.

Mrs. Cumbey served as a Corresponding Secretary and Treasurer of the National Association of Women Lawyers; Board Member and Corresponding Secretary, Northwest Bar Association; Member American Bar Association and State Bar of Michigan; Arbitrator for American Arbitration Association.

Constance Cumbey has served as Administrative Assistant and Legislative Analyst to William A. Ryan, Speaker of the Michigan House of Representatives; Consultant to Michigan State Senate Committee on Governmental Efficiency; Executive Assistant to the Mayor, Highland Park, Michigan.

Constance Cumbey is the Author of the HIDDEN DANGERS OF THE RAINBOW (Huntington House, Shreveport, Louisiana, 1983); a book on the NEW AGE movement which is currently ranked the number one best-seller in the Country.

She has written and lectured on the New Age Movement to churches, civic organizations, television, radio and college audiences since June of 1981 locally, and on a nation-wide basis and in Canada since May of 1982. She has appeared nation-wide on Christian and secular programs ranging from the PTL Club and Gary Randall Program to the Southwest Radio Church and Moody Networks. Her best-selling book has been translated or is in the process of translation into several languages and at the time of the preparation of this statement is currently ranked as the national best-seller on the Christian charts.

Constance is a born-again Christian. She has spoken to many diverse religious denominational groups ranging from Catholic and Seventh Day Adventists to Church of the Nazarene, Baptists, and Assembly of GOD audiences. She has been a featured speaker at Full Gospel and Women's Aglow conventions. I would like to extend Constance my full appreciation for her contribution to "Ominous Portents of the Parousia of Christ." May GOD richly Bless her!

CHAPTER TWENTY

The Rapture: No Double Jeopardy With GOD!

> "Behold, I shew you a mystery; We shall not
> all sleep, but we shall be changed."
> I Corinthians 15:51

One of the most interesting points of concern to true believers of this generation is of the time when Jesus will return for His church in the Rapture. It is a most joyous time for the Christians because the Rapture will be a time when Jesus will fulfill His promise to spare His faithful servants from the "darkest period of time the world will ever experience!"

Some of our present day prophets of GOD are saying that this monumental occasion will take place prior to the Tribulation (the final seven years of humanity when GOD will take out His wrath on an un-believing world). Others are convinced that the Bible is telling us that the Rapture will occur at the time when the anti-Christ removes the restored sacrificial rights of the Jews, or three and one-half years after the world announcement of the anti-Christ. Still others are firm that Jesus will come at either the end of the Tribulation or intermittently throughout the seven year period. I believe sincerely that the Holy Spirit has given me this knowledge and I am sharing it with you according to His will.

Understanding that Jesus is THE divine Spirit of GOD and that no one goes to the Father except through Jesus, the Son...let's start with the prophesies directly from the mouth of GOD!

I say the following to the readers of this book so that there may be no misinterpetation as to where my knowledge is derived. I write this book only under the divine inspiration of the Holy Spirit and the following interpetations are not intended for any personal credit...They are all for the glory of GOD!

GOD'S PROMISE TO BELIEVERS

To fully understand when the Rapture will occur, it helps

to comprehend the meaning of the words "Tribulation" and "Rapture."

The word "Tribulation" means a 'period of distress or suffering' which results from oppression (cruel or unjust authority) or persecution (to cause one to suffer for their belief.) It is also defined as a "trying experience."

The word "Rapture" means 'a state or experience of being "carried away or caught up" by an overwhelming emotion or manifestation of ecstasy.

In Matthew 24, Jesus is explaining what the end times will be like to His Disciples. Here we are not receiving second-hand knowledge of that period...we are hearing directly from the promise of GOD for what is to take place.

In Matthew 24:29, Jesus said that immediately after the Tribulation, the sun will be darkened, the moon shall not give light, the stars shall fall from heaven and the powers of the heavens shall be shaken.

In Matthew 24:30, He says that at that time, "ALL THE TRIBES OF THE EARTH WILL MOURN (be unhappy or sad.) Then in the following verse, Jesus says that "He will send His angels to gather His elect from the "four winds, from one end of heaven to the other."

You must understand these key elements in what our Lord Jesus is saying...

First, seeing Jesus' fulfillment of prophesy with His Second Coming is absolutely NO REASON FOR BELIEVERS TO "MOURN!" It would be no cause for any true Christian to be unhappy with the occurence. That alone would indicate to you that the church (the Body of Christ) is definitely not on earth at the time. All scholars of the Bible agree unanamously that the Second Coming of Christ will be at a time when all human life threatens to be lost, or in other words, the end of the great Tribulation which will come upon this world. Saying that "ALL WILL MOURN HIS COMING" tells us that believers are definitely not on the earth at that time. If we are not on earth...where are we if we aren't already with Jesus in heaven?

Jesus also said that at the time of His Second Coming "He will send His angels to gather His elect (believers) from the four winds, from one end of "HEAVEN to the other." This confirms that the church is indeed in heaven at the time! Just so, the post-tribulation theory would seem an impossibility.

Some scholars may choose to refer to "the elect" as the same as "the Chosen" (the Jewish race) of GOD, but my inspiration is saying that the elect means those he has chosen through their belief on the Lord Jesus Christ as their Savior! These "Chosen People" are the ones GOD has accepted to receive eternal life for their endurance and witness that Jesus is the Messiah...the Son of the living GOD!

Understanding that believers in Christ are not on Earth when He comes, you must acknowledge that He took them out of the world previously. In this case either half-way through the Tribulation when it would no longer be able to openly worship GOD, or prior to this 'hour of temptation.'

Those who are convinced that the Rapture will occur half-way through the Tribulation do not understand what is to take place during this period of great trial.

The ground work has already been laid for a new monetary system that will soon replace the "greenback." The computer technology exists today to place every fact about you on a micro-chip no larger than the head of a pin and this new technology will ultimately lead to a 'cashless society' in which your purchases will all be deducted automatically from your savings account. It has been astutely recognized that by the begining of 1986, checking accounts will no longer exist in the world.

It has also been estimated that a total conversion to this new system would take between five and ten years, would be efficient in most aspects of banking and would render useless the need for anyone to carry wallets once the chip is utilized.

In the meantime, credit cards are in the making that will replace money by the middle of 1985 or sooner. However, due to the fact that credit cards can be counterfeited and stolen, it would be necessary to advance swiftly to the micro-chip which shall be placed by laser beam into a person's right hand, or, for those who do not have hands, into their foreheads. The lazer could place this chip into the hand or forehead with no pain whatsoever. Then when you purchase your necessities, all you would do is place your hand under an ultra violet beam and the purchase would automatically be deducted from your banking account.

ISN'T THAT NICE?

Setting The Stage For The Antichrist!

"And he causeth all, both small and great, rich and poor, free and bond, to receive a mark IN their right hand, or IN their foreheads:

And that no man might buy or sell, save he that had the mark, or the name of the beast, or the number of his name.

HERE IS WISDOM. Let him that hath understanding count the number of the beast: for it is the number of a man; and his number is Six hundred threescore and six (666) REVELATION 13:16,17,18

6 6 6 6 6 6 6 6

It won't hurt honey. The nice government man said we have to put it on.

I know what the scriptures say... I've got to get out of here!

666
PRINTING HERE
YOUR CHOICE
HAND or FOREHEAD
$20.00
Deducted from Your Account

Analysing the previous scripture of the Book of Revelation...notice that it says IN (NOT ON) the right hand or forehead! If this information was on the hand or forehead...it could be duplicated, therefore it WILL BE "IN" the skin! It also says that it will be the number of the beast...the number of a man...the number of the anti-Christ and this number will be 666.

The numerical number for man is the number six because GOD created man on the sixth day of the week of creation! Three sixes represent the number of how many times mankind has fallen short of GOD (explained further in Chapter Twenty-One, "Hidden Secrets of the Holy Spirit".) So understanding that 666 represents man's repeated failure against GOD's covenants also tells you that the number represents mankind's desire to be anti-Christian, therefore it also represents the anti-Christ mentioned in scripture!

Larry Goshorn, president of International Robomation Intellegence, says that this system aimed at a cashless society has already been implimented in Europe and is slated for the United States as early as late 1984. We see our grocery stores going to new technology of checking groceries already and we must realize that our national debt will never be paid off with the technology of man. Goshorn has said that this credit billing system is a network of computers linked to a world-wide automated system and the first three digits are the numbers 666 (meaning international exchange). This credit billing arrangement will allow anyone to travel the world and purchase all their necessities through this micro-chip. All salaries will be automatically deposited into your accounts...no checks will ever be needed. That's all fine and dandy for humanists and atheists because they are of the earthly kingdom...but what does GOD say about those who conform to this new system?

Thou Shalt Not Receive The Mark of the Beast!

"And the third angel followed them saying with a loud voice, If any man worship the beast and his image, AND RECEIVE HIS MARK in his forehead, or in his hand,

The same shall drink of the wine of the wrath of GOD, which is poured out WITHOUT MIXTURE into the cup of his indignation; and he shall be tormented with fire and brimstones in the presence of the holy angels, and in the presence of the Lamb:

Revelation 14:9,10

So, if GOD tells His believers that we cannot accept this mark in our right hands or in our foreheads...what are our alternatives? If you are a believer in the Son of GOD, the Prince of Peace...Jesus Christ, you have no alternative but to refuse to accept the mark. What happens when we refuse the mark? Two (2) things will then take place and BOTH are for and to the GLORY of GOD!

REFUSING THE MARK of the BEAST!

First, when we refuse this mark in our right hand or forehead, it is warned in Revelation 13:17, that "no one may buy or sell unless he has the mark." That makes a lot of sense. If you do not conform to this new monetary system, no human will trade with you under any form of outdated mode of finance. If you don't have the mark, you will also be unable to retain gainful employment because there would be no way to give you a salary...you wouldn't have an account! If you have no employment and no bank account..it would be impossible for you to purchase the necessities of food and clothing for you and your family, nor would you be able to have a home to live in without being able to pay for it with an account.

This explains what Jesus meant in Matthew 24:10, where He said, "And then shall many be offended, and shall betray one another, and shall hate one another."

Can you imagine telling your family that they will no longer be able to live anywhere, nor will they be able to eat anymore or ever again participate in any worldly function? Can you imagine the quarrels that will break out? How many wives will tell their husbands to go get the mark, or, if they won't...they'll go get the mark and go on living? Can you imagine how many children will hate their parents for not providing them with their subsistence? In Mark 13:12, Jesus tells us:

"Now the brother shall betray the brother to death, and the father the son; and the children shall rise up against their parents, and shall CAUSE them to be put to death."

I have no problems refusing the mark of the beast. I know the truth of the Bible and have well schooled my family on refusing the number of the beast, however many are not even aware of the necessity for refusing the 666. If you accept Jesus Christ in your heart, He will take care of ALL YOUR NEEDS...you must have faith that He'll do just that. He promises in Luke 12:29, that you will be prepared for and you should not doubt it. In the next verse, Jesus tells us that the Father KNOWS that we will have need of these things. Jesus goes on to tell us what is going to happen then.

290

> "Fear not My little flock; for it is your Father's good pleasure to GIVE YOU THE KINGDOM."
> LUKE 12:32

Secondly, and much more important than you know, GOD said that you will be given the kingdom for your faith in Him! So, when the time comes that believers can not exist in this world without accepting the mark of the beast...The Rapture will occur and Jesus will meet His faithful in the air where we will dwell in His Father's house forever. This will also signify the begining of the Tribulation period when GOD will repay the non-believers with His wrath. To participate in the Rapture...you MUST KEEP YOUR FAITH IN THE FATHER TO KEEP HIS PROMISE TO YOU, and have no doubt! In this area we have nothing to fear because HE NEVER LIES!

> "And I heard another voice from heaven, saying, Come out of her (the earth), my people, that ye be not partakers of her sins, and that YE NOT RECEIVE OF HER PLAGUES.
> For her sins have reached unto heaven, and GOD hath remembered her inequities."
> Revelation 18:4,5

This is the time when GOD will remove His church from Earth. It will be the time when we will have no earthly means of supporting our families. Once we are taken out of the way and shielded from the wrath of GOD, the Tribulation will begin and all "hell" will break loose on earth!

The unfortunate part of the matter is that many people will not believe in Jesus nor understand the truth that is written and proclaimed by His followers (Christians), that is, until it is too late to be Raptured to Jesus in the air.

> "For the Lord Himself shall descend from heaven with a shout, with the voice of the arch-angel, and with the trump of GOD; and the dead in Christ (believers who have died) shall rise first:
> Then we (believers) which are "ALIVE AND REMAIN" shall be caught up (Raptured) together with them in the clouds, to meet the Lord in the air: and so shall we ever be with the Lord."
> I Thessalonians 4:16,17

Believers ought to understand what Jesus says in Revelations 3:7 to the church of Philadelphia (the church that has kept their faith and are righteous):

"BEHOLD, I SHEW YOU A MYSTERY; WE
SHALL NOT ALL SLEEP, BUT WE SHALL
ALL BE CHANGED,
IN A MOMENT, 'IN THE TWINKLING OF
AN EYE ..."
(I CORINTHIANS 15:51,52)

292

> "Because thou hast kept the word of My
> patience, I also will KEEP THEE FROM THE HOUR
> OF TEMPTATION which shall come upon the world to
> try them that dwell upon the Earth."
> REVELATION 3:10

> "Watch ye therefore, and pray always, that ye
> may be accounted worthy TO ESCAPE ALL THESE
> THINGS that shall come to pass, and to stand before
> the Son of man.
> LUKE 21:36

There should be no doubt of what GOD is telling His believers in these two verses. The words are "KEEP THEE FROM" and "WORTHY TO ESCAPE" this most trying experience...the TRIBULATION. The very words tell you that the believers will be called to Jesus PRIOR TO THE TRIBULATION!

Jesus doesn't tell us that if we keep His patience He will keep us from "PART" of this period...Jesus tells us that if we keep His word and patience (the Word of GOD...the Bible...the FAITH in HIM) WE WILL BE SPARED from enduring this difficult (for true Christians - impossible) TRIBULATION period. We are not going to be in the world and that's a promise from GOD!!!!!!!

In Revelations 3:8, Jesus says:

> "I know thy works: Behold, I set before thee
> an OPEN DOOR, and no man (human) can shut it:
> for thou hast a little strength, and HAST KEPT MY
> WORD (the Bible...the GOSPEL), and hast not
> denied my name!

The OPEN DOOR is the Rapture of believers and NO MAN...NO HUMAN BEING may shut this door...because once you have accepted the truth of Jesus Christ, no man can change your heart. Since no man can change the way you feel about Jesus as GOD, your treasures are not on this earth, but in heaven! Because you do not deny Him in front of men...He will not deny you in front of the Father. The following verse from Mark 8:38 explains your faith and your destiny!

> "Whosoever therefore shall be ashamed of Me
> and of My words in this adulterous and sinful
> generation; of him also shall the Son of man be
> ashamed, when He cometh in the glory of His Father
> with the holy angels."

Proclaiming Jesus Christ to yourself in private is not enough...that says that you are ashamed to tell people about Him! YOU MUST PROCLAIM HIM AS YOUR SAVIOR TO THE ROOFTOPS and tell everyone you know and some that you don't know!

When you have the Holy Spirit within you...you cannot HATE anyone...you will be COMPASSIONATE to ALL, regardless of how they will treat you! When they treat you badly...pray for them for they are not in the LIGHT. Unless you pray for them...maybe no one will. Speak to them and witness for Christ...you will be surprised to find out how many will listen to you...GOD has seen to that. Listen to the following verse and understand that it speaks of this very age:

> "And it shall come to pass in the LAST DAYS,
> saith GOD, I will pour out My Spirit on ALL FLESH;
> and your sons and daughters shall prophesy, your
> young men shall see visions, and your old men shall
> dream dreams."
> ACTS 2:17

GOD is moving upon the will of all men in these days. Some will be open to hearing the word; others will harden their hearts and lose eternal life as a result. But of those that will listen, WHAT IF YOU ARE THEIR ONLY CHANCE TO HEAR THE WORD, and because of your fear of rejection or by being ashamed of telling them the GOOD NEWS of Christ...they lose their only chance of eternal life! Be compassionate...you are doing them the most important favor they will ever hear...you will be telling them about humanity's only chance to be saved...THAT'S IMPORTANT!

It is also important that you understand that GOD is also revealing ALL HIS SECRETS UNTO THIS GENERATION! There are NO MORE MYSTERIES cepting for the DAY and the HOUR of which He will come in the Rapture, but just as that is true, He has given this believer one of His previously hidden secrets...HE HAS GIVEN US THE GENERAL TIME OF HIS COMING...PRAISE THE LORD!

> "He revealeth the DEEP and SECRET THINGS:
> He knoweth what is in the darkness, and the light
> dwelleth in Him."
> DANIEL 2:22

It is very wise for everyone, believer or not, to understand that GOD would not be imparting this knowledge upon this generation if it were not to His Glory, or if it were not of the utmost importance for His people to know.

Around the 5th century B.C., GOD told Daniel (Daniel 12:4) to seal up the prophesies until the time of the end when travel and knowledge will be vastly increased. As we are in the times that were prophesied GOD has allowed these prophetic seals to be opened and their real meaning heard by all flesh. He has spared no barriers in getting this final warning out and it has included the obvious world predicament, the many books that are being written on the end times, the increase in theology students, the 24 hour Christian cable Networks and also an increase of inspiring Evangelists.

GOD is pouring out His Spirit on all flesh (everyone). He is giving them one last chance to see what is happening and turn from the ways of man. Humanist, atheists and everyone else who fail to recognize the saving grace of Jesus Christ are heading towards their fiery destiny and they are too blind to see it. Humanists have the idea that the earth will ALWAYS BE HERE and that "man will make of it what he will." They are so blinded by the earthen ways that they fail to understand that their destiny was part of GOD's Plan since the time of man's creation...almost six-thousand years ago.

Yes, GOD is pouring out His Spirit on all humanity and whether they will admit it or not, everyone is feeling a little different.

Have you been noticing that the Word of GOD has been reaching out to places of the world that up until now it hadn't been reaching? People from all over the world are begining to recognize that Jesus Christ is indeed the Son of the Living GOD...He is GOD (John 14:7-9)!

If you understand prophesy, you'll know that 1948 began the countdown to the end times. That was the year that GOD allowed His people, the Jews, to reestablish their homeland in Israel...That was prophesized by the Prophet Ezekiel around 600 B.C.:

"And I will make them (Jews) one nation in the land upon the mountains of Israel..."
EZEKIEL 37:22

Reborn as a Nation in 1948, Israel has been continually criticized by the Palestinians, the Arabians, the Syrians, the Iraqis, the Iranians and the deceitful ones of the Soviet Union. These nations surround Israel and one day these countries will make the ultimate mistake of invading her. When they do...they are going up against GOD!

"After many days thou shalt be visited: In the LATTER DAYS thou shalt come unto the land (Israel) that is brought back from the sword, and is gathered out of many people, against the mountains of Israel, which have been always waste.

Thou shall ascend and come like a storm, thou shalt be like a cloud to cover the land, thou, and all thy bands, and many people with thee.

Thus saith the Lord GOD; It shall also come to pass, that at that same time shall things come into thy mind, and thou shall think an evil thought.

And thou shalt say, I will go up to the land of unwalled villages; I will go to them that are at rest, that dwell safely, all of them dwelling without walls, and having neither bars nor gates,

To take spoil (plunder), and to take a prey, to turn thine hand upon the desolate places that are now inhabited, and upon the people (Jews) that are gathered out of the nations, which have gotten cattle and goods, that dwell in the midst of the land."

EZEKIEL 38:8-12

The prophesy goes on to say in Ezekiel 38:16:

And thou shalt come up against My people of Israel, as a cloud to cover the land; it shall be in the LATTER DAYS, and I will bring thee against My land, that the heathen (non-believing nations) may know Me, when I shall be sanctified in thee, O Gog (Russia), before their eyes.

In verse 18 of Ezekiel GOD tells us that when they come against Israel, His fury shall know no reservation. There shall be a great shaking in the land of Israel, and the mountains shall be crumbled with all the steep places and walls. In verse 22, GOD says that He will rain upon them viciously with great hailstones, fire and brimstone...and they SHALL KNOW THAT GOD HAS DONE THIS!

You readers must understand what His word (the Bible) is telling us...this world of man...the dominion of satan is coming swiftly into fulfillment...MAN WILL STILL NOT UNDERSTAND!

Those who feel they will always have the chance to accept Jesus Christ into their hearts are surely not versed with what GOD says in Isaiah 6:9,10.

296

"And He said, Go, and tell the people, Hear ye indeed, but understand not; and see ye indeed, but perceive not.

Make the heart of this people (those who continually deny GOD) fat (stupid-foolish), and make their ears heavy (difficult to grasp) and shut their eyes (blind them); lest they see with their eyes (realize) and understand with their heart, and convert and be healed."

It is also repeated in Acts 28:24-26. Paul was preaching the GOOD NEWS of the Kingdom to the growing crowds, testifying about the Lord Jesus Christ.

"And some believed the things which were spoken, and some believed not. Acts 28:24

For those who would not believe after hearing Paul's first hand accounting of Jesus...God told Paul:

"Saying, Go unto the people, and say, Hearing ye shall hear, and shall not understand; and seeing ye shall see, and not perceive.

For the heart of this people is waxed gross (indignantly carnal) and their ears are dull of hearing, and their eyes have they closed; lest they should see with their eyes, and hear with their ears, and understand with their heart, and should be converted (come and accept Christ Jesus) and I should heal them (I should save them).
ACTS 28:26,27

So you see GOD will not always try to reach everyone. If you keep denying Christ Jesus as your Savior...one day, and that day may just be around your next corner...GOD will give up on you as one of the LOST SOULS headed for the lake of fire and brimstone. Your only choice is heaven and peace, or, if you choose, hell and torment for eternity. To me that doesn't propose a difficult decision...hopefully you, too, will read and understand.

The Year of the Lord Is At Hand!

Those who don't accept Jesus now, MAY have another chance later...that's not definite. Every-time you feel the Holy Spirit working on you and you resist Him...your heart hardens that much more and further seals your eternal fate with the fires of the burning lake (Revelation 20:15).

When you see and understand the truth...when you hear and perceive the word of GOD to be real...and, when you feel the Holy Spirt of GOD upon you, ACCEPT HIM INTO YOUR HEART RIGHT THEN regardless of the macho crowd you are with...Do not be ashamed to claim Him as your Savior...YOU MAY NOT get another chance!

If you accept Jesus now...you will be included in the Rapture of His church, you will be spared the agony of the Tribulation and most of all...YOU WILL HAVE ETERNAL FELLOWSHIP WITH GOD!

It has been determined that SOME will acknowledge Jesus as their Savior after the "Rapture," and they too shall be saved from eternal torment. But, why not accept Him now and NEVER KNOW DEATH? If you go into the Tribulation and subject yourself and your family to its trials...YOU MAY NOT COME OUT OF IT SAVED.

It is said in Daniel 7:25 of this great world dictator (the anti-Christ):

> "And he shall speak great words (vile) against the Most High (GOD)and shall wear out (make you weary) the saints (ones who love GOD) of the Most High, and think to change times and laws, and they (YOU) shall be given unto his hand until a time, and times and a dividing of time. (three and one-half years)"

The three and a half-years that you will be under this cruel world dictator will be almost unbearable to withstand...Those that will receive eternal life are those that will endure until you are martyred for your witness unto Christ Jesus. Unfortunately, many borderline Christians at this time will "become weary" under the persecution and give in to the antiChrists' leadership. These will accept the mark of the beast (666 or new monetary and coding system...computer chip) and will forever be condemned by GOD!

> "But he that shall endure unto the end, the same shall be saved."

JESUS CHRIST Matthew 24:13

So, isn't it better to accept Him now, and, by His mercy, be spared of the horrors of that period? You know it is!

Now I shall reveal the year of my inspiration...the year that has been engraved in my soul...the YEAR that the Rapture will occur. That YEAR is One-thousand, nine-hundred and ninety-one (I 9 9 I)! I am MORE than positive that this is THE YEAR that the Rapture will occur. HOW? Let me explain a little in this chapter and totally in the final chapter, Twenty-one!

First, a year ago I had no intentions of ever writing a religious book...it wasn't what my training called for. Read the FOREWARD of this book and you will understand what changed my mind, my career and my future!

Secondly, I have the Spirit of our Living GOD with me all through the writing of this book. Regardless of what some narrow-minded people will say...it is true! Anytime I needed any information or reference material from the Bible, I would open it and it would be under my fingertips.

Thirdly, GOD has verified to me through many prayers that 1991 is the year of the Rapture. He would not give me the DAY nor the HOUR of His coming...but He did give me both the YEAR along with a complete documentation (see Chapter Twenty-one).

Fourthly, I have spoken to GOD in my prayers and have been answered directly! The Holy Spirit is upon me and has changed my entire outlook on life. Yes, I still have some human characteristics, but I feel them fading swiftly. I have had such a thirst for GOD's word and knowledge that anything else seems totally irrelevant. I'm well aware that my GOD HATES LIARS and deceitful people who receive pleasure in misinforming others...A liar I am not...A deceitful person GOD knows I'm not...and of spreading misinformations - that is the furthest from my mind.

When GOD told me that the year of the Rapture will be 1991, I found it hard to believe. Why would GOD tell me of this long hidden secret? That I do not know...but I feel honored beyond words for this knowledge. When I received it, being human (temporarily anyway), I had to have the proof...if not only for my own peace of mind...for the many who will read this book...HE GAVE THAT TO ME AS WELL! GOD showed me in His Word (the Bible) the documented proof that 1991 will be the year true Christians are waiting for! If I have made any human error, it will be because I have taken the WORD of GOD literally...I believe that is exactly what He wants of us all!

GOD BLESS YOU ALL...And if it is His' WILL, "I'll see you in the air!"

CHAPTER TWENTY-ONE

God's Eternal Plan:
"Hidden Secrets of the Holy Spirit!"

"But ye Bretheran, are not in darkness, that
that DAY shall overtake you as a thief!!!
I THESSALONIANS 5:4

How many of you sports fans have watched a Monday Night NFL Football game and heard "Dandy Don" Meredith sing his now famous song "Turn out the Lights, the Party's over?" The words simply imply that the football game is almost finished and the other team HAS NO CHANCE REMAINING TO ACHIEVE A VICTORY!

Listen to the first few words and in your mind, decide for yourself if they wouldn't also be appropriate to our current world predicament!

        "TURN OUT THE LIGHTS,
        THE PARTY'S OVER.....
        THEY SAY THAT ALL
        GOOD THINGS MUST END!"

Yes, humanity has been involved in one long and dreary ballgame...one that does not recognize the fact that the festivities are over and all the good "fun" is coming into completion...IT'S OVER!!!

I relate the lyrics of the song in juxtaposition with what we have had (emphasis on the past tense) in America and are on the precipice of losing. My brothers and sisters, the hour of GOD's eternal Plan for His creation has reached fulfillment...Some are cognizant of this surety...most feel the party's refreshments are on the way to replenish and revive the fellowship...These are the exact ones who are the die-hard party-poopers that refuse to accept the final beckoning from a most weary host to get their hat and GO HOME. The Host of life's party (GOD) is now wondering to himself! He's given the final curtain call and He is marveling for those who have understood its significance. He is also weeping for those He created in His image who may lose their way home because of the fog (false Christs) that has decended upon the earth.

How many of you readers receive this FINAL chapter

may determine whether you will be guided through the haze unto an eternal Beacon, or stumble around in the vagueness of mind that WILL cause you to be blinded and lose your way home!

The unique and diabolical factions who are currently . in this late night mist want company in their evils...because misery always seeks company! There is a way to supernaturally lift this blinding affliction of sin, but, unfortunately few are making a real attempt to restore their narrowed and obscured vision! For that feeble effort...They are heading directly to HELL!

Whether you consider yourself a believer, a non-believer, a conservative or a liberal...it doesn't matter! What I am asking each of you readers to do RIGHT NOW - before you finish this final chapter, is to pause for a moment! Take a deep breath and place a mental picture in your mind...a vision of a world existence devoid of any real love...an absence of any meaningful fellowship. Picture it as a reality where there is absolutely no compassion whatsoever or any true hope or faith in anything other than the misconception that man is in control of his own destiny.

Use your wildest imagination and project yourself into a future vacuum of emptiness and despair, horror and endless deceptions. Think seriously of what this earth will be like when absolutely no believing Christians or Jews are anywhere to be found. NOW COME BACK TO THE PRESENT! That is exactly what this world will be like around the year 1991!

Everyone you will come in contact with will care less if you live or breathe. With no restraint left on Earth it will be a survival of the most fit...a world of unhappy endings and evil beings. That world is coming...that world is here!

At the moment you read this book, GOD's Plan, as old as the begining of time, has played out more than 99.8% of what is to take place...Yes, we are in the twelvth hour and there's less than a grain left in His hour glass. Believe on Jesus Christ as your Savior and you shall be given another clock...one with no hands, no face and no measurement of time! That's eternity, friends!

Any astute scholar of the Bible (believers only) will readily agree that the Bible is both divinely inspired and GOD's second greatest gift to humanity. It is much more than a book of parables and seemingly uninterpretable verses..it is GOD's eternal Plan for mankind which is made up of over one-third prophesy and two-thirds of meaningful history. If you have ever had the impression that history repeats itself...the Biblical stories will assure you of this fact. Ever wonder how our GOD feels after almost six-thousand years of rejection? Humans can't stand being denied even for a moment...How do you think GOD feels after 5,986 years of total disrespect, personal self-righteousness, individual pride and selfishness. How do you feel He looks upon all this outright defiance of His caring mercy and well-thought-out covenants and commandments? I know how He feels...because I have compassion for His overlooked kindness. With His graces, I'm soon to be with Him, but while I'm here on Earth, I lay no claim to the fantasy and material possessions of this world...my Kingdom (to borrow a quote from Jesus), is not of this world. Because I am a son of the Living GOD and made in His likeness...I CAN FEEL HOW HE IS FEELING...He has given me that blessing! I tell you in all honesty HE CARES NOT FOR WHAT IS HAPPENING ON EARTH, or in some of His churches! The odor of this stinken planet is reaching up to heaven and His wrath has been kindled.

One thing though...He is a GOD of His word, and never bears any misleading or false witness. He does as He says whether man will or not! His Plan included six-thousand years in which man could obey His covenants and find His infinite blessings, OR, choose to disobey His commandments and find themselves on the outside of His eternal reward. He gave man a choice in the Garden of Eden and the father of humanity (Adam) chose to go it alone.

If God Knew What Was Going To Happen, Why Did He Have To Give Man A Choice?

The question that I've heard being asked more than a few times has been; If GOD is so merciful and kind, why did He give man a choice if He knew what would happen in the end? You can answer that yourself in your own mortal way.

Have you ever "tested a friend" to know for sure that they are indeed a true friend? I have, and so have you! When times are the worst, only a true friend will come to the forefront with assistance...the false friends will find a thousand and one reasons why they won't help you, but the ones that really love you...shall not deny you in your time of need. You've heard the expression "a friend in NEED...is a friend INDEED!" What that means is when you are in need, those who come to the rescue are friends INDEED! Anything else and they are not friends.

So, understanding this minute analogy of GOD's friendship to us, will give you a fair comprehension of why He gave man the freedom of choosing which side of the fence he will be on! Are you really His friend? Or, are you like most in this world who only seek GOD when things go wrong in your life? Well I tell you this pure fact...He's coming for His friends...He's coming very soon, as you will see, and when He does, He will be separating His friends from those who only profess friendship; the wheat from the thistles: the corn from the stalk and the believers from the ones who don't believe! That, my friends, you can well count on!

Why Six-Thousand Years In His Plan?

There will be many learned, sophisticated and philosophical clergymen who will attack me for taking the Bible literally...that doesn't matter to me at all! I believe that GOD would not have inspired any book just for leisure enjoyment. GOD means for His people to take the Bible literally. I'll say it again with more enthusiasm...GOD WANTS HIS BIBLE TO BE TAKEN LITERALLY!!!!!!! Everything in the Bible has been divinely inspired unto men who have shown their love, friendship and faithfulness to Him...Because of that, GOD imparted His knowledge unto them!

I've had individuals in my own family circle who have been professing their allegiance to GOD, BUT, at the same time have cautioned me not to read the Bible in my simple and unsophisticated manner! "Don't take everything in the Bible literally, Rick...It wasn't meant to be taken that way!" Then I was told that many of the verses have little meaning, especially in the Old Testament. I tried to explain that the Holy Spirit had talked to me and explained His secrets...he wouldn't listen, nor was he interested in hearing WHAT I had been told, UNLESS, it had to do primarily with his professed religion. Because I love this family member very much, I won't give out the name, nor will I fail to reach out again to the person.

I will say this though. Regardless of his steadfastness, he does believe in the most important factor from GOD...and that is "that the only way to the Father is through the Blood of the Lamb...Jesus Christ!"

Why has GOD alloted mankind a round number of six-thousand years? Well, to GOD a day is like a thousand years:

"For a thousand years in thy sight are but as yesterday when it is past, and AS A WATCH IN THE NIGHT!"

PSALMS 90:4

You say it still doesn't hit home with you? You aren't really getting GOD's message? What Psalms 90:4 is telling man is that one day to Him is a thousand years of human life! You may say, what does that have to do with us? I say plenty...please read on!

In Psalm 90:4, the subject of conversation is a prayer to GOD for His mercy to mankind. Moses is the one praying:

>"And Thou hast been our dwelling place in all generations.
>Before the mountains were brought forth, or ever Thou hast formed the earth and the world, even from everlasting to everlasting, Thou art GOD.
>Thou turnest man to DESTRUCTION; and sayest, Return, ye children of men."

In Psalm 90:9, Moses says to GOD:

>"For all our days are passed away in thy wrath: we spend our years as a tale that is told."

And in the next verse Moses prophesied his feeling for GOD's wearyness and divine patience with man:

>"The DAYS OF OUR YEARS ARE THREE SCORE AND TEN (70); and if by reason of strength they be four score (80) years, yet is their strength labor and sorrow; for it is soon cut off and we fly away."

In that verse (Psalm 90:10), Moses says that OUR YEARS are three score and ten...He could have said seventy, but he chose to say THREE SCORE (60) AND TEN (10). To Moses, that meant 6,000 years for man to make a go of it on Earth. Those who are victorious and accept GOD's Plan will receive the extra ten (1,000 years.) I said to Moses...not to GOD! For it was Moses who interpeted the days of our (mankind's) years at...70. With GOD, a day is as a thousand years, and it's explained further here:

>"But, beloved, BE NOT IGNORANT (uninformed or unknowledgeable) OF THIS ONE THING, that one day IS WITH THE LORD AS A THOUSAND YEARS, and a thousand years as ONE DAY!"
>II PETER 3:8

You might wish to know the topic of interest in that verse. I believe it can be explained entirely in the following verse:

>"But the heavens and the earth, which are now, by the same word are "KEPT IN STORE" (sealed), reserved unto the fire against the "day of Judgment and Perdition (eternal damnation) of

unGodly men.

(JUMP TO II PETER 3:9)

> "The Lord is not slack concerning His promise, as some men count slackness, but is long suffering to us-ward, NOT WILLING THAT ANY SHOULD PERISH, but that ALL should come to repentance."

That verse tells you that GOD's mercy and patience is infinite; uncompromising on His command that everyone shall repent of their sins and seek His knowledge. It also should inform you that He will derive no pleasure in casting anyone, except for satan, the anti-Christ and the false Prophet, into the Lake of Fire at the Final Judgment!

In Exodus 23:l0, GOD gives us another clue as to the destiny of mankind.

> "And SIX YEARS (6,000) thou shalt sow they land (labor), and shalt gather in the fruits thereof (living on earth in the dominion of satan):
> But the SEVENTH YEAR thou shalt let it rest."

'Now, some of you shall say that GOD was giving instruction to the Chosen People on the cultivating of their lands, but the Holy Spirit is telling me that GOD has multiple meaning with almost everything He commands of us...all to the glory of His Name!

The knowledge of GOD is infinite and wond'rous and at the same time it rings purely of His sense of humor and His flare for the mystique. By that word (mystique) I mean that the Holy Spirit has given man a special esoteric (limited to a small circle of His specially initiated people) skill to interpet the true prophesies of His hidden secrets.

What I'm saying is , our Lord GOD has a flare for a sense of humor as well as one for theatrics...If you love GOD and His mysteries, He will give you the gift of interpretation. Those who do not believe in Him, will not receive the "KEY" to unravel the truth!

The reason GOD is giving man the answers today is because the tomorrows are at a premium...There are but a few left! He wants to save as many as will listen and believe what they hear after discerning the source's spirit of righteousness and honesty!

> "But know this, that if the goodman of the house had known in what watch the thief would come, he would HAVE WATCHED, and would not

have suffered his house to be broken up."
JESUS CHRIST Matthew 24:43

Why shouldn't GOD have a sense of humor or a flare for the theatrics? He made man in His image, didn't He? Sometimes, even humans like a good mystery. Sometimes we even show some form of jest in our actions, don't we? If you can understand that, you should also realize that our GOD is not always the stern, demanding and ever uncompromising GOD He has been portrayed as! Man, especially believers, have some of these same Godly traits as does the Father, but on a lesser scale. Man can not reach the plateau of GOD, nor should we try! There is only one creator...only one GOD. With Him there was no mold to be cast aside!

I get disgusted when I hear of the limited knowledge of this world's intellectual! To their human mind, "everything has to have a begining and an end! Everything must have an answer if there is a question." Such is not the story with our GOD. GOD is EVERLASTING to EVERLASTING! Figure that one out...humanist! I'll tell you this much and I'm backed by the greatest book ever produced...the Spirit of GOD...The Bible. I'll give you one thing that has a begining and an end...and that's the world, and you'd better believe that because THAT END IS NEAR...closer than you really imagine in your narrow little mind! You humanists, atheists and communist brothers had better awaken from your years of slumber before it is too late to save your wretched frames. REPENT, and you'll find out to what extent is the mercy of our GOD!

Believers will not be in the dark because they will have been well warned as to the approximate time of the coming of Jesus Christ to earth for His Bride (the believing church) in the Rapture. They won't know the day or the hour, but they will have a fairly good idea of the time!

You see, believers are watching and waiting for their GOD to return for them...the non-believer does not expect Jesus to come for them in the air...they don't believe because they aren't familiar with GOD's eternal Plan given graphically in the (literal) Bible!

If you are OF this world (secular humanists, atheists, etc.,), you have a false belief in the power and self-control of man. You are optimistic that man has your answers and because you believe that, you will also believe anything the coming anti-Christ will tell you. You will be worshipping the king of this world, in name, that is satan. He will lurk in the shadows and feed you deceiving information and ultimately you will be blinded beyond repair.

But, if you ARE NOT OF this world, you will be wise and knowledgeable of the word and promises of GOD...and GOD only! You will understand that "man" by himself, is incapable of controlling his own destiny. If you seek the face of GOD you will be given divine wisdom and extreme patience...you will know in your heart that you are much more than mortal. In essence you will come to realize that you are a "son of GOD," with powers and abilities that will defy the logistics of the human mind.

Most men will never know their true potential because they won't ask for it through the proper channel...Wisdom only comes from the Lord Jesus Christ. When you have the indwelling Holy Spirit, your logic will not make sense to the average human. Where they are concerned with the intellectuality of this world...you will be finding the beauty that can only come through GOD, thusly, you will be opened to the uncomplicated communication from our Holy of Holies, the Lord GOD Yahweh. It's all you will ever need in life to make you happy and confident.

Remember...WISE MEN STILL SEEK HIM!

The Significance Of Holy Numbers!

Throughout the Bible it becomes evident that our GOD favors the humble and lowly. He sides with the non-intellectual, the meek and those who are ever cognizant of His presence! He exaults the humble and casts out the arrogant.

Because our Father is not complicated...neither are His people who exault Him. His Plan for humanity is so simple children can easily understand His designs. If I am referred to as naive and unsophisticated for my literal approach to Biblical prophesy, I praise the Lord for your insight...To understand our GOD you must pray for this with all sincerity and know that He shall grant your requests.

GOD has been telling man for thousands of years that He is the true GOD...a GOD of patience, of truth, of kindness and of mercy and love. He also represents divine wisdom and and fair justice.

As you read His Good Book you will come to the realization that He is also extremely consistent and uncompromising with His commandments. You shall also notice the similarity between His covenants to man and the numbers three (3), six (6) and SEVEN (7). Each one of three numbers have their numerical significance to GOD's eternal "PLAN" for mankind and this will become evident as you progress in this final chapter.

In the Book of Genesis (meaning the begining), GOD explains that He created the heavens, the earth, the light that He calls day, and the darkness He calls night. He created the firmament, the great seas and divided the sea with dry land. He gave the stars and the moon for light during the darkness of night and gave us the sun during the day for both warmth and light.

On the fifth day, GOD created all the fish and the fowl, the great whales and every living creature that moves...and on the SIXTH DAY, He created His masterpiece...man!

In His very own image, GOD constructed man out of the dust of the earth and breathed upon him so that he would live...On the SIXTH DAY, the "father of all humanity (Adam)" breathed his first breath. Adam became a son of GOD and was granted special favors and dominion over all the earth and all the creatures on its' face.

GOD put Adam to sleep and took one of his ribs to create the first woman, Eve...to this day, women have one more rib than men as the symbol that woman was formed by GOD through His creation of man.

On the SEVENTH DAY, GOD rested from His labor and blessed it,making the seventh day a day of thanksgiving and worship to GOD for His kindness and mercy.

Such is the significance of the numbers SIX and SEVEN. SIX is a symbol to GOD of the day He created man. SEVEN to GOD is a sacred number, for it was on that day of the week that He FINISHED HIS LABOR.

The "THREE" Divisions Of Man!

When GOD created man on the sixth day, He did not just construct a physical being. He created a most unique moving temple of His holiness...one that was intended to have eternal life through fellowship and reverence with GOD. He made man with a body , a soul and a spirit. At that exact time, all of these portions were meant by GOD for eternity. Yes, even the body would never know death.

But man had other ideas. GOD gave him a freedom of choice to test his faithfulness and man flunked out! Adam and Eve chose to listen. to the fallen angel, satan, in lieu of his Creator's better judgment.

GOD told man that he could eat the fruit from all the trees in the Garden...but of the fruit from the "tree of knowledge," he could not eat. For on that day...man would surely die!

What GOD meant by saying that man would "surely die," was that he would die spiritually for not obeying His command. Because man chose earthen knowledge over wisdom and fellowship with GOD, He cursed mankind with spiritual death and cut the number of years an individual would reign over the earth drastically. He gave woman pain with child-birth.

The devil told Adam that he would not die if he ate from the "tree of knowledge" and man chose to believe the serpent, instead of GOD's command. THE DEVIL LIED! Because of man's disobedience to GOD, he would now have to go through life on his own, unless of course, he would repent of his sins and reestablish the broken covenant with GOD. Man was given a way in which to redeem himself of the lost graces...a manner in which he could cleanse himself of the evils he assumed on himself.

So, the first significance of the number three (3) is known to history as the BODY, which has been rendered by GOD as perishable, the SOUL, which can not be destroyed by anyone but GOD, and the SPIRIT.

The Three Stages Of God's Plan!

The very first seven which appears in the Bible was the day when GOD FINISHED HIS LABOR. If we can understand that, on that day, GOD was elated with His creation and that He sanctified the day as an eternal covenant for man to keep holy, we will not lose the importance of the number SEVEN to GOD. This particular number is the most widely utilized number in the entire BIBLE, both Old and New Testament. The number seven is conducive to both infinity and purity with GOD. It is sacred!

Aside from GOD walking with Adam, prior to the broken covenant, GOD walked with a man from the SEVENTH GENERATION of Adam, a man called Enoch...Adam's great, great, great, great grandson. By "walking with GOD" I mean that Enoch never experienced death. At the youthful age (for that time) of 365 years old...Enoch was just taken to be with GOD.   Here are the generations of Adam to Noah:

TEN GENERATIONS OF ADAM!

Adam	lived 930 years
Seth	lived 912 years
Enos	lived 905 years
Cainan	lived 910 years
Mehelaleel	lived 890 years
Jared	lived 962 years
ENOCH	lived 365 years
	NEVER DIED!!!
Methuselah	lived 969 years
Lamech	lived 777 years
NOAH	lived 950 years

The generations on the previous page are the direct bloodline into which Jesus was born.   From the creation of Adam (the father of all humanity) to the birth of Abraham (the father of many nations) to the virgin birth of the Christ (Savior of the world and mankind's last covenant from GOD), there is an interval of approximately 2,000 years!

	Approximate year of birth
Adam	4002 B.C.
Noah	2948 B.C.
Abraham	1988 B.C.
Isaac	1889 B.C.
Jacob (ISRAEL)	1825 B.C.
King David	1042 B.C.
JESUS	2 B.C.

Considering who these people were is real important. Noah, was favored by GOD, walked with Him and was chosen to save a remnant of humans around 1626, in the great flood. Noah was 601 years old when the flood subsided. The significance of Noah was that he trusted GOD; something Adam did not!

Abraham; his son, Isaac; his grandson, Jacob, (renamed ISRAEL by GOD) and his great-grandson, Joseph, all TRUSTED GOD as did the great King David (most beloved of all the Kings of Israel)! That word TRUST is the "key" to establishing any covenant with GOD.

Now Adam is considered the "father of all humanity," because he was the first human.

Abraham was considered as the "father of many nations" because it was with him that GOD tested and found true.

Jesus is the "Savior of the World." He is the risen Christ...He is GOD (John 14:7-9).

From Adam in 4002 B.C. , to Abraham in 1988 B.C., there are approximately 2,000 years of humanity, two thousand years of man's broken covenants with GOD. Abraham's birth signified the end of the first THIRD of GOD's Plan for humanity...the first two thousand years of mankind. GOD made a covenant with His trusting and faithful servant Abraham to make him a "father of many nations," and GOD kept His word.

Mankind's Second Opportunity!

With one-third of GOD's Plan consumed, Abraham began the second of three stages in GOD's eternal outreach to mankind. Surely man would understand that to be a son of GOD and inherit all the blessings of the Kingdom, he would have to make atonement for his sins against GOD by sacrificial rites.

GOD kept His promise to Abraham to make him the father of many nations when at the age of nearly 100 years old (Sarah being 90), He gave them a son...Isaac. GOD again tested Abraham's faithfulness when He commanded him to take his ONLY SON to a mountain and sacrifice Isaac to GOD. Again Abraham trusted in the Lord and his merciful GOD stopped Abraham from killing the youngster....Abraham was truly tested and came through much to the delight of GOD! God told Abraham that, through Isaac, He would make his seed like the stars in the heavens and of this, GOD also kept His word.

Through the loins of Isaac, Jacob was born and begat twelve sons:

Ruben - Simeon - Levi - Judah - Dan - Naphtali
Gad - Issachar - Zebulun - Asher - Joseph & Benjamin

These twelve sons of Jacob (renamed by GOD..Israel) are the original 12 tribes of Israel. It was through the loins of Judah that, seven hundred years later, King David was begotten and, carrying it out further...Joseph, the husband of the Virgin Mary and the foster father of Jesus Christ, was born.

Why Must Man Continue To Fail?

The nation of Israel was included in GOD's second stage. Man consistently showed GOD that he was incapable of having a real relationship with Him. This confirmed, beyond any doubt, that mankind was destined for hell unless GOD could supernaturally change their way of thinking.

All during this time, GOD retained a remnant of faithful men who sought His word with every fiber of their being. GOD knew that on their own, man had little chance of ever overcoming the powers of the one that controlled the earth...satan!

For four-thousand years, man had to make atonement for their own sins through the rites of sacrifice, but GOD knew that that would not be enough to save humanity.

Around the year 2 B.C., GOD had had enough of man's corrupt nature. He decided to see first hand, in the body of man, just what kind of temptations man had to overcome in his search for the Spirit of GOD. GOD came to earth in the body of man and in the name of Jesus the Christ...the Messiah prophesized in Isaiah 53...for recognition by you Jewish brothers. That prophesy was made more than six-hundred years before the birth of Christ in Bethlehem. The prophesy of Isaiah was fulfilled with the first coming of the Messiah...most Jews didn't believe it because satan had clouded their vision with false prophets.

With all the miracles Jesus performed in the sight of men, including many of the non-believers, he was denied by many. The First Coming of Christ Jesus signalled the third and final chapter of GOD's Plan for mankind. Man's last hope was to believe that Jesus came to earth for one reason...the personal atonement of sin!

GOD knew that man was basically evil and evil by association with the deceitful one, satan, the king of the earth. If GOD had come to earth and told people that He was GOD...no one would have been able to perceive it. So GOD took on the name, Jesus, and did wonderful miracles during his time on earth. Jesus lived on earth for 33 years and in itself...thirty-three years is not the product of chance. Even by the amount of years (3-3), GOD was telling man that the two 3s, signalled that two-thirds of His Plan was fulfilled and the final two-thousand years, or the last third of His Plan began when Christ physically came to Earth in 2 B.C. Christ was crucified around the year 30 A.D.

The Significance Of The Numbers

If you understand that the number three (3) represents the divisions of the body of man, the number of times the Holy Temple in Jerusalem will be both built and destroyed and the three distinct 2,000 year intervals of GOD's Plan for humanity...you're on the right track.

Now if you understand that the sacred symbol for man is the number SIX (the day GOD created Adam...the sixth day), you will come to the forefront of this acknowledgment: To GOD, a thousand years is like a day (Psalms 90:4 and II PETER 3:8) and considering that GOD made man on the sixth day of creation (Genesis 1:26) or near the end of the 6,000th year (6 X 1,000 years), and forsaking presumption, GOD has given man 6,000 years from Adam to repent of their sins and come back home!

If you consider the fact that of the 6,000 years, 5,986 have been already used up...you'll see that the remaining fourteen years are the LAST FOURTEEN, or the end of human time...the end of GOD's Plan for mankind!

So, if all this is true (and I feel strongly that I have been receiving divine information), we can determine that the final year in human history should be in the year 1998 (the end of the 6,000 year period of GOD's Plan).

Considering that and also acknowledging what the Bible tells us about the period of great Tribulation, to find the year of the Rapture, we deduct this last SEVEN years from 1998 and for us pre-Tribulationists, the year of the Rapture should be 1991.

Shortly prior to 1991, the anti-Christ should be proclaimed to all the world and apostasy in the church should have reached a fever-pitch!

It should be well noted that Jesus said that "of that day or hour, knoweth no man, no, not the angels of heaven, but the Father only." We should not presume anything, but GOD did say that in the end times His believers would have a fairly good idea by the fulfillment of the prophesies, of when He would return for His church. We see most of the prophesies being fulfilled before our very eyes and all the unfulfilled prophesies shall escalate as the final years move into history!

Man, as a whole, has not sought the face of GOD. Humanity will not learn how our Father HATES corruption. You can readily understand that by what He did to the world in the days of NOAH. In the days after the flood GOD destroyed the Tower of Babel when Nimrod and others wanted to be like GOD and reach up to the heavens. They were practicing every perverse deviation known to the mind of that era and GOD smashed the Tower and scattered the people to all parts of the earth, each speaking different languages. Witchcraft, astrology and devil worship were prevalent in those days.

In the days of Abraham and Lot, God destroyed Sodom and Gomorrah because of perverted desires of the people. GOD couldn't even find ten good people in the whole city. Lot, his wife and two daughters were the only good ones left, but evidently his wife didn't know how to obey the angels... She must have had second thoughts about leaving the city, or, was just curious to see if the word of GOD would be fulfilled. SHE DIDN'T HAVE FAITH and was turned into a pillar of salt!

NOW LEARN A LESSON FROM LOT'S WIFE ON OBEDIENCE TO GOD'S COMMANDS:

> "Then let them which are in Judaea flee to the mountains
>
> Let him which is on the housetop not come down to take anything out of the house:
>
> Neither let him which is in the field return back to take his clothes.
> JESUS CHRIST Matthew 24:16-18

Christians...take heed! That's the advice from our GOD about the time when He comes for us in the Rapture. Don't look back because you won't be leaving anything here on earth...you're not OF this earth – sons of the Living GOD belong in heaven!

Symbols Of Broken Allegiance!

We know the number SIX is the symbol for man. Understanding that GOD'S Plan has three (3) distinct stages, what do the numbers 666 tell you? That's right! The anti-Christ in Revelations 13:18! But knowing that our GOD has a flare for theatrics...couldn't it mean something else as well?

When the THREE SIXES are used together they represent the THREE STAGES (3) that ole number SIX (man) has FAILED OUR GOD! For three 2,000-year periods man has had the penchant for evil...EVIL SPELLED ANY OTHER WAY IS...6...6...6. In that frame of mind you can now realize that the 666 is definitely representative of some who could care less about GOD's patience, GOD's love or GOD's fellowship...They represent an ANTICHRIST!

How Does The Sacred Number "SEVEN" Fit In?

God created the Earth and everything in it including man in SIX DAYS...on the SEVENTH HE RESTED, blessed the day and made it Holy!

Understanding that, will help you acknowledge the correlation between the six (man) and the seven (purification)!!! Let's see if this diagram helps explain what we have so far...

MAN	MAN	MAN
SIX	SIX	SIX
Stage #1	Stage #2	Stage #3
ADAM	ABRAHAM	JESUS
2,000	2,000	2,000

Those who are familiar with Biblical prophesy know that the Holy Temple in Jerusalem has been built and destroyed TWO TIMES...and, it has been prophesized to be rebuilt and destroyed one more time! That's three, too!

The holy number for reestablishing purity with GOD is SEVEN.

Not only is it a BLESSED NUMBER, it represents the day of.........the.........week........a........person.........is CLEANSED!...PURIFIED!...REESTABLISHED IN THE GRACES

314

OF GOD through the sacrificial rites.

°We know that Enoch was a man who loved and trusted GOD and also was the SEVENTH generation of Adam.

°We know that the SEVENTH day of our present week is reserved for the worship of GOD...and, it's supposed to be a day of REST!

°We know what Psalms 90:10 says about the days of our years being three score...AND...ten!

°We know that the Tribulation is SEVEN years in duration and that it will be a time of punishment and PURGING the non-believers...another word for PURGE...is PURIFYING!

°We know that in the four thousand years prior to the First Coming of the Messiah in 2 B.C., men of this earth had to purify themselves by sacrificing animals in the Temple to GOD!

> "If thou buy a Hebrew servant, SIX DAYS
> he shall serve (labor):...AND in the SEVENTH
> year he shall go out free for nothing."
> EXODUS 21:2

°We know that GOD saved and delivered the Jews from the Pharaoh in Egypt, after saving them, killing the first born of each family in Egypt and PASSING OVER (Passover) the Hebrews when they placed blood on their doors. As a remembrance of that period, GOD told the Jews to celebrate it forever by "eating unleavened bread for six days and feasting on the SEVENTH! Anyone eating leavened bread from the first day until the SEVENTH will be cut off from Israel! EXODUS 12:15

°GOD confirms the seven to be holy when He says in Exodus 29:30..."And that son that is priest in his stead shall put them on seven days (holy garments), when he cometh into the tabernacle in the holy place."

°SEVEN DAYS shalt thou consecrate (to make sacred) them Exodus 29:35

°SEVEN DAYS thou shalt make an atonement for the altar, Exodus 29:37

°Six days may work be done; but in the SEVENTH is the Sabbath of rest. Exodus 31:15

°"Wherefore the children of Israel shall keep the sabbath, to observe the sabbath (SEVENTH DAY) throughout their generations, 'for a perpetual (EVERLASTING)' covenant." Exodus 31:16

°The similarities between the SEVEN and SEVENTY are explained in Exodus 1:5..."And all the souls that came out of the loins of Jacob (Israel) were SEVENTY souls:

°The purifying for a sin offering is explained in Leviticus 4:6..."And the priest shall dip his finger in the BLOOD, and sprinkle of the blood SEVEN times before the Lord, before the veil of the sanctuary."

°Leviticus 8:33..."And ye shall not go out of the door of the tabernacle of the congregation in SEVEN days, until the days of your consecration (purification or atonement) be at an end; for SEVEN days shall he consecrate you."

°In Exodus 24:16..."And the glory of the Lord abode (rested) upon mount Sinai, and the cloud covered it six days: and the SEVENTH day He called unto Moses out of the midst of the cloud."

°Understand this in the making of the holy candlestick for the sanctuary in Exodus 25:32-40:

"And SIX branches (signifying man) shall come out of the sides of it; three branches of the candle stick out of one side (each one thousand years or 3,000 years) and three branches of the candlestick out of the other side:
Three bowls made like unto almonds, with a knop (knob) and a flower in one branch (GOD's love for mankind); and three bowls made like almonds in the other branch, with a knop and a flower: so in the six branches that come out of the candlestick.
And in the candlestick shall be four bowls made like unto almonds, with their knops and their flowers.
And there shall be a knop under two branches of the same (divisions of 3 - 2s or 3 X 2,000 years), and a knop under two branches of the same, according to the six (man) branches that proceed out of the candlestick.

There knops and their branches shall be of the same: (equal intervals - equality) and it SHALL BE "ONE" beaten work of "PURE" gold. (This signifys no breaks in the artistry...GOD is one with us)

And thou shalt make the SEVEN lamps thereof: and they shall light the lamps thereof, that they may give light over against it."

The similiarities between the number SEVEN and purification are much too numerous to list in this book. Skipping all the way to the Book of Revelation we see the significance of seven prophesized in the END TIMES of the world.

°John has been exiled to the island of Patmos and has a vision from GOD....

°....."And I turned to see the voice that spake with me, and being turned, I saw SEVEN golden candlesticks. (GOD's covenant with the seven churches, each as he is ONE with them." (Revelation 1:12) NOTE: these SEVEN churches also represent the churches of today. Read what GOD says about each church...then ask yourself if your church is applicable!

°....."And in His right hand SEVEN stars (the angels of the seven churches): and out of His mouth went a sharp "two-edged" sword (Judgment): and His countenance (mood) was as the sun shineth in His strength."

°.....Then Jesus tells John to write to the SEVEN churches of Ephesus, Smyrna, Pergamos, Thyatira, Sardis, Philadelphia and Laodiceans. In each case, with the exception of the church of Philadelphia (who are the ones who HAVE KEPT HIS WORD...the Gospel...and have not denied His name), He had something against their doctrines. "Does your church TEACH THE GOSPEL? If not you may be deprived of the open door GOD speaks of in Revelation 3:8"

°.....And I saw in the right hand of Him that sat on the throne a book written within and on the backside, sealed with SEVEN seals. Revelation 5:1

°Revelation 6 tells of the SEVEN seals.....

°In Revelation 8:2..."And I saw SEVEN angels which stood before GOD; and to them were given SEVEN trumpets."

°....."And I saw another sign in heaven, great and marvelous, SEVEN angels having the SEVEN last plagues; for in them is filled up the wrath of GOD (after the seven last plagues, GOD's wrath will be finished)." Revelation 15:1

°Revelation 15:7 says..."And one of the four beasts gave unto the SEVEN angels SEVEN golden vials (bowls) full of the wrath of GOD who liveth for ever and ever."

GOD'S PLAN COMES TOGETHER!

It was not my intention to over-emphasize the meaning of the "holy number SEVEN" in the eyes of GOD. By now you have a fairly good idea of its significance with GOD's call to purity among His people. By repenting of your sins and asking GOD (Jesus Christ) into your heart, you will SAVE your eternal soul and be purified in the eyes of our Lord GOD. By accepting Him now into your heart...you won't even have to read any further...it won't concern you because during the Tribulation you won't be here on earth...you'll already be in heaven worshipping our GOD for His mercy and kindness.

Up to now we have learned the significance of some of the numbers that are pertinent to GOD's Plan for humanity. Most will not believe what they are reading because MOST do not know the GOD I know, nor do they seek the Light that shines from Him with wisdom.

GOD has told me that He has a present day Prophet here on earth at this time...This mortal man has great insight into prophesy and his name is HAL LINDSEY. GOD recommends that each one of you become familiar with all of Dr. Lindsey's books because all are the truth about the end times and each in detail.

GOD placed Hal Lindsey here on earth to write about the Bible's prophetic scenerio and how it will unfold...believe what you read in his books. GOD has told me that his interpetations are accurate!

Hal has been attacked by every secular humanist in the Country and has been scorned as a "man of doomsday predictions" by many of these "great" philosophers and "intellectuals!" Believe nothing of what you hear that is of negative vibration about Lindsey because it simply isn't true!

If you really know the Holy Spirit of GOD and pray to Him as you should...you will also know that these words I speak are all truthful!

The Seventh Year Of Rest & The Millennium!

By now you have possibly guessed what the seventh year of rest is. Reminding you that to GOD a human day is as a thousand years,we realize that we have used up 5,986 already. In 1991 (if you believe as I do that the believers in Christ will be Raptured before the begining of the Tribulation), or there abouts, Jesus will come for His church (believers). At that time, apostasy in the churches will be blatant and more and more believers will have fallen away, or, misled away from once known truths about Christ and His teachings.

About this time, just shortly prior to the Rapture, the antiChrist will be revealed to the world. I feel it will come after a period of extreme darkness that will have covered the earth. This may be a limited nuclear exchange, "great times of devastating FAMINE" over most of the earth and I believe that the famine will begin this year in areas of the world that have never known such hardship! By 1986, this famine will have reached epic proportion and many will die as a result. The United States will also feel the hunger pains for the first time in their history and as a result of this "grave famine," many shall eat forbidden fruits!

By 1988, the earthquakes will multiply in intensity from what we have seen in recent generations. There will be earthquakes in cities and countries that have never before experienced such calamity, and the entire world will be ripe for uniting into a "one world government," that will set the stage for the coming antiChrist.

This antiChrist will rise from complete obscurity with all the world's solutions and come in as a man of GODLY splendor. Because of his satanic powers, he will work great miracles throughout the world. I feel that we will hear about this man around the year 1989 or 1990, perhaps sooner.

The new monetary system currently being reviewed is a product of this vile aggressor...it is his creation and its aim is against the Messanic Jews (Jews who witness for Christ) and all Christians.

GOD is warning everyone right now through His many wise current day prophets of what is happening in our world. Christians and Messanic Jews will all know the every move of this new system, because they are in the LIGHT of the LAMB and are spiritually tuned in on His wavelength!

The seventh year of rest "IS" the Millennium, my brothers and sisters in Christ!

"...And six years (6,000 to our GOD) thou shalt labor, and shall gather in the fruits thereof;
But the SEVENTH (the Millennium - 1,000 years) year thou shalt let it rest!
EXODUS 23:10

"...He shall purify himself on the third day (touching a dead body), and on the seventh day., "he shall be clean: but if he purify not himself on the third day he SHALL NOT BE CLEAN."
NUMBERS 19:12

Face it brothers...it's either repent now of the sin, or, pay for it with your soul later! If you've ever wondered why the moral and spiritual values are not getting better here on planet earth? Read what Jesus says in John 14:30:

".....Hereafter I will not talk much with you: for the prince (notice the small "p" on prince...the "prince of darkness" - satan) of this world cometh, and hath nothing in Me."

Jesus verifys the explanation of the candlestick in John 15:5...

"I am the vine (center of the candlestick), ye (believers) are the branches: He that abideth in Me, and I in him, the same bringeth forth much fruit: for without me ye can do nothing."

".....Ye have not chosen Me, but I have chosen you, and ordained you, that ye should go and bring forth fruit (bring people to Christ), and that your fruit should remain: that whatsoever ye shall ask of the Father in My name, He may give to you."

".....If ye were OF the world, the world would love his own: but because ye ARE NOT of the world, but I have chosen you out of the world, therefore the world hateth you."
JOHN 15:19

In those last two verses of the Gospel of John, Jesus documents the fact that those who follow Him are not of this world...If you are not OF this world...you must be a son of GOD!!! He also says that ANYTHING you ask of the Father in the name of Jesus...it shall be granted. Now that's a promise from a GOD who doesn't know how to lie...who doesn't know how to deceive.

God's Crosscheck of The 666!

Turn in your Bible to the Book of Revelation, chapter 13, verse 18, for the total verification of the year of Christ's birth, the documentation of the year of the (preTribulation) Rapture, the year of Adam's creation and finally, the year of the Parousia (Second Coming) of Christ.

We know by now that our GOD loves us and protects those who love Him...He also gives His knowledge to those who ask for it and this particular Source of wisdom – has no boundaries or limitations!

"Here is WISDOM. Let him that hath understanding count the number of the beast: for it "IS" the number of a man (triple 6); and his number is Six hundred threescore and six."

Take the number 666 and place it in a position which will allow this number to read the same in three different directions. These are the THREE STAGES OF GOD'S PLAN, the three directions that man has taken to avoid compliance to the covenants of GOD.

Since man is so interested in the three sided pyramid and its supposed powers...since mankind in so interested in the Trilateral Commission in this age and also the devious "NEW AGE" conpiracy and their three-sided deceptions...Let's look at the three sides of the FALLING SHORT OF GOD...let's look at the 666 as an unholy and infamous trinity...........

```
6  6  6    Diagonal  6        6          Horizontal
6  6  6              6        6          6  6  6
6  6  6              6   6 Verticle
___________
1  9  9  8
```

When you total the sum of the three-sided 666, it comes out as a verification of the final year in human history...the year One thousand, nine hundred and ninety eight. This should be the year of Christ's Second Coming with the wrath of GOD...Take away two thousand years from 1998 and you have the year of the Virgin Birth of Christ in His First

Coming as the Messiah in 2 B.C. Subtract the 6,000 years that GOD gave mankind to seek the purification of the living soul and you will come out with the year GOD created Adam...the year 4,002 B.C. To find the year of the great Tribulation (if you believe that the Rapture will be prior to the Tribulation) you remove the prophesied seven years from 1998 and it tells you that 1991 will be the preTribulation Rapture.

You wonderful believers in Christ will not be deceived because you seek the LIGHT that is GOD. There is no way possible that you can be misled following our Christ Jesus and through the guidance of the Holy Spirit...you will know who the antiChrist is right away when he is revealed...You'll know because you will be looking for him due to the mercy in GOD's prophesy.

We who know Him cannot deny Him...we would rather die than to say we don't know Him.......We have the Holy Spirit dwelling within us because we can feel Him moving over us like a blanket of extreme assurance and warmth...Once you have this feeling...you could not possibly seek anything more, and certainly nothing less.

If you are reading this book and feel happy at what you are reading....YOU KNOW JESUS CHRIST. If you are uneasy about the facts you have heard....YOU NEED TO KNOW HIM....If you are in despair because of what you now read, you are realistic but belong to this earth...And if you do not know Jesus Christ as your personal Savior and are not now asking Him to come into your heart and soul...YOU ARE VERY FOOLISH INDEED!

I urge, NO...I plead and pray that everyone that reads this book and doesn't know the Lord Jesus Christ will pray this sinner's prayer and come to know Him RIGHT NOW! Don't put it aside with the idea that you'll do it tomorrow...you may not have a tomorrow! If you walk out of your house and drop dead without accepting Jesus into your heart...you will be eternally doomed to the Lake of Fire! Please accept Jesus RIGHT NOW...Pray with me RIGHT NOW and be eternally FREE!

> "Dear GOD, You have said that anything we ask for in the name of Jesus will be granted and we ask right now that you release satan's bonds on everyone that is reading this prayer to you. I ask that you bind the powers of satan and banish his hold on these people forever. I ask in the name of Jesus, the risen Christ, that the readers of this book will be free and find the real truth that is only from your mercy. If their children have been under the vile clutches of lucifer, break the evil bonds

and bring them all into Your protective mercy.

Lord, we agree that we are sinners and deserve nothing, but right now we repent of our sins and ask you sincerely for forgiveness. I ask that you cure the many readers who are afflicted with the darkness of satan. If they are bound by the evils of homosexuality, alcoholism, perversions of the flesh, addicted to illusionary drugs, set them free and allow them into your merciful and loving fold. If they are involved with satanic worship...show them the light and convert them to your rightful ways. Father, speak to their hearts and give them the courage and the strength to break away from demonic influence of this world.

If they are in a church that doesn't preach the WORD of GOD, warn them and get them into one that is preaching the GOSPEL.

Oh Father, we thank You for Your kindness and we thank You for setting these readers free. And we ask these things and know that we will receive them because we are asking for them in the name of Jesus...Amen and Amen.

If you just prayed that prayer, Jesus Christ is now in your heart. Call one of the prayer lines and share your new witness with someone. If you can't get through...CALL ME and I will pray with you...If the tears are rolling down your cheeks at this moment — it's because you now know Jesus...CALL and go out and proclaim Him to the rooftops...because once you really have accepted Jesus...He will never forsake you...and, He shall never leave you...GOD BLESS YOU!

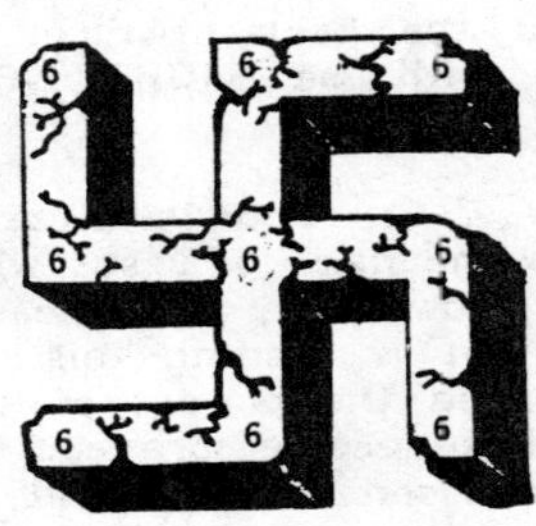

MATTHEW 13:41,42
THE SON OF man shall send
forth HIS angels, and they'll
Gather out of HIS KiNGdom
All things that offend, and
them which do iniquity;
And shall cast them into
a furnace of fire: there
Shall be wailing and
Gnashing of teeth...
"I NEVER KNEW YOU!"
REV. 3;8
I Know thy works: behold, I
have set Before thee an open
door, and no man can shut
it: for thou hast a little
Strength, and hast KEPT
MY WORD...
"ENTER IN...MY BELOVED!"

CHAPTER TWENTY-TWO

Sheol: Satan's Altar Call To Sinners!

"Therefore hell hath enlarged herself, and opened her mouth
without measure; and their glory, and their multitude, and their
pomp (vainglory), and he that rejoiceth, shall decend into it."
Isaiah 5:14

"Hell and destruction are never full;
so the eyes of man are never satisfied."
Proverbs 27:20

"The wicked shall be turned into hell, and all
the nations that forget GOD!"
Psalms 9:17

"Withhold not correction from the child: for if thou
beatest him with a rod, he shall not die.
Thou shalt beat him with the rod, and
shalt deliver his soul from hell."
Proverbs 23: 13,14

"Her house is the way to hell, going
down to the chambers of death."
Proverbs 7:27

Those fools who say that heaven and hell are here on earth have little knowledge of scripture. Those who do not believe in GOD are strong advocates that man has control of his destiny on earth. To them, life just ceases to exist when they die. If I had their unGodly attitude I wouldn't want to believe that there was a hell (sheol) either...because without repentance, that's their eternal destination.

I got news for you today. Sheol literally and physically does exist! There actually is life and living death after our lives expire. I would never make such a statement without verification from the mouth of GOD. GOD is merciful and understanding. He loves us more than we will ever know. Anyone that would give up His only Son for us unworthy people...has to love us!

This book is the result of GOD's divine mercy. He has spoken personally to my heart and has said that multitudes will come to know Him through it. GOD has told me personally that the souls that are presently lost will be revived by the power of the Holy Spirit by their faith in what they are reading and most of all, they will be saved by WHO they will come to believe in...the Lord Jesus Christ!

It doesn't matter if you are an orthodox Jew, a staunch Roman Catholic, a Baptist, an Evangelical, a Pentacostal, a Methodist or a Presbyterian or Moslem. He has spoken to me through the Power of His Holy Spirit and commanded me to write this book and be open to His Word only in its preparation. He commanded me to pray to Him with my prayer language and do it from within my very soul.

He has shown me wisdom and knowledge that I never dreamed existed. I cannot pray to Him without floods of tears pouring down my cheeks with the utmost compassion for the many souls that are heading for the chambers of torment. They MUST be pulled out of their darkness...eternity is a very long and agonizing period of time to be spending apart from the love of GOD!

GOD has told me that He desires me to go to the ends of the earth and bring Him back His lost sheep who have gone astray from His Word! I have promised Him that I will do as He commands of me. You know many of us in the Body of Christ (the Church) have forgotten that the atheists, the punk rockers, the liberals, the socialists and communists were also created by GOD. We must not forget that they, too, can be saved...if we try and reach out.

In past years, many of these people have professed to hate Jesus Christ and everyone who witnesses for Him. Now, GOD has poured out His Holy Spirit on ALL flesh and even some of these non-believers will come to believe in these final days. Many of the Evangelists and Pastors who have contributed to this book will testify to this fact.

With so many great men like Oral Roberts, Billy James Hargis, Hal Lindsey, Paul Crouch, Dwight Thompson, Gary Greenwald, Demos Shakarian, Jimmy Swaggart, Pat Robinson and the many thousands of gifted speakers who are praising His Holy Name, I asked Him ...why me? He spoke to my soul and said, "Because I know that you will do as I ask of you!"

When I look at the many people who are without His knowledge...my soul weeps to reach out to them and let them know GOD loves them and wants them to turn away from their sins.

What if you died tonight and never had accepted the only Hope you have for eternal life? If you are walking in evil, as Pastor Greenwald said in chapter nine, the devil can take you to his chambers anytime he wishes to...you MUST believe that! I pray in the name of Jesus that you will put away your sins

326

and come to Jesus Christ before it's too late.

As you have learned from the last two chapters, GOD works many times in multiples of seven (the length of time it takes for purification). Understand that this year is 1984 and if I have heard His word correctly, we have but 14 years remaining until He comes in His wrath. The final seven years are the period of Tribulation and unless you accept Him today and believe on Him with all your heart , it may be impossible for you to partake in His Rapture in the year 1991., which is seven (7) years from right now.

Change your ways now and live for Him only! Purify yourself now in these last seven years before the Rapture and join us when we meet Him in the air. The final seven years of humanity will be humanly unbearable. GOD has told me many of the things that are going to take place during this finishing chapter of mankind and believe me it's not a place that you'd want to be.

There were many times in the writing of this book that I didn't feel it was worthy of glorifying Him...He reassured me that it was and if it were to only save ONE SOUL FROM SPENDING AN ETERNITY IN SHEOL...ISN'T THAT WORTH IT? When I heard those words in my spirit...I could not control the tears that gushed from my eyes. Unless you know Him in your soul, you won't understand what I am saying to you. He told me the year that He was coming in the Rapture and it's not a coincidence that He has also given this message a week of years prior to this time.

Pastors, Evangelists and Priests must step up their efforts at saving souls. Saving souls is much more important than knocking each other's rituals. GET BACK TO THE WORD or all those in the congregation may miss out on salvation. Your deeds won't make it to heaven...believing on Him will get you there!

Some Prophesy After The Rapture!

> The righteous perisheth, and no man layeth it to heart: and merciful men are taken away (caught-up), none considering that the righteous is taken away FROM the evil to come.
> Isaiah 57:1

When Jesus Christ comes for His faithful in the air, this prophesy tells us that many won't even blink an eye. They won't even consider WHY we have left this earth...but it will happen whether you'll believe it or not! When GOD told me of some of the things that are going to happen after the

Rapture...I was totally frozen with the chills that went down my back, but kept praying for this knowledge. He told me to tell the people that the time for His harvest is near. Even though GOD has given the year of the Rapture...if you hesitate accepting Him into your heart...there's no guaranteeing that you won't drop dead tomorrow thinking that you still have seven years to make up your mind. DO IT TODAY...DON'T HESITATE...TO HESITATE COULD MEAN THAT YOU WILL BE LOST...FOREVER!

GOD has told me that this punk rock movement is much more than just evil music...it is one of the foundations that this antiChrist will be accepted by multitudes of people.

He told me that there will be such a famine in the world that those who now have plenty will be searching for food in the gutters of the cities.

He told me that the anti-Christ will become known around the year 1989 or 1990, that he will be a religious man on the outside and evil within. He will be praised by many right away and much of it will be through subliminal suggestion to the subconscious mind.

He will introduce a new religion which will appeal to over 80% of the world's population, including those who have been outright protesters of any worship of the Deity. It will be such a perfect religion that he will sweep away many of confused Christians. Preachers listen with an open heart to what I am saying.

He showed me that this famine will be so devastating that cannibalism will be accepted by most of the world and that new born babies will be on the stoves in boiling pots.

After the Rapture occurs, the antiChrist will change morality laws and allow anything man's heart would desire. Murder will be accepted...No woman will be safe from being raped and offered up in strange, sacrificial rites to many different gods. They will be hunted down by vicious criminals and literally eaten alive and their blood will become a delicacy.

Human body parts will be sold in stores. It will be an existence which knows no barriers. In 1986 this world-wide famine will begin spreading into the rich areas of the earth.

Begining this year, the entire world's climate will begin changing drastically and there will be evil signs everywhere as men are reduced to desperation...those who don't know GOD!

By the early months of 1987, arcade video games will begin trasmitting subliminal thoughts to the children on a more escalated scale. It will all be evil.

Natural disasters will begin to multiply, earthquakes in places that have never had them, tornados also in areas of the world who have never before thought they existed.

This new monetary system that is coming into focus will

328

lead eventually to the micro-computer chip being inserted by a laser beam into the right hand or in the forehead. I believe that this transformation will be required by the year 1991, or shortly thereafter.

Those who are here on the earth who refused to accept this "mark of the beast" will be ridiculed, persecuted and many of them will be murdered or sacrificed as living offerings to idol gods.

Persecutions against believing Christians and Jews will begin to escalate around the world in 1985. By 1986, the United States will be the only place left on earth who still may outwardly preach the gospel in public. Laws are currently being drawn up for the world-wide elimination of public worship to GOD!

Homosexuality and other degrading influences will multiply tenfold by the year 1988 in relation to what it is today. By 1990, Churches of Satan will be as plentiful as those of GOD.

Animal sacrifice will be restored by the early 1990s in many parts of the world and will eventually lead to human sacrifice by 1992.

Mass healings will begin taking place in the open and in GODly places of worship and will be mimicked with the punk rock movements with their music.

By 1990, there will be ordinances in the United States whereby children of believers must attend special schools of the state...private schools will be eliminated totally.

Grave robbery will become an alternative for food by mid-1995 and anyone professing their belief in Jesus Christ will literally and physically be nailed to public places as a warning to others in that same year.

Syria will invade Israel in the year 1990 and will kill many men, women and children before the anti-Christ (who will come to power through Rome but not of Italian decent) will step in with an amazing truce that will bring peace to all the world. By 1992 there will be no more war (at least temporarily) in the world.

Plagues will come with no cures and by 1990 there won't be one GOD-fearing man in a governmental office in the United States.

There will be an abrupt change in the Vatican and I believe that the present Pope will step down and be replaced.

The Rapture in 1991 will be explained by the anti-Christ as his doings. He will explain away the disappearance of millions of men, women and children by telling the people they were evil, would not conform to receiving the new system and he simply did away with them.

Mass assassinations of strategic and essential government officials will begin by 1989 and peak in 1990...many of the

Everything she was telling me about Jesus and that rapture must be the truth. One minute she was here— the next minute gone!!
SAD AFTERTHOUGHT
DECISION
"BEHOLD, I SHEW YOU A MYSTERY; WE SHALL NOT ALL SLEEP, BUT WE SHALL ALL BE CHANGED, IN A MOMENT, 'IN THE TWINKLING OF AN EYE ...'"
(I CORINTHIANS 15:51,52)
King of the Jews
ACCEPT HIM NOW!
ETERNAL LOVE
It won't hurt honey. The nice government man said we have to put it on.
I know what the scriptures say... I've got to get out of here!
"ENDURE!"
666
PRINTING HERE
YOUR CHOICE
HAND or FOREHEAD
$20.00
Deducted from Your Account

assassins will be trusted secret service agents.

There will be a marked increase in churches falling away from the truth about Jesus Christ in the year 1988...some will do a complete turnaround from one month to the next. Many people will begin worshipping GOD privately in the home by 1990 and 1991.

More and more people will be studying the occult practices of Hinduism and other mind control studies. By 1989, few commercials won't have some message of the antiChrist and how good he is for the world.

After 1990, no Christian programs will be allowed on national TV and by 1991, or there abouts, there will be no more religious training left anywhere in the world. Simply speaking, we won't be here to operate the equipment!

After the Rapture in 1991, there will be many bold new believers in Jesus Christ springing up everywhere...they will then understand that the word of GOD is the real truth...unfortunately all new believers shall be martyred between 1992 and the restoration of the third Holy Temple in 1994 or 1995.

From 1988 through early 1991, vicious gangs of criminals will descend on any one witnessing for Jesus Christ, even in the United States.

New believers after 1991 will be unmercifully used as guinea pigs for new food developements. No children will be born after 1995 that will not be considered food, except by the few believers who will still be on the face of the earth. They, too, will be slaughtered by bands of government agents in the name of the people.

By the end of 1995, there shall be no Christians left on the face of the earth.

By 1995, the antiChrist will be deemed to be GOD and all the world will worship him in the newly built temple. Anyone breaking his new laws shall physically be sacrificed to him.

After 1995, there will not be one sane human in the world. All will be killing each other to eat. It shall not rain on earth for the final seven years of human history.

All men on earth will begin drinking the blood of their latest victims and this shall be a "toast" to the powers of the anti-Christ.

This is what I have received from earnest prayer. To my human imagination, it doesn't seem possible that such a grotesque transition could ever take place in only seven to fourteen years. I cannot even perceive such cruelty against mankind but I won't question the Authority in which it was given to me. Life in the 1990s is not something that I want to participate in. No sane person would wish that on their worst enemy. Please accept the Lord right now and don't reprove me for this inspiration. We must reach out to those poor lost souls who don't even understand that they are on the dark side of Biblical prophesy. We must make them believe it...but more importantly, we must show them the Light that is Jesus Christ. Through His graces only shall they find eternal life. GLORY TO GOD in the Highest! Now let's look past this present life to the final resting place of, or shall I say the final tormenting place of all who fail to believe in the Lamb of GOD! That place does exist...it's called by some sheol...and it's called by others...hell...either way you choose to refer to it...IT'S A REALITY!

A PLACE CALLED DEATH!

Again I would like to publically extend my appreciation to Brother Gary Greenwald of Eagle's Nest Ministries in Santa Ana, California, for his additional contribution to the making of this final portion of the book. Pastor Gary...THANK YOU for your kindness and interest in the work of GOD!

There's a punk rock band called AC-DC which kind of sums up the final chapter of unrighteousness in their song called "Highway to Hell!" The lyrics go like this:

> Don't need no reason...
> Don't need no rhyme...
> Ain't nothing I'd rather do...
> Going down..it's party time...
> My friends are gonna be there,too!

According to Pastor Gary, "Yes, their friends are going to be there, too, if they are living for satan." He continues..."But I want to tell you that hell is not a big party place like your "friends" would have you believe.

They'd have you believe that there's going to be all the fun and games you could ever imagine. It simply isn't GOD's accounting!"

Personal Accountings Of Hell!

Dr. Maurice Rollins, a top cardiologist (heart specialist) who is the Clinical Associate Professor of Medicine at the University of Tennessee, has talked with many heart patients who have clinically died and been resuscitated (brought back to life.)

He says in his book, "Beyond Death's Door!" that about 50% of the revived persons have mentioned going to a place of great darkness, filled with grotesque moaning and writhing bodies, crying out to be rescued from this place with an overwhelming feeling of eerie and nightmarish terror. He said that at least 50% of the persons who were clinically dead and revived would talk about it...others would not.

One person who had a life after death experience said that he was summoned out of the hospital emergency room by a giant and several inflight figures. The patient said that he decended through a tunnel-like passage which eventually emptied into a cavern piled high with glowing hot rocks.

He told Dr. Rawlings he experienced unbearable heat and felt oosing, slimy, writhing creatures slithering all over his feet.

Another time, Dr. Rawlings tells of a man who came into the hospital for a checkup and told a nurse...

"I think you had better help me. I have chest pains and I think I'm about to die!"

At first the nurse thought he was joking, but as she giggled...he died. Dr. Rawlings was just outside the door when he was called by the frantic nurse. He came in and worked feverishly to revive the man. Suddenly the man screamed...

"Don't stop!" Patients usually yell at the doctor to stop hurting them and beg him to stop, but this man wanted desperately to come back to life.

"Why don't you want me to stop?" asked Dr. Rawlings.

"I'm in hell!" screamed the man.

"You mean you're scared of going to hell?"

"NO! NO! I'm in hell! I'm in Hell! Don't let me go!

As Doctor Rawlings looked at his patient closely for the first time, he realized he had not seen such terror on a man's face in 25 years.

"How do I stop going to hell?" screamed the hysterical man.

"I'm not a preacher." grunted Dr. Rawlings, continuing his frantic efforts to save the man.

"Please tell me how to stop going to hell!" begged the man almost pathetically.

"I guess you pray a Sunday school prayer." replied the Doctor."like this...Lord Jesus, forgive my sins and come and live in me. If you spare my life...I'll be hooked on you. If you take my life...take me to heaven!"

With that the man died again. Six times the doctor brought him back before succeeding to keep him alive. But that man tipped over into the next life and saw what hell was like.

Two Minutes Of Hell Upon Request!

I think one of the most graphic descriptions of hell was by Doctor Ebey (the 1978 O.P.S.C. Physician of the year), who was allowed by GOD to glimpse "hell's waiting room" for two hideous minutes.

GOD spoke to him and told him he would be allowed to see hell so he could go tell the people they had to escape. GOD said, "You must be able to tell them that they can choose heaven or hell, but tell them that I died to close hell and open heaven just for them! They must choose between my love and eternal life or satan's lies and eternal death. Tell them that there is yet a little time...but very little." The voice was as one calling their sheep...then He was gone and Doctor Ebbey's two minutes in hell began.

Doctor Ebey's Accounting Of Sheol!

"Suddenly I was in hell. I knew I was trapped in the bowels of the earth - instantly I was in a stone coffin, four feet by six and one-half feet high," said Dr. Ebey, "The terror was instantaneous and indescribable. With a sickening thud I felt my feet hit the rock floor. My lightning fast mind added to the horror of this total isolation in stone by telling me all the answers to my sudden questions.

Cast as an unsaved sinner, I was on death row in solitary confinement by my own choice. Satan had invited me and I had accepted. I allowed myself to die without accepting the love of Jesus Christ about which I had heard of many times. This is the pit of the first death...the holding tank of horror...satan's stronghold for sinners.

I tried to scream but there was no voice. I pounded the walls and the ceiling - no escape! Total blackness - total silence - total stench. I was terrified.

The stench had to be from demons - sure enough...I looked down and saw clearly with the minds eye of my fallen spirit body - many little spider-like demons about my feet.

Among them were several deformed, cat and dog-like creatures with black feces-matted fur. Despite their constant movement, each one fastened its gaze upon me as the smaller ones swarmed up the walls beside my face. Behind each eye were flames. The stench was nauseating. My mind told me they were chained demons of satan and they all agreed, saying "We are the chained demons...we're here to haunt and taunt you in hell...And buddy buddy,..we'll do it!" Their actual language was so foul it cannot be repeated.

The next day I asked Jesus to erase all their demonic language...and He did!" explained the Doctor. The minutes wore on...

"You could have accepted GOD as your Father and Jesus as your Savior," said the demons, "We read the book...you're trapped with us now...and buddy,..we'll make this your hell!

SATAN'S CHAMBERS OF TORMENT
SHEOL

Ah hah! You fool! Then I noticed the cold - the kind that sickens and chills every cell, just enough to ache...but not enough to get numb. There was no way to get warm...not in this dark, dank pit!" explained Dr. Ebbey, "and the smell. Horrid, nasty, stale, rotten, evil...all mixed together. It was concentrated. Somehow I knew instantly that these were the odors of my pit mates...stinking, crawling demons that seemed mentally delighted in making one wretched.

The immensity of this depravity in which they were living was appalling. I would now have an eternity of inescapable nausea besides all the rest of this hell. My terror mounted until I was ready to collapse with utter hopelessness. I was an eternally lost soul..all by my own choosing. I screamed and tried to cry out, but not a sound came forth.

The clammy, wet cells and the tight walls held me crushed for eternity without escape, without a Savior, without anything to maintain my sanity. AND THEN IT WAS OVER! That was just two minutes in hell's waiting room, and then it was OVER! What if that was your eternity? There's going to be many who will live there as a permanent, inescapable torment. Don't let it be you!"

> And the sea gave up the dead which were
> in it; and death and hell delivered up the dead
> which were in them: and they were judged
> every man according to their works.
> And death and hell were cast into the lake
> of fire. This is the second death.
> And whosoever was not found in the book
> of life was cast into the lake of fire...
> REVELATIONS 20:13,14,15

Will You Be Stuck In Hell For An Eternity?

From the "Hell Report," a Miss "D" was conducted to a place of which she described in the most terrifying language and declared that the horrid shrieks of lost spirits still seemed to sound in her ears. As she approached the burning pit, a tremendous effort was made to draw her into it, but she felt herself safe under the protection of her guardian angel.

She recognized many in the place of torment whom she had known on earth. Some having been considered Christians. There were princes and peasants, rich and poor, learned and unlearned, all writhing together in a dreadful, unquenchable fire, where all earthly distinctions and titles were forever at an end.

Among them, she beheld a Miss "W," who had occupied a prominent station in society, but had died during the transe of misdeed. She said that "Miss W" saw her approach. Her shrieks were appalling...they were beyond the power of language to describe and she made a desperate, but unsuccessful attempt to escape. "Punishment for lost souls." She said.

Miss "W" represented a symbolizing of the respective sins which occasioned their condemnation.

Be not deceived; GOD is not mocked: for whatsoever a man soweth, that shall he also reap.

For he that soweth to his flesh shall of the flesh reap corruption; but he that soweth to the Spirit reap life everlasting.
GALATIANS 6:7,8

But after thy hardness and impenitent heart treasurest up unto thyself wrath against the day of wrath and revelation of the righteous judgment of GOD;

Who will render to every man according to his deeds.
ROMANS 2:6

In other words, however wicked your unrepented sins were, or whatever they were, that was the portion of torment you would be in.

Miss "W" was condemned for her love of money.

But they that will be rich fall into temptation and a snare, and into many foolish and hurtful lusts, which drown men in destruction and perdition.

For the love of money is the root of all evil: which while some coveted after, they have erred from the faith, and pierced themselves through with many sorrows.
I TIMOTHY 6:9,10

Being condemned for the love of money, I had every reason to believe, was befitting her sin and she seemed to be robed in a garment of gold...all on fire.

Mr. "O", whom she saw, was lost through intemperance. He appeared to be punished by devils administering to him some boiling liquid. He had loved drink; and now they were making him drink a boiling liquid. She said that there was no sympathy among those unhappy spirits. Their was unmixed hatred in all its frightening forms prevailing in every part of the fiery regions.

DOES THAT SOUND LIKE A PLACE OF LOVE? DOES IT SOUND LIKE THE SPLENDOR OF HEAVEN? Does that sound like GOD's glorious kingdom where Jesus said, "Behold I go to prepare a place for you, that where I am, you may be also? In my Father's House, there are many mansions."

There's going to be GLORY...HOLINESS is going to be in heaven. There's going to be singing and praise...glorious ecstasy and enjoyment. THERE'S GOING TO BE A PARADISE. Would you give all that up to follow rock music? Would you give all that up for anything this world has to offer? Anyone i their right mind of logical thought...surely would not give up eternal bliss with our Lord Jesus Christ. Tell the devil to go jump in the lake of fire...you want no part of anything he has to offer now, or in the future.

Kids...get rid of those evil images of the beast you play with. Get rid of those punk rock and any rock music albums you may have. Start living for Jesus and obey His every wish! There's a future worth fighting for with Him! GOD Bless you! Let's pray!

FATHER,
I PRAY IN THE NAME OF JESUS THAT THESE CHILDREN OF YOURS WOULD GET THEIR ALBUMS, THESE ROCK MUSIC IMAGES OF THE BEAST, THIS PORNOGRAPHY AND ALL THESE OCCULTIC THINGS OUT OF THEIR HOMES. WE PRAY THAT THEY WILL HAVE NOTHING TO DO WITH THESE ABOMINATIONS, LORD, FOR WE WANT TO GO TO HEAVEN. WE WANT TO BELIEVE THAT JESUS DIED FOR ALL OF OUR SINS AND WE WANT TO HAVE ETERNAL LIFE THROUGH THAT BELIEF. WE BIND EVERY WORK OF SATAN RIGHT NOW, EVERY CONFUSING, LYING SPIRIT THAT WOULD TRY TO TELL YOU THAT YOU WANT TO PARTY AND HAVE FUN, BECAUSE JESUS WANTS TO GIVE YOU LIFE AND THAT'S MORE ABUNDANT. HE WANTS TO GIVE YOU THE MOST ENJOYMENT IN LIFE THAT YOU CAN HAVE. AND IF YOU WOULD LIKE TO RECEIVE JESUS AS YOUR LORD AND SAVIOR, IF YOU BELIEVE TODAY THAT GOD SENT JESUS INTO THIS WORLD TO DIE ON THAT CROSS AND SHED HIS SPOTLESS, PERFECT BLOOD THAT ALL YOUR SINS MIGHT BE FORGIVEN, IF YOU SINCERELY BELIEVE THAT HIS BLOOD IS A COVERING FOR ALL YOUR SINS, IF YOU BELIEVE THAT GOD SENT JESUS INTO THIS WORLD SO THAT YOU WOULDN'T HAVE TO BE DESTROYED AND IF YOU ACCEPT JESUS' SACRIFICE TODAY...YOU CAN HAVE ETERNAL LIFE THROUGH HIS BLOOD. YOU ARE NOW A CHILD OF GOD! AMEN AND AMEN!

And Jesus said unto him, "VERILY I SAY UNTO THEE, TO-DAY SHALT THOU BE WITH ME IN PARADISE."

LUKE 23:43

EPILOGUE

As this gift from the Holy Spirit of GOD comes to its fulfillment, I can't help but wonder how many of His children have received His message? GOD has told me in prayer that those who truly know Him...will know that this book has come directly from Him.

In this book, GOD has given you HIS message...not the author's. He has informed the wayward sheep of this world that the human kind has never possessed the answers to make it on this Earth without His blessings. He told this writer in solemn promise and from deep, spiritual prayer that His people will be multiplied dramatically as a result of this inspiration...and I know that my GOD never lies. I say this to the reader of this book in all honesty...Don't even hint that this author wrote this testimony as an individual profit maker...you would be in grave error of judgment. The Holy Spirit of our GOD wrote every page, every paragraph and every word and it's all to His glory. If there is no profit realized by Hall Publishing Company – but it saves the precious soul of only ONE person...this toil has well been worth it!

In this book, GOD has made you awaken to many factors that most have been taking for granted for far too long now. He's told you WHO you have to fear in this world, HE'S told you WHY you need more than man; HE'S informed you WHEN we lost our sanctity; HE'S told you WHERE to be looking for His graces and HE'S told you HOW you may attain the eternal longevity of your soul. All that's left now is FOR YOU TO BELIEVE...and LIVE FOR HIM ONLY!

In relation to eternity, your life span is but a granule of sand on the bottom of the sea. How you live this microscopic period of time will determine your potential for immortality.

The Holy Spirit of GOD has shown you the necessity of turning your back on the evils of satanic practice. Through His graces in this book, He has supplied the names of many evangelists, pastors and preachers in this Country who also care that you make the right decision to live your remaining days for the Lord Jesus Christ. He is the only way to the Father's House...the ONLY WAY to the immortality of the living soul. I cry out from earnest prayer to the many people of this earth that have no direction or supportive structure in which to make this crucial decision. Believe on Jesus Christ and have the confidence and knowledge that YOU ARE SAVED by His protective Blood!

GOD is leading you to His Living Waters of the Kingdom but He also gave you the freedom of making your own choice. You can choose to continue paying your dues to satan and dwell in the fires of hell for ever...OR, you can give your life to GOD and have more confidence in your little finger than most will ever have in their entire bodies...that confidence comes with GOD's territory...the real promised land in eternity!

Years ago, I was a hopeless sinner, too. I heard His calling to turn away from my sins many times...but each time I told Him that I wasn't ready. What I was really saying was that I wanted to live a life of sinful pleasures in the flesh over accepting His free gift of real living! I always had intentions of being on His side eventually...I'm just glad that GOD had patience with me to wait and give me the time...something He didn't have to do. If I would have died without accepting Jesus Christ into my heart...I would have been forever a lost soul. When I think back on my delay...I see how very foolish I really was. If you should die tomorrow without first getting on your knees and ASKING JESUS INTO YOUR HEART...you shall never have another chance for redemption...you'll never have another opportunity to tell Jesus that you're sorry for your sins. You'll be within the chambers of horror forever...that's a very long time to burn in torment.

I know of your everyday temptations in life...I know the hesitation you have for really believing on Jesus. You hear that Jesus was only a good prophet and that there was no chance of Him either being GOD incarnate with the name of Jesus or the product of virgin birth. You hear it because those you have been listening to are walking in total blindness...they have lead you to the precipice of eternal damnation. I don't care if the man that tells you that Jesus is not GOD is your rabbi, your pastor, your priest, your preacher or your evangelist....HE IS WRONG! Don't take my word for it but understand first what is meant by the short scripture in I JOHN 2:22 and JOHN 14:7   Your answer is found there in simple words:

"WHO IS A LIAR BUT HE THAT DENIETH THAT JESUS IS THE CHRIST!"

"IF YOU HAD KNOWN ME, YE SHOULD HAVE KNOWN MY FATHER ALSO: AND FROM HENCEFORTH YE HAVE KNOWN HIM, AND HAVE SEEN HIM."

So, if someone has misinformed you into believing that

WHO IS A LIAR BUT HE THAT DENIETH THAT JESUS IS THE CHRIST....(I John 2:22)

LET NO MAN DECEIVE YOU BY ANY MEANS: FOR THAT DAY SHALL NOT COME, EXCEPT THERE COME A "FALLING AWAY FIRST..."
(I THESSALONIANS 2:3)

Jesus is not the Messiah...rebuke that man...turn your back on him and get out as fast as you can. Take your soul across the street where they preach the word of GOD! Tell the congregation too...they are also GOD's lost children and deserve better for their eternity.

If your church leader is one of the many humanist preachers (70% of seminary students in the past 23 years) that say there was no virgin birth of Christ Jesus; there was no GOD incarnate by the name of Jesus; there was no ascension; there were no miracles; there will be no rapture...no first or Second Coming of Jesus Christ....TELL THEM RICK HALL IS CALLING THEM A "LIAR!" TELL THEM...YOU KNOW BETTER!

Recommended Spiritual Reading!

"The HOLY BIBLE!" by the LORD GOD ALMIGHTY
"God Still Heals Today!" By Oral Roberts
"The Cross & the Sickle!" by Billy James Hargis
"Hidden Dangers of the Rainbow!" by Constance Cumbey
"The Late Great Planet Earth!" by Hal Lindsey
"The Rapture!" by Hal Lindsey
"Satan is Alive & Well On Planet Earth!" by Hal Lindsey
"There's a New Name Written Down in Glory!" and. . .
"The Satan Connection!" by Jimmy Swaggart
"The Punk Called Rock!" by Gary Greenwald
"Marijuana: The Heavenly Deception!" Gary Greenwald
"The Secret Kingdom!" by Pat Robinson
"Adventure in Adversity!" by Paul Billheimer
"Worse Than Hell/Better Than Heaven!" by Jerry Barnard
"Beyond Death's Door!" by Dr. Maurice Rollins

Recommended Christian Viewing!

PRAISE THE LORD (TBN - Channel 40...6 in Las Vegas)
(also all programs on their 24 hour network)
THE "700" CLUB (CBN - Channel 28)
ORAL ROBERTS CRUSADE (Sunday, ABC 12 noon PST)
JIMMY SWAGGART CRUSADE (Sunday, ABC 8:30 am PST)

I sincerely pray that the readers of this book have found it much more than entertaining...I have faith that you have discovered your salvation through GOD's message that is contained with it! Place your faith in the ONE that is everlasting to everlasting and learn GOD's eternal "Plan" for humanity...Above all recommended spiritual reading...THE BIBLE has no equal...READ IT AND LIVE! MAY GOD RICHLY BLESS YOU ALL!

Additional Food For Thought!

Dear Reader

If you have ever had the inner impression that the world around us was not designed for you - you are wise. This earth is the dominion of the "prince of darkness" and it doesn't take a genius to recognize the fact that the road to hell is wide and many shall follow its pathway to destruction.

If you are one of the many people who have been existing...devoid of any personal committment to the Lord Jesus Christ - you are not a sincerely happy person.

GOD has told us that in the end times of the world His people would know that Jesus is GOD...and GOD is Jesus. That is happening now. Messanic Jewish organizations are popping up everywhere and more and more individuals are begining to accept Christ Jesus as their Messiah. Why would this happen? Jesus was crucified more than 1,954 years ago...why after such a long time are the Jewish people understanding the truth? The answer is that GOD has poured out His Holy Spirit on ALL flesh and many Jews are now in the light because they will not believe the lies of their ancient forefathers who bribed Roman guards and tried to keep the truth from the masses.

The Books of the Holy Bible were all written by Jews. There is not one Book of the Bible that can be proven to have been written by a Gentile. If you are a Jew and do not want to understand what I am saying...call your own people and allow them an opportunity to mail you some material which will save you and your house from the fires of hell. We are in the generation that will witness the Second Coming of the Lord Jesus to earth...Be one of the 144,000 who will be saved...better still - be one of the many Christian Jews who will not endure the Tribulation period.

I know that there will be many angry letters from rabbis and staunch, single-minded Jews on this subject. I don't appologize for getting your attention. Contact Avi Snyder of the JEWS FOR JESUS Organization in Studio City, California 91604 (213) 766-9379, or JEWS FOR JESUS, 60 Haight Street, San Francisco, California 94102 (415) 864-2600...ask for Moishe Rosen.

Jews Testify For Christ!

Let's hear from some Jewish brothers and sisters who have come into the Light on Jesus Christ. Even in Israel, over 15,000 Jews have presently come to know the truth.

According to Vickie Kress of JEWS FOR JESUS in San Francisco, California, "If being born hasn't given you much satisfaction...TRY BEING BORN AGAIN."

"You are all eligible for this experience. GOD wants all of us to have this opportunity," says Mrs. Kress, in one of her mailers, "All you have to do is trust...that's all! And you will become a new creature with a fuller and happier life!

Trust Who?

"Trust in Jesus Christ," says Vickie, "Ask Him to come into your life and be the ONLY SPIRITUAL RULER in it. Your ruler must not be your friend, nor your guru, nor your mother, nor the Pope, or your rabbi or any other mere human being!

Why Should I Trust Jesus?

"Jesus alone is GOD, who became man, as it was foretold in the Old Testament," she goes on, "In the Books of Micah 5:2, Isaiah 9:6, Isaiah 53:, Zechariah 12:10, etc.,etc., it tells us that Jesus is the Messiah of the Jews and the Savior of all people who ask Him into their lives!"

"I know as Jews you have heard it before," says Mrs. Kress, "This may sound familiar since it's been available for centuries... How long are you going to wait to trust someone who will revolutionize your life and give you love from above? Not only that but Jesus guarantees a special bonus offer of eternal life. We are JEWS FOR JESUS! Doubters are welcome."

From another Jewish brother, Moishe Rosen, also from San Francisco, California...he says, "Why not JEWS FOR JESUS? We're happy to tell it - after all, Jesus is alive and well and is coming back soon to bring peace to earth!!"

"I know many of you orthodox Jews are probably saying - Oh, Brother...but I say that this is no put-on...we're serious," says Rosen, "Jesus is the Messiah of Israel.

Hey Wait A Minute! Jews Don't Believe In Christ!

"Who says we don't?" Explains Moishe, "Some Jews DO BELIEVE JESUS IS THE MESSIAH! WE DO!!! Knowing Jesus helps the Jew to understand our heritage better...after all, He is a Jew,too! I know most Jews don't believe in Christ as the Messiah and you are right when you say it...but, when has TRUTH ever been determined by a MAJORITY VOTE?"

"Many Jews don't even believe in GOD!" Rosen goes on, "And others have NEVER looked at all the prophesies in the Old Testament (mentioned above).

"Many Jews have never even looked at the New Testament or realize that it's a Jewish Book! JESUS "IS" your MESSIAH!" explains Rosen, "Jesus will make you Kosher. I once said, "I was born a Jew and I'll die a Jew," but to me the Jewish thing was simply...Saturday instead of Sunday, Pesach instead of Easter, The Shema instead of "Our Father," and circumcision instead of baptism. It was always SOMEthing instead of the JESUS thing."'

"Nobody understands our religion very much...not even us," says Rosen. "When you ask a rabbi "what's a Jew?, he'll just say, Oy - don't ask!...There's one thing we Jews all know: we've got to keep our own religion...we've got to stick together!"

"Some people see Judaism as a kind of Christless Christianity (even many Jews)," explains Moishe, "To me, Judaism was pretty much the same as Christianity, only WITHOUT JESUS!

Christianity minus Christ equals JUDAISM
Judaism plus Christ equals CHRISTIANITY
......0.......plus 0.......equals...."O"

"Because the one thing that I and ALL my Jewish friends could say for certain was that the JESUS-thing was not a JEWISH-thing," Rosen goes on, "But, I found that there's more than "non-Jesusness" that makes a Jew a Jew! It was the day I found that BELIEVING IN JESUS was indeed...THE JEWISH THING! He is our MASHIACH (Messiah) and our KAPOREH (atonement)."

"He is the one whom the Prophet Isaiah (53:5) spoke about when he said:

"He was wounded for our transgressions,
He was bruised for our inequities:
The chastisement of our peace was upon Him;
And with His stripes we are healed."

(and that was written by a very Jewish prophet!)

"Jesus is what makes some of us want to be MORE JEWISH...ever wonder what 'more' Jewish could mean?!?" Explains Rosen, "We believe more than ever in the GOD of Abraham, Isaac and Jacob, in the survival of the Jewish people and in the divine establishment of the State of Israel. The words of the Jewish prophets have helped us to believe in Jesus...Read and SEE FOR YOURSELF:

God Never Says. . . "Don't Ask!"

I extend my appreciation to Moishe Rosen and Vickie Kress of JEWS FOR JESUS. Another fantastic organization for Messanic Jews is also a cable television show on CBN (channel 28 in Vegas) called "THE JEWISH VOICE" with its host, David Hill. They can be reached at Post Office Box 6, in Phoenix, Arizona 85001, or by calling 1 (602) 867-8300 or 867-8700...SHALOM!

I thank you for reading this book, but I appreciate it much more when you realize that its construction was not from the mind of any human being. GOD selected me as one of His present day "scribes" to give His divine message to all humans who will listen and understand its value.

I hope that you have gained much insight into our current world positioning in time, but, more important than any other intellectual gain, is WHERE WILL YOU GO FROM HERE? If you have not as yet accepted the "Son of man," "the Messiah," "your Mashiach," "the Bread of Life," "the Living Waters," "the Son of GOD," or "JESUS our GOD".....do so NOW with me as we pray:"

Father GOD,
I admit that I don't have the answers to solving the problems of this world. I admit that I have been caught up in earthly pleasures of the flesh and desire to know my GOD in heaven. I have sinned against You and my fellow man and ask through Your graces for forgiveness. On my knees, I ask that Jesus Christ will come into my heart, my spirit and my soul. I ask You Father to change my worthless life and make me whole in the name of Jesus. I confess my inequities to You now. . . and I reprove any authority that I have allowed satan to have over me or my family. Father, You said that anything asked for in the name of Jesus will be granted. . .I believe that Jesus Christ died on Mount Calvary for all the sins I have ever committed and that by His Blood, these sins are all washed away. I ask that Jesus Christ will come upon me and dwell within my very soul for eternity. I ask for Your assistance in my life in all matters...my family, my business and my friends...I give it all to You to do with as to Your will. I will live for You only for the rest of my days with the confidence that I have been given eternal life through Jesus. You are number one in my life. . .that's the way I want it! I ask these things in the name of JESUS. . . .
Amen and Amen.

If you just said that prayer.......you may rest assured that it was heard and you are now an important member of the Body of Christ......I love you...new bother or sister in Christ and may GOD richly bless your every move!

THE UNITED STATES OF AMERICA
IN GOD WE TRUST
LIBERTY
FAMILY
FREE
GOD
THOU SHALT NOT

Love Me and
OBEY
MY LAWS!

SOME PARTING ADVICE!

By now you can well understand that this book was not written through the mind of mortal man. It was intended to make you, the reader, aware of the evils that are constantly around you. GOD loves each one of us and wants us to obey His Plan for living. If we are truly "Children of GOD," we can not deny this wish!

Each day you are being encompassed with false and misleading information from the "national news media." What they tell the people is what they are told to tell them and, it will generally not include our GOD. DO NOT BELIEVE WHAT YOU READ IN NATIONAL NEWSPAPERS OR FROM THE NETWORK NEWS!

If they were for the people, and not just the representative of a few families, they would report the true feelings about America's yearning to get back to their GOD in every way possible. We are slowly, but surely, coming into an era of one world government and, one world religion. You can bet that Jesus Christ will not be the centerpiece in this new faith. Why isn't this obvious transition being reported?

When 200,000 "real Americans" showed up in Washington, D.C., in support of Vocal Public School Prayer this past March, why didn't ABC, NBC and CBS give it the proper coverage?

Ask yourself, why Walter Mondale is getting all the attention from the "national media" when he has been FOR everything the 80% IS AGAINST?

With the Trilateral Commission, the Council For Foreign Relations and the New Age Movement in the minds of most Christians...why don't you hear anything about it from the national media?

The American people are being railroaded, duped and have been blantantly abused by these misinformations and nothings being done about it!

Through GOD's manifestation of the Holy Spirit within me, He has imparted His wisdom and instructed me to write this book and warn His children of this Country's falsehoods. There will be numerous attacks against this cautionary testimony...some even from men who profess to be "of GOD," but DO NOT BE MISLED BY THEIR ERRONEOUS STATEMENTS. Our GOD has said, "if they are not with Me, they are against Me."..Understand His meaning!

The prophesy I have entered into the book will come true because their origin is not from human imagination...but from the Will of the Holy Spirit of GOD!

GOD wants those who love Him to get their house in order to receive Him...because He comes very soon. When He does, He will separate His believers from His enemies. The tree that didn't produce good fruit was thrown into the fire...you must remember that scripture!

I love each one of you and hope that you have made the RIGHT decision about the begining of the rest of your life. I hope that you will seek the "FACE of GOD" and, cease listening to those who do not know Him!

Many church leaders around this country are too proud to admit that their ministries have been falling on deaf ears. Their congregations come to church on Sundays out of obligation or because their conscience tells them that it is the right thing to do. They attend unenthusiastically and continue to be clock-watchers; waiting for their weekly hour to be fulfilled so they can go home and get back into the "ways of the human."

I have good news for your congregation! Our GOD doesn't want it that way and there is something you can do about it at this very moment.

GOD has anointed Rick Hall to bring your church into a renewed understanding of the "Will of GOD in these final days of humanity." When you come to the reality that your church group needs a revival...cast off your pride and arrange for Rick to light the fire that will continue to burn on until our Lord comes for us.

You may be a Pastor with a great love for our GOD, but, somehow over the years you have been feeling that your message just isn't getting across to the masses. There is something you can do about it and if you don't, many of those weekly souls are going to be lost forever. A living soul is a terrible thing to waste!

Rick will come to your church or synagogue and give your faithful a new reason to shout GOD's message to the rooftops. There's a new world coming and it's the obligation of church leaders to ready their congregations. The real message GOD has for

His people in these final days should not be obscure or supressed; it's a beautiful message that MUST BE TOLD if they are to live eternally.

Rick has not been ordained or anointed through human school of theology...if that will embarrass you, by all means don't seek his assistance. But, if GOD has told you through prayer that what has been said in this book is truly His opinion of this world, don't hesitate another moment to ask Rick to come to your church and inspire your beloved following. Rick has been ordained and anointed by the Holy Spirit of GOD to shout GOD's message throughout the land and awaken GOD's true believers to instant reality.

There's only one thing that should stand above all else in these days; that is bringing the lackadaisal to the knowledge that only a little time remains to get our houses in line with GOD's everlasting intentions and understanding the eternal significance of the saving of just one soul from damnation.

This is an age when all believers should be rejoicing and praising GOD for His patience with us...why isn't it happening? It is an extremely happy time for all believers because we are that generation that will meet our GOD in the air in the not too distant future. ARE YOU CONFIDENT THAT YOU WILL BE INCLUDED?

You must understand something of the utmost importance! As you look over your congregation this Sunday, look past the facial expressions and human mannerisms. Look into their very soul and ask GOD are they really saved? GOD will allow you to see their living soul if you ask Him for this grace. If they are not truly saved...you must do something about it!

If you sincerely want GOD to inhabit your congregation and really desire a revival with all your heart...the next move is up to you!

Rick isn't timid; in fact he's _very_ enthusiastic with GOD's message. He won't stand reticent and you can count on him keeping the total attention of your congregation while he lectures. He may even run up the aisle and do a headstand if that's what it takes to make your following understand the value of their soul to our GOD! If you church leaders plan to stifle Rick's message from GOD or desire to soften the blow for the sake of those with weak hearts...you don't want Rick to lecture to your congregation! However, if you want your church to become alive in both word and action...GOD has blessed him with the Spirit for that task!

Where is it written that GOD's message is dull? Where is it written that only theologians have messages from the Almighty? Our GOD is speaking to everyone in these days but the trouble with most is that they aren't listening! When Rick finishes with your church there'll be no question in your heart that GOD was surely there and that the message you will have received was direct from His Holy Spirit! You'll never need another cause to revive the spirit of your church again.

If you want this for your people call Rick Hall today and get the fire kindled...he's only a phone call away! ◻

GOD has told me to make up a true list of His Ten Commandments and make them available to any reader for whatever they will send in as a gift (See inside back-cover.) GOD's original Ten Commandments have been assembled for your family's knowledge and adherence to their principles. If you would like a "scroll of these Commandments" for your home, simply mail in your love gift to HALL PUBLISHING COMPANY, P.O. Box 19020, Suite 277, in Las Vegas, Nevada 89132. GOD's Commandments are in three colors and on parchment...ready to be framed and placed on the walls of your home. Whatever gift GOD tells you to send my Company will be honored.

"And thou shalt teach them diligently unto thy children, and shalt talk of them when thou sittest in thine house, and when thou walkest by thy way, and when thou liest down, and when thou risest up.
And thou shalt bind them for a sign upon thine hand, and they shall be as frontlets between thine eyes.
AND THOU SHALT WRITE THEM UPON THE POSTS OF THY HOUSE, and ON THY GATES!"
DEUTERONOMY 6:7-9

I assure you that my Company did not make up these superlatives as a means of profitability...the reason they are available to you is for their divine knowledge you will receive from understanding them. I wish I could give every American one of these beautiful scrolls free, but their costs of printing and shipping doesn't allow such a luxury.

HALL PUBLISHING COMPANY has special rates for all Christian church groups and Jewish Organizations. Please call Rick Hall in Las Vegas, Nevada at (702) 737-0040 for bulk ordering rates.

FOR YOUR THREE-COLOR SCROLL OF GOD'S TEN COMMANDMENTS ON PARCHMENT (actual size 8 X 10), MAIL ANY AMOUNT AS A LOVE GIFT TO ASSIST US WITH THE FINANCIAL BURDEN IN THE PROMOTION OF THE KINGDOM OF GOD!

MAIL TO: HALL PUBLISHING COMPANY
Post Office Box 19020
Suite 277
LAS VEGAS, NEVADA 89132

MAY GOD RICHLY BLESS YOU!!!

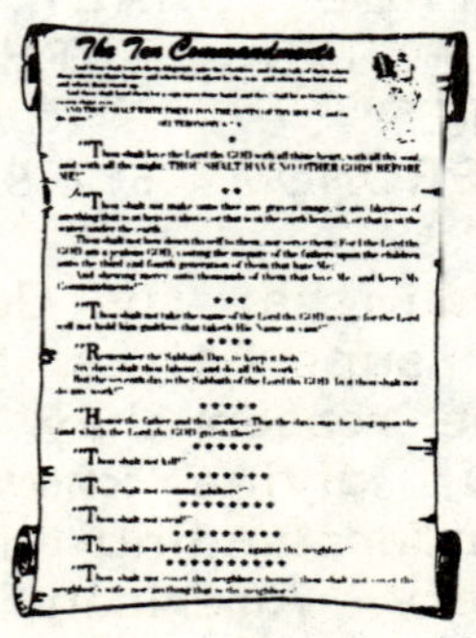

About The Author

R. (Rick) Henry Hall, is a former professional gambler and contributing sports-editor and sportswriter for Gaming International – Atlantic City, New Jersey. Rick has written many sports' oriented articles for Gambling Times (Hollywood), H & H Sporting Times (Oklahoma City, Oklahoma), the Expert's Gambling Newsletter (Los Angeles, California) and writes a sportsletter for Pro Football Insiders in Las Vegas. In his own words. . . he explains, "My past is just that – history! GOD has other plans for my future! Praise GOD!"

NOTE: This inspirational book can be purchased in bulk rate by Christian and Messanic Jewish Organizations for "love gifts and fund raising!" Rick Hall is also available for personal testimony. . . where ever and when ever GOD calls through His Elect. . . the wonderful children of GOD! According to Rick. . . "I have the Spirit of the Living GOD and WILL TRAVEL anywhere in the world in the glorification of His Name!"